NOAH AND HIS BOOK(S)

Society of Biblical Literature

Early Judaism and Its Literature

Judith H. Newman, General Editor

Editorial Board

Mark J. Boda
George J. Brooke
Esther Glickler Chazon
Steven D. Fraade
Martha Himmelfarb
James S. McLaren
Jacques van Ruiten

Number 28

NOAH AND HIS BOOK(S)

NOAH AND HIS BOOK(S)

Edited by

Michael E. Stone, Aryeh Amihay, and Vered Hillel

Society of Biblical Literature
Atlanta

NOAH AND HIS BOOK(S)

Copyright © 2010 by the Society of Biblical Literature

All rights reserved. No part of this work may be reproduced or transmitted in any form or by any means, electronic or mechanical, including photocopying and recording, or by means of any information storage or retrieval system, except as may be expressly permitted by the 1976 Copyright Act or in writing from the publisher. Requests for permission should be addressed in writing to the Rights and Permissions Office, Society of Biblical Literature, 825 Houston Mill Road, Atlanta, GA 30329 USA.

Library of Congress Cataloging-in-Publication Data

Noah and his book(s) / edited by Michael E. Stone, Aryeh Amihay, and Vered Hillel.
    p. cm. — (Early Judaism and Its literature ; no. 28)
    "This book is a joint enterprise emerging from Michael Stone's senior seminar during the years 2003–2005. The seminar was devoted during those two years to a study of the traditions about a book or books of Noah and about Noah himself. The subject is enormous, as will be seen from the chronological and geographical range of the material assembled here. Two questions were defined that focused the discussion and, consequently, the material presented in this book. The first was to assess references to a Noah writing in the Second Temple period, including segments of existing works that scholars had in the past attributed to a Noah writing. As a corollary of this, the traditions of Noah in other Second Temple period works were studied, first, to gain insight into their character and, second, to see whether distinct enough traditions survived in those, often incidental, references to witness to the existence of a Noachic writing or writings"—Data View.
    Includes bibliographical references and indexes.
    ISBN 978-1-58983-488-0 (paper binding : alk. paper)
    1. Noah (Biblical figure)—Legends—History and criticism. 2. Noah (Biblical figure)—In rabbinical literature. 3. Bible. O.T. Genesis V–IX—Criticism, interpretation, etc. 4. Christian literature, Early—Syriac authors—History and criticism. 5. Dead Sea scrolls. I. Stone, Michael E., 1938-. II. Amihay, Aryeh. III. Hillel, Vered.
    BS580.N6N6125 2010
    222'.11092—dc22   2010013972

18 17 16 15 14 13 12 11 10   5 4 3 2 1
Printed in the United States of America on acid-free, recycled paper
conforming to ANSI/NISO Z39.48-1992 (R1997) and ISO 9706:1994
standards for paper permanence.

Dedicated to All the Members of the Seminar
1967–2005

Contents

Abbreviations ix

Introduction 1

PART 1: FRAGMENTS AND DOCUMENTS ASSOCIATED
WITH A "BOOK OF NOAH"

The Book(s) Attributed to Noah
 Michael E. Stone 7

A Reconsideration of Charles's Designated "Noah Interpolations" in
1 Enoch: 54:1–55:1; 60; 65:1–69:25
 Vered Hillel 27

Is 1 Enoch 6–11 a "Noachic" Fragment? A Scholarly Discussion
 Michael Tuval 47

Traditions of the Birth of Noah
 Aryeh Amihay and Daniel A. Machiela 53

A Note on 1Q19: The "Book of Noah"
 Claire Pfann 71

The Noah Cycle in the Genesis Apocryphon
 Esther Eshel 77

Is 4Q534–536 Really about Noah?
 Jeremy Penner 97

The Rebirth of a Book: Noachic Writing in Medieval and
Renaissance Europe
 Rebecca Scharbach 113

Part 2: Noah Traditions

Noah and the Flood in the Septuagint
    Benjamin G. Wright III — 137

Distinctive Traditions about Noah and the Flood in Second Temple Jewish Literature
    Nadav Sharon and Moshe Tishel — 143

The Role of Noah and the Flood in *Judean Antiquities* and *Against Apion* by Flavius Josephus
    Michael Tuval — 167

Philo's Interpretation of Noah
    Albert C. Geljon — 183

Noah in Rabbinic Literature
    Aryeh Amihay — 193

Noah and the Flood in Gnosticism
    Sergey Minov — 215

Some Jewish Noah Traditions in Syriac Christian Sources
    Daniel A. Machiela — 237

The Literary Presentation of Noah in the Qur'ān
    Erica Martin — 253

A Shelter amid the Flood: Noah's Ark in Early Jewish and Christian Art
    Ruth Clements — 277

Part 3: Miscellaneous Noah Texts and Traditions

Noah in Onomastic Traditions
    Vered Hillel and Michael E. Stone — 303

Mount Ararat and the Ark
    Michael E. Stone — 307

Bibliography — 317
Contributors — 351
Index of Ancient Sources — 355
Index of Authors — 375

Abbreviations

Primary Sources

1 Clem.	1 Clement
4 Bar.	4 Baruch (Paraleipomena Jeremiou)
ʿAbod. Zar.	ʿAbodah Zarah
ʾAbot R. Nat.	ʾAbot de Rabbi Nathan
Abraham	Philo, *On the Life of Abraham*
Ag. Ap.	Josephus, *Against Apion*
Agriculture	Philo, *On Agriculture*
ALD	Aramaic Levi Document
Alleg. Interp.	Philo, *Allegorical Interpretation*
Ant.	Josephus, *Jewish/Judean Antiquities*
apGen	Genesis Apocryphon
Apoc. Ab.	Apocalypse of Abraham
Apoc. Paul	Apocalypse of Paul
b.	Babylonian Talmud
B. Meṣiʿa	Baba Meṣiʿa
Ber.	Berakot
Cherubim	Philo, *On the Cherubim*
Confusion	Philo, *On the Confusion of Tongues*
Creation	Philo, *On the Creation of the World*
Did.	Didache
Drunkenness	Philo, *On Drunkenness*
Eccl. Rab.	Ecclesiastes Rabbah
ʿErub.	ʿErubin
Ep.	Epistle
Faust.	Augustine, *Contra Faustum Manichaeum*
Flight	Philo of Alexandria, *On Flight and Finding*
Gen. Rab.	Genesis Rabbah
Giants	Philo of Alexandria, *On Giants*
Giṭ.	Giṭṭin

Haer.	Irenaeus, *Adversus haereses*; Hippolytus, *Refutatio onmium haeresium*
Heir	Philo, *Who Is the Heir?*
Hom. Gen.	Origen, *Homilae in Genesim*
Ketub.	Ketubbot
L.A.E.	Life of Adam and Eve
m.	Mishnah
Moses	Philo of Alexandria, *On the Life of Moses*
Migration	Philo, *On the Migration of Abraham*
Moses	Philo, *On the Life of Moses*
Ned.	Nedarim
Noe	Ambrose, *De Noe et arca*
Pan.	Epiphanius, *Panarion*
Parad.	Ambrose, *De paradiso*
Pesaḥ.	Pesaḥim
Pirqe R. El.	Pirqe Rabbi Eliezer
Planting	Philo of Alexandria, *On Planting*
Posterity	Philo of Alexandria, *On the Posterity of Cain*
Prelim. Studies	Philo of Alexandria, *On the Preliminary Studies*
Q.G.	Philo of Alexandria, *Questions and Answers on Genesis*
Rewards	Philo of Alexandria, *On Rewards and Punishments*
Roš Haš.	Roš Haššanah
Sacrifices	Philo of Alexandria, *On the Sacrifices of Cain and Abel*
Sanh.	Sanhedrin
Sib. Or.	Sibylline Oracles
Sobriety	Philo of Alexandria, *On Sobriety*
t.	Tosefta
T. Levi	Testament of Levi
T. Naph.	Testament of Naphtali
T. Reu.	Testament of Reuben
Taʿan.	Taʿanit
Tanḥ.	Tanḥuma
Ter.	Terumot
Tg. Ps.-J.	Targum Pseudo-Jonathan
Tim.	Plato, *Timaeus*
Unchangeable	Philo of Alexandria, *That God Is Unchangeable*
Virtues	Philo of Alexandria, *On the Virtues*
Worse	Philo of Alexandria, *That the Worse Attacks the Better*

ABBREVIATIONS

Secondary Sources

AB	Anchor Bible
ABD	*Anchor Bible Dictionary*. Edited by David Noel Freedman. New York: Doubleday, 1992.
AbrN	*Abr-Nahrain*
AbrNSup	Abr-Nahrain: Supplement Series
AJSR	*Association for Jewish Studies Review*
AJSL	*American Journal of Semitic Languages and Literature*
ALGHJ	Arbeiten zur Literatur und Geschichte des hellenistischen Judentums
ANF	*The Ante-Nicene Fathers: Translations of the Writings of the Fathers Down to A.D. 325*. Edited by Alexander Roberts and James Donaldson. 10 vols. 1885–87. Repr., Grand Rapids: Eerdmans, 1989.
ANRW	*Aufstieg und Niedergang der römischen Welt: Geschichte und Kultur Roms im Spiegel der neueren Forschung*. Part 2, *Principat*. Edited by Hildegard Temporini and Wolfgang Haase. Berlin: de Gruyter, 1972–.
AOAT	Alter Orient und Altes Testament
AJJS	*Australian Journal of Jewish Studies*
BAR	*Biblical Archaeology Review*
BIOSCS	*Bulletin of the International Organization for Septuagint and Cognate Studies*
BJS	Brown Judaic Studies
BKAT	Biblischer Kommentar, Altes Testament
BKP	Beitrage zur klassischen Philologie
CBQ	*Catholic Biblical Quarterly*
ConBOT	Coniectanea Biblica: Old Testament Series
CP	*Classical Philology*
CRINT	Compendia rerum iudaicarum ad Novum Testamentum
CSCO	Corpus scriptorum christianorum orientalium
DJD	Discoveries in the Judaean Desert
DSD	*Dead Sea Discoveries*
EDSS	*Encyclopedia of the Dead Sea Scrolls*. Edited by Lawrence H. Schiffman and James C. VanderKam. 2 vols. New York: Oxford University Press, 2000.
EEBS	Ἐπετηρὶς ἑταιρείας βυζαντινῶν σπουδῶν
FC	Fathers of the Church
FRLANT	Forschungen zur Religion und Literatur des Alten und Neuen Testaments

GCS	Die griechische christliche Schriftsteller der ersten [drei] Jahrhunderte
HSM	Harvard Semitic Monographs
HTR	*Harvard Theological Review*
HUCA	*Hebrew Union College Annual*
ICC	International Critical Commentary
IDB	*The Interpreter's Dictionary of the Bible*. Edited by George E. Butterick et al. 4 vols. Nashville: Abingdon, 1962.
JAAR	*Journal of the American Academy of Religion*
JANESCU	*Journal of the Ancient Near Eastern Society of Columbia University*
JAOS	*Journal of the American Oriental Society*
JBL	*Journal of Biblical Literature*
JE	*The Jewish Encyclopedia*. Edited by Isidore Singer. 12 vols. New York: Funk & Wagnalls, 1906.
JJS	*Journal of Jewish Studies*
JNES	*Journal of Near Eastern Studies*
JQR	*Jewish Quarterly Review*
JRH	*Journal of Religious History*
JSJ	*Journal for the Study of Judaism in the Persian, Hellenistic, and Roman Periods*
JSJSup	Journal for the Study of Judaism Supplement Series
JSNT	*Journal for the Study of the New Testament*
JSOR	*Journal of the Society of Oriental Research*
JSOT	*Journal for the Study of the Old Testament*
JSOTSup	Journal for the Study of the Old Testament Supplement Series
JSP	*Journal for the Study of the Pseudepigrapha*
JSPSup	Journal for the Study of the Pseudepigrapha Supplement Series
JSQ	*Jewish Studies Quarterly*
JSS	*Journal of Semitic Studies*
JTS	*Journal of Theological Studies*
LCL	Loeb Classical Library
LSJ	Liddell, Henry George, Robert Scott, and Henry Stuart Jones. *A Greek-English Lexicon*. 9th ed. with rev. supp. Oxford: Clarendon, 1996.
LSTS	Library of Second Temple Studies
NHMS	Nag Hammadi and Manichaean Studies
NHS	Nag Hammadi Studies
NovT	Novum Testamentum

NPNF	*Nicene and Post-Nicene Fathers*
NTS	*New Testament Studies*
NovTSup	Supplements to Novum Testamentum
Numen	*Numen: International Review for the History of Religions*
OTL	Old Testament Library
OTP	*The Old Testament Pseudepigrapha.* Edited by James H. Charlesworth. 2 vols. Garden City, N.Y.: Doubleday, 1983.
PAAJR	*Proceedings of the American Academy of Jewish Research*
PO	Patrologia orientalis
PS	Pseudepigrapha Series
PTS	Patristische Texte und Studien
PVTG	Pseudepigrapha Veteris Testamenti Graece
RB	*Revue biblique*
RevQ	*Revue de Qumran*
RHPR	*Revue d'histoire et de philosophie religieuses*
SBLDS	Society of Biblical Literature Dissertation Series
SBLEJL	Society of Biblical Literature Early Judaism and Its Literature
SBLSCS	Society of Biblical Literature Septuagint and Cognate Studies
SBLTT	Society of Biblical Literature Texts and Translations
SJLA	Studies in Judaism in Late Antiquity
SNTSMS	Society for New Testament Studies Monograph Series
STDJ	Studies on the Texts of the Desert of Judah
StPB	Studia post-biblica
SVF	*Stoicorum veterum fragmenta.* Edited by Hans Friedrich August von Arnim. 4 vols. Leipzig: Teubner, 1903–24.
SVTP	Studia in Veteris Testamenti pseudepigraphica
TSAJ	Texte und Studien zum antiken Judentum
VC	*Vigilae Christianae*
VT	*Vetus Testamentum*
VCSup	Supplements to Vigiliae Christianae
VTSup	Supplements to Vetus Testamentum
WBC	Word Biblical Commentary
WMANT	Wissenschaftliche Monographien zum Alten und Neuen Testament
ZAW	*Zeitschrift für die alttestamentliche Wissenschaft*
ZDMG	*Zeitschrift der deutschen morgenländischen Gesellschaft*
ZNW	*Zeitschrift für die neutestamentliche Wissenschaft und die Kunde der älteren Kirche*

Introduction

This book is a joint enterprise emerging from Michael Stone's senior seminar during the years 2003–2005.[1] The seminar was devoted during those two years to a study of the traditions about a book or books of Noah and about Noah himself. The subject is enormous, as will be seen from the chronological and geographical range of the material assembled here. Two questions were defined that focused the discussion and, consequently, the material presented in this book. The first was to assess references to a Noah writing in the Second Temple period, including segments of existing works that scholars had in the past attributed to a Noah writing. As a corollary of this, the traditions of Noah in other Second Temple period works were studied, first, to gain insight into their character and, second, to see whether distinct enough traditions survived in those, often incidental, references to witness to the existence of a Noachic writing or writings.

The second main purpose of the papers presented was to examine Noah traditions and documents after the destruction of the temple. On the one hand, once again the purpose was to get a picture (this time, in view of the enormous amount of material surviving, a less exhaustive one) of how Noah and Noah writings were portrayed in a series of Jewish, Christian, gnostic, Samaritan, qur'anic and other sources. The role of the Noah traditions in early modern discussions of geological strata and the seemingly eternal search for Mount Ararat and Noah's ark have not been documented here, nor were rabbinic and medieval Jewish sources squeezed until the last drop of juice was extracted. The Muslim tradition is represented basically only by the material in the Qur'an proper. The medieval Christian sources, too, are rather sampled than exhausted. Doubtless, the learned reader will find other, glaring omissions.[2] In addition, comparative material from the ancient Near East and the

---

1. A previous publication of the seminar is Stone, Wright, and Satran 2000.

2. The work by Dorothy M. Peters, *Noah Traditions in the Dead Sea Scrolls: Conversations and Controversies of Antiquity* (SBLEJL 26; Atlanta: Society of Biblical Literature, 2008), appeared too late to be taken into account.

classical tradition has been introduced by the various authors but has not been the object of an independent study.

The reason for this is the nature of the volume. It was written and edited by members of the senior seminar, but no compromises were made on this account with scholarly standards. However, the human resources required to study the complete range of everything ever said about Noah were not available, nor could they, in all likelihood, have been assembled at any other university. We aspired to be as exhaustive as feasible as far at the predestruction sources go, but only to provide a responsible representation of the later sources. Even then, some essays by former members or nonmembers of the seminar were included.

A former member, Erica Martin, contributed the chapter on the qur'anic materials. Albert Geljon of Leiden kindly answered our invitation to write on Philo's Noah, and Benjamin G. Wright III, another former seminar member, contributed the study of Noah in the Septuagint. All other essays were written by members of the seminar.

The three editors shared the work, and they share the responsibility for the imperfections, such as there are. Aryeh Amihay served as secretary both of the seminar and of the editorial board and kept us all in control of the very complex material and coordination. Vered Hillel worked on bibliography and knocked a very diverse series of essays into a standard format and shape. Michael Stone did the first scientific editing of the manuscripts, guiding their transformation from seminar presentations to scholarly chapters. Amihay, Hillel, and Stone read and edited all the manuscripts. Thanks are expressed to Ruth Clements, who assisted in many ways, particularly in questions of format and bibliography. Lauren Stevens was responsible for the final updating and polishing of the manuscript and pounced on many inconsistencies that slipped by the editors. Thanks are duly expressed to them.

The copyright holders kindly granted permission to quote the following material: from Louis H. Feldman, *Flavius Josephus, Judean Antiquities 1–4: Translation and Commentary* (Leiden: Brill, 2000), the translation of *Ant.* 1.105–108 on pages 37–38, *Ant.* 1.92–95 on pages 33–35, *Ant.* 1.72–74 on pages 26–28, *Ant.* 1.110–112 on pages 39–40; from John M. G. Barclay, *Flavius Josephus, Against Apion: Translation and Commentary* (Leiden: Brill, 2006), the translation of *Ag. Ap.* 1.128–131 on pages 70–81; Harm W. Hollander and Marinus de Jonge, *The Testaments of the Twelve Patriarchs: A Commentary* (Leiden: Brill; 1985), page 101 verse 6 "For thus they" until page 102 verse 7 "unto heaven," page 301 verse 4 "so that you" until verse 5 "and fruits" (line 5 from the bottom), page 431 verse 3 "Therefore was also" until verse 4 "righteous brother" (by permission of the authors); Michael E. Stone and Gary A. Anderson, *A Synopsis of the Books of Adam and Eve: New and Revised Edition*

(Atlanta: Scholars Press, 1999) page 91E, from verse 49:2 "Michael the archangel" until verse 50:2 "will be fired."

Jerusalem, Tevet 5796
January 2009

Part 1: Fragments and Documents Associated with a "Book of Noah"

The Book(s) Attributed to Noah*

Michael E. Stone

There has been considerable scholarly debate in recent years over whether or not a book of Noah existed. This question is of interest not least because if such a book of Noah did exist, it would be one of the most ancient Jewish works outside the Bible. A book of Noah is cited by Aramaic Levi Document (ALD) 10:10, and, since ALD is dated to the third century or early second century B.C.E., a source document of ALD must have been even older.[1] Pieces of the puzzle of the "dark age" of the history of Judaism in the fourth and third centuries B.C.E. are gradually being found and fitted together, and if the book(s) of Noah turns out to have existed, it will fill in a significant part of this puzzle. Moreover, the relationship between Enoch and Noah, and between the documents bearing their names, demands our attention, though it is beyond our scope in this essay. The disappearance of the book(s) of Noah is a further part of this enigma. If such a work existed and if it was so ancient, then why did it disappear? Is this historical happenstance, or does it reflect changes in the streams of Judaism in the fourth and third centuries, changes that are still beyond recovery? Such issues sharpen the question: Did a book of Noah exist?

The present writer, indeed, expressed a guardedly positive response to this question in a study published in 1999 in which he addressed both explicit references to the book of Noah in ancient pseudepigrapha and also textual

---

* This paper is presented in honor of John Strugnell, whose contribution in learning and teaching the Dead Sea Scrolls and Second Temple Period Jewish literature is *non pareil*. The article originally appeared in *DSD* 13:4–23. It is republished here with errata and additional notes.

1. The early date (early second century B.C.E. at the latest) of ALD has recently been challenged by Kugel 2007. The crux of his argument rests on the relationship between ALD and Jubilees, on the one hand, arguing that ALD is dependent on Jubilees, and on the supposedly Hasmonean date of ALD implied by the application of royal, i.e., Judahite language to Levi, on the other. These issues are complex, and I intend to broach them in a future publication. Suffice it to say here that I remain unconvinced by Kugel's demurrers on my dating. On one aspect of the issue, see n. 22 below.

fragments, not explicitly attributed to a book of Noah, but that many scholars consider "Noachic."[2] In the present essay, I do not seek definitively to resolve issues of the composition, indeed of the very existence of a book(s) of Noah, but to contribute to the solution of this contentious issue. To do this, it seems to me most reasonable to take as the point of departure those places in ancient literature where the title "Book of Noah" or a book associated with Noah is mentioned explicitly. A close examination of those texts should provide an initial insight into the question implied by the title of the present essay.

The study here, then, is directed solely toward instances in which the title or the book is actually mentioned. This seems to me to be methodologically justified: it is necessary in my view to distinguish between two categories of texts relating to the book(s) of Noah: (1) those in which the title or a book of Noah is clearly mentioned in an ancient source; (2) those in which scholars, in the course of their study of ancient sources, have come to regard passages of certain works as coming from a Noachic source, even though such an attribution is not explicit in the original. In the search for clarity, it may eventually become necessary to divide the second category itself into two subcategories: texts in which Noah is the central actor or speaks in the first person; other texts that for one or another reason have been regarded as belonging to Noachic literature. In the present study, however, I will consider only the unambiguous cases in group 1, that is, those instances in which the title "Book of Noah" or a book transmitted by Noah is actually mentioned.[3]

Genesis Apocryphon

The only surviving copy of the Genesis Apocryphon (1QapGen or 1Q20) is a first-century manuscript from Qumran Cave 1. The work is older than that, but more cannot be said securely about its date (see n. 15 below). In the fifth column of the Genesis Apocryphon, line 29, the reading has been found [פרשגן כתב מלי [נוח" [copy of] the Book of the Words of Noah," of which the first word is a restoration. Richard Steiner wrote a detailed discussion of this title, the only book of Noah title surviving in Hebrew or Aramaic from antiquity.[4] Steiner points out that it occurs following a blank line and so seems

---

2. Stone 1999, 136–41; 2000, 613–14. In 1996b, I already assembled much material relating to the book of Noah (283–88). See earlier Stone 1971.

3. Hindy Najman (1999, 382 and n. 6) suggests that Noah writings are mentioned in Jub. 8:11 and other places because of the special role of writing: "It is central to *Jubilees'* notion of divine speech that it be accomplished in writing—indeed, Noah received, recorded and then transmitted the already revealed heavenly tradition." Such an attitude, of course, bears neither positively or negatively on the question we are seeking to answer here.

4. Steiner 1995.

to be the beginning of a new section that continues, as far as we can tell, until column 17. This material, though fragmentary, is first-person narrative, and it differs from the Noah narrative occurring in columns 2–5 of the same scroll. The subject there is the wondrous birth of Noah, but the narrative is set in his father Lamech's mouth, so the material about Noah is predominantly in the third person.[5]

Chapters 106–107 of the book of Enoch also contain material dealing with Noah's birth. Intriguingly, that narrative, too, is in the third person,[6] set in the mouth of Enoch, Noah's great-grandfather. The material in 1QapGen columns 2–5 is, therefore, most probably not drawn from the same source as that which starts with the title "[copy of] the Book of the Words of Noah" at the bottom of column 5 of that scroll. The change of framework and speaker, the blank line, and the beginning of a new section seem to indicate this more than does the variation of grammatical person, and they mark the beginning of a different literary source.

Before the identification of the phrase "Book of the Words of Noah" in column 5 line 29 in the Genesis Apocryphon, García Martínez opined that 1QapGen columns 1–17 "contains a summary of the lost *Book of Noah* which is independent of Jubilees."[7] He argued that the Genesis Apocryphon is independent of Jubilees, so the Noah material in it is not drawn from Jubilees but from a source it shared with Jubilees.[8] That source, he maintains, was the book of Noah.[9] Steiner and others have elucidated the implications of the

---

5. The relationship between Enoch and Noah is discussed in Nadav Sharon and Moshe Tishel's "Distinctive Traditions about Noah and the Flood in Second Temple Jewish Literature" in the present volume.

6. Scholars have attributed other material in the book of Enoch to a book of Noah, and this material will be dealt with in a separate study (see also Vered Hillel's "A Reconsideration of Charles's Designated 'Noah Interpolations' in 1 Enoch: 54:1–55:1; 60; 65:1–69:25" in the present volume). It has, of course, been the object of considerable attention in the past, starting notably with the observations of Charles 1906, subsequently modified in Charles 1912, xlvi–xlvii. See also James 1920, 11–12.

7. García Martínez 1992, 40. On doubts raised about one specific point of García Martínez's reconstruction, see Scott 1997b, 372.

8. This is surmised on the basis of halakic argument by Werman 1999, 173–76. She argues that material shared by Jubilees, ALD, and 1QapGen was drawn with adaptations by Jubilees from the other two works. She concludes: "*Jubilees* knows of a Book of Noah only by hearsay, from these secondary sources that contradict one another as to the nature of this putative work" (181). This conclusion goes beyond the outcome of her convoluted argument there.

9. García Martínez 1992, 40. He supports his contention by a comparative analysis, 40–43. See further Stone 1996b, 286–88. No stand is taken on the existence of a book of Noah by Morgenstern, Qimron, and Sivan in their edition of the material (1995, 32).

new reading; García Martínez's position should consequently be modified, and, if a book of Noah is cited by 1QapGen, the phrase "Book of the Words of Noah" in column 5.29 was most likely its title or, less probably, an introductory lemma.

Dimant singled out the story of Noah's birth as a likely candidate for inclusion in the "Hebrew narrative midrash," the existence of which she postulates, but she denies that this story comes from a book of Noah.[10] I prefer for the moment to leave the determination of this aside but note that it seems to be significant that the narrative of Noah's birth is usually presented in the third person. This may have been the case in 1Q19 frg. 3, the so-called "Book of Noah" from Qumran Cave 1, though the literary framework is lacking that would enable us to transform this tentative assertion into a definite one.[11] In 1 En. 106–107 the incident is related by Enoch, and within that first-person literary framework, it is third person narrative.[12] The same is true of 1QapGen column 2, except that there the narrative is set in Lamech's mouth. In 2 En. 71, which is the comparable story of the birth of Melchizedek, the narrative is in the third person and is included within a discourse.[13] This consideration, it seems to me, effectively diminishes the argument based on first- or third-person style as determining whether the birth story was part of a book of Noah.[14]

It is still possible to maintain that the story of Noah's birth was not necessarily part of a book of Noah. After all, the story is either anonymous, as in 1Q19 (but that is probably due to the fragmentary state of 1Q19), or set in the mouth of Noah's father or grandfather. Later it even circulated separately, in Latin at least.[15] In 1QapGen it is not included in the material following the

---

10. Dimant 1998 is extremely skeptical of the existence of a book of Noah, while gladly admitting the possible existence of "a more comprehensive Hebrew narrative midrash, written perhaps in a style similar to the Aramaic Genesis Apocryphon, which would have included at least some of the materials dealing with Noah, such as his miraculous birth" (146). Her difficulties lie in the specificity and singular nature of the document she posits to be implied by the title "Book of Noah." Hers is an overly rigid understanding of the latter term. A slightly later article making the same points in more detail is Werman 1999.

11. See Barthélemy and Milik 1955, 84–86 and 152.

12. For similar reasons, the fragmentary "third person" narrative of 1Q19 should not be taken too seriously.

13. Here I will not discuss Orlov's (2000b) proposal that the displacement of the birth story from Noah to Noah's nephew Melchizedek resulted from contention about the role of Noah. That view is worthy of detailed discussion elsewhere.

14. See Dimant 1998, 164; in 1QapGen 10:2 ,Noah is spoken of in the third person. It is interesting to compare the first-person Noah material in columns 5–6 with the first-person Enoch material in the preceding columns 2–3.

15. James 1893. He regards it as a fragment of a Latin version of the book of Enoch (146), while Milik doubts whether such an integral translation ever existed (1976, 80–81).

title "Book of the Words of Noah" but occurs in the Lamech material, three columns earlier. What that title in column 5 of the Genesis Apocryphon does is strengthen the probability of the existence of an ancient book of Noah, parts of which may occur in or have served as a source of the succeeding columns of 1QapGen. It does not make the inclusion of the birth story in such a book of Noah more likely.[16]

The usual response of those who would deny the significance of the title's occurrence in ancient sources is to remark that some of the Enoch quotations in Testaments of the Twelve Patriarchs are not drawn from any Enoch work we know and so are fabrications. Consequently, they infer, the mention of the title book of Noah in 1QapGen and Jubilees is equally likely to be the invention of the authors of these works. This argument is, of course, illogical. It is quite possible that the Enoch quotations in Testaments of the Twelve Patriarchs were drawn from an Enoch work that has not survived.[17] Moreover, and even more tellingly, Testaments of the Twelve Patriarchs is a later Christian document, probably from the second century C.E.[18] Its practice in citation cannot be used either to discredit or to verify citations made in 1QapGen, which was written at least three centuries earlier and in very different circles.[19] Instead, seeking comparable instances of citation in ancient sources, we should perhaps consider the quotations of Aramaic Levi Document itself and of Jubilees by the Damascus Document, which are genuine, though sometimes periphrastic.[20] This bears upon all the ancient references to a book of Noah that we will discuss later.

Milik does adduce quite a lot of evidence for knowledge of Enoch material in Latin. Lawlor 1897 argues that the Latin version is not a translation from 1 Enoch, but from a book of Noah (see 174–75, 224–25). I have not reached a definite conclusion on this point.

16. The birth of Noah, and in particular the later forms of the story, is discussed in the present volume by Aryeh Amihay, "Noah in Rabbinic Literature," and Jeremy Penner, "Is 4Q534–536 Really about Noah?" Most recently, see also the discussion of later developments of this material by Orlov 2007, 371–75, 382.

17. See Lawlor 1897.

18. I accept M. de Jonge's views on the date and origins of Testaments of the Twelve Patriarchs. These are set forth very lucidly and documented by Kugler 2001, 35–39. A full list of de Jonge's numerous writings on the topic may be found in DiTommaso 2001, 919–75.

19. Fitzmyer would date the work most probably to the first century B.C.E., but, in fact, there is no evidence except that it is older than its manuscript, 1Q20. That manuscript is dated by paleography to the Herodian period. See Fitzmyer 2000.

20. See Greenfield 1988. In addition, the Damascus Document clearly refers to Jubilees (CD 16:3). Other Qumran texts also apparently refer to Jubilees or another work of the same title, with varying degrees of certainty: see 4Q228 f1i:4; 4Q270 f6ii:17; 4Q271 f4ii:5; and 4Q384 f9:2. On the question of "fake" citations, see also Kaufman 1932.

Aramaic Levi Document

In ALD 10:10 we read that the series of ritual commandments given by Isaac to Levi were taken from τῆς βιβλίου τοῦ Νῶε περὶ τοῦ αἵματος, "Of the Book of Noah concerning the Blood." Greenfield, Stone, and Eshel remarked on the ambiguity of this phrase, which might be read either as a title, "Of 'The Book of Noah concerning the Blood,'" or as "of 'The Book of Noah' concerning the blood,'" where the last words designate the subject of the book of Noah.[21] Whichever interpretation is correct, this is the oldest explicit reference to the book of Noah, for ALD is to be dated to the third or very early second century B.C.E. at the latest.[22] Although the phrase we have cited did not survive among the Qumran fragments of ALD, nor in the Genizah Aramaic folios, but only in an excerpt from a Greek translation, there is no reason to doubt its originality.[23] The Aramaic might have been כתב נוח (cf. 1QapGen

---

21. Greenfield, Stone and Eshel 2004, 180.
22. Ibid., 19–20.
23. It does not seem that the ideas proposed by Kugler 2008 make any difference to this conclusion. His conclusions seem to go beyond the evidence he adduces, and a "Qumran" reading or recension of ALD cannot be taken as demonstrated, though of course it is possible. Indeed, in principle, each copyist of a work in fact produces an interpretation, and no text-form is identical to any other. An example of a systematic attempt to clarify such differences for one work is the research of Levison, 2000. Greenfield and I showed the existence of at least two recensions of ALD at Qumran on literary grounds in 1996, 43–45, 54–60. So it has a complex literary history, not more than some other works at Qumran, such as S (The Community Rule) and D (The Damascus Document). Kugler's claim of a Qumran recension to serve sectarian purposes is unproven. The lack of a fragment from some anyway fragmentary witnesses does not show its deliberate composition and insertion in another witness as part of a sectarian recension. This is otherwise demonstrated only by a single variant between a first-person singular and a first-person plural. Kugler is correct that there were different text-forms, though strangely he does not relate his "Qumran" text-form to the different Qumran Aramaic recensions discerned on literary grounds. Instead, he argues on narrow grounds for a theory of Qumran retelling of ALD that is not implausible but that remains unproven. Even if he is right and such a retelling existed, we can, and should, still talk of ALD as a single work. The long and short recensions of Hebrew Jeremiah are just that. The work remains one work, and there is good reason to try to place its parts in some sort of order and not just to deconstruct them into discrete manuscripts. There are sixty-four manuscripts of the Armenian version of Testaments of the Twelve Patriarchs. They differ from one another, sometimes by the dynamic of copying and sometimes by deliberate recensional activity, with literary and ideological purposes. Are we then to say the work cannot be edited but must be published as sixty-four different compositions? Surely there are other ways of presenting the evidence. So Kugler's article must be appreciated for raising our consciousness about recensional and tendentious readings of ancient documents, but regarding what happened at Qumran as different

5:29). It seems from ALD that this book of Noah contained all the teaching that ALD attributed to Isaac (i.e., 6:1–10:10) and that Isaac had received from Abraham. Abraham, in turn, so the story goes, drew it from the book of Noah. In 10:3 we read, "[f]or my father Abraham commanded me to do thus and to command my sons," while in 10:10 we find: "[f]or thus my father Abraham commanded me, for thus he found in the writing of the [B]ook of Noah concerning the blood."[24] The conclusion of Isaac's teaching is found in 10:10. Next comes the blessing he pronounced in 10:11–14, which has its own beginning, "And now, beloved child...."

The detail, length, and tight structure of this passage of priestly teaching make it probable, in my view, that it comes from a source document, and the title of that source document is explicitly said to be "Book of Noah." This teaching was also cited by Jubilees, as we shall see in the next paragraph.

Jubilees 21:1–10 records part of the priestly instruction given by Abraham to Isaac. This is another form of the priestly teaching given by Isaac to Levi, according to ALD.[25] In Jubilees, Abraham concludes the first part of this instruction with the words: "for so I have found written in the books of my forefathers (in the words of Enoch and the words of Noah)."[26] R. H. Charles remarks, "There was probably no ground for the statement made by our author."[27] Yet, one wonders. It seems very likely that, since this chapter of Jubilees is dependent on ALD, the reference to "words of Noah" has been taken from there (ALD 10:10). The additional mention of Enoch is either an expansion of the information in ALD or else Jubilees knew a tradition that the words of Enoch were transmitted through Noah.[28]

---

from what happened in other contexts of transmission seems to be unwarranted. At the very most, *non liquet*.

24. All citations from Aramaic Levi Document are drawn from the edition mentioned in note 21, above.

25. The relationship between these two passages will be explored in a subsequent study. Observe, however, that in *TLevi* 9:3, which is radically abridged in comparison with ALD, Isaac attributes part of the teaching to Abraham, without any reference to Noah. However, as has been noted above, *TLevi* is secondary to ALD. V. Hillel in the following chapter of the present volume discusses the Noachic fragments in 1 Enoch, and in her paper "Demonstrable Instances of the Use of Sources in the Pseudepigrapha" in Hempel (forthcoming), she addresses most recently the issue of the interrelations between ALD, Jubilees, and Testaments of the Twelve Patriarchs.

26. Sparks, 1984, 68.

27. Charles 1902, 134.

28. On this line of transmission of antediluvian knowledge through Noah to Abraham and Levi, see Stone 1999. See also Jub. 7:38–39, but no book is transmitted there. On transmission of Enochic material through Noah, see Orlov 2007, 119–31.

The Book of Jubilees

The book of Jubilees was composed sometime in the first third of the second century B.C.E. We have a complete text of it in Ethiopic, fragments in Latin, and a substantial number of fragmentary copies from Qumran.[29] Jubilees 10:1–14 is a passage dealing with the demons that afflicted Noah's children after the flood. Noah prayed to God for help (10:13), and God commanded an angel to teach Noah all the remedies against them (10:10).

> 10:12 And we explained to Noah all the remedies against their diseases, together with their seductions, and how to heal them with herbs. 10:13 And Noah wrote down everything in a book, as we instructed him about every kind of remedy; thus were the evil spirits kept from doing harm to Noah's sons. 10:14 And he gave everything he had written to Shem, his eldest son; for he loved him most of all his sons.[30]

This passage then relates that Noah wrote a book of remedies and transmitted it to his son Shem. A very similar passage was included in the medieval Jewish medical work Sefer Asaf Harofe,[31] and it was translated into English

---

29. See introductory remarks in VanderKam 2000b.

30. Translation by Charles, revised by Rabin in Sparks 1984, 42. For 10:4, VanderKam, in his translation, reads, "He gave all the books that he had written to his older son Shem for he loved him much more than all his sons" (1989, 59). Betsy Halpern-Amaru observes in a personal communication that the Ethiopic in 10:13 has the singular "book," while in 10:14 it has the plural. "It seems that there are multiple books and that in an 'orderly' way he kept different 'books' for the various traditions he would pass on" (letter of 7 April 2005). Yet, as she observed in a later communication, the textual basis for "books" is ambiguous, and VanderKam accepts Charles's reading and does not read "books." As for the plural, Halpern-Amaru points to the use of the plural in Jub. 45:16, where Jacob transmits "books" to Levi (letter of 11 April 2005). This latter reading does not seem to me to bear on the issue of the book(s) of Noah.

31. It was introduced into the scholarly discussion by Jellinek 1938, 3:xxx–xxxiii and text on 155. See general discussion in Lewis 1968, 12–14. Werman (1999) regards this as a separate source from Jub. 10:1–14, asserting that "the author of *Jubilees* used material from … the Introduction of the Book of Asaph, but with changes" (172). Of course, since Jubilees antedates Sefer Asaf Harofe by more than a millennium, she must mean that the source used by Sefer Asaf Harofe was that used by Jubilees. In fact, Werman was far from the first to put forth this proposal; Charles had already done so in 1902, xliv; see also Himmelfarb 1994, 127. She points out that the story (without any mention of a book) was known to George Synkellos (128; Adler and Tuffin 2002, 36). This assertion demands that the issue of the transmission of the material found in Sefer Asaf Harofe be addressed energetically. A beginning of this labor has been made by Himmelfarb 1994.

by Martha Himmelfarb.³² The parallel to Jubilees in Sefer Asaf Harofe concludes:

ויכתב נח את הדברים האלה על ספר ויתנהו לשם בנו הגדול
And Noah wrote these things in a book and gave it to Shem, his oldest son. (cf. Jub. 10:14)

Intriguingly, Sefer Asaf Harofe adds two further book of Noah references of its own in this passage. At the opening it reads: "This is the book of remedies that the ancient sages copied from the book of Shem son of Noah. It was transmitted to Noah on Mount Lubar of the mountains of Ararat after the flood."³³ The mention of Mount Lubar is a distinctive tradition, and this name of "one of the mountains of Ararat" only occurs elsewhere in ancient Jewish literature in Jubilees and 4QpseudoDaniel^b. It is mentioned in the Byzantine Chronography of George Synkellos as the place of Noah's burial (cf. Jub. 10:15).³⁴ It is not mentioned in Jub. 10:1–14, which is the pericope to which Sefer Asaf Harofe is parallel. However, it does occur in the next pericope in Jubilees, where it is the site not of revelation of the book of Noah but of some other incidents. This leads us toward the conclusion that Sefer Asaf Harofe was familiar with more of Jubilees-allied traditions than the "medical" passage it is quoting.³⁵ The second reference to a book of Noah in Sefer Asaf Harofe is found in the continuation of the passage quoted above, where the transmis-

---

32. Himmelfarb 1994, 129–30 published the first English translation of this passage. On pages 130–31 she clearly assumes that the material in Sefer Asaf Harofe draws on a Hebrew source of Jubilees that has been tailored to fit the interests of the author of Sefer Asaf Harofe.

33. זה ספר הרפואות אשר העתיקו חכמים הראשונים מספר שם בן נוח אשר נמסר לנח בלובר ההר מהררי אררט אחרי המבול (Jellinek 1938, 3:155), Here I have departed from Himmelfarb's translation. It is to be noted that Mount Lubar is mentioned in the verse following this passage in Jub. 10:15, in connection with Noah's burial. It is also mentioned in Jub. 5:28, 7:1, and 7:15 and further in 1QapGen 12:13 and 4Q244 f8:3 (4Qpseudo-Daniel^b), also apparently in connection with Noah. On Mount Lubar, with a possible etymology, see Steiner 1991.

34. On which, apparently, Synkellos draws; see Adler and Tuffin 2002, 63.

35. See above. As already noted, it is conceivable that both Jubilees and Sefer Asaf Harofe are dependent on a third document. Himmelfarb (1994, 127–36) argues vigorously in support of this view. Another interesting analysis of this passage in the context of *hekhalot* and magical texts may be found in Swartz 1994, 225–26. The question of the origin and date of Sefer Asaf Harofe is debated, but apparently it comes from soon after the middle of the first millennium C.E. See Muntner 2007. A detailed study is Aviv Melzer's doctoral thesis of 1972. On the date, see 34–57.

sion of the book is traced down to Galenus.³⁶ The reference to a Noachic book in Jub. 10:14, therefore, is accompanied by a medical/demonic explanation of the human state, which also occurs either in a derived form or drawn from a similar source, in the much later Sefer Asaf Harofe.

The Similitudes of Enoch

Similitudes (Parables) of Enoch is the least readily dated and located of the parts of 1 Enoch.³⁷ However, it seems to have been written about the turn of the era or a little later. Similitudes of Enoch (1 Enoch) 68:1 sets the following words in Noah's mouth: "And after this my great-grandfather Enoch gave me the explanation of all the secrets in a book and the parables that had been given to him, and he put them together for me in the words of the book of the Parables (Similitudes)." This statement, coming toward the end of the Similitudes of Enoch, is apparently intended to give it authority. It is intriguing that it occurs in this particular position. The surrounding text has been characterized as Noachic, a claim that will be discussed elsewhere.³⁸ I find myself uncertain about the relationship between this Noachic text and the Enochic context. Whether the surrounding text is Noachic or not, indubitably this particular claim was set in Noah's mouth, who alone could have said "my great-grandfather Enoch." Noah claims that Enoch gave him explanation of all the secrets in a book.³⁹ Thus the expression in Jub. 21:10 is not unparalleled, and the idea was current that Enoch and Noah both had and transmitted books that were connected with one another.⁴⁰

Tabula Gentium

In recent years James M. Scott has drawn attention to the *tabula gentium*, the division of the earth among Noah's three sons in Gen 10.⁴¹ This passage

---

36. Some further references to the book of Noah in medieval literature will be discussed in the appendix below.

37. On the date of Similitudes, see most recently Boccaccini 2007.

38. See Hillel in this volume, 27–45.

39. This line of transmission is mentioned in Jub. 7:38. 1 En. 108:1 speaks of a book Enoch wrote for Methuselah and all who would come after him.

40. These issues were dealt with in a broader context in Stone 1999, especially 138–40. That paper was concerned primarily with the role of Noah as transmitter of antediluvian knowledge. On similar transmission in later sources, see the discussion of Jub. 21:10 above. An early, perceptive, and learned discussion of the Noachic material in 1 Enoch is Schmidt 1926. He discusses 1 En. 68:1 on pp. 122–23.

41. Scott 1997b.

was extensively developed in Jub. 8:10–9:15, apparently in the fragmentary column 12 of 1QapGen, and further elaborated in later sources.[42] Scott correctly points out that, according to Jubilees, this division was inscribed in a book, as Jub. 8:11 says, "When he summoned his children, they came to him—they and their children. He divided the earth into the lots that his three sons would occupy. They reached out their hands and took the book from the bosom of their father Noah."[43] Scott makes the following points concerning this passage. First, the explicit mention of a book in Jub. 8:11 (and, I venture to add, 8:12) means that the division of the earth was included in a "book of Noah."[44] Second, such a book of Noah is distinct from books of Noah on other topics.[45] He also observes that the division of the earth was the subject of the fragmentary 1QapGen columns 16–17, which confirms the antiquity of this material. Moreover, Gen 10 is already found to have influenced 1QapGen 12:10–12, although it is in tension with it at a number of points.[46]

The above are all the uses of the title "Book of Noah" or explicit references to such a book in Jewish literature from the Second Temple period.[47] The question remains to be discussed whether these references are fabricated in order to add a patina of authority to the works citing them or whether they indeed refer to an ancient document(s) that actually existed. As I have said, I prefer to assess the use of the titles separately rather than to deal with the titles together with various unattributed literary pieces that scholars have assigned to Noah.

From the analysis above, it emerges that there are four substantial pieces of unique text that ancient documents attribute explicitly to a book of Noah. These are: (1) the extensive material in 1QapGen 5:29–17;[48] (2) the cultic material attributed to the book of Noah in ALD 6:1–10:10 and the text that is

---

42. E.g., Stone 1981, 271–77, and works cited by Scott 1997b, 370 n. 8; Charles 1902, 68. See also Eshel 2007.

43. Jub. 8:12 continues, "In the book there emerged as Shem's lot…" (VanderKam 1989, 52).

44. Scott thus advances García Martínez's argument considerably; see Scott 1997b, 269–70.

45. Ibid., 370.

46. Ibid., 371–72. The *tabula gentium* material entered Midrash Aggadah associated with R. Moses the Preacher and is discussed by Himmelfarb 1994, 121–23. It was also used in the Ethiopic tradition; see Cowley 1988, 31–33.

47. I have also included a discussion of Jub. 8:11–12, in which an untitled book by Noah is mentioned.

48. The material in cols. 2–5 of 1QapGen is not presented there as part of a book of Noah.

most probably derived from it in Jub. 21;[49] (3) the magico-medical material that Noah wrote in a book, according to Jub. 10:1–14, which material and attribution are also found in Sefer Asaf Harofe; and (4) the *tabula gentium* that Noah is said to have written in a book (Jub. 10:11–12). First Enoch 68:1, which seems to be part of a subscription to the Similitudes of Enoch, raises issues about the relationship between Enoch and Noah and is problematic and thus best left out of the present discussion.

One of the most vigorous opponents of the existence of a book of Noah has been Devorah Dimant.[50] I shall discuss her arguments in detail, not because they are better or worse than those of others, but because they are typical. Dimant surveys the references to Noachic books in Jub. 10:21 (surely an error for 10:13), 21:10 and T. Levi 2:3 (Greek). (I assume that by this last reference she intends ALD 10:10; old section 57.)[51] She asserts that "fictional postulation of such works in pseudepigraphic and legendary writings cannot be taken as historical evidence, unless there exists reliable, independent confirmation."[52] I find this assertion to be bizarre. Why should citations that are explicitly said to be drawn from a Noachic document, and each of which is associated with a very distinct body of material, be regarded *ab initio* as "fictional postulations"? Dimant offers no reason except that the references are made in "pseudepigraphic and legendary writings." Indeed, she does not adduce the strongest argument of which I know, namely, the existence of unidentifiable Enoch citations in Testaments of the Twelve Patriarchs. This has been taken (albeit unjustifiably, in my view) to throw doubt on all quotations in ancient sources. As I have shown above, this argument itself is not

---

49. Above I have dealt with the additional attribution to Enoch found in Jub. 10:21. See also the paper by C. Werman referred to in n. 8 above.

50. See above, n. 10.

51. Testament of Levi refers to a "book of Enoch" twice, in 10:5 and 16:1, but nowhere to a book of Noah. Following T. Levi 2:3 in one manuscript is a Greek expansion that is actually part of ALD, but it does not contain the reference to a book of Noah either. That occurs in the long passage following T. Levi 18:2 in the same Greek manuscript of Testaments of the Twelve Patriarchs. So, I am forced to assume that Dimant is confused here. In addition, on pages 144–45, Dimant enumerates passages that have commonly been assumed to derive from a book of Enoch. I forbear to treat this part of her argument.

52. Dimant 1998, 145. I suspect that L. Schiffman would hold a similar view. Compare his article on pseudpigrapha (2004), where his "book" in ALD 13:4 is the result of a misunderstanding: see Greenfield, Stone, and Eshel 2004, 206. In general, the instances I am discussing in this article are more complex than his categories would suggest. The mysterious "writing" mentioned (if the editors are correct) in 4Q243 is unclear. See the discussion in DiTommaso 2005, 128–29. His connection of this writing with Adam's testament is speculative, but it does not seem to have been Noachic either.

convincing.⁵³ Indeed, I maintain that a citation formula, title, or subscription that is associated with a substantial and distinct block of text has a good claim to be considered genuine, unless the work in which it occurs is rife with obviously forged citations. This is not the case in Jubilees, which mentions only books of Enoch and Noah, except for Jubilees itself in the superscription and books of Jacob in the subscription. 1QapGen mentions the book of Enoch twice on column 20, and these two mentions, in addition to the reference to the book of Noah, are its only surviving references to books. Thus the burden of proof falls on scholars who would deny the authenticity of the book of Noah titles and sections a priori, not on those who would assert it.⁵⁴

The second argument adduced by Dimant is that the fragments of the book of Noah "diverge in form and detail" and are "of diverse character." This case is made not just on the basis of the titled passages but also on the basis of other unascribed passages that scholars have attributed to a book of Noah.⁵⁵ Yet, it seems to me that, even should we group the titled and untitled passages together, this consideration is not convincing. On the one hand, there is no need for there to have been only one Noachic book (or "booklet"). Second, and more telling, we have not a few works from antiquity that contain material of very diverse character. Suffice it, perhaps, to mention the Book of the Watchers in 1 Enoch. If, for example, we had only fragments of chapters 1, 3, 7, 22, and so on of the Book of the Watchers, would we not be able to make Dimant's argument about their divergence in form and detail and their diversity of character and infer that they do not derive from the same document?

It is my conclusion, therefore, that unless contrary evidence emerges, the titles discussed above do designate an ancient literary work (or works) that has not survived in full but that is being cited. This being the case, in a future study I hope to discuss the relationship of fragments attributed by scholars to a Noachic work to these assured Noachic fragments. A final remark should be made on the Noachic document(s). It was a very old work, of the third century B.C.E. at least, and perhaps older. It fell out of use early, it seems,⁵⁶ and for

---

53. The title "Book of the Words of Noah" in 1QapGen was unknown to Dimant, for it was deciphered after she wrote her article, but the instance in 1QapGen is no different from those she rejects.

54. The case might be different were these merely passing references. However, in these major, ancient instances, a block of textual material, distinct from its context, follows the reference to the book of Noah.

55. See the similar remarks in Fletcher-Louis 2002, 36.

56. 1Q19, which is preserved in a first-century manuscript, is a Noah birth story, with much in common with 1QapGen 2–3 and 1 En. 106–07, as I have observed. The title "Livre de Noé" was given by the first editors. I shall discuss this story in a future study, but it is not, in my view, necessarily or even particularly probably drawn from a book of Noah.

that reason survives only in these citations. It also seems to have fallen more or less completely out of the memory of the fathers of the church, though a couple of possible references to it survive.[57] In later Jewish traditions, a book of Noah is mentioned in a number of sources, as well as in medieval and subsequent Christian traditions. Of these mentions, many are later inventions.[58]

If the argument proposed here is accepted as a point of departure, further study is required in order to clarify the contents and character of the book of Noah, as far as is possible. As indicated above, the literary fragments that scholars have attributed to a Noachic source must be investigated anew, and the corpus of texts relating to the birth of Noah should be considered once more. Issues of considerable importance cannot yet be determined. These include the relationship between both the figures and the writings of Enoch and Noah. This is still unclear and will remain so until the literary issues surrounding the book of Noah have been resolved. It is possible that different traditions of learning are here involved, and it is possible that the Noah material was taken over by the Enochic material. If that is the case, and if such a development has a sociological correlative, the question of why remains to be addressed. It may never be answered fully, but even to pose the question is significant for understanding the early development of postexilic Judaism.

Some similar problems with the figure of Noah occur in later sources, particularly in 2 Enoch, and the replacement of Noah in the birth story by Melchizedek is most striking[59]—and it is not the only case. Therefore, it will be necessary also to examine traditions about Noah and later Jewish and Christian retellings of the Noah story, which may preserve elements of old Noah traditions.

For the moment, the modest aim of this paper has, I believe, been achieved. It seems to me more than likely that a book or books of Noah existed in the third century B.C.E. or earlier. Some material drawn from this document is preserved in ALD, Jubilees, and the Genesis Apocryphon.

---

57. However, see below, in the last section.

58. Fabricius 1713, 240–77; Migne 1856, cols. 640–49. See Schmidt 1926, 113, who discusses many of the references. Compare Stone 1982a, 88–103.

59. See Orlov, cited in n. 13 above. He tends, however, to see polemic and confrontation between traditions in very many instances. This often involves thinking of a single paradigm against which various groups react, while the actual socioreligious reality might have been more complex. His work, however, is very perceptive and stimulates innovative ways of thinking about tradition development.

Appendix: Some Later Instances of "Book of Noah"

In this appendix I give some preliminary information on certain significant medieval sources relating the existence of a book of Noah. These sources do not have any weight in answering the question whether a book of Noah existed in the early postexilic period. They can only illustrate how the medieval Noah traditions developed. The idea of a book of Noah was not foreign to medieval Jews, Samaritans, and Christians. I do not intend the appendix to be exhaustive but to indicate the riches that may be drawn from later traditions.

Sefer Harazim and Sefer Raziel

Sefer Harazim is a work of magical character dated to the first millennium C.E., probably toward the middle of that millennium. It has survived in fragments from the Genizah and was published with many variants by Mordechai Margaliot in 1966. An English translation was prepared by Michael Morgan and published in 1983. At the start of this work we read:

> זה ספר מספרי הרזים שנתן לנוח בן למך בן מתושלח בן חנוך בן ירד בן
> מהללאל בן קינן בן אנוש בן שת בן אדם, מפי רזיאל המלאך בשנת ביאתו
> לתיבה לפני כניסתו. ויכתבהו באבן ספיר באר היטב וממנו למד מעשה פלאים
> ורזי דעת
>
> This is a book of the books of mysteries that was given to Noah, son of Lemech, son of Methuselah, son of Enoch, son of Jared, son of Mehalalel, son of Kenan, son of Enosh, son of Seth, son of Adam, from the mouth of the angel Raziel in the year in which he came to the ark, before entering (it). And he wrote it on sapphire stone very clearly, and from it he learned wonderous acts and secrets of knowledge [etc].

Noah's role as transmitter of a book of primordial knowledge is clear here,[60] and he is the one who records the secret knowledge, dictated by the angel Raziel, whose name means "secret of God."[61] This is the most prominent chain

---

60. In Pirqe de Rabbi Eliezer ch. 8 (Jerusalem: Eshkol, [n.d.]), [24]–[26], which is translated in Friedlander 1981, 52–54), a similar genealogy is given for the transmission of "the principle of intercalation" (called in Hebrew סוד העבור "the secret of intercalation").

61. There are many variants to the text of Sefer Harazim. The chief one, noted by Margaliot on p. 113, reads: "This is a book of secrets of knowledge that was revealed to Adam from the mouth of the Angel Raziel in the three hundredth year of the life of Jared, son of Mahalalel, son of Kenan, son of Enosh, son of Seth, son of Adam." Intriguingly, this genealogy stops in the generation before Enoch. Margaliot, however, considers this variant to be secondary; see his note on p. 65. The text was published earlier by Jellinek 1938, 3:159, drawn from Sefer Raziel; see ibid., 3:xxxii.

of tradition to be found in Jewish magical literature.⁶² Michael Swartz has contrasted it with the chain of tradition of the *hekhalot* books, which starts with Moses.⁶³ Intriguingly, he points out that the Moses tradition is also connected with healing, and he has also explored its relationship with Sefer Harazim (pp. 28–29). Of course, all this is not evidence for the existence of an ancient book of Noah. I adduce it to illustrate how the Noah traditions developed. The role played by the material from Jubilees or allied with Jubilees in the crystallization of this specific Noachic material in Sefer Harazim and Sefer Raziel is most significant.

The same angelic name, Raziel, is set on a book that Jellinek cited in his presentation of the book of Noah.⁶⁴ This is a later work, published in Amsterdam in 1701. Margaliot verified the Amsterdam edition against the manuscript and confirmed Jellinek's reading in Beth Hamidrasch.⁶⁵ The passage cited by Jellinek is quite long and contains much interesting material. The book was revealed by the angel Raziel to Adam, following his prayer of repentance upon his expulsion from Eden.⁶⁶ The book contained secrets of the future and nature and the course of history. The text continues:

> And the angel Raziel opened the book and read it to Adam. And it came to pass when he heard the words of this holy book from the mouth of the angel Raziel, he fell upon his face trembling. And he said, "Adam, rise and be strong. Do not fear and be not in awe! Take this book from my hands, and be preserved through it, from it you shall have knowledge and understanding. And make it known to everyone who is worthy of it and it will be his portion."
>
> [21] At the time when Adam took this book, fire burned on the bank of the river, and the angel ascended to heaven in a fiery flame. Then Adam realised and knew that he was an angel of God and that this book was sent from the presence the Holy King. And he kept it in pure sanctity.
>
> And after four generations Enoch, son of Jared, arose and had understanding in the awe of God and conducted himself in purity. He used to wash and sanctify himself in living water (fresh water) and beseech the Creator of all. And in a dream, the place where the book was hidden was revealed, how it was to be handled⁶⁷ and what its function was and its pure sanctity. And he arose early and went to a cave and delayed until midday and through

---

62. Swartz 1994, 212–17.
63. Ibid, section 2.
64. In fact, in an early printing, Sefer Harazim is called "Book of Noah"; see Margaliot 1966, 59–60. See further Blau 1906.
65. See Margaliot 1966, 65 n. 1.
66. Jellinek 1938, 156–67.
67. Ibid., 158.

the sun's power his soul came there, so that the local people should not perceive [יבינו] him. He besought God Blessed be He and ascended (to heaven) in purity and held to the pure Name. And when he understood it, his eyes enlightened all his ways, and he conducted himself through it and continued until he became like the holy ones on high and he was separated from the inhabitants of the earth and was not, for God took him.

For through this book he instructed and gave knowledge of the orbits and the constellations and all the luminaries that serve for each month, and the names by which each orbit is called, and the angels that serve in the four seasons of the year, and he learned the names of the earth and the names of the heaven and also the names of sun and moon. And he continued to honour it with all his might and he learned all wisdom, more than Adam the first man, and he learned that all the generations that came after him did not have strength to withstand it, for it is mighty and glorious. And he hid it until Noah, son of Lamech, arose, a completely righteous man [צדיק תמים] in his generations. And in the 500th year of his life the earth was corrupted by the violent action of the generations and all flesh corrupted their way upon the earth and the cry of the earth rose up to heaven before the throne of glory of the Holy One Blessed be He, and Noah found grace in the eyes of the Lord.

And then Raphael, the holy archangel [שר] was sent to him and he said to him, "I was sent through/by the word of God to you to heal the earth and to make known what will be and what (a man) should do and escape." Then he gave him this holy book and taught him how to handle it and what its function was, and what was the sanctity of its purity.

And he said to him, "Hear the word of the Lord. Since you were found to be a perfectly righteous man in your generations, behold, I have given you this holy book and I have made known to you all its secrets and mysteries, to do it in sanctity and purity and modesty and humility, and from it you shall learn to make (an ark) of gopher wood. And you shall enter, you and your sons and your wife and the wives of your sons, to hide for a short time, until the wrath shall pass." And Noah took the book from the hand of Raphael the holy archangel [שר], and when he learned in it the letters that were engraved, the spirit of the Lord rested upon him and he made the ark by length and width with the knowledge that he learned through this holy Name [...].

Then Noah, son of Lamech, hid it before he came into the ark [...]. Then he opened his mouth with the spirit of wisdom and understanding and he blessed the Lord God, the great, mighty and awesome king.[68]

The text continues to relate the transmission of the book to Shem, Abraham, Isaac, Jacob, Levi, Moses, Aaron, Phinehas, and all the generations. So here we have a legend of a book of Noah, revealed to Adam and transmitted

---

68. Ibid., 156–58.

to Enoch, to Noah, and then to Levi and through him to the priestly line. It contains many points of interest for the student of Second Temple period texts, and its full exegesis must await a future study. The sources used by Sefer Raziel, however, are much more extensive than those preserved in Sefer Harazim. Particularly striking is the section on Enoch as well as the transmission from Noah through Abraham to Levi and his sons. The text gives no extracts from the Noachic book but indicates that it is a repository of secret knowledge, including the divine Name by which Noah built the ark. Because of the etymology of Raphael, the connection of Raphael with the revelation of the book to Noah evokes the section from Jub. 10 and its parallel in Sefer Asaf Harofe, even though this angel is not mentioned in the latter work.

THE BOOK OF ASAṬIR

In the medieval Samaritan history entitled The Book of Asaṭir, we read in chapter 3:

> And Noah sat in Adam's place after Adam's death. In the seventh year (of his life or after Adam's death?) he learned three books of the covenant: the Book of the Signs, the Book of the Constellations and the Book of the Wars, this is the Book of the Generations of Adam.[69]

The work is discussed by J. T, Milik, who sees in the reference to the Book of the Signs (ספר האותות) a possible hint that Adam created the true calendar.[70] He would interpret the three Noachic books to be related to Enochic writings: "we can recognize in these without much difficulty the earliest compositions attributed to Enoch: the sacred calendars ... the astronomical treatise (1 En. 72–82) and the Vision of Enoch (1 En. 6–19)."[71] I do not find Milik's identifications convincing, the less so since Asaṭir relates the three works to Noah and *not* to Enoch. It is intriguing, however, that here once more we have books associated with Noah in a medieval tradition.[72]

---

69. The Aramaic text with a Hebrew translation is given by Ben-Ḥayyim 1943; 1944.
70. Milik 1976, 64–65.
71. Ibid, 67–68.
72. Moreover, Milik is surely correct in finding the association of the Book of Signs with Enoch to be significant. I take exception only to his specific identification of the three books that Noah learned with specific parts of 1 Enoch.

Other References

Hugh J. Lawlor points out that Tertullian, in *De cultu feminarum* 3, apparently knew of no work he regarded as Noachic.[73] On the other hand, "Augustine, speaking of Enoch and Noah in *City of God* 18.38," says that the only reason their writings are not canonical is their excessive antiquity. The Zohar, Berešit, 1.37b and 55b refers to a book of secrets revealed by the angel Raziel to Adam, who transmitted it, via Seth, to Enoch. Noah does not figure in this transmission.

---

73. Lawlor 1897, 179–80.

A Reconsideration of Charles's Designated "Noah Interpolations" in 1 Enoch: 54:1–55:1; 60; 65:1–69:25

Vered Hillel

The book of Noah and Noah traditions have long intrigued scholars and have recently led to considerable scholarly debate and a growing number of publications.[1] The book of Jubilees (10:3; 21:10), Genesis Apocryphon (col. 5, line 29), and Aramaic Levi Document (10:10) mention a book(s) of Noah,[2] while Jubilees, 1 Enoch, and various Qumran fragments preserve Noah traditions.[3] As early as 1893, R. H. Charles distinguished certain passages in the Similitudes of Enoch (1 En. 37–71) as Noachic fragments belonging to the book of Noah or the apocalypse of Noah mentioned in Jubilees. Using a specific set of criteria, he determined that 1 En. 54:7–55:2; 60; and 65:1–69:25 are such interpolations. Characteristically, Charles liberally proposed interpolations and emendations together with his criteria to help him arrive at his conclusions.

Charles has been criticized for this type of "cut-and-paste" treatment of texts[4] and for paying too much attention to historical allusions and theological doctrines and too little attention to literary structure and symbolism.[5] He has even been accused of "hindering the study of Second Temple Judaism."[6] While many of these comments may be true, we need to remember that Charles wrote in a time when the source-critical principles of Wellhausen dominated

---

1. For a bibliography of publications until 1999 devoted to Noachic traditions, see DiTommaso 2001, 427–30; see also Orlov 2000b, 207 n. 1.
2. See Stone 2006a.
3. Jub. 7:20–39; 10:1–15; 1 En. 6–11; 54:7–55:2; 60; 65:1–69:25; and 106–107; 1Q19; 4Q534–536; 4Q252–254.
4. Black 1985, 238; de Jonge 1953, 31–36.
5. Collins 1986, 348.
6. Charlesworth 2002, 227.

the German and the British scholarly traditions[7] and when Christian scholars, who were in the majority, approached texts with their own bias and presuppositions searching for the background of Christianity and/or the historical Jesus.[8] These ideas created an anti-Jewish portrayal of Second Temple Judaism characterized by stereotypes gleaned from the New Testament and tendentious polemics that did not begin to change until after the Second World War. In essence, Charles, like all scholars, was a product of his time.

Since Charles, new "criticisms" (form, text, literary, structural, etc.) and methods drawn from the social sciences, as well as archaeological discoveries such as the Dead Sea Scrolls and the Cairo Genizah, have modified the methodology by which texts are studied and the point of view from which they are approached. Despite these advances, Charles's work on the Apocrypha and Pseudepigrapha remains seminal and is consulted by students and scholars alike. A case in point is his 1912 translation of and commentary on the Ethiopic text of 1 Enoch. This work remained the standard edition of 1 Enoch until 1978, when Michael Knibb published a new edition based on Rylands Ethiopic MS 23. Subsequently in 1985, Matthew Black, building on Charles's 1912 edition, published a revised translation and commentary; in 2001, George W. E. Nickelsburg published part 1 of the Hermeneia commentary on 1 Enoch, which unfortunately does not include the Similitudes, and in 2005 Nickelsburg and James C. VanderKam published a new translation of the whole book.

Also seminal are Charles's designated "Noah interpolations": scholars either adopt them without question or reject them without demonstrating why the designation is invalid. This article investigates Charles's designated Noah interpolations in the Similitudes in light of his own criteria and methodology to see if his arguments hold. In his 1912 edition, Charles listed seven criteria (emended from his 1893 edition) used to determine three Noah interpolations in the Similitudes.[9]

Charles's Criteria

1. The interpolations always disturb the context in which they occur.
2. They profess to be a revelation to Noah.

---

7. Already in the eighteenth century the British and German schools were collaborating. Ideas worked out in Britain were quickly translated into German and disseminated among the Protestant faculties of theology. For more information, see O'Neil 1992, 726.

8. For bibliography on the details of the anti-Jewish interpretation of Judaism, see Nickelsburg and Kraft 1986, 10. See also the discussion in Sanders 1977, 1–19 esp. 1–12.

9. Charles 1912, 106–7; 1893, 146–47.

3. There are definite dates in the additions; as in 60:1: "In the year 500, in the seventh month on the fourteenth of the month in the life of Enoch."
4. The demonology is different.
5. The interpolator seeks to adapt his additions to their new contexts and accordingly incorporates in them many terms and phrases from the Similitudes but misuses technical terms and phrases, either through ignorance or set purpose.
6. The interpolator misunderstands the Similitudes and combines absolutely alien elements.
7. The Similitudes follow the LXX chronology; the interpolations follow the Samaritan chronology.

This essay first evaluates the integrity of Charles's criteria, then examines his three designated Noah interpolations (54:7–55:2; 60; 65:1–69:25) in light of these criteria. Two points to bear in mind before beginning our investigation are that: (1) the extant Ethiopic text is a third-generation translation; it is a translation of a Greek translation of a Semitic original; and (2) the surviving manuscripts are often confused and corrupted.

Section 1: Integrity of the Criteria

Criteria 2 and 3: Attribution and Definite Dates

According to Charles's criteria, the interpolated passages profess to be a revelation to Noah; as a result, he also attributes to Noah any passage related to the flood or the first judgment. This is true of 54:7–55:2, which does not mention Noah by name but focuses on the flood and thereby is linked to Noah and satisfies Charles's second criterion as an interpolation.

It is clear from 60:1 and 60:8 that chapter 60 is erroneously attributed to Enoch instead of Noah.[10] The mention in verse 8 of the visionary's great-grandfather, the seventh from Adam, and the dating "in the year 500," which is drawn from Gen 5:32,[11] could apply only to Noah, as according to both the LXX and MT, Enoch was 365 years old when he walked with God (Gen 5:22–23). Noachic and Enochic traditions often occur together, and in some

---

10. The erroneous attribution to Enoch instead of Noah has been argued since Dillmann 1853. Suter (1979b, 32, 154) does not accept this as a wrong attribution; cf. Dimant 1998, 144–46.
11. Noah was 500 years old when his sons were born.

texts the "words of Noah" follow closely on the "words of Enoch."[12] There is interdependence between Noachic and Enochic material; some type of affinity lies behind the "Enoch-Noah axis." Even the texts that seem to show a theological polemic against Noah (e.g., 2 Enoch) are based on some type of "original" Noachic material.[13] Although the "original" Noah motifs and themes are substantially rewritten in it, they nevertheless exhibit parallels to the Noah material.[14] The same is true in 1 En. 60, where the Noah material has been reworked to read as an Enochic vision. Interestingly, definite dates like those given in 60:1 and 60:8 are only found in Charles's designated "Noah fragments." Elsewhere in the Similitudes, only general phrases such as "in those days" or "all the years of the world" are used.

Of the passage 65:1–69:25, only 65:1–68:1 is attributed to Noah. While Noachic attribution could possibly apply to the discourse between Michael and Raphael in 68:2–69:25, it seems unlikely, as both Noah and the flood suddenly vanish when the discourse begins, leaving no indication that the passage is connected to Noah. The introductory phrase to the discourse, "And on that day," also signals a break in the section, as it points to the last judgment instead of the first. While no definite dates are used in either section, two distinct time-related phrases are mentioned: "in those days," which appears only in 65:1–68:1; and "on/from that/this day," which is relegated to 68:2–69:25. This corresponds to the attribution division just mentioned. Thus only the first section (65:1–68:1) can be attributed to Noah.

CRITERION 4: DIFFERENT DEMONOLOGY

Charles contends that the demonology in the additions is different from that of the Similitudes proper. It is difficult to assess this criterion, as Charles's arguments are as bewildering as the demonology in the text. His line of reasoning must be teased from his commentary just as the demonology from the text; nothing is stated explicitly. The demonology in the Similitudes includes the fallen angels and their leader Azazel, satans, Satan, and the angels of punishment. Satan and satans only appear four times in 1 Enoch and then only in the Similitudes: Satan appears as the leader of the angels of punishment (53:3) and as the ruler who subjugates the hosts of Azazel (54:6); the satans are the accusers of (40:7) and teachers of violence (65:6) to those who dwell on the earth. The angels of punishment are instruments of retribution for the condemned who oppressed humankind and led them astray (53:3; 56:1; 62:11;

---

12. Kvanvig 1988, 71–86; Stone 1999; Jub. 21:10.
13. Orlov 2000a; 2000b. For a slightly modified position, see Orlov 2005.
14. Orlov 2000b.

63:1). However, in 66:1 they have power over the waters that are released to punish those who dwell on the earth.

Charles classifies these references into two groups of evil agencies: the satans, comprised of the satans and the angels of punishment, led by Satan;[15] and the fallen angels, led by Azazel. This classification allows Charles to propose three roles for the satans: (1) accusers who have access to heaven (40:7); (2) punishers of the condemned (53:3; 56:1; 62:11; 63:1); and (3) those who lead people astray (69:4, 6).[16] The first two functions, accusers and punishers of the condemned, appear only in the Similitudes proper and stand in opposition to their function in the interpolation as those who lead astray (69:4, 6). Thus the term is used differently in the interpolation.

The reference to the angels of punishment in 66:1, which was omitted from Charles's argument summarized above, also supports his criterion. In the Similitudes, the satans interact with those who dwell upon the earth (40:7; 65:6) and the angels of punishment with the condemned, the hosts of Azazel, and the kings and the mighty. However, in 66:1, a designated Noah interpolation, the two terms have been confused. Here the angels of punishment, instead of the satans, are paired with those who dwell on the earth: the angels of punishment have control over the waters that will bring judgment and destruction on those who dwell on the earth. The two groups, satans and angels of punishment, have been fused. While the Similitudes allude to their amalgamation, the interpolation executes it. Consequently, the demonology in 66:1 is different from the Similitudes and thus qualifies the verse as an interpretation.

The two lists of fallen angels in 1 En. 69 also exhibit differences in demonology that indicate that they are interpolations. The first list in 69:2-3, which lists the angels who were placed over the elements of the cosmos, is the same, with some variations, as that in 6:7 and is generally considered to be a secondary insertion.[17] According to Suter, this list probably did not originally refer to fallen angels. Although this would indicate redactional activity, it does not provide information on the use of the list in the Similitudes. Charles contends that this list refers to the angels who fell in the time of Jared, but it is not clear how he reached this conclusion. Regardless of its status or to whom it refers, the list contains no information pertinent to our evaluation of criterion 4.

The second list (69:4-15) parallels one in 8:1-3. Both lists give the names of the angels along with their function in leading humankind astray. In the Book of the Watchers (8:2), men are led astray into godlessness and

---

15. See Charles 1912, 78 (40:7); cf. Black 1985, 200 and references there.
16. Charles 1912, 78.
17. For example, see Charles 1912, 136; Knibb 1978, 136. Knibb thinks the variations are due to inner-Ethiopic variants of the names in 6:7 (1978, 76,159).

fornication, while in 69:4–6 Jeqon and Asbeel lead the sons of god to defile themselves with the daughters of men and Gadreel leads Eve astray. Accordingly, both Jeqon and Asbeel existed before the sins of the Watchers and Eve. Consequently, either the list does not refer to the fallen angels as stated in 69:2 (Jeqon and Asbebel are the cause of the Watchers going astray) or the demonology in the list is different from that of the Similitudes.

Several other incongruities exist between the two lists of names; for example, Gadreel has assumed the role of Azazel (or Asael) as the angel in charge of making weapons of war (8:1; 69:6) and Kasdeja the role of Samjaza as the angel in charge of enchantments and root-cuttings (8:3; 69:13). But the most significant for our investigation is the leader of the fallen angels. In the Book of the Watchers, Semjaza is the leader of the fallen angels (6:3; 8:3; 9:7) and Azazel is responsible for all unrighteousness and corruption on earth (9:6; 10:4–9; 13:1–2), while in the Similitudes Azazel is the leader of the fallen angels (54:5; 55:4). To the contrary, 69:4 designates Jaqon as the leader, indicating that the demonology in the list in chapter 69 is different from the rest of the Similitudes. While the incongruities uphold Charles's criterion that the demonology is different in the interpolations, it not clear that they can be attributed to a book of Noah or a Noah tradition. However, Suter's assertion that 69:4–12 represents "the original form of the tradition" and the names in 8:1–3 are the "result of redactional assimilation"[18] lends credence to this theory.

CRITERION 5: TECHNICAL TERMS

Charles claims that the interpolator adapts many technical terms and phrases from the Similitudes but misuses them. Bear in mind that the terminology "misuse of technical terms" is a quote from Charles and not a value judgment on our part.

Term 1: "Those Who Dwell on the Earth"

This phrase is used most prominently in the Similitudes to indicate the elect, the righteous, those who have eternal life, whereas in the three passages that Charles attributes to Noah, the phrase designates the unrighteous, the wicked, those being judged, or merely their geographical location as inhabitants of the physical world. In 54:7–55:2, "those who dwell on the earth" refers to the wicked inhabitants on earth who are judged in the flood; in chapter 60, the phrase designates their geographical location; and in 65–69 it indicates both

---

18. Suter 1979b, 73.

the unrighteous, wicked people (65:6, 12; 66:1; 67:8) and their geographical location (67:7; 69:1).

Term 2: "Angels of Punishment"

The role of the "angels of punishment" only occurs in one interpolated passage, 66:1, where it also deviates slightly from its regular usage in the Similitudes. All four times that the "angels of punishment" appear in the Similitudes, they punish the condemned (53:3; 56:1; 63:1; 66:1). Three times (53:3; 56:1; 63:1) they deal with the eschatological, second judgment, and once (66:1) with the first judgment. In 66:1 (a Noah fragment), they have control over the waters. Hence, the angels of punishment are related to the flood, the first judgment by water, and consequently to Noah and ultimately to Noachic traditions.

Term 3: "Lord of Spirits"

The "Lord of spirits" is a unique term found only in the Similitudes. Although the term probably stems from Num 16:22, its closest parallel in Jewish literature appears in 2 Macc 3:24. "Lord of spirits" occurs 104 times in the Similitudes, 28 of which appear in Charles's interpolated sections. In most instances, "Lord of spirits" refers to the all-knowing, wise God who interacts with the figure(s) who appear(s) with him. He is not an austere deity who acts alone to judge and condemn. On the contrary, he gives wisdom, knowledge, mercy, and revelation to the Righteous One, the Elect One, elect ones, and so on, who, in turn, depend on him. The angels surround him, and the righteous dwell with him. He is extolled, praised, and blessed. Some believe in his name, while others deny it. Punishment proceeds from him, but he is not said to perform the action.

In the second, less frequent use, the Lord of spirits is impersonal and independent. He himself judges and punishes; there is no interaction between him and the figures who appear with him. This second, less frequent use appears only in the sections designated by Charles as Noah fragments. So in 54:7–55:2 the Lord of spirits is an impersonal figure connected with the judgment of the temporal world. He executes the punishment of those "who dwell on the earth" and "under the ends of the heaven" by opening the chambers and the foundations of water. Even though the Head of Days is mentioned in this section, there is no interaction between him and the Lord of spirits.

The title "Lord of spirits" also appears three times in chapter 60 (once in v. 6, twice in v. 25). Here he acts independently to judge and to punish those who dwell upon the earth. Although his mercy and longsuffering are mentioned, his patience has run out. It is time for judgment! There is no hint of praise or adoration of the Lord of spirits or of the righteous or elect accompanying him. Instead, he acts alone to judge and to punish those who deny his name. As in 54:7–55:2, the characteristics of the Lord of spirits in chapter 60 fall within the secondary usage, which only appears in Charles's Noah passages.

Significantly, in 65:1–69:25, the third Noah passage in question, both understandings of the title have been very cleverly woven together. The Lord of spirits is presented as the all-knowing God and judge (65:9–11), as the plumb line of judgment for those who deny his name (67:8), as the angry judge (68: 4–5), and as one who is thanked and praised (69:24). In all five references, the Lord of Spirits is an impersonal deity who is talked about but with whom there is no interaction. Even his role as the all-knowing God, extolled and praised, is passive. Although clearly adapted to its context, the use of the "Lord of spirits" as impersonal and independent in 65:1–69:25 is consistent with the less frequent use of the title and is distinctive of Charles's designated Noah interpolations.

Term 4: "Head of Days"

The title "Head of Days" appears less frequently than "Lord of spirits" and then only in the second part of the Similitudes, in visions inspired by Dan 7.[19] Of its eight occurrences, five times the "Head of Days" is connected with the "son of man,"[20] and three times he acts alone.[21] Primarily, the Head of Days is described as "ancient, primordial, from the beginning of all time and eternal" (46:1; 48:2; 71:10, 12, 13), as in Dan 7:9.[22] In contrast, Charles's designated Noachic interpolations (47:3; 55:1; 60:2) emphasize the literal interpretation of the figure's role as the majestic Chief or Head. The first-person narrative in 54:7–55:2, in which the Head of Days speaks and acts alone, reflects none of the characteristics derived from Dan 7. Instead, it emphasizes his omnipotence. Consequently, the passage echoes the second usage and the so-called interpolations.

Contrary to the other occurrences where the "Head of Days" and the "son of man" appear together (46:1; 48:2; 71:10, 12), in chapter 60 there is no relationship between the two; they are totally independent figures. Here the Head of Days is seated on the throne with the angels and the righteous surrounding him (v. 2), while the son of man figure does not appear until later, after the throne-room vision and the introduction of Leviathan and Behemoth (v. 10).

---

19. Dillmann 1853, 156.
20. 1 En. 46:1; 48:2; 71:10, 11, 12. For the relationship of the two phrases, see Charles 1893, 127 n. 1; 1912, 85.
21. 1 En. 47:3; 55:1; 60:2.
22. Black 1985, 193; cf. Charles 1893, 127.

This differs from the most common usage in the Similitudes, where the two figures are associated and work in tandem. Another deviation in chapter 60 that points to a Noah interpolation is the way in which the Head of Days is depicted as a majestic chief accompanied by angels and by the righteous and not as the eternal, primordial being.

Term 5: "Son of Man"

The "son of man" figure, the last term we will address, is the most intricate. The significant corpus of scholarly writing on the "son of man figure" extends well beyond the scope of this paper. Even a limited study of the figure within the Similitudes elicits divergent scholarly opinions.[23] Because of these complexities, we will limit our comments to a general description of the term's use in the Similitudes and its comparative use in 60:10, the only time it appears in Charles's interpolations. Most often in the Similitudes, the "son of man" is more than simply a "human figure";[24] he is a redeming, eschatological figure whose defining characteristics are righteousness and election.[25] He is the judge of the world whose appearance will expose every hidden thing and will signal the revelation of good and the unmasking of evil. These characteristics are derived from Dan 7.

However, in 60:10 the "son of man" does not reflect the eschatological figure of Dan 7 but resembles a form of address peculiar to the book of Ezekiel, where the human prophet is called "son of man." Like Ezekiel, Enoch himself is called "son of man." In 60:10, Enoch plays no eschatological role and exhibits none of the characteristics usually ascribed to the son of man in the Similitudes. Above all, he is not a revealer of all things, but quite the reverse. He is a human seeking to know and understand hidden things. This usage of the term "son of man" has no parallels in the Similitudes, not even in other designated "Noah passages."[26]

Clearly the technical terminology is used differently in the designated interpolations than in the body of the Similitudes. Thus, according to the single criterion of the "misuse of terminology," it seems that Charles was justi-

---

23. On the term "son of man" in the Similitudes, see Nickelsburg 1992b, 138–40; VanderKam 1992b, 174–85; Collins 1980; and Casey 1976. See also Boccaccini 2007.

24. See note 23.

25. 1 En. 46:2–7; 48:2–10; 62:5–14; 63:11–12; 69:26–29.

26. A possible exception is 71:14. However, most scholars consider chapters 70 and 71 a double epilogue and not part of the original Similitudes. VanderKam (1992a, 177–79), on the other hand, finds these two chapters integral to the text and crucial to one's understanding of the phrase "son of man." See, for example, Boccaccini 2007.

fied in drawing a distinction between the interpolations and the body of the Similitudes.

Criterion 6: Combination of Alien Elements

Charles correctly observes that the "interpolator misunderstands the parables and combines absolutely alien elements." For example, 67:4–5 locates the "burning valley" in the west among the mountains of metal. This combination of elements is found in chapters 52–54: Enoch is swept away toward the west, where he sees mountains of metal (52:1–2). Next to these mountains is a deep valley in which the angels of punishment are making Satan's instruments (53:1–3). Enoch then turns to "another part of the earth," where he sees a burning valley into which the kings and mighty were being cast (54:1–2). To the contrary, in chapter 67 the fallen angels are cast into the burning valley that lies in the west among the mountains of metal. Also note that in 54:1 the burning valley lies in a different, unknown direction from the mountains. The writer not only combines details of the valleys and mountains of metal but also incorporates flood traditions (54:7–55:2) to create an entirely new scenario in which all the elements from chapters 52–54 coalesce: the burning valley, the great convulsion of waters, and the punishment of the kings and the mighty.

Section 2: Interpolated Sections

We shall now proceed to apply all of Charles's criteria to his interpolated "Noah" passages: 1 En. 54:7–55:2; 60; and 65:1–69:25. We will examine the context of each "interpolation" (criterion 1), then see how all the criteria, including those discussed above, come to bear on a single passage. It is important to remember that, although a significant part of the Similitudes is a reworking of earlier Enochic traditions drawn from the Book of the Luminaries[27] and the Book of the Watchers,[28] the Similitudes is distinct from the rest of 1 Enoch, among other things, in its origin, in its use of the names of God, and its view of eschatology.[29] The Similitudes is the second of 1 Enoch's

---

27. Chapters 1–16 and 17–36 in the Book of Luminaries closely parallel the first parable in the Similitudes, chapters 38–44.

28. The Similitudes 41:3–8; 43–44; 60:11–24; and 69:22–24 parallel the Book of the Watchers. Similarly, the "Noachic" narratives in 65–67 are related to stories in 83–84 and 106–107.

29. For an explanation of the chief characteristics that differentiate the Similitudes from the rest of 1 Enoch, see Charles 1893, 106–7. See also Boccaccini 2007.

five major divisions and is usually itself divided into three major blocks (first parable, 38–44; second parable, 45–57; and third parable, 58–69), plus a brief introduction (37:1–4), an epilogue (70), and an appendix (70–71).[30]

1 Enoch 54:7–55:2

Criterion 1: Disturbs the Context

According to Charles's criteria, the interpolated passages profess to be a revelation to Noah (criterion 2), so any passage related to the flood or the first judgment is also attributed to Noah. This is true of 54:7–55:2. The verses do not mention Noah by name, but they do focus on the flood. As a result, the passage is linked to Noah and satisfies Charles's second criterion as an interpolation. He also states that this section disturbs the context of the second parable (45–57; criterion 1). The preceding verses, 53:1–54:6, address the final judgment: the condemnation of the watchers; the resurrection of the dead; and a deep, burning valley prepared for Azazel and his armies. Suddenly, 54:7–55:2 begins discussing the first judgment, the punishment of the flood. Then in 55:3 the text returns to the final judgment, that is, to the angels on the day of tribulation and pain, to the judgment of Azazel and his hosts, and to the deep valley, thereby connecting 55:3 back to 54:6.

The change from the second judgment to the first in this passage definitely disturbs the context, and when the section is removed, the remaining material flows well together. However, the first judgment material has been cleverly worked into the context. This passage imitates 1 En. 8–10 in the Book of the Watchers; in both instances, the flood material is introduced after the account of the condemnation and temporary incarceration of the Watchers.[31] So, although the material may be out of context, it is not out of place.

The first-person utterance by the Lord of spirits in 55:3 concerning the judgment of Azazel and his armies is problematic. While the declaration smoothly follows the first person narrative in 55:2, it connects clumsily with 54:6, where the angel of peace is speaking about the Lord of spirits. Four or five words of this text are confused and corrupt, with some parts of the text missing.[32] Charles translates the corrupt text "this is in accordance with my commandment" and attaches it to the end of 55:2, as he understands the phrase to refer to the "pledge of faithfulness."

---

30. That 71:1–17 is generally considered an appendix, see Stone 1984a, 401 n. 97, 403 n. 106. Milik 1976, 90, proposes different divisions.
31. Black 1985, 184.
32. Charles 1906, 99.

And He sware by His great name: "Henceforth I will not do so to all who dwell on the earth, and I will set a sign in the heaven: and this shall be a pledge of good faith between Me and them for ever, so long as heaven is above the earth. *And this is in accordance with My command.* 3 When I have desired to take hold of them by the hand of the angels on the day of tribulation and pain because of this, I will cause My chastisement and My wrath to abide upon them, saith God, ... the Lord of Spirits...." (emphasis added)

On the other hand, Black, like other translators, follows the traditional verse division and places the phrase at the beginning of 54:3.[33] He assumes that a reference to Azazel and his host is missing. Thus he emends Charles's reading to: "And this is my command [with regard to the host of Azazel] when I am pleased to seize them by the hand of the angels." Black's emendation smoothes the transition between 54:6 and 55:3, showing that the text flows as a whole without the Noah passage in 54:7–55:2. However, there is no need to try to smooth or justify all the inconsistencies in an ancient text, so Charles's suggestion is tenable.

Summary

Only three of Charles's criteria apply to 1 En. 54:7–55:2: context; attribution; and the "misuse of technical terms." The section, based on its subject of the flood, the first judgment, interrupts the flow of the context and indirectly professes to be a revelation to Noah. Its distinctive use of these technical terms "Lord of Spirits," "Head of Days," and those "who dwell on the earth" reflects a secondary usage found only in the so-called interpolations. These findings uphold Charles's designation of this section as an interpolation. The fact, noted above, that the text flows more or less smoothly after the interpolation is removed, corroborates this conclusion.

1 Enoch 60

Criterion 1: Disturbs the Context

The textual complexities[34] and lack of distinct unity[35] make it difficult to determine the overall position of chapter 60 within the third parable and thus whether or not it disturbs the context. The chapter begins with Enoch's

---

33. Black 1985, 220.
34. Charles 1906, 108; Martin 1906, 124; Knibb 1978, 148; Black 1985, 230–31. Charles actually places v. 25 between vv. 6 and 7 in the translation (1912, 114–15).
35. Knibb 1978, 143; cf. Black 1985, 225.

(Noah's) vision of the heavens that quake so violently that all the heavenly hosts are disquieted and he is prostrate with fear. Subsequently, Michael sends an angel[36] to raise Enoch up and to warn him of the impending judgment and punishment, during which two monsters, Leviathan and Behemoth, will either be food for or devour the victims. A short excursus on the mysteries of nature (thunder, lightning, snow, hail; 60:11–23) interrupts the description of Leviathan and Behemoth material, which concludes in the first part of verse 24. The subject then returns to the eschatological judgment and punishment, and in chapter 61 suddenly introduces two angels who measure paradise and the righteous.

These opening verses of the third parable consist of several units of traditional material. K. William Whitney Jr. demonstrates this in the following chart:[37]

58:1–3	Eschatology	Introduction
59:1–3	Cosmology	Lightning and thunder
60:1–6	Eschatology	Heavenly throne room and judgment
60:7–10	Eschatology	Behemoth and Leviathan
60:11–23	Cosmology	Heavenly secrets
60:24ab	Eschatology	Behemoth and Leviathan
60:24c-25	Eschatology	The judgment
61:1–5	Eschatology	Measuring of the righteous
61:1–3	Eschatology	The elevation of the Chosen One

The rapid shifts between eschatological and cosmological concerns may indicate the displacement of original material.[38] Nickelsburg proposes regrouping the material thematically by relocating 60:11–13 to follow 59:1–3 immediately, thus reuniting the two cosmological units as well as that of Leviathan and Behemoth.[39] Although the textual integrity of an apocalyptic work should not usually be judged by thematic consistency, Whitney states that at the very least the two references to Behemoth and Leviathan should be treated as an original unity.[40]

Even if we accept Nickelsburg's emendations, they do not solve the textual difficulties. Several questions still remain: (1) How should 60:24–25 be handled? Should the corrupt text be emended by repositioning the verses to follow the Noah material in verses 1–6, or should they remain in place? (2)

---

36. Probably the angel of peace named in 60:24.
37. Whitney 2006, 46–47.
38. See Whitney 2006, 47 esp. n. 58 for bibliographical references.
39. Nickelsburg 1981, 219.
40. Cf. Knibb 1978, 143 n. 60.6.

How should the Leviathan/Behemoth material be interpreted: does it apply to the flood or the eschaton? Knibb explains that verses 24c and 25 are out of place in most manuscripts, probably due to missing words that were reinserted in verse 25.[41] He joins 24ab to verses 7–10 because they answer the question about the two beasts posed in verse 9, and he connects verses 24c–25 to the Noachic material that broke off in verse 6.[42] In 1893, Charles recognized the textual problem and inserted verse 25 after verse 6, thereby connecting the verse with the Noah material. Although Charles mentioned the displacement of verse 24, he did not emend the text. In contrast, Black, following Dillmann, sees no need to emend the text because they interpret the Leviathan/Behemoth material as pertaining to the first judgment, to the flood. He interprets the passive verb "to feast" (*yessēsayu*) in 60:24 to mean "to be supplied with food," not to provide food for the righteous, as other commentators maintain.[43] Accordingly, the role of the two monsters was to devour the victims of the flood. This interpretation describes the first judgment and removes the need to emend the text: the cosmological material in verses 11–23 becomes less intrusive because the flood deals with the cataclysm of nature.[44] Thus, according to Black and Dillmann, all of chapter 60 refers to the flood and as such can be attributed to Noah and Noachic traditions.

Conversely, Whitney and Knibb understand the Leviathan/Behemoth material to refer to the eschaton. Whitney, based on verbal tenses, terminology, and parallels found in 4 Ezra 6:49–52 and 2 Bar. 29:4, has convincingly demonstrated this position.[45] According to 4 Ezra and 2 Baruch, Leviathan and Behemoth are huge monsters created on the fifth day as food for the righteous during messianic times.[46] Whitney concludes that these texts all stem from a common tradition that was set in primordial times.[47] This interpretation accounts for the tension in 1 En. 60:7–10, 24ab but is suspect because it derives from the author's attempt to impose an eschatological context on the originally primordial material.

Besides the false attribution, the verse describes the abode of Behemoth as being in Dendayn. Many attempts have been made to clarify the location

---

41. Knibb 1978, 148 n. 60.24.
42. Knibb 1978, 143 n. 60.6, 148 n. 60.24.
43. Black 1985, 225, 230–31; Dillmann 1853, 183–84, 190–91. For dissenting opinions, see, e.g., Whitney 2006, 56.
44. Black 1985, 230–31.
45. Whitney 2006, 50–51.
46. This tradition seems to be a reworking of Ps 74:14. See Bousset and Gressmann 1966, 285. The Bablylonian Talmud (B. Batra 74a) also understands the two monsters to be food for the righteous in messianic times.
47. Whitney 2006, 57.

and name of this desert.[48] Whitney shows how Dendayn is of "considerable antiquity" and a much earlier form of the similar tradition found in 4 Ezra 6:51.[49] Furthermore the association with Enoch (v. 8) indicates that the work arose from the community of "ancestral heroes." If we accept this assessment along with the correct attribution of Noah, we can deduce that some type of Noah tradition lies behind this chapter and possibly even a "book of Noah."

No matter how one interprets or emends chapter 60, the opening verses of chapter 61 are problematic: the identity of the two angels[50] is not immediately obvious. It is clear that they do not refer back to the hosts of angels in 60:1, because their characteristics are different. Scholars resolve this uneven seam in various ways: Dillmann simply links these angels to the angels that appeared previously in the Similitudes; Charles characteristically explains their sudden appearance by "some preceding part now lost."[51] Black proposes that they are a "midrashic treatment" of Zech 2:1–3, and Knibb is silent. If, on the other hand, Nickelsburg's proposed relocation is accepted, then the passage in 61:1–5 dealing with the angels' measuring of paradise and the righteous would directly follow the Leviathan/Behemoth unit. This order is similar to the eschatological blessings that follow the Leviathan/Behemoth material in 2 Baruch. Though such an emendation smoothes the uneven seam, it does not explain the sudden appearance of the two angels. Even with the restoration of "Noah" for "Enoch," it is not clear that the entire chapter or even parts ever belonged to an original book of Noah.

Summary of Chapter 60

The textual complexities of this chapter complicate the assessment of Charles's criteria more than any other section. How one resolves important issues concerning the Similitudes and its language influences the decision as to whether the passage is interpolated Noah material or not. Based on the definitive dates given (criterion 3), the material clearly should be ascribed to Noah (criterion 2). However, the author has thoroughly reworked the material and applied it to Enoch. Thus it is difficult to discern precisely what is Noachic tradition. Whether or not the passage is out of context depends on one's interpretation of the Leviathan/Behomoth material. If the passage refers to the final, eschatological judgment, it does not interrupt the flow of the text, seeing that it

---

48. For example, Dillmann 1853, 30, 184; Charles 1913, 115–16; Milik 1971, 348; Black 1978, 231–32; 1985, 227.

49. Whitney 2006, 53–55, 57.

50. Some manuscripts read "those angels."

51. Dillmann 1853; Charles 1912, 119.

relates thematically to chapters 59 and 61 and therefore cannot be classified as an interpretation. However, if one accepts Whitney's assessment of the Leviathan/Behemoth material, as I do, the passage refers to the first judgment. This assessment, coupled with his contention that the legend contains primordial material of "considerable age," verifies the criterion and makes this passage an interpolation related to ancient Noah traditions. The technical terms in chapter 60 reflect the secondary usage, which equates them with the "interpolated" passages. Consequently, I conclude that chapter 60 relies on some type of Noah tradition that has been thoroughly reworked by the author. Although the chapter may reflect a book of Noah, it cannot be tied to a specific writing.

1 Enoch 65:1–69:25

Criterion 1: Disturbs the Context

This section deals mainly with three subjects: the impending flood and the deliverance of Noah (65:1–67:3); the punishment of the fallen angels (67:4–68:1); and the judgment of the fallen angels and the secrets they disclosed (68:2–69:25). The narrative shifts between first person and third person: 64:1–2 is a first-person narrative by Enoch; 65:1–2a briefly shifts to a third-person narrative about Noah; and 65:2b-68:1 is a first-person narrative by Noah.[52] The material then turns to a discussion between Michael and Raphael about the judgment and the aftermath thereof (68:2–69:25).

Enoch and Noah appear together in 65:1–68:2: Noah cries out to Enoch, his grandfather—actually, his great-grandfather—who is located at the ends of the earth, in order to find the reason for the impending destruction of the earth.[53] Enoch explains to Noah that the destruction is coming because the earth has been corrupted by the teaching of the angels and the satans, then gives him (Noah) a promise of redemption (65:6–12). As a sign of confirmation, Enoch shows Noah that the angels of punishment who hold the power over the waters prepared to bring judgment and destruction are restrained by the Lord of spirits (66:1–2). Noah temporarily leaves Enoch's presence (66:3). The two appear together again in 68:1, where Noah receives the book of secrets and parables from Enoch. In the intervening chapter (67), Noah expounds Enoch's revelation and reiterates God's promise to him. This time

---

52. Black (1985, 239) regards vv. 1–3 as a first-person narrative based on the reading of Eth^t, which he regards as the correct reading. Dimant classifies this section as a discourse and not a narrative (1998, 145).

53. In 1 En. 83–84, Enoch relates to Methuselah a dream vision he had concerning the flood.

Noah receives the revelation directly from God; Enoch is not the intermediary. In 68:2–5, Michael and Raphael discuss the severity of the judgment of the secrets and of the fallen angels, while chapter 69 lists the names and functions of the fallen angels and satans.

It is clear that 65:1–69:25 deals with two separate traditions (65–67 and 68–69). Chapter 64 shifts from the preceding description of the eschatological judgment of the kings and the mighty (chs. 62–63) to the following Noah material (chs. 65–67). Another transition is found in 68:1, in which Enoch entrusts Noah with a book of parables. This verse is an apparent interpolation, as it assumes that the Similitudes already exists, that it tries to smooth the seam between the following Michael-Raphael discourse and the preceding Noah material, perhaps to lend authority to the Michael-Raphael tradition.

Chapters 65–67 clearly deal with the first judgment, and chapter 68 is assigned to the time of the flood because it discusses the judgment of the angels who are identified as the Watchers. Chapter 69 is assigned to the first judgment because it names the fallen angels and satans and because it reworks 1 En. 6:6–8, which definitely refers to the flood. These separate traditions have been adapted into a coherent literary unit that can stand as a whole, independent of its context. When removed from their context, the text flows smoothly from chapter 63 to chapter 70. Although out of context, these verses are not out of order. They have been carefully worked into the Similitudes. The judgment of the angels is described in 55:3–4 as a warning to the mighty kings, whose own judgment appears in chapter 62. Somewhere between chapter 55 and chapter 62 the mighty kings became two entities, the mighty and the kings. The kings and the mighty resurface again in the middle of the judgment of the fallen angels in 67:8, tying them together by *Stichworte*.[54] Nevertheless, their association with the first judgment disturbs the context of the Similitudes and satisfies Charles's first criterion as a Noah interpolation.

Summary of 65:1–69:25

Our examination of this passage in light of Charles's criteria shows that it consists of two separate traditions—chapters 65–67 and 68–69—that have been intricately woven together to create one literary unit that refers to the time of the flood. Section one reflects Noah traditions that probably came from a book of Noah. The second section, however, represents an independent tradition that cannot be traced to a book of Noah or even to a Noah tradition.

---

54. Black (1985, 238–39) points out that "connection of pericopae by Stichworte is a familiar literary device in the growth of traditions." Charles (1912, 135) thinks that this may be a play on words between angels (מלאכים) and kings (מלכים).

Although the two sections deal with different subjects, together they interrupt the flow of the context, thereby fulfilling Charles's first criterion. Both sections use specific time-related phrases but do not give explicit dates, so the relevance of criterion 3 is questionable. Chapters 65–69 satisfy Charles's second criterion as an interpolation, in that they deal with the flood and specifically with Noah in 65–67. The technical terminology is misunderstood in this passage (criterion 5); nonetheless, the terms have been cleverly adapted into the context and into the Similitudes as a whole. Unique to this section are the demonology and the manner in which the author combined elements (i.e., the metal mountains and the burning valley): both reflect a secondary usage and therefore an interpolation.

Conclusion

Devorah Dimant denounces Charles's recognition of 54:1–55:1; 60; 65:1–69:25 as traces of the lost book of Noah without examining his criteria for such designations.[55] The above examination reveals that her assessment is faulty. Conversely, our examination of the criteria that Charles proposes upholds their integrity and shows that : (1) 54:7–55:2 is an interpolated Noah passage that probably can be traced to a book of Noah; (2) chapter 60 relies on some type of Noah tradition, but the material, which has been attributed to Enoch, has been so thoroughly adapted that it is an integral part of the Similitudes; and (3) 65:1–69:25 consists of two sections (65–67 and 68–69:25) carefully woven together to form a literary unit. Chapters 65–67 are Noah traditions that probably reflect a book of Noah, and chapters 68–69 are an independent Michael-Raphael tradition that is made to look like a Noah tradition.

Dimant partially basis her denunciation of the designated Noah fragments on David W. Suter, who does not think that 54:7–55:2 and 64:1–69:12 belong to a book of Noah but are a midrash of Isa 24:17–23.[56] Although Suter does not agree that this material belonged to a book of Noah, his exegesis of the passage confirms Charles's designation of these two sections as interpolations and relates them to the flood, which makes them Noah traditions. He correctly points out the literary and structural reasons to view chapter 60 as an integral part of the third parable.[57] Thus, we concur with Charles that 1 Enoch contains Noah interpolations. One further observation is in order. Charles erroneously concludes that the Noah material has no right to form a part of

---

55. Dimant 1998, 144.
56. Suter 1979b.
57. Ibid., 133–35; cf. Dimant 1998, 146.

the text of Enoch.[58] This conclusion is unnecessarily extreme. While the Noah interpolations may be out of context, they have been so thoroughly adapted that they are not out of place.

---

58. Charles 1912, 129; cf. 106–7.

Is 1 Enoch 6–11 a "Noachic" Fragment? A Scholarly Discussion

Michael Tuval

Most scholars working on 1 Enoch agree that the chapters called the Book of Watchers (chs. 1–36) belong to one of the earliest strata of the Enochic corpus, possibly being predated only by the Book of the Luminaries (chs. 72–82).[1] Most of these scholars also adhere to the view that chapters 6–11 comprise the earliest stratum of the Book of Watchers. The aim of this essay is to reevaluate the hypothesis first formulated by R. H. Charles concerning the possible Noachic provenance of these chapters in the light of some recent studies. As is well known, in his 1912 commentary on 1 Enoch, Charles speculated on the possible existence of a book of Noah, to which the various fragments, identified by him as "Noachic" and now embedded in the book of Enoch, belonged.[2]

In distinction from his many other suggestions concerning the structure of 1 Enoch and the history of its traditions, Charles's identification of various Noachic fragments in 1 Enoch has not met with a scholarly consensus. This is especially true in the case of 1 En. 6–11, for reasons that will be mentioned in due course.[3]

It would certainly be unfair to say that Charles's hypothesis in relation to 1 En. 6–11 was promptly consigned to total oblivion. Indeed, it has been reevaluated a number of times by various scholars, whose work will be discussed below. At the same time, it should be said that no definitive statement has been made and no scholarly consensus reached. The indeterminate status of the question has led to the situation where some scholars preferred to ignore the issue completely. Thus, to mention only the most conspicuous cases, the Noachic hypothesis was not even mentioned in relation to chapters 6–11 in such major treatments of 1 Enoch as J. T. Milik's *The Books of Enoch* (1976)

---

1. See Milik 1976, 4–41; Nickelsburg 1992a; 2001, 7–8, 165–72; Collins 1998, 47–62.
2. Charles 1912, xlvi–xlvii, 13–14. See also Charles 1913, 168–70.
3. See also the paper of Vered Hillel in this volume on Charles' procedures and on "Noachic" passages elsewhere in 1 Enoch.

and George W. E. Nickelsburg's recent *1 Enoch 1* (2001). It seems that these important scholars thought that the question neither had much relevance to their research on these chapters, nor did it have anything to contribute to the tradition-historical criticism of the Book of Watchers.[4]

It should be emphasized that, in contradistinction to their treatment of chapters 6–11, neither Milik nor Nickelsburg ignores the question of the provenance of the Noachic traditions in other parts of the book of Enoch.[5] This makes the reexamination of the evidence for 6–11 all the more compelling.

Since much form-critical work has already been done on these chapters, I will not try to trace the history of their development but rather deal with them as a single unit.[6] Thus, I am not particularly interested here in the *Sitz im Leben* of the various traditions embedded in the narrative, such as the historical background of the myth of the Watchers, nor in the relationship between its different strata.[7] The unity of 6–11 has been recently emphasized and discussed at length by Devorah Dimant, and it will shortly become clear that the following discussion is much indebted to her analysis.[8]

At the beginning, I would like to reiterate the main points that led Charles and some other scholars to think that these chapters (whether in their entirety or in part) came from a distinct source that predated the book of Watchers and that they were incorporated into it at a later stage. It should be emphasized, however, that not all of these scholars believed that these chapters originated from a lost book of Noah. Actually, most of them do not think that a book of Noah ever existed. The main reasons for their skepticism will be considered later.

First, from the compositional point of view, it is quite obvious that 6:1 introduces totally new material and that what follows differs stylistically from chapters 1–5 and belongs to a different genre. It has also been recognized by most scholars that 12:1-2 is a seam and serves to bring Enoch into the story of the Watchers, in which until this point he has not been mentioned at all. In addition, the narrative of 6–11 is a self-contained unit, making perfect sense

---

4. In another major commentary, Uhlig (1984, 506, 516) just states that chapters 6–11 stem from an earlier book of Noah but does not discuss the matter at length.

5. Thus, Milik deals with the question of the book of Noah in 1976, 55–60; Nickelsburg discusses the matter in 2001, 539–50. Both discuss the issue mainly in relation to 1 En. 106–107.

6. In addition to the studies by Charles, Collins, and Nickelsburg listed above, see Collins 1982; Dimant 1974; 1998; 2002; 2006; Molenberg 1984; Newsom 1980; Nickelsburg 1977; Suter 1979a. For a more comprehensive bibliography, see DiTommaso 2001, 394–401.

7. See Nickelsburg, 2001, 165–72; Dimant 1974; 2002.

8. Dimant 2002.

on its own, without any inherent need for what precedes it in chapters 1–5 or for what follows in chapter 12.[9]

Second, as has already been mentioned above, in distinction from all the rest of the Book of Watchers, in chapters 6–11 the figure of Enoch is not mentioned even once, and the only named human character who plays any role in the narrative is Noah.[10]

Third, these chapters are an elaboration of the "sons of God" myth from Gen 6:1–4, where it precedes the description of the earth's corruption and the subsequent flood. In 1 En. 6–11, the fall of the Watchers is actually used to explain the earth's corruption. The flood, then, is a punishment for the sins of the Watchers. These chapters follow the biblical text much more closely than do any other parts of 1 Enoch.

Fourth, it seems that other Noachic narratives in latter chapters of 1 Enoch are dependent on 6–11, and it is also likely that the author of the book of Jubilees uses this material in 7:21–25.[11]

In light of these points, I beg to disagree with the view of Florentino García Martínez, who, while accepting that the author of 1 En. 6–11 drew on a lost book of Noah, seeks further to identify smaller Noachic fragments that in his view came from that book.[12] In my opinion, Dimant sufficiently demonstrated the unity of 6–11 in her above-mentioned article, and if the book of Noah ever existed, no reason why all of the material in these chapters could not have originated in it is evident.

Lest any confusion result, I must emphasize that Dimant herself does not adhere to the view that chapters 6–11 come from a book of Noah, and she is extremely skeptical concerning whether it really existed at all.[13] On the other hand, she is certain that chapters 6–11 come from an independent "parabiblical work" that was used by the author/compiler of the Book of Watchers.[14] At this point, then, the discussion is over the name of that parabiblical work.

It seems that one of the main reasons that Dimant and other scholars are hesitant to postulate the existence of a book of Noah in antiquity is the lack of agreement of different sources mentioning it concerning the kind(s) of material it contained.[15] In the opinion of these scholars, the divergence between the sources as to the contents of the book of Noah compromises the

---

9. All these peculiarities are discussed at length by Dimant 2002.
10. As already noticed by Charles 1912, 14.
11. Ibid, xivii, 14.
12. García Martínez 1992, 26–36.
13. See also Dimant 1974, 122–40; 1998, esp. 144–46, and most recently, 2006.
14. See Dimant 2002.
15. The most detailed defense of this view is Werman 1999.

very probability that a book of Noah ever existed outside the imagination of the authors of these sources or of modern scholars. Therefore, the skeptics suggest that the authors of Aramaic Levi Document, Jubilees and the Genesis Apocryphon did not use a real "book of Noah" but invented it in order to gain more credence for their statements.

In response to the first point, I would like to say that, in light of the recent discussion by Michael E. Stone,[16] I do not see any reason why the same composition could not have contained different types of traditions or even different genres. Indeed, if a book of Noah existed, it could have easily been of a composite nature. As has been pointed out by Stone, there are plenty of examples of this phenomenon in biblical and postbiblical literature, such as, among others, the book of Deuteronomy, the book of Jeremiah, and 1 Enoch itself.

As far as the invention of never-existing sources is concerned, although I do understand and appreciate the caution of the scholars who think that it is quite possible that the authors of ALD, Jubilees, and Genesis Apocryphon invented the book of Noah to add verisimilitude to their statements, I do not see any reason to postulate axiomatically the nonexistence of sources in every case. It is well-known that pseudepigraphy was a widespread phenomenon in the period under discussion.[17] Indeed, it is possible that nonexistent sources were composed and then "quoted,"[18] but at the same time it is also known that not all sources quoted in the Second Temple documents are fictional. Thus, for example, it is widely accepted that the author(s) of the Damascus Document quoted Jubilees and ALD.[19]

Objections of a different kind from those of Dimant and Werman have been raised by Moshe Bernstein in his article "Noah and the Flood at Qumran" (1999). After a detailed discussion of the different materials dealing with Noah and the flood in the Qumran corpus, Bernstein asks his concluding question—Was there a "book of Noah" at Qumran?—and answers no. In his view, "[a] reasonable alternative hypothesis to the predication of the existence of a large-scale 'Book of Noah' from which these other works made selections is the possibility that different events or aspects or themes of the Noah story

---

16. Stone 2006a, reprinted as pages 7–25 in this volume. See also Stone 1999.

17. See Speyer 1970; 1971; Stone 1984a, 427–33; 2006b.

18. For an example of one such "source," see D. R. Schwartz 1990, 200–207. "The chronicle of the high priesthood of John Hyrcanus" in 1 Macc 16:24 might well be another example.

19. CD 16:3, 4:15–19. However, as in the case with the quotations from a "book of Noah," Dimant also thinks that CD does not quote Jubilees; see Dimant 2006, 242–48.

were expanded beyond their pentateuchal scope at some early date and then circulated in a variety of forms either orally or in writing."[20]

While there is nothing inherently impossible in this alternative hypothesis, several points should be emphasized. First, this explanation makes more sense if one presupposes that a "book of Noah" never existed. If its existence could be proved, this hypothesis would be less convincing. Second, even if a book of Noah existed, it did not necessarily have to include all the various traditions mentioning Noah and the flood—either at Qumran or anywhere else. Moreover, if such a book did in fact exist, nothing would prima facie exclude the possibility that such material as 1 En. 6–11 originated from it.[21]

In the context of this discussion, I would also like to raise a terminological issue. As has been mentioned, Dimant has made a good case for chapters 6–11 being a part of a "parabiblical work," although she does not believe this parabiblical work to be the book of Noah. She agrees that it blames the Watchers for the corruption of the earth, mentions Noah, and interprets the flood as the punishment for the Watchers' sins. However, if such a parabiblical work had ever existed (and in light of Dimant's treatment of these chapters, its existence is more likely now than ever before), how can we be sure it was not called "Book of Noah"—whether by its author(s), its redactors, or its ancient readers? In many cases we simply do not know what the ancients called their compositions. Can we even be sure that 1 Enoch was called the "Book of Enoch" by its authors and redactors?

In light of the recent discussion of the book(s) of Noah by Stone,[22] it seems that most objections to its/their existence have been overcome. However, although this makes the identification of 1 En. 6–11 with a portion of the book of Noah more likely, it must be admitted, that a clear-cut decision one way or another is hardly possible at this stage. The purpose of this essay is to emphasize the likelihood that 1 En. 6–11 may point us toward the more ancient book.

---

20. Bernstein 1999, 229.

21. The comparison with the various Enochic materials might be useful here: not all Enoch traditions occur in the book(s) of Enoch. Some are attested in Ben Sira, Jubilees, Pseudo-Eupolemus, etc. Moreover, not every passage in 1 Enoch discusses Enoch, and large portions do not mention him at all. So, if we only had fragments or quotations in an ancient source, the arguments of Dimant, Werman, and Bernstein could be marshaled to prove that a "book of Enoch" did not exist, when, of course, several "books of Enoch" did in fact exist.

22. Stone 2006a.

Traditions of the Birth of Noah*

Aryeh Amihay and Daniel A. Machiela

The birth of Noah is recounted in a brief and straightforward manner in Gen 5:28–29, as part of his antediluvian genealogy and providing an explanation for his name (i.e., as a *midrash shem*).[1] The story of Noah's birth was expanded, however, into a much more extensive narrative in ancient times, as is evident from the similar accounts found in 1 En. 106:1–107:3[2] and the Genesis Apocryphon (also known as 1QapGen and 1Q20) 2–5,[3] in addition to several other early Jewish texts.[4] In this narrative, Noah is born with a striking appearance and praises God upon his birth. This leads his father, Lamech, to fear that the child is of angelic descent, and Methuselah, Lamech's father, journeys to Enoch, his own father (and Noah's great-grandfather) to receive an answer on this matter. Enoch assures him that Lamech is the father and provides a

---

* The following is the fruit of our work in the Thursday Night Seminar of Prof. Michael E. Stone, 2004–2005, which dealt with Noah traditions. We gained invaluable insights, references, and methodological tools from Prof. Stone's guidance while working on this paper. Its flaws are solely our own.

1. There are, however, idiosyncrasies in comparison with the other names listed in the genealogy. See Skinner 1910, 124–34; Sarna 1989, 44; and Cassuto 1961, 287–90.

2. Quotations from 1 Enoch are taken from Nickelsburg and VanderKam 2004. For other translations, see Black 1985; Charles 1913; Isaac 1983; Knibb 1978; Nickelsburg 2001. A synoptic translation to English of all versions can be found in Stuckenbruck 2007.

3. The scroll was first published, although only in part, by Avigad and Yadin 1956. Later publications of the same or other parts of the scroll include Jongeling et al. 1976, 75–119; Beyer 1984, 165–86 (1994, 68–70; 2004, 89–101); Greenfield and Qimron 1992, 70–77; Morgenstern, Qimron, and Sivan 1995, 30–54; and Fitzmyer 2004. New editions are currently under preparation by Daniel A. Machiela and Esther Eshel. The English translation provided here is that of Fitzmyer.

4. E.g., 1Q19, and perhaps 4Q534–535 (see below). For more on the comparative material, see Machiela 2007, 43–50. This dissertation has been published as Machiela 2009 but may be accessed in pdf format at: http://etd.nd.edu/ETD-db/theses/available/etd-07022007-205251/.

prophecy alluding to the deluge and to Noah's role as the survivor of it.⁵ It is noteworthy that this narrative was not developed or even preserved in later Jewish traditions.

The purpose of this paper is to discuss the various components making up the expanded birth story of Noah in early Judaism, taking special note of any features found in later literature or that might be traced back to the biblical account. In conclusion, we will address the relation between the account given in 1 En. 106–107 and other accounts of Noah's birth and its possible implications for the question of a discrete book of Noah, with which these texts are often associated.

1. Noah's Mother

Noah's mother is not mentioned by name in 1 Enoch, but the mere notification of her presence in 106:1 is significant. The explicit element of a wife is an expansion vis-à-vis the biblical narrative, since in Genesis Noah's birth is mentioned in the framework of a genealogical list in which fathers beget sons and the role of the mother is disregarded. In 1 En. 106–107, however, it is precisely Lamech's fatherhood of Noah that is in doubt, making his wife's role crucial for the dramatic unfolding of the story.

The role of Noah's mother is expanded much further in the Genesis Apocryphon, where she is named Batenosh. Although the text is badly damaged, enough is preserved in the Apocryphon to see a clear connection with the version in 1 Enoch, at the same time allowing us to discern some important differences, such as Batenosh's heightened function in the story.

Although Lamech's suspicion of Batenosh is not taken directly from the brief report of Noah's birth in Genesis, it does take up the tradition preserved in the biblical story of the sons of God taking wives for themselves from the daughters of men (Gen 6:1–4). This story, or the tradition it reflects, together with the extraordinary appearance of the child to be discussed below, provide the basis for Lamech's suspicion.

In the Genesis Apocryphon, Batenosh confronts Lamech's suspicion and rebukes him for it, reminding him of her sexual pleasure as a proof of her fidelity. Her monologue is extensive, and despite her vehement, emotional assertion she stresses her respect for and submissiveness to Lamech, whom she addresses twice as "my brother and my lord," (1QapGen 2:9, 13).⁶ This is

---

5. For interpretations of the birth story, see VanderKam 1992a, reprinted in 2000a, 396–412; Nickelsburg 2001, 536–50; Stuckenbruck 2007, 606–89.

6. Avigad and Yadin (1956) do not include the full address in the second instance, but it may now be read with some hesitation on more recent, narrowband infrared photo-

probably intended to evoke in Lamech feelings of both love and responsibility, at the same time imploring that he will acknowledge her own affection (exhibited in her sexual pleasure) and deference to his role as "lord."

The name of Batenosh appears once more, with slight variation, in Jub. 4:28, where she is called Betenosh.[7] The Jubilees account is much shorter than either 1 Enoch or the Genesis Apocryphon, remaining much closer to Gen 5:28–29, although the additional detail that Betenosh is the daughter of Barakel is introduced.

2. Conception by Angels

Noah's remarkable physical appearance at birth, coupled with his ability to speak, leads Lamech to suspect that he is not the father of the child. The connection between the child's appearance and his conception is clearly stated in 1 En. 106:5. There Lamech observes that the child resembles "the sons of the angels of heaven" and continues in verse 6, "I think that he is not from me, but from the angels."

This connection is also explicit in the extant passage of the Genesis Apocryphon, where Lamech reports in the first person, "it occurred to me that the conception was from the Watchers, and the seed from Holy Ones, and to Nephil[in...]" (1QapGen 2:1). In line 2 he adds, "and my mind wavered concerning this infant."[8] It is clear that the speaker here is Lamech, because 2:3 continues with the resumptive "Then I, Lamech."

In 1 Enoch Lamech's concern is assuaged quickly by his grandfather Enoch (106:18). This feature also has a parallel in the Genesis Apocryphon. Although not as well preserved as the confrontation between Lamech and his wife in column 2, 1QapGen 5:3–4 contains the words, "]n[ot] from the sons of Heaven, but from Lamech your son." The Apocryphon repeatedly stresses the veracity of this fact by invoking the word "truly" (קושט) at a number of points throughout Enoch's testimony.[9] The word "truth" appears twice in 1 Enoch as well (106:18; 107:3), in order to convince Lamech that Noah was not begotten by angels. This particular aspect of the story figures much more prominently in the Genesis Apocryphon than in 1 Enoch.

---

graphs. See Machiela 2007, 80. See also Fitzmyer 2004, 69, 130; Nickelsburg 1998, 144. Note that Methuselah uses a similar address to his father as a precaution, in case Enoch is cross at his disturbance (col. 2, lines 24–25).

7. On the different vocalizations of the name, see Fitzmyer 2004, 127 (who prefers Bitenosh). For further discussion of the name, see Stuckenbruck 2007, 621.

8. Literally, "My heart within me was changed" (Fitzmyer 2004, 126).

9. Note the use of this word to emphasize Noah's righteousness as well. See Bernstein 2005, 52.

Despite the fact that Noah's conception turns out to be entirely human in these works, the doubt imputed to Lamech makes it worth mentioning several accounts of angelic or divine conception in ancient times. One thinks immediately of Jesus of Nazareth, who was not only said to be the son of God but also plays a dual role as both human and deity akin to Noah's (and Enoch's) exaltation elsewhere in the Enoch traditions.[10] We are also told that Jesus was conceived miraculously.[11] Of course, this analogy should not be unduly exaggerated. For instance, the point of the story about Noah's conception is ultimately his humanity, while it is precisely the opposite with Jesus. Moreover, divine conception carries negative connotations in the Noah story, an element not present in the story of Jesus' nativity.[12]

There are other examples of joint human-angelic conception in ancient Jewish traditions as well. Of course, the possibility of such union is first suggested by Gen 6:2-4. Although Noah was not born from the sons of God, the fact that women could, and indeed did, beget children from angels appears to be one of the oldest traditions in the Bible.[13]

Another account of divine conception is of the birth of Cain. Targum Pseudo-Jonathan rephrases Gen 4:1 as follows: "And Adam knew his wife Eve, that she had conceived by Samael, the angel of the Lord."[14] There are multiple exegetical techniques employed here. One is taking the verb "to know" (ידע), which is used regularly as a euphemism for sexual intercourse in the Bible, back to its original sense. Adam did not "know" Eve (i.e., have intercourse with her), but rather he *knew that* Eve had intercourse with Samael. In addition, the Targum seems to be playing on the biblical explanation of Cain's name, relating it to divine origin: Eve proclaims that she produced a man with the Lord. This could be understood as a poetic expression of the awe in front

---

10. Enoch's exalted status is conveyed most clearly in 1 En. 70-71. Noah's exaltation may be seen in the Animal Apocalypse (1 En. 89:1).

11. Matt 1:18—2:12; Luke 2:5-20; see also the account of John the Baptist's birth in Luke 1:5-78. See Nickelsburg 2001, 540. For further bibliography on these passages, see the following commentaries on these passages: Davies and Allison 1988; Fitzmyer 1981, 303-448. Note also Fitzmyer's comment on the significance of this narrative for the study of Qumran as background of Christianity (Fitzmyer 2004, 123). See also nn. 39, 52.

12. This notion is probably due to the disruption of cosmic order, implied already in the narrative of the Nephilim in Gen 6:1-4. Cf. Eshel 2003, 78; Davidson 1992, 316-22; Stuckenbruck 2004; 2007, 666. For the sociological background of this theology, see Suter 1979.

13. See Gunkel 1997, 56-59; Westermann 1984, 363-83.

14. For the text, see Clarke 1984. Further comments on this Targum and its variations are to be found in Shinan 1992b, 130-31.

of the miracle of birth, but the Targum prefers to understand it literally in this case.[15]

By adding this information about Cain's conception, the Targum is providing an explanation for the source of evil, utilizing an idea already present in Gen 6:2–4 and developed more fully in 1 Enoch, Jubilees, and elsewhere. The Targum's explanation of Cain's origin is mentioned in several later sources.[16] The relation between angelic conception and the origin of evil in these sources helps illuminate the desire to prove that Noah had a purely human conception, despite his miraculous appearance at birth.

One last relevant example of divine conception is the story of the birth of Melchizedek, Noah's nephew, in 2 En. 23.[17] In this account, Noah's brother Nir rebukes his wife Zophanima for infidelity upon learning that she is pregnant. She denies any infidelity and further rejects having any knowledge of how the pregnancy came about. Consequently, the mistrusted Zophanima dies of sorrow, and the child emerges of its own accord, sitting beside his dead mother and praising the Lord. Like the story of Noah's birth in 1 Enoch and the Apocryphon, the mother is unjustly blamed of infidelity; however, very much unlike these accounts, we are explicitly told that Nir did not have intercourse with his wife from the day he assumed the mantle of the priesthood. It is evident that the reader is expected to believe that Zophanima did not know how she was impregnated and therefore assume that the child was, in fact, of supernatural origin. Thus, in contrast to the presumed negative connotations attending supernatural conception in the stories of Cain and Noah, the divine conception of Melchizedek (like Jesus of Nazareth) was understood positively, perhaps being another Christian trait of 2 Enoch.

3. Description of the Baby

Several features of Noah's miraculous birth are shared by other traditions. We shall discuss each of the following separately, although at points they are interconnected: (1) the child's physical traits; (2) the light accompanying his birth; and (3) his immediate ability to speak, stand, and utter praise to the Lord.

---

15. See García Martínez 2003; 2004.
16. E.g., Pirqe R. El. 21, perhaps implied in the Life of Adam and Eve. See García Martínez 2003, 29.
17. On the comparison between 2 Enoch and earlier Noah traditions more generally, see Orlov 2000b (repr. Orlov 2007, 361–78); Dimant 1998, 131; Himmelfarb 1993, 41. Orlov contends that shifting the features of a miraculous birth from Noah to Melchizedek is part of an anti-Noachic polemic. See Orlov 2007, 371–75.

3.1. Physical Traits

Almost nothing remains of the description of Noah's physical attributes at birth in the extant passages of the Genesis Apocryphon, but Lamech's response to his son's alarming appearance at the beginning of column 2 implies that they were once described at the end of column 1.[18] This coheres with what we find in 1 En. 106–107.

First, Enoch lists several remarkable physical features. Early in the narrative we read, "And when the child was born, his body was whiter than snow and redder than a rose, his hair was all white and like white wool and curly" (106:2). Later on (106:5), Lamech tells his father that the child resembles the sons of God: "his form is strange, not like us." Similar assertions are implied by the Genesis Apocryphon.[19]

Lamech's statement is significant not only for Noah's description in 1 En. 106:2 but also for Second Temple period angelology. By providing such a description, and then a few verses later stating that the child looks like an angel, we are offered a glimpse of how the narrator envisaged an angel at the time this story was written.[20]

It may also be possible to garner insights into Noah's description from other biblical sources. For example, the contrast of the white and red of the child's flesh brings to mind the description of the lover in Song 5:10, "My beloved is brilliant and red; he stands out among the multitudes."[21] Many commentators have understood the adjective צח to be a designator of quality (i.e., "radiant"), such as Brenner's opinion that both terms are a depiction not of contrasting colors but rather of different, complementary personal traits.[22] While this may be the original intent, Song of Songs has a very ancient tradition of allegorical interpretation dating back to at least the first century C.E.,[23]

---

18. *Contra* Fitzmyer, who interprets Lamech's suspicion as deriving from "such remarkable beauty" (Fitzmyer 2004, 123). What we have here is Lamech's fear and confusion (explicitly stated in col. 2, lines 1–3; col. 5, line 16), not admiration. Cf. Fitzmyer's quote of Rosenthal on 126.

19. See 1Q20 col. 2; 5:5, 7, 10.

20. See Stuckenbruck 2007, 607–10, 626. However, Stuckenbruck does qualify this by stressing that Lamech thinks that Noah is of the angels but not an angel himself (636–38). This is also apparent in the emphasis that Noah is not of the Nephilim, reflecting that this was Lamech's true fear (633, 654). On this matter, see also Fletcher-Louis 2002, 37–49.

21. The translation is our own.

22. Brenner 1982b. For an English version, see Brenner 1982a, esp. 73–75. For the previous view, see Murphy 1990, 164–65; Pope 1977, 531–34.

23. Alexander 1996b, 15. This point has been more recently and elaborately discussed by Stone 2007b.

according to which the lover is identified as God. If a similar tradition underlies the colors used to describe Noah in our texts—which seems a distinct possibility—the belief that this verse describes divine attributes may have been held as early as the time these chapters of Enoch were composed.[24] The fact that the next verses in Song of Songs (5:11–12) describe the lover's hair and eyes—the same features employed to describe Noah—reinforces the possibility that the writer has this passage in his purview.

We might also note the metaphorical meaning of these specific colors in Isa 1:18: "Come now, let us argue it out, says the LORD: though your sins are like scarlet, they shall be made white as snow; though they are red like crimson, they shall become like wool." Here we see that, while a modern view of the archetypal contrast of colors may be black and white, for biblical and parabiblical authors it was red and white.[25] Consequently, the description of Noah's flesh may not only suggest his similarity to an angel but also carry theological importance, the contrast in his flesh reflecting the notion of good and evil residing together.[26] This would coincide with other contrasts woven into this narrative, such as the idea that the origin of evil stems from the intermixture of angels and humans. It may also portend the cleansing of present evil by the flood.

Of course, the features of Noah's hair are reminiscent of the Ancient of Days (עתיק יומין) in Dan 7:9.[27] Here the Ancient of Days' garment is as white as snow—a specification echoed in 1 En. 106 (though in reference to Noah's flesh)—and his hair compared to lamb's wool, like the description of Noah's

---

24. For the dating of the 1 Enoch chapters, see Nickelsburg 2001, 118–19 (our chapters discussed on 542); Alexander 2002, 69.

25. See also Lam 4:7.

26. See Nickelsburg 2001, 543. Stuckenbruck (2007, 627) cautions here against assigning specific attributes or symbolisms to each color but does agree that the impression as a whole bears significance.

27. This is not to say that 1 Enoch is drawing from Daniel, nor the opposite. Whether 1 Enoch is earlier than Dan 7:9 or thirty years later, it is unlikely that the book of Daniel would have reached an authoritative stance to justify its usage by the author of 1 Enoch (as the book of Genesis did, for example). The resemblance between these metaphors reflects a shared literary background and interest, not a literary dependence. See Stuckenbruck 2007, 628. For discussions of the relation between the visions in Enoch and Daniel, see Collins 1992; Grelot 1978; Henze 2005; Reid 2004; Koch 2007; Stuckenbruck 1997; 2001; VanderKam 2006, 291–307. Note also the similarity of the divine epithet "Most High" in 1Q20, col. 2, line 4 and Daniel (Fitzmyer 2004, 127). As for the question of usage of scripture in the book of Enoch, see Alexander 2002, 57–68; VanderKam 1993 (repr. in VanderKam 2000a, 276–304).

hair upon birth.²⁸ There is, however, an interesting point of divergence here. One could say that, since the Ancient of Days has hair like wool, Noah's hair is a sign of his heavenly or angelic appearance. Yet while the white hair of the Ancient of Days befits his age (or, perhaps, agelessness), Noah, as a newborn, would not be expected to have white hair.

This may perhaps be explained by the passage in Jubilees where "the heads of the children shall be white with grey hair, and a child of three weeks shall appear old like a man of one hundred years" (Jub. 23:25). Noah's white hair could thus be a contrast of youth and old age somewhat similar to the contrast of red and white (signifying good and evil) evoked in the description of Noah's flesh. It may also be significant that this chapter of Jubilees speaks of the effects of sin at the end of days—an age with which Noah's generation is identified repeatedly in Second Temple literature.²⁹ The continuation of events in Jubilees reinforces this connection: "In those days the children will begin ... to return to the right way. The days will begin to become numerous.... There will be no old man ... because all of them will be infants and children" (Jub. 23:26–28).³⁰ Although Jubilees is not referring to Noah in this passage, the vision echoes suitably Noah's birth and its context,³¹ illuminating the depiction of his birth in 1 Enoch: he is born in a time of sin and fornication and returns, as it were, to the path of righteousness, thereby heralding a new era.³²

Another special appearance of a newborn that has been identified intermittently with Noah is found in 4Q534–536 and is dealt with in detail

---

28. Following Sokoloff's (1976) argument that נקא should be understood as a word for sheep and not as "pure." See also Collins 1993, 301.

29. That is, the generation of the flood is equated with the sinners of the end of time, as the flood itself is a prototype for the Day of the Lord. See, e.g., 1 En. 83–90; 4 Ezra 4:1–28, 9:4–22; Sib. Or. 3:93–161. See Collins 1997, 30–51; Nikiprowetzky 1987; Stone 1990, 63–67, 292–301.

30. Translation from VanderKam 1989, 2:148–49.

31. For the function of Noah's birth narrative in the eschatological views of 1 Enoch, see Nickelsburg 2001, 539–40, 543; Stuckenbruck 2007, 620. Stuckenbruck also stresses that Enoch begins his prophecy by describing past events, providing the background for the significance of Noah's birth (662–63). On the birth narrative in the Genesis Apocryphon, cf. Falk 2007, 49. This fits well with the vision in Jub. 23 and with the tension of past and future in general in apocalyptic literature. For relations between Jubilees and 1 Enoch, see Nickelsburg 2001, 72–73; van Ruiten 1999, 79–82.

32. Note also the wish to gain a life-span that existed in antediluvian times (VanderKam 2001, 58–59). For the context of this vision in the theology of the book of Jubilees, see Segal 2007, 292–99. Cf. Frey 1997.

elsewhere in this volume.[33] It is worthwhile noting for our purposes that the extant text begins with a physical description including the color red and the mention of hair (4Q534 col. 1, lines 1–2). While these features are also found in 1 En. 106, they are not presented in the same way, and not enough has been preserved to say just how this description progressed and thus would have looked as a whole.

4. Light Appears with Birth

Noah's birth is accompanied by a profusion of light in our texts. The source of the radiance is described twice in 1 Enoch: "When he opened his eyes, the house shone like the sun" (106:2), and "[h]is eyes are like rays of the sun, and glorious is his face" (106:5). Enoch speaks of the same features in 1QapGen 5:12: "he lifted his face to me, and his eyes shone like [the] su[n…]." The parallelism employed in 1 En. 106:5 (and perhaps at one time in the Genesis Apocryphon as well) heralds and significantly heightens the exalted role that Noah is ascribed in these works, seeming to imply some sort of quasi-divine status. In the Hebrew Bible and New Testament, shining eyes are characteristic of angelic beings (Dan 10:5; Rev 1:12–16). The use of this trait of the angel in Daniel is significant, since both 1 Enoch and the Genesis Apocryphon share much in common with that book. Another interesting parallel is that of Moses' shining face in Exod 34:29–35. In some respects, this passage reflects even more closely the attitude of our works, since Moses is a human being infused only for a time with the heavenly attribute of facial radiance. Furthermore, it is a direct sign of his status as chosen by God.

Light at Noah's birth is also found in 1Q19. Despite the fragmentary nature of the preserved text, we are fortunate enough to have Lamech specified by name on the same fragment as the phrase "the rooms of the house like shafts of sunlight" (frag. 3, line 5).[34]

Light shining at the birth of an infant is a feature attributed to several other figures. We might first mention Cain, whose angelic conception has been discussed above. The Life of Adam and Eve recounts that Eve "brought forth a son who shone brilliantly" (21:3),[35] and his special appearance is noted

---

33. Jeremy Penner, "Is 4Q534–536 Really about Noah?" in this volume. See further bibliography on this text there.
34. See Barthélemy and Milik 1955, 84–86; Stuckenbruck 2007, 629.
35. This is the translation of the Latin text, provided in Anderson and Stone 1999, 24E. The Armenian version reads: "Then, when she bore the child, the color of his body was like the color of the stars." A similar version is found in the Georgian text: "Eve arose as the angel had instructed her: she gave birth to an infant, and his color was like that of the stars."

in Pirqe R. El. 21. In explaining how Adam knew that Eve had been impregnated by an angel, we are told that Adam looked at the child's face and saw that he resembled the upper ones and not the lower ones. Here we are not only reminded of Lamech's suspicion, but the text also seems to imply that the child was radiant, as in the Noah texts.[36]

We also possess a tradition of Abraham shining at birth, but the existing record of this tradition is not as ancient. It is found in Jellinek's *Bet Ha-Midrasch*, where he writes that the manuscript on which he drew was first printed in Constantinople in 1519.[37] This is likely a much later tradition than the other stories dealt with above, and it contains an abundance of motifs from variant traditions, such as the persecution of male newborns by Nimrod, hiding in a cave, and a miraculous birth. What we seem to have here is a cluster of traditions, Christian and Jewish, gathered together in order to be reworked and redeployed in reference to Abraham.[38]

Moses is yet another hero who is said to radiate light at his birth.[39] The most ancient evidence of this tradition is found in the Talmud (b. Sotah 12a–13a), but apparently derived from tannaitic sources, and is later repeated in Exodus Rabbah. The starting point for this midrash is a juxtaposition of the statement that Moses' mother "saw that he was good" (Exod 2:2) with the statement that "God saw that the light was good" (Gen 1:4).[40] According to another version of this story, Moses' father recognized that the newborn was a savior due to the light that filled the house upon his birth. Although in the midrash this tradition relates most directly to the statement that Moses was good, it is clear that in a narrative sense it foreshadows the brilliance of Moses' face following his encounter with the Lord at Sinai, noted above.

---

36. Although it is possible that this tradition implies that Adam saw a strange figure, as Lamech saw Noah in 1 Enoch, there are no references to angels having strange appearances in this composition. The only reference to their physical appearance describes them as burning fire (Pirqe R. El. 4).

37. Jellinek 1938, 1:25–34.

38. For discussions of Noah traditions in Jewish medieval literature, see Rebecca Scharbach, "The Rebirth of a Book: Noachic Writing in Medieval and Renaissance Europe," in this volume.

39. Cf. Shinan 1997. For the relation between this tradition and the Jesus birth stories, see Hughes 1997; Kensky 1993.

40. On this expression, see Feldman 2002, 278–80. The other explanations provided for the statement that he was good are that his mother saw that he was prepared for prophecy or that he was born circumcised. The tradition of Moses being born circumcised is interesting, as it is said of Noah in 'Abot de Rabbi Nathan and perhaps in 4Q535 as well. For 'Abot de Rabbi Nathan, see Aryeh Amihay, "Noah in Rabbinic Literature," in this volume; for 4Q535, see Penner in this volume.

None of these natal traditions—Cain, Abraham, or Moses—include the element of eyes emanating rays of light, but they do provide a general description of luminescence strikingly similar to Lamech's statement in 1 En. 106:5. Cain should again be distinguished from the others in this group, since his shining marks his ignoble, although supernatural, origin, while the others are both of human origin and are righteous characters who play a significant role in establishment of the true worship of God.

Despite the rather late source of Abraham's birth story, it seems appropriate to note that the three heroes who shine at birth share other characteristics as well. This alignment of any one patriarch with others by means of parallelism (thus constructing a broad template of patriarchal righteousness) is characteristic of Second Temple literature. That Noah's role as transmitter of knowledge is intensified and stressed far more here than in the Bible is part of this trend.[41]

5. The Baby Stands and Speaks Immediately

Another remarkable trait of Noah is his youthful manifestation of adult faculties. Unlike other animals, which learn to stand just hours after their birth, the human newborn takes years to master the human traits of standing upright, walking, and speaking. In our texts, however, Noah is an astounding exception. His instantaneous speech marks him as outstanding, and the fact that his first words are addressed to the Lord of righteousness marks him as a wise and prophetic individual.[42]

We find similar traits in some of the other figures mentioned above: Cain stands up and walks immediately, going to gather flowers for his mother (L.A.E. 21:3). Abraham learns to walk when he is ten days old, somewhat of a late bloomer in comparison to Noah and Cain, but he also recognizes God on his own, according to several traditions.[43] In addition, Melchizedek, Noah's nephew in 2 Enoch, has the appearance of a three-year-old child upon his birth, and he also praises the Lord as his first utterance (2 En. 23:22).

Here, too, it is clear that Cain should be singled out. He (apparently) does not have the faculty of speech, and we would not expect him to praise

---

41. Stone 1999. For the relation between Abraham, Noah, and Moses, see Rendtorff 1999. Dimant (1998, 123–24) is correct in pointing to Noah's parallelism with Adam, too, but it is not surprising that this is not expressed in the birth narrative, as Adam was never born, thus making this point irrelevant for our discussion.

42. Nickelsburg 2001, 543; Stuckenbruck 2007, 653–54.

43. This is told in the Testament of Abraham, several times in Genesis Rabbah, and also in the tale brought in Jellinek's *Bet Ha-Midrasch* mentioned above (n. 37).

the Lord, since he will eventually be identified as evil. Thus exempting Cain, we have traditions of Abraham, Noah, and Melchizedek sharing the trait of prophecy in connection with their miraculous birth.

6. Noah's Name Midrash

Genesis 5:29 provides the first name midrash (etymological explanation of his name) for Noah. Here Lamech declares that his name shall be Noah (נֹחַ; √נוח), since "this one will bring us comfort [נחם; יְנַחֲמֵנוּ] from our labors, and from the toilsome struggle of our hands against the soil, which the Lord has cursed." This formulation is quoted in Jub. 4:28 and reworked in 1 En. 106:18 and 107:3.[44]

As noted already by Rabbi Yohanan "The midrash is not a name, and the name is not a midrash" (Gen. Rab. 28.2). He refers here to the discrepancy between the root נחם, which is part of the explanation of Noah's name, and the root נוח, which is the root underlying the name. VanderKam has discussed this problem extensively in his study of the birth of Noah.[45]

It is interesting to observe how the explanation of the name is reworked in 1 Enoch. In Genesis, Lamech employs the imperfect tense to designate his hope that the newborn will provide some relief from the hardships and toils of life. However, in 1 Enoch it is not Lamech alone who names his son, but Noah's great-grandfather Enoch as well, thus giving the name a doubled explanation. Enoch first explains the name by citing the fact that Noah will survive the flood and "be your remnant, from whom you will find rest" (106:18). This is closer to the meaning of the root נוח than the explanation provided in Gen 5:29. At the end of the story, however, Lamech names his son (107:3) in a way that echoes the explanation provided in Genesis. This shows that the author was aware of the etymological problem in Gen 5:29 and tackled it by providing a twofold explanation.

7. Noah—Survivor Who Is a Savior

Having discussed the various components of Noah's miraculous birth in 1 Enoch, we turn to two features of Noah that are not related solely to his birth but that have to do with his exalted status and are also evident in this narrative.

---

44. See further discussion on the onomastic tradition by Michael E Stone and Vered Hillel, "Noah in Onomastic Traditions," in this volume.

45. VanderKam 1992a, repr. in 2000a, 396–412. See also Black 1985, 322–23; Fitzmyer 2004, 143; Nickelsburg, 2001, 546–48; Stuckenbruck 2007, 674–76.

The first may seem a self-evident feature of Noah's character, namely, that he is simultaneously a savior and a survivor, or remnant.[46] There are several texts that isolate this trait as Noah's most prominent characteristic, such as Ezek 14:12–20. Together with Job and Daniel, he is mentioned as someone who would be saved from any plague or calamity that God would bring on the earth. Although modern scholars have pointed out that the choice of these three specific men is due to the fact that they were considered three universal (i.e., non-Israelite) righteous figures,[47] it is noteworthy that traditional Jewish commentators considered their common denominator to be a connection with some significant destructive event and their ultimate salvation from it. Rashi says: "For these three saw three worlds. Noah saw the world built, ruined, and (re)built. Daniel saw the temple, or [a different explanation for Daniel] himself, originally prince of princes, led to the lions' den and returned to his original prominence, and so Job who saw himself settled, ruined, and settled (again)."[48] We have here evidence of later Jewish exegetes who considered the fact that Noah was chosen to survive the flood as a special trait of his character, undoubtedly tied to his blamelessness.

Similarly, Sirach says of Noah that "in the time of wrath he was taken in exchange [for the world]; therefore was he left as a remnant upon the earth" (44:20). This text, along with Ezek 14, clearly recognizes that Noah's survival is at the same time the redemption of all humanity. Due to his righteousness, he survived the flood, thus enabling the continuity of the human race.[49] Noah as a survivor is mentioned twice more in 1 Enoch. His survival of the flood is alluded to in the Animal Apocalypse (1 En. 89:1–9) and also in the Book of

---

46. On Noah as a remnant, see Nickelsburg 2001, 546–47; Stuckenbruck 2007, 609, 669–70.

47. Cf. Noth 1951; Spiegel 1945; and, more recently, Wahl 1992. This has also been accepted by the major commentators on Ezekiel such as Zimmerli 1969, 320–21 (for English translation, see Zimmerli 1979, 314–15); Brownlee 1986, 206–7; Eichrodt 1970, 188–89; Greenberg, while recognizing the non-Israelite nature of the three, also criticizes his predecessors (1983, 257–58).

48. Radak follows Rashi on this point, while other commentators such as Yossef Kara and Eliezer of Beaugency stress their righteousness. Noah's righteousness as his major trait was stressed by various commentators. Philo says his name means righteous (*Worse* 121; cf. Nickelsburg 2001, 548); Ephrem the Syrian says that Noah was an example to his sons by his virtue, keeping his virginity for five hundred years (*Commentary on Genesis*, section 6). Several rabbinic Midrashim state that Noah's birth marked the beginning of a fruitful agricultural period (Gen. Rab. 25; Tanhuma Bereshit). See also b. Sanh. 113b; t. Sotah 10:2.

49. VanderKam 1980; 2000a, 411; Nickelsburg 2000, 251. This is once again tied in early Christian traditions to the parallels between Noah and Jesus. See Origen, who says: "our Lord, the true Noah, Christ Jesus" (Genesis homily 2 in Heine 1982, 76). Cf. Lewis 1968, 101–20; Moberly 2000, 345–56.

Parables, where the notion of his election on the basis of his righteousness is specifically stated (1 En. 67:1). Since this motif is also mentioned in the prophecy given by Enoch to Methuselah (1 En. 106:15-18), it seems linked to Noah's astounding birth. The quotation "and he shall not die in the day of evil" (ולא ימות ביום רשעא), which appears in 4Q536 (frag. 2, col. II, line 11), is reminiscent of this prophecy given by Enoch. It also bears the notion of singling someone out, bringing to mind the words concerning Noah in Ezek 14:14.

8. The Knowledge of Noah

In discussing the light accompanying Noah's birth, we noted that Noah's affiliation with Abraham and Moses also evokes his role as transmitter of knowledge to humanity. This trait seems to play an important role in Second Temple literature and is probably intended to solve a historical problem that arises from the accounts given in Genesis. Genesis 4:20-22 recounts the development of human knowledge, assigning different crafts to descendants of Cain. After the flood, all these craftsmen should have perished, and the Bible does not provide an explanation as to how these skills were acquired once more. This seems to be the reason that Noah's role as a transmitter of knowledge becomes important in later traditions.

The main stories of Noah's birth—1 Enoch and the Genesis Apocryphon—do not elaborate the motif of Noah's knowledge and wisdom, although the fact that he is able to talk and praise the Lord upon birth might be considered indicative of it. Furthermore, the emphasis on the fact that he and his family will be the sole survivors of humanity anticipates the significance of his knowledge. Upon Noah's birth, Enoch issues a prophecy that distinguishes Noah from the rest of humanity. If Enoch is the archetype of the righteous man who was translated to higher spheres due to his unique traits, Noah is to be his successor and messenger on earth. If Enoch gained knowledge from this translation, as is specified in the birth narrative (1 En. 106:19; 107:3) we might also deduce that Noah should also gain some of this knowledge as part of his role.

The relation between Noah as a transmitter of knowledge and narratives concerning his birth may be drawn together in 4Q534-536 (if, indeed, they refer to Noah). These fragments, directly following the description of his remarkable appearance (4Q534, frag. 1, col. I, lines 4-8), provide an extensive description of the main character's knowledge.

It is also of interest that this text attributes the knowledge of "three books" to the individual in question.[50] Noah's relation to a book(s) is mentioned in Jub. 10:14 and the Genesis Apocryphon (see below). Finally, it should be men-

---

50. García Martínez 1992, 8-9, 19-20.

tioned that 4Q534–536 also mentions the knowledge of secrets (4Q534, 1, I, 8; 4Q536, frags. 2+3, lines 8–9), a motif also employed in 1 Enoch's account of the birth of Noah (106:19; 107:3).

9. The Role of Enoch in Noah's Birth

Enoch's role in Noah's birth story was stressed in the preceding two sections. His role is instrumental in Noah's distinction as the survivor-savior, and he is even more prominently placed in the descriptions of Noah's knowledge. Not only is he the one who utters the prophecy regarding Noah's future role, thereby assigning him the task of transmitting human knowledge to future generations, but he is apparently also the source of much of that knowledge. That this is the case is merely implied in 1 Enoch, but it is stated more explicitly in some later traditions. The question of Noah's knowledge is not addressed directly in 1 En. 106–107, but Enoch's knowledge is dealt with extensively in the book as a whole. Indeed, this is the reason Methuselah seeks his advice regarding the newborn Noah. Directly following the birth narrative, we encounter a new account in which Enoch writes a book for Methuselah "and for those who would come after him" (1 En. 108:1). We are also told of Enoch providing a book to Noah in 1 En. 68:1. Whoever incorporated Noah's birth narrative into the book of Enoch was probably aware of this connection and of Noah's role as a messenger situated between Enoch and humanity.

Enoch provides Noah with knowledge more explicitly in Pirqe Rabbi Eliezer, where he is said to have given him the secret of the Ibbur, the intercalation of the lunar calendar. This late text probably draws upon or reworks an ancient tradition, possibly one of those contained in 1 Enoch or Jubilees.

Conclusions

The special connection between Enoch and his great-grandson Noah is significant for the question of the relation between 1 En. 106–107 and the rest of the book of Enoch, as well as the relation between 1 En. 106–107 and the Genesis Apocryphon. From the beginning of the study of 1 Enoch, it has been noted that the book is made up of a number of distinct components, not all of which relate seamlessly to each other. In this case, 1 En. 106–107 is a new, separate unit—a non sequitur of sorts—not closely related to what precedes and follows it.[51] This serves as an indicator that these chapters are an insertion, and we can now say so with more assurance due to the Genesis Apocryphon. The fact that we have two parallel texts, one of the major points of diver-

---

51. Milik 1976, 55; Nickelsburg 2001, 3–8, 539.

gence between which is the main speaker, supports the conclusion that in 1 En. 106–107 we find the reworking of an earlier narrative for the purpose of incorporation into the broader composition of 1 Enoch.[52]

In any case, we have here multiple attestations of Noah's birth story and yet another sign of Noah's significance during the Second Temple era. The accumulation of shared components in these sources with 4Q534–536 leads us to conclude that it is quite likely that 4Q534–536 is yet another narrative relating to the birth of Noah, reworking and expanding existing traditions such as those found in the Genesis Apocryphon and 1 Enoch.[53] If we add 1Q19 to these, we have no less than three, and most likely four, distinct but related accounts of the birth of Noah in Hebrew and Aramaic from the Second Temple period.

The remarkable number of Noachic birth stories (given our general paucity of ancient written sources), especially when compared with the brief account given in Genesis, begs once more the question of a hypothetical book of Noah that may have served as their shared source. Whether such a book ever existed has been the cause of ongoing debate.[54] The main arguments against the existence of such a book have been the diversity of materials attributed to the book of Noah, the fact that such a book has not been found, and problems of dating the various sources that allegedly drew from the book of Noah.

This study has attended to a marked preoccupation with Noah's birth, which plays only a part in the broader interest in the figure of Noah during this period. All texts know something of Noah's spectacular natal appearance, implying the possibility of celestial origins. However, all texts expand on this differently, focusing on traits and persons according to their taste. It is highly probable that these texts drew from a common well of traditions.

Assigning this source to a book of Noah has been made especially complicated for the birth narrative by the discovery of the words כתב מלי נוח

---

52. On the relation of the Genesis Apocryphon to Enoch, see Machiela 2007, 43–50. Cf. Bernstein 2005; Nickelsburg 2001, 541–42; Stuckenbruck 2007, 607. See also, on the style of the Genesis Apocryphon and its adaptation of various traditions, Bernstein 1996; Falk 2007, 26–106; Fröhlich 1998, 88–96; Lehmann 1958; Miller 1991; VanderKam 1978.

53. See García Martínez 1999, 94–95.

54. Barthélemy and Milik 1955, 84; Baxter 2006; Bernstein 1999, 226–31; 2005, 53; Bhayro 2006; Charles 1913, 163; Davidson 1992, 118; Dimant 1998, 144–46; 2006, 231–42; Fitzmyer 2004, 122; Fletcher-Louis 2002, 53; García Martínez 1992, 24–44; 1999, 88–89; Lewis 1968, 10–15; Milik 1976, 56; Nickelsburg 1998, 156–58; Puech 2001, 117–27; Schmidt 1926; Scott 1997b, 368–81; Segal 2007, 152; Steiner 1995, 66–71; Stone 2000; 2006a (see reprint in this volume); Stuckenbruck 2007, 610–14; Werman 1999.

preserved in the Genesis Apocryphon.[55] What would seem to be the title of a book is found only *after* the birth account, thus excluding the birth narrative from the "book." On the one hand, this seems logical, since we might expect that "The Book of the *Words* of Noah" would include only things that were written after his birth (even if only shortly after it, considering he knew how to speak immediately).

On the other hand, there is the issue of what we might call the lost source that recounted the birth of Noah and that was known to numerous authors. Jubilees 10:14 implies the existence of several books of Noah, and this suggests one possible solution to the problem: assigning the birth narrative to another book, distinct from that to which the Apocryphon refers. We are unable, in fact, to say whether the fount of these many tellings of Noah's birth was in a book of Noah, a work associated with Enoch, or even some other composition. Moreover, the title of the work is of no real importance. It is important, however, that we have considerable grounds for believing that the birth of Noah, as reflected in 1 En. 106–107 and the Genesis Apocryphon, was part of a broader antecedent and reflects the tendency to intensify Noah's role and significance in Second Temple Judaism.

55.1 QapGen 5:29. Cf. Steiner 1995; Stuckenbruck 2007, 610–14.

A Note On 1Q19: The "Book Of Noah"
Claire Pfann

1Q19, a collection of twenty-one Hebrew fragments, was first published in 1955 by J. T. Milik in DJD 1.[1] The manuscript as published comprised five somewhat substantial fragments containing three or more lines of text and sixteen smaller fragments. Milik arranged the fragments into two groups, apparently based on content and paleographic features. Although the name Noah is not preserved on any of the fragments, Milik entitled the manuscript "Le Livre de Noë," based upon the explicit mention in fragment 3 of Lamech and Methuselah, the father and grandfather of Noah, the implicit description in fragment 1 of conditions on the earth prior to the flood, and the apparent list of angels in fragment 2. Milik further noted the affinities of this text to the accounts of the birth of Noah in 1 En. 106–107 and in the Genesis Apocryphon.[2]

1Q19 is the only text from late antiquity dealing with the birth of Noah to have been preserved in Hebrew. The composition of this text in Hebrew and its potential relationship to its Aramaic sister-texts as source, derivative, or companion remains undefined. Michael Stone notes, "1Q19 does combine a number of the elements from part 1 of 1 Enoch that scholars believe are ultimately derived from a Noachic work. However, 1 Enoch was composed in Aramaic, as the Qumran fragments of it attest, while 1Q19 was written in Hebrew. We cannot determine whether 1Q19 was a 'Book of Noah' or another work embodying Noachic material."[3]

Furthermore, what has puzzled scholars since the *editio princeps* of this collection of fragments is the apparent change in content and character in

---

1. In Barthélemy and Milik 1955, 84–86. Fragment 2, known as 1Q19 *bis*, was early separated from the main manuscript. Its photo was published by John Trever 1965, pl. VII, and its transcription by Milik in Barthélemy and Milik 1955, 152.
2. See Aryeh Amihay and Daniel Machiela's "Traditions of the Birth of Noah" in this volume.
3. Stone 2000, 613–15.

fragments 13–21, which lack any distinctively Noachic character. Fragments 1–3 deal with themes and individuals familiar from biblical and extrabiblical accounts of Noah. The wickedness of humankind and impending judgment (frag. 1), the intercession of the archangels (frag. 2), and the birth of a miraculous child (frag. 3) are well-known motifs associated with Noah and the flood. With fragment 13, a shift from narrative to hymnic material takes place as language, including כבוד, הדר, תפארת, and בחיר, is introduced. Any explicit connection with Noah traditions disappears, as such hymnic or poetic material is lacking in the known Noah passages in the Bible, 1 En. 106–107, and 1QapGen ar, for example. As Stone notes, "The combination of Flood motifs with the story of Noah's birth is highly suggestive. The remaining fragments of 1Q19, however, do not seem to have any recognizable relationship to material connected to Noah and Enoch."[4] The language of fragments 13–21 is reminiscent, rather, of Berakhot, Mysteries, Shirot Olat Hashabbat, and other poetic compositions. Indeed, Crispin Fletcher-Louis (2002) has recently pointed out the presence of such "angelomorphic" language as reflective of a theme occurring, in his opinion, across a wide range of Second Temple Literature, including 1 Enoch, Jubilees, Ben Sira, 4QInstruction, and other texts. In these texts, the heavenly or divine aspect of a human figure is stressed. Furthermore, in 1Q19, the use of the *niph'al* of √כבד and √נשא with passive meaning evokes a sense of the future glorification or exaltation of an individual by divine agency.[5] Due to the fragmentary nature of the text, this individual cannot be identified with certainty. Within Second Temple literature, only a few individuals were expected to have an "exaltation experience," in particular, the Messiah (cf. Dan 7 and 4Q246 Aramaic Apocalypse, the "Son of God" text, both in Aramaic and in both of which the *niph'al* with passive meaning is used to indicate divine agency). Milik tentatively suggested that these fragments contained a song of Methuselah and referred to the miraculous child who had just been born. However, no other text preserves an enthronement or exaltation theme connected with Noah.

This paper suggests that 1Q19 as published by Milik is, in fact, at least two separate manuscripts. A close examination of the photographs of the fragments reveals several distinctive features that indicate the presence of at least two scribal hands. These features include line height, letter height, and letter shape. The line spacing in fragments 1–12 is 10 mm on average, where measurable, while that in fragments 13–21 is 11 mm on average. More important

---

4. Stone 2000, 613.

5. I am indebted to my husband Stephen J. Pfann for elucidating the character of these fragments and their implications and for compiling the alphabet chart that follows.

is the fact that the average letter height in fragments 1–12 is 4 mm, while that of fragments 13–21 is 3 mm.

When we set out exemplars from the main fragments side-by-side, the distinctiveness of each scribal hand is clearly visible. In the figure on the following page, the larger letters on the right are taken from fragments 1 and 3, dealing with the birth of Noah, while the smaller letters on the left are from fragments 13 and 15, the hymnic section. After even a cursory examination, the dramatic difference in letter height is seen, as well as the fact that the scribal hand of fragments 1 and 3 is characterized by slanting or curved descenders, while that of fragments 13 and 15 features vertical or straight descenders, particularly in ד, ו, and י. Other letters, in particular א, ב, and כ, also help to support the distinction between the scribal hands.

The א in fragments 13 and 15 contains a highly stylized, inverted v serif on the upper right arm, while the same arm in the א of fragments 1 and 3 exhibits merely a thickening or triangulation.

The ב in fragments 1 and 3 contains a pronounced curved upper stroke, and the lower cross stroke extends well to the right of the vertical stroke. In the ב of fragments 13 and 15, these features are less pronounced.

The כ of fragments 1 and 3 contains a short upper cross stroke and a long base stroke, while the כ of fragments 13 and 15 is quite squared, with the upper and the lower strokes almost equal in length.

Milik did not date the scribal hand(s) of 1Q19, but Stephen Pfann has suggested that the hand of fragments 1–11 is a semiformal Herodian hand dating to the end of the first century B.C.E. or beginning of the first century C.E., with some features typical of the rounded or rustic scribal hands of that period. Fragments 13–21 likely date to the second quarter or mid-first century C.E., based particularly on the squared or even slightly squat, rectangular form of many of the letters (e.g., ב, כ, ד, שׁ).[6]

Milik himself seems to have been cognizant of some distinction in paleographic features within the manuscript, for his grouping of the smaller fragments within the two groups (frgs. 1–12 dealing with the birth of Noah, frgs. 13–21 containing hymnic material) shows that he recognized the compatibility of each subgroup. Given his tremendous expertise, the question remains why he did not identify the fragments as two separate manuscripts from the start.

How does this analysis of 1Q19 bear on the study of Noah traditions in Second Temple period literature? First of all, it is clear that, on the basis of line height, letter size, and palaeographic features, 1Q19 comprises two dis-

---

6. Personal communication with the author. He feels that frg. 12 may not belong to either manuscript.

NOAH AND HIS BOOK(S)

אאאא אאאאאאא
בבבב בבבב
    ג
גגג גגגגגגג
ה ההההההה
ווו וווווווווו

  חח

זזז זזזזז
כב בבבב ך
ל לללל
  עס
  גנ
  ע
  ז

פ

ררר רררררר
ש ששש
תח תתתתת

The Scribal Hands of 1Q19
Fragments 13, 15 Fragments 1, 3

tinct manuscripts that I demarcate as 1Q19a and 1Q19b. Furthermore, the palaeographic division among the fragments is supported by a division in subject matter, vocabulary, and style. While these observations cannot move us forward in determining the origin or relationship of the Noah traditions present in 1Q19a, 1 En. 106–107, 1QapGen^a, or 4Q534–536, they do liberate us from having to devise a hypothesis by which we can incorporate hymnic material (1Q19b) within the Noah traditions, for which no parallels exist.[7] Furthermore, they yield a new, tantalizing, though decidedly meager, manuscript describing, in a manner perhaps similar to that of 4Q246, the future exaltation or enthronement of an individual, perhaps the Messiah. As a result, we might dub this newly discovered composition "1Q19b Exaltation [or, Glorification] Hymn."

TABLE 1: PALAEOGRAPHIC ASSESSMENT OF 1Q19

Fragment	Line Height	Letter Height	Descenders	Triangulated א
1	10–11 mm	4 mm	curved/hooked	lacking
2	9 mm	4–5 mm	curved	lacking
3	10–11 mm	4 mm	curved	lacking
4	———	4–5mm	curved	———
5	9–10 mm (only one example)	4 mm	curved	———
6	10 mm	4 mm	curved	———
7	———	4 mm	curved	damaged
8	10 mm	4 mm	curved	———
9	———	4 mm	curved	———
10	———	4 mm	———	———
11	10 mm	4 mm	straight	———

---

7. It may be worth noting that 2 En. 71:18–19 relates the miraculous birth of another child, the priest Melchizedek. In this account, the child is born as a fully developed three-year-old, wearing the "badge" of the priesthood (ephod? breastplate?) and already capable of speech. The text mentions that he "blesses God," reminiscent of Noah's blessing of God upon birth in 1 En. 106, although no poem or hymn of praise is recorded.

12	——	4 mm	straight?	——
13	11–12 mm	3 mm	straight	present
14	10 mm	3–4 mm	straight	——
15	10–11 mm	3 mm	straight	present
16	——	3 mm	——	——
17	——	——	——	——
18	——	3 mm	——	——
19	——	3 mm	straight/NA	damaged
20	——	3 mm?	——	——
21	——	3 mm	straight	——

THE NOAH CYCLE IN THE GENESIS APOCRYPHON*

Esther Eshel

INTRODUCTION

The Genesis Apocryphon—an Aramaic parabiblical text—recounts, with additions, omissions, and expansions, some of the stories from Gen 5–15.[1] The scroll, opened in 1956, contains the remains of twenty-two columns, but it was originally longer; the sheet to the right of column 22 was clearly cut away in antiquity, and the text of column 22 breaks off in the middle of a sentence. It is now generally accepted that text survives from at least one additional column that preceded column 1. This earlier column has been labeled 0. The work is generally attributed to the second or first century B.C.E., but based on my study of this composition, an earlier date in the third century should not be ruled out.[2] Like the other Aramaic texts found at Qumran, the Genesis Apocryphon is not considered sectarian.[3]

1. THE CONTEXT OF THE GENESIS APOCRYPHON

The surviving text of the Genesis Apocryphon retells the narratives of the

---

* This paper was written while I was a Kennedy-Leigh Fellow at Oxford Centre for Hebrew and Jewish Studies, Oxford University.

1. See Bernstein 2005.

2. For the latest edition of the Genesis Apocryphon, see Fitzmyer 2004. The readings and translation of the Genesis Apocryphon are based on this edition. However, certain readings were arrived at by the author in conjunction with Moshe Bernstein; others were formulated in the course of working on this essay, together with the readings and translations made in the Ph.D. dissertation of Machiela 2007; see now Machiela 2009.

3. Note that Noah waited until the fifth year to drink the fourth-year wine (1QapGen 12:13–15; see also Jub. 7:1–2), as required in sectarian law, rather than in the fourth year, as in rabbinic law. See Kister 1992. On the other hand, a reference to Noah's endogamy in choosing his children's spouses (col. 6) may point to general, nonsectarian, Second Temple practice.

patriarchs corresponding to Gen 5:18–15:5, that is, from Enoch to Abram's vision of the stars. It does so mainly through first-person narration by Lamech, Methuselah, Enoch, Noah, and Abram. Recently, Daniel Falk suggested that the preserved text could be divided into three stories—a story of Lamech, a story of Noah, and a story of Abraham—but finally concluded: "It is preferable to view the *Genesis Apocryphon*—at least as preserved for us—as structured around two stories: a Noah cycle and an Abram cycle." Thus, according to his understanding, "[t]he Lamech section is best seen as part of the Noah cycle, and its purpose is to more fully place the story of Noah in the context of the sons of God myth from Gen 6.1–5."[4] As for the text's style, he notes: "it is part of the narrative's style to allow characters to speak in their own words." Nevertheless, since he traces a change in the middle of Abram's narrative, from column 21:23 until the end of the existing text, to an impersonal narration, he concludes that "the narrative voice does not seems to be an entirely reliable guide to the intended structure."[5]

My reading of the first two columns shows that the picture is more complicated. Columns 0–1 include parts that do not seem to belong to Lamech's speech, such as a speech in first-person plural, which seems to best fit the Watchers' appeal, for example, ונקבל אסר [ושבועת]א די אסרנא [על נפשנא], "we took an oath [and a vow] that we bind [ourselves (?)]" (0:2–3), and וכען הא אנחנא אסירין, "And now we are prisoners" (line 8). Furthermore, the first-person appeal to God, referring to his anger or his decision to destroy the world, seems to fit Enoch's appeal to God rather than that of Lamech, to be compared with 1 En. 12–16. The Enoch cycle includes apocalyptic visions referring to God's deeds that will take place at ביום דינא רבא וקץ, "[…] at the Day of the Great Judgment and End" (4:12), to be compared with 4QEnGiants[f] (4Q206 2–3) frag. 1 xxii:2–3 ועד זמן יום קצא ד[י] דינא רבא די מנהון יתעבד, "and until the time of the Day of the End o[f] the Great Judgment which will be exacted of them" (1 En. 22:4);[6] as well as with 4QEn[c] (4Q212) frag. 1 iv:22–23: ומן [בתרה שבוע עשרי דבשבי]עה דין עלמא וקץ דינא רבא] יתנקם[...], "And af[ter it, the tenth week, in the se]venth [part of which] an eternal Judgment and the (fixed) time of the Great Judgment [shall be executed in vengeance…]" (1 En. 91:15).[7] It also includes various visions regarding Noah's future and the misdeeds of humanity (5:16–19)

The Enoch cycle features some elegant interweaving of first-person narration: Lamech's first-person reaction to Noah's exceptional appearance (he

---

4. Falk 2007, 30.
5. Ibid, See earlier Bernstein 1998, 145.
6. Milik 1976, 229–30.
7. Ibid., 266, 269.

feared he was the son of an angel) followed by his confrontation with his wife Bitenosh (col. 2); Enoch's assurance to Lamech through Methuselah that Noah is indeed his son (5:2–23); and Lamech's final reaction to Enoch's assurance (5:26–27). Therefore I suggest assigning the first six columns to Enoch rather than to Lamech, thus dividing this composition into three cycles, which seems to me more suitable in terms of both structure and content:

The Enoch cycle (cols. 0–5:27)
The Noah cycle (cols. 5:29–18:22)
The Abraham cycle (cols. 18:24–22:?)

This division is further supported by the physical marker of blank lines left between the cycles, that is, in column 5 line 28, at the end of the Enoch cycle, and in column 18 line 23, at the end of the Noah cycle.[8] Of these three, although poorly preserved, no less than thirteen columns of the Noah cycle survived, while only four to five columns of each of the other two cycles have survived. There is, however, no reason to doubt that both of the other cycles were originally much longer. As for the proposed Enoch cycle, one might suspect that column 0 was preceded by additional passages devoted to the story of the Fallen Angels, which together with the surviving reference to this myth, might be added to other such compositions that are so dominant in the Qumran library.[9] It is worth noting in this context that references to the Watchers are found on numerous occasions in the surviving parts of this composition, especially in columns 0–1, and are not confined to the Enoch cycle. This is also the case with the words of Lamech (2:1, 16) and probably in the words of Enoch referring to ביומי ירד אבי, "for in the days of Jared my father" (3:3),[10] as in his answer to Methuselah (5:3–4). The Watchers also appear in Noah's vision (6:19–20).

The remains of the Genesis Apocryphon, of which the beginning and end have not been preserved, thus comprise three cycles: the Enoch cycle; the Noah cycle; and the Abram cycle. Therefore, it might originally have included additional cycles that are now lost. From the extant text, we can see a well-written story, with smoothly connected individual components that share both themes and terminology. Thus, the Noah cycle seems to be an integral part of the composition, not an independent work taken from a written source

---

8. Armin Lange has suggested that in col. 18:23–24 there was a *vacat* of 1.5 line, which probably marked the beginning of the Abraham story at line 25; see Lange 1996, 192 n. 10.

9. See Stone 1999, 133–49.

10. Compare with 4QEn[a] 1 iii:4–5 (1 En. 6:6): [ונחתו די מאתין כלהן והוו] ירד ביומי; see 4QEn[c] 5 ii:17–18 (1 En. 106:13).

and introduced as a whole into the Genesis Apocryphon. This, in turn, does not exclude the possibility that the Genesis Apocryphon used earlier sources, which is probably the case in the Enoch cycle, where clear connections with 1 Enoch are found. Being one of the earliest and most detailed sources dedicated to the figure of Noah, one might assume that the Genesis Apocryphon was used by later compositions, such as Jubilees.

The Genesis Apocryphon draws significant parallels between the main characters, and I suggest that this literary technique be termed a "chain of traditions." The way the story is told, Enoch, like Noah, struggles with a sinful generation, that of the Fallen Angels and their sinful offspring. He also seems to be singled out as the only righteous person, as Abram will later be singled out with respect to Sodom, serving as the mediator between the sinners and God and bringing their appeal to heaven. Like Abram, he also has immediate communication with God, being vouchsafed various visions regarding the future of humanity that can be compared with Gen 15. By the same token, Noah is described in terms close to those applied to Abram, being the ultimate righteous individual who has a vision regarding the future of humanity.

With regard to shared terminology, the following main locutions stand out.

1.1. Enoch and Noah

(1) The root אסר, meaning both "to swear" and "to bind," is found in the Enoch cycle used for both sin and punishment of the Watchers (col. 0:2, 8, 12). Yet a third meaning of this root, "to gird," is used in Noah's biography וחצי אסרת בחזון קושטא, "I girded my loins with a vision of righteousness" (6:4).

(2) In connection with Enoch's visit to heaven, it says that עדבה פליג, "he shares his lot (with the angels)" (2:21). This terminology derives from Josh 15 and is used later to describe Noah's division of the world among his sons, as in לשם נפק עדבא תניאנא, "For Shem emerged the second lot" (1QapGen 16:14), as well as [ו]יפת פלג בין בנוהי, "[And] Japhet divided between his sons" (1QapGen 17:16).[11]

(3) The reference to רז "mystery" is found in both stories: רז is first mentioned in the Enoch cycle in the Watchers' appeal in column 1, רז רשעא, "the mystery of wickedness" (1:2; and just רזא in lines 3, 7). Later, when Enoch speaks to his son Methuselah, he says ברך אחוי ברזא דנא[...], "[...] your son make known by this mystery" (5:21). Methuselah then tells it to his son

---

11. עדב is used by Targum Jonathan to Joshua to translate Hebrew גורל (Josh 15:1; 16:1), as well as תחום "portion," found numerous times as the translation of Hebrew גבול in Targum Jonathan; see VanderKam 2000a, 488.

Lamech: ועם למך ברה ברז מלל, "and he spoke with Lamech his son about a mystery" (5:25). When we move to the Noah cycle we hear again: וטמרת רזא דן בלבבי, "I hid this mystery within my heart" (6:12); see ALD 4:13 אף וטמרת דן בלבי וכל אינש לא גליתה, "And I hid this, too, in my heart, and I revealed it to nobody." רז probably has a neutral meaning, and it gets its value weighting from its context. Thus, while in the Watchers' context the mystery has a negative sense, to be compared with the Watchers' story according to the book of Watchers, 4Q201 iv: 4–5: וכלהן שריו לגלי[ה רזין לנשיהן, "[And they all began to reveal] secrets to their wives" (1 En. 1:4/8?),[12] in our context of both Enoch and Noah it is given a positive sense.

1.2. NOAH AND ABRAM

(1) When Noah exits the ark, after the flood, he says, [אדין] אנא נוח נפקת והלכת בארעא לאורכהא ולפותיהא, "[Then] I Noah went out and walked on the land by its length and by its width..." (11:11), which is clearly taken from God's command to Abraham קום והתהלך בארץ לאורכה ולרחבה (Gen 13:17), described in the Genesis Apocryphon as קום הלך ואזל וחזי כמן ארכהא וכמן פתיהא, "Rise, walk about, go and see how great is its length and how great its width" (21:13–14). Abram obeys this command: ואזלת אנא אברם למסחר ולמחזה ארעא ... ואזלת ליד טור תורא למדנחא לפותי ארעא, "So I, Abram, went to go around and look at the land ... and moved along Mount Taurus toward the east through the breath of the land" (21:15–16).

(2) God's promises to Noah are clearly taken from those to Abraham in the Bible; thus, God says to Noah: (11:15) אל תדחל יא נוח עמך אנא ועם בניך די להון כואתך לעלמים, "Do not fear, O Noah, I am with you and with those of your sons who will be like you forever," which is based on Gen 26:24: אל תירא כי אתך אנכי וברכתיך והרביתי את זרעך בעבור אברהם עבדי, "do not fear, for I am with you and will bless you and make your offspring numerous for my servant Abram's sake," as well as on Gen 15:1a: אל תירא אברם אנכי מגן לך, "Do not fear, Abram, I am your shield."[13] Furthermore, the second part of this verse, שכרך הרבה מאוד, "your reward shall be very great" (15:1b), can be found earlier in the Genesis Apocryphon, when God promises Noah יקר ואגרו אנה משלם לך, "honor and reward I am paying to you" (7:5).

(3) In one of his dream visions (14:9–19), Noah sees a large cedar tree with three branches. The interpretation of the dream identifies the different

---

12. Cf. רזי פשע in 1QH^a 13:38; 24:9; 1Q27 1 i:2; See Bernstein 2005, 45 n. 15, which also refers to 2 Thess 2:7.

13. See also ולבניך מן בתרך ... אל תדחל "to your sons after you for all ... do not fear" (8:33–34).

parts of the tree. Thus Noah is the cedar, and the three shoots are Noah's three sons. Shem can be identified as the first scion, described as coming forth from the cedar and growing to a height (14:10). A cedar also plays a role in Abram's dream vision (19:14–21) when, just before he and Sarai descend to Egypt due to the famine in the land of Canaan, Abraham has a dream. In his dream Abraham sees a cedar, which people are trying to cut down, and a palm tree, which is left alone. This dream reflects Abraham's awareness that his life is in danger. His response is to ask Sarai to protect him by claiming that they are brother and sister.

(4) When Noah divides the world among his sons, Arpachshad's allotment (17:11–15) is the same as that in Abraham's tour of the Promised Land as described in the Genesis Apocryphon (21:16–19).

Furthermore, not only does the author use parallels between the main three characters, but I would like to suggest that within these cycles one also finds secondary characters that serve transitional functions. Each of these is used as a "link" connecting the earlier and later main figures, thus creating an even closer connection between the cycles. Thus one might characterize Lamech as a "secondary figure" who serves as the connection between Enoch and Noah, by appealing to Enoch in regard to Noah's miraculous birth. The end of the Noah cycle and the beginning of the Abraham cycle have not survived, but I would like to suggest, based on the Noah story, that we might tentatively expect parts of columns 17–18 to be devoted to the figure of Shem as the "secondary character."

Shem's special role is first found when he is identified with the first scion, on which Noah's name will be called (14:12). Thus, as in the case of Noah, Shem and his descendants are also called "a plant of truth" (14:13). Later, when Noah wakes from his dreams, he goes and tells them to him: ואתעירת [לל]ה אחון[ת] וכולא ברי לשם אנה לית[ואז ... שנתי מן נוח א]נ, "Then I], Noah, [awoke] from my sleep....]I went to Shem, my son, and relat[ed] everything to [him]" (15:21–22). God's promise earlier to be with Shem and his descendants is being referred to, when God promises Noah, "I am with you and with those of your sons who will be like you forever" (11:15).

Shem's special role seems to be further developed by the author of Jubilees, particularly in the detailed description of Shem's portion found in Jub. 8:12–21. This includes Noah's happy reaction, especially when he makes his portion the best, including the three main mountains, and being in the center of the world (see below).

2. Noah Cycle

After the title נח מלי כתב [ג]ש[פר], "A [co]p[y] of the words of Noah" (5:29), which probably marked the beginning of the Noah cycle,[14] there remain very few decipherable letters, providing no indication of the content of the last six and a half lines of that column (5:29a-36). When the text is readable again, at the beginning of column 6 line 1, we are already in Noah's biography: "And in the furnace of my gestation I flourish to truth, and when I left my mother's womb I was rooted in truth" (6:1). Thus one might infer that the previous lines dealt with Noah's birth, to be compared with its earlier description of that event by his father Lamech (col. 2), as well as in 1 En. 106–107. As a whole, the story of Noah covers almost thirteen columns of thirty-six lines each column: a total of more than 260 lines.

The following table summarizes the above-mentioned subjects with their parallels.[15]

Subject	1QapGen	Genesis	Jubilees
Noah's righteousness from early life	6:1–5	(6:9)—	(10:17)—
Noah's marriage	6:6–7	—	4:33a
Noah's children	6:7–8	5:32; 6:10	[4:33b]
Marriage of Noah's children	6:8–9	—	—
Noah's first set of visions	6:9–22	—	
Noah find favor	6:23	6:8	[5:5, 19]
God's planned destruction	6:24ff.	6:6–7, 11–17	
God blesses Noah	6:?–7:6	(9:1–2): after the flood!	—
Noah rejoices (?)	7:7–9	—	—
God responds (?)	7:10–15	—	—

---

14. Some argue that this part of the Genesis Apocryphon originated as an independent composition, probably from the book of Noah. See Steiner 1995, 66–71. For a discussion of the possible existence of a lost book (or books) of Noah, see Stone's comments on pages 8–11 of this volume (= 2006a, 5–9), where he also relates to earlier studies.

15. See Falk 2007, 31–32.

Noah's second set of visions	7:16ff.– 9:?	—	
Noah and the flood	9:[?]–10:1	7:11–12	[5:24–27]
Noah and his family praise God	10:1–10	—	
The ark rest on Hurarat	10:11–12	8:4	5:28
Noah offers sacrifice	10:12–13	8:20	6:1b-2
Details of sacrifice	10:13–17	—	6:2–3
God accepts sacrifice (?)	10:18–?	8:21–22	[6:4]
Noah watches at the ark's door	11:1–10 (?)	—	—
Noah's survey of the land	11:11–12	—	—
Noah blesses God	11:12–14	—	—
God blesses Noah	11:15ff	9:1–7	6:5–9
God's covenant with Noah	11:?–12:6	9:8–17	[6:15–16]
Noah descends the mountains (?)	11:7–9	(9:18)	
Noah's second generation	12:9–12	10:1–11:11	
Noah plants a vineyard	12:13	9:20	
The fourth year's wine	12:13–14		
Fifth-year wine celebration and prayer	12:14–19	—	7:1–2
Noah's second set of visions	12:19–15:21		
Noah wakes from his dreams, blesses God, tells to Shem	15:21ff		
Division of the land	end of col. 15–17:24?		

This table shows quite clearly that, while some detailed descriptions expand upon a very small biblical base, such as Noah's righteousness mentioned in Gen 6:9, נח איש צדיק תמים היה בדרתיו, other elements have no parallel at all, not only in Genesis, but also in other parallel accounts, such as 1 Enoch and Jubilees.

Another significant difference is that Noah is described only in a positive way, being in close contact with God. Thus, the biblical description of Noah being drunk and shamed, starting with וישת מן היין וישתכר ויתגל בתוך אהלה, "He drank the wine and became drunk, and he uncovered himself within the tent" (Gen 9:21), and ending with וייקץ נח מיינו, "When Noah woke up from his wine" (9:24), is reinterpreted in the Genesis Apocryphon columns 12–15, in an opposite manner, where ויתגל is interpreted in the sense of having a vision (from גלה/גלי "to reveal"),[16] and Noah is described as having a set of symbolic dream visions, starting with his statement "and I was lying on my [...]" (12:19), perhaps his side or his bed. This formula can be compared to God's command to Ezekiel, "Lie on your left side" (4:4), as well as to Dan 7:1, which states, "Daniel saw a dream and a vision of his mind in bed." Even more closely related is Levi's statement in the Aramaic Levi Document: "Then [...] I lay down, and I remained o[n...]" (4:3), which is immediately followed by a vision (4:4ff.).[17] This set of dream visions ends by saying: ואתעירת אנא[נוח מן שנתי ושמשא רמה ואנה]נוח[... למברך אל עלמא]... וא[זלית אנה]...ל[ה][אחו]ת[ברי וכולא לשם, "[Then I,] Noah, [awoke] from my sleep, and the sun [...]" (col. 15:21).[18] Thus, after waking up, not only does Noah not curse Canaan, but he blesses God and goes to tell his dreams to Shem.[19] In the following very fragmentary text (15:23ff.), Noah apparently speaks to Shem, mentioning the righteous one and God. Here I would assume that a major part of the bottom line of column 15 (lines 23–36) and maybe even parts of the beginning of column 16 were devoted to our "secondary figure," who is Shem. Nevertheless, one cannot rule out the possibility that Noah's curse of Canaan was included in the nonpreserved lines at the end of column 15. If so, one might speculate that it was based on Noah's set of dream visions in which he was informed of Canaan's future violent deeds; thus Noah might have cursed him for that rather than for his father's deeds.

---

16. To be compared with 4Q201 iv: 4–5: וכלהן שריו לגלי]ה רזין לנשיהן, "[And they all began to reveal] secrets to their wives"; for a detailed discussion of this interpretation, suggested by Machiela, see Machiela 2007, 211–18.

17. Greenfield, Stone, and Eshel 2004, 66–67.

18. See Fitzmyer 2004, 92–93.

19. *Contra* Bernstein (1996, 43), who hypothesizes that Noah's drunkenness and its ensuing embarrassment is to be reconstructed in the missing parts of 1QapGen.

In the Noah cycle, three unique phenomena occur that merit our attention. These are the "two-ways" terminology, Noah's dream visions, and the division of the world.

2.1. The Two-Ways Terminology

The beginning of the Noah story is lost, and its first surviving text starts with his biography:

> [...] And in the furnace of my gestation I flourished to truth; and when I left my mother's womb, I was rooted in truth and I conducted myself in truth all my days, and I walked in the paths of eternal truth. For I was instructed (?) by the Holy [One(s)], to w[alk] on the path of the way of truth, and to warn me away from the path of falsehood which leads to everlasting darkness. [...] I girded my loins in a vision of truth and wisdom [...] all the paths of violence. (6:1–5)

This description is unique in many ways: a poetic structure, similar to biblical *stichoi*, with parallels and contradictions, to be compared with the wisdom poem of ALD 13, using paired words and parallel phrases, which is already known from earlier Aramaic poetry.[20] Within these lines we find the following "ways" terminology: מסלה, שביל, אורח, נתיב.[21] We also find adjectives describing the right way, using קושט "truth" or אמת "truth."[22] This, in turn, is contrasted with the adjectives describing the wrong way as שקר "falsehood," חשוך "darkness," or חמס "violence."[23]

The concept of walking in "the path of truth" has its roots in the biblical דרך אמת, "way of truth," mentioned in Gen 24:48. The metaphor of the two ways, of the paths of good and of evil, first appears in Deut 30:15–30, where the

---

20. See Greenfield 1979, 49–51; Greenfield, Stone, and Eshel 2004, 102–9, 201–6.

21. Two of these—מסלה and נתיב—are Hebrew words found in this Aramaic composition. The inclusion of both Hebrew and Aramaic terms brings to mind the name-midrashim of Levi's sons in ALD (ch. 11) and his grandson Amram (12:4), which include both Hebrew and Aramaic etymologies. Thus Merari, who has triple onomastic midrash, the first of which is ארי מר לי עלוהי לחדה, "for I was bitter on his account particularly," where מר לי, "I was bitter" (11:8) is a Hebraism, probably based on Ruth; as well as that of Jochebed, on whom it says לכבוד לישראל, "for glory for Israel" (11:10), which is a midrash based on the Hebrew word כבוד. In those cases we suggested either a usage of earlier Hebrew source or a name-midrash made by "a literate Jew of the third century BCE"; see Greenfield, Stone, and Eshel 2004, 184–193.

22. Again, a Hebrew term.

23. This rich imagery of the two ways includes both Hebrew and Aramaic terms; see above, n. 21.

ways of life and death are related to obedience or disobedience of divine commandments. This metaphor also "runs like a thread through Prov 1–8."[24] These ancient texts (as well as Jer 21:8, which interprets Deut 30:15 in an ironic exegesis[25]) "appear to employ the two ways as a construct for envisioning alternative behaviors rather than to constitute a fixed two-ways literary form."[26]

Noah's testimony as walking in the path of truth in the Genesis Apocryphon is to be compared with ALD 3, where Levi says in his prayer:

> 3:4 And now my children are with me,
> And grant me all the paths of truth.
> 3:5 Make far from me, my Lord,
> the unrighteous spirit,
> and evil thought and fornication....
> 3:6 Let there shown to me, O Lord, the holy spirit,
> and grant me counsel, and wisdom and knowledge and strength,
> 3:7–8 in order to do that which is pleasing before you....
> 3:9 And let not any satan have power over me,
> to make me stray from your path.

As we argue in our edition of ALD, "It is related to the idea of the two ways, one good and one bad ... but is distinct from it in its use of the idea of the two spirits."[27]

Another early source in which this motif occurs is Tobit. As part of his programmatic statement, Tobit states, "I, Tobit, walked the paths of fidelity and righteousness all the days of my life" (1:3).[28] The same motif appears later in Tobit's testamentary instruction to his son Tobias:[29]

> Be mindful of (God) the Lord, my boy, every day of your life
> Do not seek to sin or transgress His commandments.
> Practice righteousness all the days of your life,
> and tread not the paths of wickedness.
> For those who act with fidelity will prosper in all they (you) do.
> To all those who practice righteousness. (4:5–6)[30]

---

24. Nickelsburg 2001, 455.
25. See Holladay 1986, 573–74.
26. Nickelsburg 1999, 98. For a detailed discussion of the Jewish sources of the "two ways" in Did. 1–6, see van de Sandt and Flusser 2002, 140–90.
27. Greenfield, Stone, and Eshel 2004, 34.
28. Where G^{II} = G^{I}; the translation is based on Fitzmyer 2004, 98.
29. According to G^{II}, which unless noted, is usually identical with G^{I}.
30. Fitzmyer 2004, 163, according to G^{II}, where G^{I} reads, "For if you act in fidelity, success will attend all you do. To all those who practice righteousness."

For almsgiving preserves one from death and keeps one from going off into darkness. (4:10) [31]

A third reference is found in Tobit's instructions to Tobias: "On every occasion praise God and beg him that your ways may be made straight and all your paths [G¹ + and plans] may lead to prosperity" (4:19).

Unlike Tobit, which, as mentioned, relates the path of righteousness to Torah, in the Genesis Apocryphon, as in ALD, no reference to the divine commandments is found. But not only is Genesis Apocryphon's description of the two ways more detailed; it also introduces a significant new element, the eternal nature of both good and evil: "I walked in the paths of *eternal* truth," which is contrasted with the "path of *everlasting* darkness." Accordingly, the Genesis Apocryphon represents the bestowing of an eschatological dimension on the two-ways motif, to be compared with Levi's prayer in ALD 3:17, asking God [למעבד] ..., דין קשט לכ]ל עלם "... And make (me) participant in your words, to do true judgment for all times."

Next, I would like to adduce another parallel to the two-ways imagery, which is found in Jubilees, and to argue for its possible reference to the far more detailed description in the Genesis Apocryphon. As we saw above, in its early biography of Noah, the Genesis Apocryphon documents how he walked in the path of truth. Jubilees' initial recounting of the story of Noah's ark relies on 1 Enoch (6–16; 86–88) but also quotes Gen 6:8 (Jub. 5:5: "He was pleased with Noah alone"). Jubilees returns to the Noah story in 5:19, which reads:

> To all who corrupted their ways and their plan(s) before the flood, no favor was shown, except to Noah alone, because favor was shown to him for the sake of his children whom he saved from the flood waters for his sake because his mind was righteous in all his ways, as it has been commanded concerning him. He did not transgress from anything that had been ordained for him.

I suggest that the two-ways terminology underlies this description, in which Noah's righteous way ("his mind was righteous in all his ways") is contrasted to that of others who chose the wrong way ("To all who corrupted their ways and their plan[s]").[32] Furthermore, the addition of nonbiblical elements using the two-ways terminology to explicate Noah's righteousness echoes the Gen-

---

31. Ibid., 164.

32. The addition of "and plans" seems to have originated in Tob 4:19, where G^II reads: "On every occasion praise God and beg him that your ways may be made straight and all your paths may lead to prosperity"; G^I reads: "your paths *and plans*."

esis Apocryphon: "and I walked in the paths of eternal truth" (6:2), as opposed to "the path of falsehood that leads to everlasting darkness [...]" (6:3).[33]

I would like to suggest that the author of Jubilees might have used and adapted the Genesis Apocryphon in his portrayal of Noah. Thus, both texts describe Noah as walking in the righteous path, but Jubilees shifts the emphasis to what is significant in his worldview, namely, that Noah follows God's commands: "as it has been commanded concerning him. He did not transgress from anything that had been ordained for him." As we have seen, this element is also found in Tobit's biography. Another element shared with Tobit is the existence of a reward for following the right way: Jubilees, "because favor was shown to him," and Tobit, "For those who act with fidelity will prosper in all they do. To all those who practice righteousness" (4:6). But, as opposed to the Genesis Apocryphon, this context contains no eschatological theology.

2.2. Noah's Dream Visions

In contrast to its biblical source, one outstanding feature of Noah's biography in the Genesis Apocryphon is the large number of divine communications to Noah, including dreams. Thus, according to the Genesis Apocryphon, Noah had two sets of dream visions. The first antediluvian vision (6:11–12) is concerned with "the conduct of the sons of heaven" (6:11), and since it is a

---

33. Further, VanderKam discusses the difficult phrase "favor was shown to him" (Jub 5:19; 1989, 2:34) having the "Hebrew נשא פנים underlie the Ethiopic words," explaining it in "a positive sense, 'to be gracious to' (Gen 32:21)." I would like to argue that Jubilees here is probably corrupt. The biblical phrase is ונח מצא חן בעיני ה' (Gen 6:8), translated by Jubilees as "he was pleased with Noah alone," to be translated literally: "Noah alone found favor before his eyes" (5:5; VanderKam 1996, 33). This verse is referred to in the Genesis Apocryphon 6:23: | ואש[כחת אנה נוח חן רבו וקושטה, "And I Noah found favor, greatness, and truth." We might trace Jubilees' version's development as follows: מצא חן was understood as parallel with נשא חן, the latter also found in the phrase מצא חן לפני, e.g., Esth 2:17. Being paralleled with נשא חן לפני, where לפני = פנים, thus creating the wrong phrase פנים + נשא. It is interesting to note that the verb התהלך in the phrase את האלהים התהלך נח (Gen 6:9) is translated in LXX as εὐηρέστησεν, from εὐαρεστέω, meaning "to please." The same verb is used earlier in the same phrase regarding Enoch ויתהלך חנוך את האלהים (Gen 5:22, 24), as well as later, with regard to Abram: התהלך לפני והיה תמים (Gen 17:1; see 24:40), as well as in Joseph's reference to his ancestors: האלהים אשר התהלכו אבתי לפני אברהם ויצחק (Gen 48:15), and in Sir 44:16: חנוך נמצא תמים והתהלך עם ייי (MS B), translated to Greek as Ενωχ εὐηρέστησεν κυρίῳ. Thus it seems that all share the same exegesis, which might be as old as or even older than Jubilees. One might wonder whether this shared title of Enoch, Noah, and Abram was behind our author's parallel descriptions of these characters.

mystery, he then hides it and does not tell anyone.³⁴ Next, Noah is visited by "[an em]issary of the Great Holy One" (6:15) who seems to explain to him the behavior of the sons of God and its result in the bloodshed of the Nephilim (דמא די אשדו נפיליא; 6:19). This vision and Noah's subsequent communication with God seem to explain to him why God decided to destroy the world as a result of the fallen angels' misdeeds. The surviving portion of this vision is nonsymbolic in nature.³⁵

The second set of visions includes symbolic dream visions. Although poorly preserved, Noah's dream visions in the Genesis Apocryphon columns 12–14 include at least three separate dreams. In composing this dream sequence, the author of Genesis Apocryphon did not follow one specific biblical source; rather, he drew the various images found in these visions from different biblical visions belonging to this genre. The first dream refers both to an object made of gold, silver, stone, and pottery as well as iron, from which everyone is breaking off pieces, and "chopping every tree and taking it for themselves." It reads as follows:

> ⁸[…] the wild beasts […] and the creeping creatures of the dry land were passing […] [⁹gold and silver,] stone and pottery were chopping and taking of it for themselves. I watched those of gold and silver [¹⁰…] iron, and were chopping every tree and taking it for themselves. I watched the sun and the moon, ¹¹and the stars, chopping and taking of it for themselves. I watched until the earth and the water habitant ¹²terminated it." (13:8–12)³⁶

This dream bears striking parallels to Nebuchadnezzar's dreams of the statue made of iron and clay in Dan 2 and of the great tree in Dan 4, a study that is beyond the scope of this article. The second dream vision reads as follows:

> ¹³I turned to observe the olive tree; and behold the olive tree grew in height and for many hours […] great foliage¹⁴[…] appeared among them. I contemplated the olive tree, and behold the abundance of its leaves[…] ¹⁵[…] they tied on it. And I wondered tremendously at this olive tree and its leaves. I wondered […] ¹⁶[the four] winds of the heaven blowing strongly, and they mutilated this olive tree, removing its branches, then breaking it. First [came] ¹⁷western [wind], and struck it and cast off its leaves and fruit, and scattered it in (all) directions. After it (came) […]. (13:13–17)

---

34. The same terminology is used in ALD 4:13b: "And I hid this, too, in my heart, and I revealed it to no one," which concludes Levi's vision(s).

35. It might have been followed by another heavenly communication, which might have included building instructions (see למבנה in 7:19).

36. Fitzmyer 2004, 88–89.

This dream concerns a large olive tree that is being destroyed by the "[four] winds of heaven" (13:16). This reference to the "[four] winds of heaven" is related to Balshazzar's dream of the four beasts in Dan 7. The large gap in the Genesis Apocryphon (13:18–14:8) probably contained the interpretation of the olive-tree dream and perhaps some additional dreams. Again, although the dream of the olive tree clearly relies on various biblical prophecies, including the image of the olive tree used to represent Israel in Jer 11:16, without its interpretation I can provide no further detail as to its meaning.

The third, and most significant, dream for this discussion, that of the cedar tree in column 14, combines both the elements of symbolic use of the cedar for persons and the prediction of future events. The details of the dream itself have not been preserved; it can, however, be reconstructed from its partially preserved interpretation. That reads as follows:

> [...] ⁹[and now] pay atten[tion] and listen! You are the gre[at] cedar, [and] the [cedar] standing before you in a dream on the top of mountains ¹⁰[...] truth. A branch which sprouted from it and grew to a height. Three s[on]s [...] ¹¹[... And as for the fact that] you saw the first scion reaching to the stump of the cedar [...] and the tree from it [...] ¹²[...] all his days he will not part from you, and your n[am]e will be called in his seed [...] ¹³[...] will grow into a plant of truth for all [times (?)...] ¹⁴[...] standing forever. And as you, seeing the scion reaching the st[um]p [...] ¹⁵[...] and that which you saw [...] the last scion [...]¹⁶ *vacat* [...] from the edge of their foliage it enters the foliage of the first. Two sons [...] ¹⁷[...]from the [ea]rth [...] on the north [...] And what you saw part of their foliage entering into the foliage of the first [...] ¹⁸[...] they were placing in his land [...] and not [...] ¹⁹and I told the secret until [...] (14:9–19).

In this dream Noah sees a large cedar tree with three branches. The interpretation of the dream identifies the different parts of the tree. Thus Noah is the cedar, and the three shoots are Noah's three sons. Shem can be identified as the first scion, described as coming forth from the cedar and growing to a height (14:10). The further characterization of Shem as "the first scion reaching to the stump of the cedar" (14:11), which is interpreted in this son's name-midrash, introduces the metaphor of an upright planting. Regarding Shem, the Genesis Apocryphon states: "(he will not part from you), and your n[am]e will be called in his seed [...]" (ובזרעה יתקרה ש[מ]ך) (14:12). The following line denotes Shem, and his descendants, "a plant of truth" (14:13).[37] The cedar-tree vision of the Genesis Apocryphon also contains predictive ele-

---

37. On the use of tree imagery in the Noah cycle in Genesis Apocryphon, and its parallels, see Eshel 2009.

ments. It foretells the future of Ham and Japheth, according to which they will depart from their father, moving "left," that is north, and "right," to the south. This probably refers to Japheth going to Europe and Ham to Africa, as implemented in the division of the world described in columns 16–17 (see below). After a blank space in the text, we find yet another development involving prediction in the cedar image. Using the image of "some of their boughs entering into the midst of the first one" (14:17), the Genesis Apocryphon foretells acts of aggression to be conducted by the descendants of Ham and Japheth against Shem. This part of the vision probably refers to the period when Canaan inhabited the southern part of Syria. Jub. 10:28–34 describes how Canaan violently seized "the land of Lebanon as far as the river of Egypt." This land was originally assigned to Shem, and because Ham took it, he was cursed by his father and brothers. One might assume that the same explanation for Noah's curse of Canaan is to be found in the Genesis Apocryphon, namely, due to his violent capture of the land not assigned to him (not the shameful act of his father Ham). Unfortunately, due to the fragmentary condition of the scroll, such a reference did not survive. Furthermore, according to Jubilees, Madai, one of Japheth's sons, negotiated with Shem's sons Elam, Asshur, and Arpachshad to be allowed to settle within the patrimony of Shem (10:35). No reference to the conflict or negotiations between the brothers has been preserved in the columns of the Genesis Apocryphon treating the division of the world among Noah's descendants.

2.3. The Division of the World

The last part of Noah's story is the division of the earth. At least two columns—16 and 17 as well as perhaps some of the almost lost 18—are devoted to the division of the earth among Noah's sons. Accordingly, the author of the Noah story endows this topic with considerable weight. The section following Noah's awakening from his dream visions (15:21) is illegible, and the next decipherable part is the conclusion of Japheth's portion. Elsewhere I have discussed the *mapa mundi* in detail, mainly comparing the descriptions found in the Genesis Apocryphon (cols. 16–17), Jubilees (8–9), and Josephus (*Ant.* 1.122–147).[38] In short, those sources reflect both reliance on Gen 10 and a shared cartographical basis for their construction of the world,[39] namely,

---

38. Eshel 2007.
39. Such constructs also appear in Pseudo-Philo, *L.A.B.* 4:1–10, *Sib. Or. 1* 3: 110–14; Acts 2:9–11, and later, in *Gen. Rab.* 37:1–8. The *War Scroll* (1QM 2:10–14) also contains a Gen 10–based list of nations to be fought in the third phase of the thirty-three-year war. See Y. Yadin 1962, 26–33. 1QM 10:14–15 also alludes to the division of the world.

an updated version of the ancient, sixth-century B.C.E. Ionian world map, based on Dicaearchus's (ca. 326–296 B.C.E.) division of the world by a median running through the Pillars of Hercules, the Taurus Mountains, and the Himalayas.[40] Of these texts, the Genesis Apocryphon is, in my opinion, the oldest surviving Second Temple period text mapping the inhabited world.[41]

Both Jubilees and the Genesis Apocryphon provide detailed descriptions of each son's allotment, with many parallels, including shared terminology, mainly land-related terms taken from Josh 15. Nevertheless, there are significant differences between the Genesis Apocryphon and Jubilees, some of which enable us to draw conclusions with regard to the interrelationship of these texts. The most crucial difference lies in the actual lots given to each son and in the prominence Jubilees ascribes to Jerusalem. According to Jubilees, Shem received all of Asia Minor, together with Syria, Phoenicia, and Palestine, whereas according the Genesis Apocryphon, the region of Asia Minor belonged to Japheth. In that respect, Genesis Apocryphon accords with the map of Shem's lot according to Josephus (*Ant.* 143). Moreover, the surviving text of the Genesis Apocryphon documents no concept of Jerusalem's superiority.

In Lud's allotment, the Genesis Apocryphon mentions "the Sea of the East" (ים מדנחא; 17:10). The "Sea of the East" can be identified as Jubilees' Mauq Sea, the present-day Sea of Azov. This reference to the Sea of the East reflects the orientation from Greece, namely, with Delphi at the center. Thus, as opposed to Jubilees, which converts the Ionian map to a Jewish perspective, placing Jerusalem at the center of the world, the Genesis Apocryphon retains the focus of the original Ionian map. Only someone using Greece as a reference point could refer to the Sea of Azov as "the Sea of the East."

Some scholars suggest that the author of Jubilees utilized and adapted the Genesis Apocryphon for his needs or that both authors used a common source.[42] I argue that the distinct development of the world division in each of these texts emerges more strongly from examining the differences between them rather than from the similarities. The Genesis Apocryphon is the older source, and the original Ionian map can still be traced in it. This text was later used by the author of Jubilees, and he converted it to fit his Jewish perspective, awarding Shem the major portion and function—as he received all of Asia Minor, together with Syria, Phoenicia, and Palestine—and placing Jeru-

---

40. Alexander 1982, 204; Feldman 2000, 43.
41. See Fitzmyer 2000, 1:302. Fitzmyer argues for its literary dependence on Jubilees, therefore suggesting a possible first century B.C.E. dating. See, however, Stone 2006a, 9 (page 11 in the current volume).
42. See van Ruiten 2000.

salem at the center of the world. Thus, both the identification of mistakes and a conceptual shift in the nature of the *mapa mundi* indicate that the Genesis Apocryphon served as a source for Jubilees.

CONCLUSION

As we have seen, the Noah cycle covers the major portion of the surviving columns of the Genesis Apocryphon, that is, no less then twelve columns. Not only is the presentation of the Noah material very different from its biblical parallel, but it is unique in comparison with other known Jewish traditions about Noah. The portrait of Noah according to the Genesis Apocryphon is that of a patriarch, structured in parallel with both Enoch and Abram. Noah, according to Genesis Apocryphon, was a righteous patriarch, communicating with heavenly beings, who had various dream visions in which he was informed about both past events, such as the sin of the Watchers, as well as future events, such as the division of the world among his sons. Apparently, some of his visions also referred to eschatological events, among them the final judgment. This positive description of Noah seems to lead the author to change the biblical story from the shameful result of his drunkenness to a glorious set of visions.

Furthermore, Noah's story is interwoven into the Genesis Apocryphon as an integral part, with both thematic and linguistic interconnections with the other cycles of Enoch and Abram. As I have argued, between these three main characters there were probably two "secondary characters," that of Lamech and probably Shem, who served as "links" that connected these cycles.

Finally, a comparison of the major parallels between the Genesis Apocryphon and Jubilees shows some possible contacts between the two compositions, and a close study of its parallels leads to the tentative conclusion that, in most cases of shared traditions, the most reasonable explanation is the use of the earlier traditions found in Genesis Apocryphon by the later author of Jubilees.

APPENDIX: THE ORIGINAL LENGTH OF THE GENESIS APOCRYPHON

Matthew Morgenstern has argued for a calculation of the original length of the Genesis Apocryphon based on the letter *qoph* found on the upper side of column 17, which is a first column of a sheet on which six columns were written (cols. 17–22), and the letter *tsade* written on the sheet on which seven columns were copied (cols. 10–16). Since these two letters are in sequence, he assumes that it numbered the sheets sewn together. On this basis, he made the calculation that the original text was very long and that we are lacking between 70 to 105 columns, that is, between fourteen to fifteen sheets, which according to his calculation is about 9 meters.[43] To that one should add, according to Morgenstern's assumption, three more sheets at the end (marked as *resh-shin-taw*), with eighteen to twenty-one additional columns. Thus, this scroll will have had no less than 115 columns, which would measure no less then 25 meters all together![44]

This reconstruction for one scroll seems to be impossible. Based on Morgenstern's calculation, Fitzmyer commented, "one wonders whether it contained other texts along with the *Genesis Apocryphon*."[45] However, it is preferable not to accept Morgenstern's claim regarding the extreme length of the scroll.

The longest surviving scroll, 11QT, is reconstructed as 8.75 meters long,[46] while 1QIsa[a] is 7.34 meters. Thus, although the Genesis Apocryphon has relatively wide columns, including up to seven columns per sheet and each column has between thirty-four and thirty-six lines, it is still hard to believe that the scroll was as long as suggested by Morgenstern.

I therefore suggest that these letters found at the top of the sheets were in use only by the one who prepared the parchment for writing, as his own practical signs. Even if we assume that he started his marks with *aleph* (even that assumption is not necessarily the case), he was probably marking the sheets he was making at a certain period, to fill a specific order or the like, and not necessarily marking them for one scroll alone.

---

43. Morgenstern 1996, 345–47.

44. Based on Morgenstern's calculation of the second and third sheet measuring 63–64 cm, together with the preserved twenty-three sheets, there will be an additional ca. 14.5 m, and presumably three more sheets are missing at the end (of *resh-shin-taw*) which are ca. 2 m. Going with the minimal calculation of an average of six columns per sheet, probably one column is missing before the surviving col. 0, thus having six columns in the first sheet before col. 5, and probably at least one more sheet after col. 22, with about six more columns. This yields a scroll of no less than thirty-five columns of 2.5 m, which is the average size of a scroll.

45. Fitzmyer 2004, 38.

46. Another proposed reconstruction of an extremely long scroll was put forth by Tov; see Tov 2004, 76, with regard to 4QRP[a–e]. Tov posits that this scroll originally contained all of the Pentateuch and reconstructs an original length between 22.5 and 27.5 m. This reconstruction might not be correct, since we have no indication that the whole Pentateuch was included in RP.

Is 4Q534–536 Really about Noah?

Jeremy Penner

1. Introduction

That the Second Temple period is marked by an active interest in the patriarchs is evident from the proliferation of biblical retellings and legends found in the Apocrypha and Pseudepigrapha. The same abundance is true of Noah.[1] Since their discovery, the Dead Sea Scrolls, particularly the Genesis Apocryphon, have added significant new material to the corpus of Noachic traditions found in Second Temple period. Another text, 4Q534–536, might also be included in this growing collection of material, but the identity of the central figure within this text remains elusive and under considerable discussion.[2]

The purpose of this paper is twofold: (1) it will attempt to bring some clarity to the identity of the figure in 4Q534–536; evidence given to support the claim that the text is about Noah will be weighed as well as alternative theories; (2) if a conclusion favoring Noah is reached, this paper will then seek to determine what, if anything, 4Q534–536 contributes to our understanding of Noachic traditions in the Second Temple period.

---

1. Noah is often referred to as a patriarch of Israel during this period. See, for example, Jub. 19:24; Josephus, *Ant.* 1.106; Tob 4:12. Ben Sira also includes Noah in his praise of Israel's ancestors (Sir 44:17).

2. Starcky 1964, 51–66; Carmignac 1965, 199–217; Fitzmyer 1965, 348–72; Greenfield 1973, xx–xxi; Grelot 1975, 481–500; Milik 1978, 91–106; García Martínez 1992, 1–44; Wise, Abegg, and Cook 1996, 428; Caquot 1991, 145–55; Davila 1998, 367–81; Zimmermann 1998, 170–204; Abegg and Evans 1998, 191–203; Puech 2001, 117–70; Dimant 2006, 239–41.

2. Text and Context

2.1. 4Q534–4Q536: A Short History of Interpretation

4Q534 was first published by Jean Starcky in 1964, who assigned this manuscript the siglum 4QMess ar.³ He published only the first two columns of the text (frags. 1–2), which include a physiognomic description of an unknown figure's miraculous birth and some events that take place during his adult life. After reading a certain "three books," he will gain wisdom "that will go to all the peoples, and he shall know the mysteries of all the living" (4Q535 1 i 8). Now endowed with sage-like wisdom, he will also face much opposition but will remain unharmed because of his acquired wisdom and because he is the "elect of God" (בחיר אלהא). Starcky's initial impulse was to identify the figure as messianic, as he saw strong parallels between the motifs and events of his life and the life of Jesus, in particular the use of the title בחיר אלהא.⁴

In the following year (1965), however, Joseph A. Fitzmyer challenged Starcky's reading of "elect of God" (בחיר אלהא), concluding that "it is not *per se* evident that the title 'Elect of God' was Messianic in Qumran circles."⁵ He further observed that many of the literary motifs in 4Q534, such as the miraculous birth, a long life, books, destruction, an emphasis on wisdom, and the presence of Watchers, are very similar to the motifs found in Noachic literature of the same period, and therefore concluded that the figure is in fact Noah (see, e.g., 1 En. 6–11; 54; 65–69; 106–108; Jub. 7:20–39; 10:1–15; 21:10).⁶

This proposal gained some support, and shortly thereafter J. T. Milik took Fitzmyer's proposal a step further, arguing that 4Q534 belonged to a lost book of Noah.⁷ In addition, he also identified four other manuscripts belonging to the book of Noah: two more copies of 4QMess ar (4Q535–4Q536), 4Q561, and 4Q186.⁸ Thus, according to Milik, "These four Aramaic manuscripts (and

---

3. Starcky 1964, 51–66.

4. For example, both figures are miraculously born, they both grow in wisdom, and both are proclaimed as the "elect of God" (cf. John 1:34; Luke 23:35). Starcky also thought that 4Q534 was relying on the themes present in Isa 42:1 and 61:1, texts that were also interpreted in the New Testament to refer to Jesus, thus adding further evidence of the messianic identity of the figure in 4Q534 (Starcky 1964, 59).

5. Fitzmyer 1965, 354.

6. Ibid., 371.

7. Grelot also agreed with Fitzmyer in 1975, 498.

8. Cf. Milik 1978. García Martínez reached a similar conclusion to Milik's in 1992, 1–44 (a translation of García Martínez 1981, 195–232) but did not include 4Q561 and 4Q186 as texts belonging to a book of Noah.

the Hebrew version of 4Q186) belong to a 'Book of Noah' in which the birth of the Patriarch (with an astrological section giving a series of horoscopes), and probably his whole life, was narrated in great detail."[9]

Since then Puech has verified that 4Q534, 4Q535, and 4Q536 are copies of the same document, but not 4Q186.[10] He also kept Fitzmyer's proposal of the identity of the figure as Noah[11] and emended the title of the text from 4QMess ar to 4QNaissance de Noé (following Milik; see note 9).

2.2. Is 4Q534–536 Really about Noah?

Some scholars still prefer to identify the figure in 4Q534–536 as someone other than Noah, primarily because of his title as בחיר אלהא. In his book *Messianische Texte aus Qumran* (1998), Johannes Zimmermann, following Starcky's initial suggestion, argued in favor of a messianic figure in 4Q534–536.[12] Wise, Abegg, and Cook have also concurred, positing that the " 'chosen one' is a messiah, if not the messiah."[13]

Other possible identities of the unknown figure have also been claimed. Jonas Greenfield, for example, briefly speculated that the figure could be Melchizedek, as his miraculous birth story in 2 (Slavonic) Enoch is somewhat similar to the birth story of the figure in 4Q534–536 (2 En. 69–73, esp. 71). Greenfield also points out that the traditions found in 2 Enoch and later Jewish texts firmly place Melchizedek within the Enochic genealogy by conflating the priest-king of Salem with either Shem, the son of Noah (in rabbinic literature), or with Nir's son (in 2 Enoch).[14] Targum Pseudo-Jonathan on Gen 14:18, for example, states that "Shem, the son of Noah, is the righteous king [or Melchizedek: מלכי צדק] of Salem" (see also Targum Neofiti on Gen 14:18;

---

9. Milik 1976, 56. Later Milik (1992, 357) renamed the text "Naissance de Noé."

10. Puech 2001, 120–21. Puech, however, while acknowledging some similarities between 4Q534 and 4Q561, argues that they are not copies of the same manuscript and that their relationship at this point is uncertain. See also the similar arguments of Zimmermann 1998, 190.

11. Puech, 121.

12. Zimmermann 1998, 170–204.

13. Wise, Abegg, and Cook 1996, 428.

14. The child in 2 (Slavonic) Enoch is supposedly already three years old when delivered. He is named Melchizedek by Noah and his brother Nir. In a night vision, Nir is told of the impending flood and that an angel will bring Melchizedek into Paradise to escape the flood. 2 (Slavonic) Enoch also makes clear that Melchizedek will eventually return through Noah's genealogical line as a postdiluvian priest (ch. 71), and in the end-time he will return a third time as a messianic priest. Cf. 2 En. 69–73.

b. Ned. 32b).[15] Thus the equation Shem = Melchizedek would implicitly place Melchizedek within a diluvian context, which also seems to be the context of 4Q534–536, especially in light of the motifs "devastating waters" (4Q534 1 ii 14) and "Watchers" (4Q534 1 ii 16, 18). Finally, Greenfield saw the title "elect of God" and phrases such as "his wisdom will be known to all the nations and he knows the secrets of all the living" to further evince his claim, as they could have easily been used to describe Melchizedek.[16]

But upon further consideration, Greenfield's proposal seems unlikely. It is true, as Greenfield remarks, that we see an increased interest in Melchizedek at Qumran, especially in such texts as 11Q13. But a connection between Shem and Melchizedek is unattested in any sources contemporary with 4Q534–536. Moreover, one can observe that the two names are never conflated in historical narrative dealing specifically with the flood. In rabbinic literature, the conflation occurs only in narratives that originally refer to Melchizedek (i.e., Gen 14:18), and in 2 Enoch, Melchizedek ascends to paradise before the flood comes. Again, because of the fragmentary state of the text of 4Q534–536, it is difficult to determine the historical period that it describes. In light of what appear to be diluvian references as well as a testamentary-type scene (in 4Q536), in which the figure implores his audience to write down his words, it seems unlikely, though not impossible, that the text is about Melchizedek.

In an article in 1991, André Caquot speculated that the unknown figure is none other than Enoch and that the text is announcing his return (as "*Henoch redivivus*").[17] He observed that the figure in 4Q534–536 is described in terms similar to Enoch in the Parables of Enoch, again referring to the title "chosen one" (1 En. 46:2). He also points out that both figures reveal divine knowledge (see 46:3; 51:3), an important function of Enoch.[18]

As part of his argument, Caquot also prefers a difficult reading of the phrase וכול חשבוניהון עלוהי יסופו ומסרת כול חייא שגיא (4Q534 1 i 9), translating it as "et tous les calculs les concernant s'accompliront d'après lui et si grand que soit le numbre de tous les vivants il sera…[selon?] ses calculs."[19] Thus, by

---

15. See Orlov's helpful article written on the matter (2000a, 23–38). He writes, "As shown, *2 Enoch* presents Melchizedek as a continuation of the priestly line from Methuselah, son of Enoch, directly to the second son of Lamech, Nir (brother of Noah), and on to Melchizedek. *2 Enoch* therefore considers Melchizedek as the grandson of Lamech" (28).

16. See Greenfield 1973, xxi.

17. Caquot, 1991, 145–55.

18. Others have also noted similarities between 4Q534–536 and the Parables of Enoch. See, e.g., Zimmermann, 1998, 196–97, who suggested that 4Q534 might provide a link to Parables at Qumran.

19. Caquot 1991, 148. His reading of 4Q534 1 i 9 depends on the particular meaning he gives to the word מסרת, which is based on the supposed existence of a second root

reading the phrase וכול חשבוניהון עלוהי as referring to the total number of humans that must come into existence before the destruction of the world, Caquot is able to speculate that the figure in 4Q534–536 is privileged with the same information as given to Enoch (according to 2 En. 23:5).[20] But the meaning of מסרת as "le nombre," on which he depends for his interpretation, is unattested except in Samaritan Aramaic, and in the end Caquot's linguistic arguments are not convincing (see n. 19).

Another attempt to discern the identity of the figure in question was undertaken by James Davila, who compared 4Q534–536 to later Hebrew physiognomic tractates from the late antique and medieval period.[21] Instead of the Messiah, Melchizedek, or *Enoch redivius*, Davila found the figure to be more comparable with anonymous *merkabah* mystics attested to in later Hebrew physiognomic literature. His argument is based, again, on a comparative analysis: both Hebrew physiognomic literature and 4Q534–536 describe certain physical features such as moles and hair, to predicate their future. Other motifs, such as celestial ascent,[22] divine revelation, wisdom, and chosenness, are also comparable to *merkabah* mystics. He further notes examples in Hebrew physiognomic literature of mystics who enter into the study of the Bible (i.e, Torah, Prophets, Writings) later in life, which he suggests is also comparable to the figure in 4Q534 (1 i 4–5), as he also gains esoteric wisdom from studying a certain three books later in his career.[23] Thus, Davila reads the "three books" in 4Q534 1 i 5 as "Torah, Prophets, and Writings," as in T.-S

מסר that is equivalent to the Hebrew root פקד (150). I have not been able to follow his argument here.

20. Caquot 1991, 155. 2 En. 23:5 states, "Sit and write all the souls of mankind, however many of them are born, and the places prepared for them for eternity, for all souls are prepared for eternity before the formation of the world.... And I wrote all these things exactly, and I wrote 366 books."

21. Davila 1998, 367–81. He compared 4Q534–536 to the following documents: "The Physiognomy of R. Ishmael," published by Scholem 1953, 459–95; Oxford 240 165b–166b, published by Scholem 1953 and Gruenwald 1970, 301–19; T.-S. K 21, published also by Gruenwald 1970, 306–17; and T.-S. K 21.95.L ,published by Schäfer 1984, 135–39; 1988, 84–95.

22. Davila (and also García Martínez) suggests that the figure described in 4Q534–536 experiences an actual ascent into heaven for the purpose of revelation. This argument is based on the difficult reading of [א]ארכובת as "upper sphere" in 4Q534 1 i 6, but this reading is not at all clear, and there are other possibilities. Puech and Fitzmyer prefer to read [א] ארכובת (knees), which is perhaps a sign of veneration (i.e., one has approached the hero on his or her knees). For the discussion of this word, see Davila 1998, 373, 375–76; García Martínez 1992, 9–10; Puech 2001, 138; and Fitzmyer 1965, 357.

23. See T.-S K 21 A1. 6–10, published by Gruenwald in 1970, 307. In this text, the figure falls from a rooftop, breaks his head, but miraculously does not die, after which he

K 21 A.16–10. He cites 4QMMT C 9–10 as evidence for such a division, arguing that "If 'Moses' (the Pentateuch) was considered a single book [ספר] and 'David' (the Hagiographa) a single unit, then the collection of the 'Prophets' could easily have been thought of as a unit as well."[24] Eugene Ulrich, however, has convincingly argued that seeing such a tripartite division of scripture in 4QMMT is difficult. Moreover, even if 4QMMT refers to such a threefold division of scripture, it seems unlikely that each set of writings would have been considered a single "book."[25]

Davila's article is important, as it attests to the growing awareness of the existence of physiognomic, astrological, and mystical traditions within Judaism before the rabbinic period.[26] The question remains, however, if the parallels that Davila draws to our attention actually change our understanding of both the character of the unknown figure and the surrounding narrative to such an extent that a Noachic identification is no longer tenable. To state the question differently, is it implausible that Noah's birth could also be described in physiognomic terms? There is still much to learn through comparative study of physiognomic texts of the Dead Sea Scrolls and later Judaism, including an analysis of the role that this type of literature fulfills in both contexts.[27] But, given the fact that 4Q534–536 was composed in a milieu fascinated with retelling the legends of the biblical patriarchs, it seems better to ascribe the description in the text to Noah or some other biblical figure rather than to a mystic.[28] It remains to be seen why these retellings could not include a physiognomic treatise of a patriarch such as Noah, especially since we see a similar (but not identical) interest in physical characteristics in the Noachic

---

begins study of the Torah, Prophets, and the Writings (יכנס לבית רבו וילמד תורה ונביאים וכתובים).

24. See Davila 1998, 375.

25. See Ulrich 2003, 202–14. There are two other references to a tripartite division of scripture in the second century B.C.E.: the prologue to Ben Sira and 2 Macc 2:13–14. Although the issue is complex, it seems that in both cases it is untenable to read each division of scripture as a "book." See also Berthelot 2006, 1–15, who argues that 4QMMT C 10–11 is a reference to authors, not divisions of scripture.

26. See Alexander 2006.

27. For an examination of the physiognomic material from Qumran with Greco-Roman and Babylonian traditions, see Popović 2006; 2007.

28. One could argue, however, that the existence of anonymous figures in 4Q186 and 4Q561 demonstrates the opposite. But some scholars have speculated that these texts are physiognomic treatises (see Holst and Høgenhaven 2006, 39–42), in which case we would expect the anonymity of the individuals described. The extended description of the individual in 4Q534–536, and his rather specific identifying characteristics, however, suggest someone of great importance, or at least not anonymous.

birth material in 1 Enoch and Genesis Apocryphon, and also because we see a growing interest in physiognomic sciences at Qumran in general.

There is much to commend in the hypotheses mentioned above, but in each hypothesis problems remain that are difficult to explain. In the absence of a more appropriate alternative, and given the fact that 4Q534–536 seems to be referring to a diluvian context in which cities are destroyed, it is likely that the figure in 4Q534–536 is indeed Noah. While a single clinching argument demonstrating the figure to be Noah does not exist, when the evidence is viewed in a sum total, the argument is more convincing. The following is a list of arguments why the figure in 4Q534–536 is Noah.

2.2.1. The Miraculous Birth

Using the miraculous birth and the physiognomic descriptions of the infant in 4Q534–536 (see 4Q534 1 i 1–3, 1 ii 1–5; 4Q535 3 1–6; 4Q536 1 1–2) to identify the figure as Noah is both helpful and difficult at the same time. On the one hand, miraculous Noachic birth stories are attested in other Second Temple literature, such as Genesis Apocryphon, 1 En. 106, and 1Q19, and can therefore be used to set a precedent for the presentation of a Noachic figure in 4Q534–536. On the other hand, the details of the birth narrative in 4Q534–536 do not match other stories of Noah's birth. In 4Q534–4Q536, for example, the infant is described as having red hair, a lentil (i.e., mole?) on his face, and small birthmarks on his thigh. He is born in "the fifth hour" of the night, comes out "whole"[29] at a weight of "350 shekels," and "sleeps until half his days are done." In contrast, 1 En. 106:2–3 states:

> When the child was born, his body was whiter than snow and redder than a rose, his hair was all white and like white wool and curly. Glorious was his face. When he opened his eyes, the house shone like the sun. And he stood up from the hands of the midwife, and he opened his mouth and praised the Lord of eternity.[30]

One might be able to reconcile the differences between 4Q534–536 and the other Noachic birth stories by reading these texts through the compositional

---

29. 4Q535 3 2 mentions that the infant is born "whole/perfect" (...שׁל[ם). Is it possible that this description is similar to the description of infant Noah in 1 En. 106:3? That is, could the word שׁלם refer to his ability to stand and give praise to God already at birth or to his being born circumcised?

30. All translations of 1 Enoch are from Nickelsburg 2001. See also 1Q19 3, where the child illuminates the room with his glory, and in Genesis Apocryphon where the child is described as having eyes like the sun (v 12).

interests of the authors. In 1 Enoch, Noah is described as angelic because the author is attempting to contrast Noah with the Watchers, and also to foreshadow the salvific mission that Noah has been chosen to undertake.[31] Lamech unsurprisingly suspects Noah of being the offspring of a Watcher because of his angelic appearance. He goes to Methuselah, who in turn travels to the "ends of the earth" to ask Enoch about the truth of Lamech's son Noah (106:8–18).[32] Enoch, however, explains to Methuselah that Noah is in fact Lamech's child, and he will "be righteous and blameless. And call his name Noah for he will be your remnant from whom you will find rest" (1 En. 106:18). Thus, in its present context, the imagery used to describe Noah's birth signifies his righteous perfection as well as his salvific mission to be carried out six hundred years later. It was on account of the Fallen Angels that the world will be destroyed, but it will also be saved on account of an angel-like man, Noah.[33]

The physiognomic context surrounding the birth story in 4Q534–536 may dictate other features of the infant that are common to this particular genre, which may also help explain the differences from other birth stories. Moreover, unlike 1 Enoch, the description in 4Q534 also eliminates narrative suspense: through physiognomy one can recognize immediately the chosenness of the child. In the end, however, both birth stories have the same aim; that is, both texts use physical descriptions of the child to predict/foreshadow his salvific role in God's plan to wipe clean the sins brought by the Watchers.[34]

2.2.2. "Elect of God"

The title "The elect of God" is ascribed to our figure in 4Q534 1 i 10. Fitzmyer has correctly noted the term "elect of God" should not be read as an equivalent

---

31. "His body was whiter than snow and redder than a rose, his hair was all white and like white wool and curly. Glorious was his face. When he opened his eyes, the house shone like the sun. And he stood up from the hands of the midwife, and he opened his mouth and praised the Lord of eternity (1 En. 106:2–4, translation from Nickelsburg 2001, 536).

32. These events also seem to parallel those in 1Q19, which discuss the corrupted state of humanity before the flood, and Noah's birth, in which the child caused the "rooms of the house to shine like rays of the sun," also a possible hint at his angelic-like appearance. Lamech's suspicions regarding Noah's origins are also recorded in the Genesis Apocryphon (ii).

33. See Fletcher-Louis 2002, 35–37; Nickelsburg 2001, 539–50.

34. García Martínez also suggests that the differences in the Noachic birth stories are due to differing compositional interests. He suggests that Noah's hair was changed to white because of the "influence of the *Book of Dreams* of *1 Enoch*, in which white is constantly used in the zoomorphic stories to designate the just, and is particularly applied to Noah" (García Martínez 1992, 23).

to the title "Messiah."[35] While it is true that we find this title applied to Jesus in Luke 23:35 and in some manuscripts at John 1:34,[36] we should not assume the title to be messianic. Its use in both the Hebrew Bible and in Second Temple literature suggest instead that the term is broader in meaning, indicating the divine calling of an individual for some significant purpose.[37] The title occurs once in the Dead Sea Scrolls, where it refers to the community.[38] There is one other attested usage in the Parables of Enoch (46:3–4), but since the text is usually dated to the end of the first century B.C.E., it is probably too late for our purposes.[39]

The title is certainly suitable for Noah, who is called both "righteous" and "just," and he alone is credited with preserving the human race. Jubilees describes Noah as the only person "whom God saved from the waters of the flood on his account; for his heart was righteous in all his ways, according as it was commanded regarding him, and he had not departed from aught that was ordained for him" (Jub. 5:19). A description of Noah in 1 En. 106:17–18 is similar:

> And he will cleanse the earth from the corruption that is on it. And now tell Lamech, "He is your child in truth, and this child will be righteous and blameless; And "Noah" call his name, for he will be your remnant, from whom you will find rest. He and his sons will be saved from the corruption of the earth and from all sins and from all iniquities that are summated upon the earth in his days...."[40]

In 1QapGen vi 1 Noah states that "in the womb of her who bore me I came out for uprightness; and when I came forth from my mother's womb, I

---

35. Fitzmyer 1965, 354.

36. This title appears in such manuscripts as Codex Sinaiticus, OL, OS, and some church fathers, while the majority of Greek witnesses read "Son of God." See Brown 1966–70, 1:57, who argues that the change in title demonstrates a christological development.

37. The title is applied to Moses (Ps 106:23); David (Ps 89:4); the servant of the Lord (Isa 42:1); Israel (Isa 45:4); pious ones (Isa 65:9, 15, 22); Joshua saves God's chosen (Sir 46:1).

38. "And those who derided and insulted the 'Elect of God' (or God's Chosen), will go the punishment of fire" (1QpHab x 13).

39. See a recent discussion on dating the Parables in Suter 2007, 415–443, and Stone 2007a, 444–49. The motif of "chosen" frequently occurs in Parables, but the motif also occurs numerous times in 1 Enoch outside Parables. See, eg. 1 En. 1:1, 8–9; 25:5; 93:3; 94:4.

40. See also Puech's discussion of the figure's identity. He also concludes: "De même qu'Hénoch reçut mission d'annoncer aux Veilleurs leur châtiment (1 Hén. 12:4), de même Noé, son descendant, est-il désigné et préparé pour annoncer le châtiment des fils d'Adam" (2001, 123).

was planted for uprightness. All my days I have practiced uprightness, and I have been walking along the paths of everlasting truth; and with me the Holy One has been...."

In these sources Noah's righteousness and election for the divine task are strongly emphasized, and it is not difficult to conclude that the title "elect of God" could have been given to Noah. Moreover, we find in 1 Enoch that the terms "righteousness" and "chosen" are very closely parallel, probably in an effort to demonstrate an exceptionally close relationship with God. The recognition of Noah's righteousness combined with his divine purpose could have easily led the author of 4Q534–536 to endow Noah with the title "elect" or "chosen of God."[41]

2.2.3. The Three Books

After reading a certain three books, the unknown figure will "acquire prudence and learn understanding..." (4Q534 1 i 6). That the author of 4Q534–536 had a specific "three books" in mind is probable. Pierre Grelot suggested that the three books are the Enochic works the Book of Watchers, the Astronomical Book, and the Book of Dreams.[42] This proposal has received some support,[43] especially as this trilogy is likely alluded to in Jub. 4:17–22, where the author explains the origin of the books: Enoch was "the first among men who learned writing and knowledge and wisdom" (Jub. 4:17), and he wrote it down concerning "the signs of the heaven according to the order of the months" (Jub. 4:18 [Book of Astronomy]); "And he saw what was and what will be in a vision of his sleep as it will happen to the child of men in their generation until

---

41. 1 En. 1:1 writes of Enoch: "The words of the blessing with which Enoch blessed the righteous chosen who will be present on the day of tribulation to remove all the enemies; and the righteous will be saved." The terms 'righteous' and 'chosen' are also paralleled (outside the *Parables*) in 1 En. 1:8–9; 5:4–9; 25:4–5; 93:3. In *Parables*, cf. 1 En. 38:2–4; 39:6–7; 48:1–2; 61:12–13, 15; 62:12–15; 70:3.

42. Grelot 1975, 498. Other suggestions concerning the identity of the three books have been put forward. Fitzmyer argues that the three books "are probably apocalyptic, and not specific, real books; rather they allude to such writings as the 'books of the living' (Enoch 47:3), the book of man's deeds (Ps 56:9; Dn 7:10; 1 En. 90:17) and the 'heavenly tablets' (Jub. 30:22; 1 En. 81:1–2) to which the Intertestamental Literature often makes reference" (1965, 363–64); Carmignac (1965) suggested that three books may refer to a sectarian trilogy, such as The *Book of Mediation* (1QSa i 7; CD x 6), *The Rule of the Community* (1QS), and *The Damascus Document* (CD); Davila suggested the three books may refer to the Torah, Prophets, and Writings, but also conceded that if 4Q534–536 is about Noah, then Grelot's suggestion is most likely correct (1998, 375).

43. Milik 1976, 94; García Martínez 1992, 9; Puech 2001, 124.

the day of judgment" (Jub. 4:19 [Book of Dreams]); "And he was therefore with the angels of God six jubilees of years. And they showed him everything which is on earth and in the heavens, the domain of the sun. And he wrote down everything, and bore witness to the Watchers" (Jub. 4:21–22 [Book of Watchers]). Milik further added to Grelot's proposal by arguing that the Kitab al-Asaṭir, an eleventh century C.E. (or later) Samaritan work, also preserves the tradition that Noah learned the three books of Enoch: "In 7 years, he [Noah] learned the three Books of creation: The Book of the Signs, The Book of Astronomy, and The Book of Wars which is the Book of the Generation of Adam."[44] Milik's suggestion is quite interesting but should not be pushed too far, as it is difficult to say whether the three books in the Asaṭir are indeed the three books of Enoch, especially given the late date of the composition.[45]

In addition to the possible references to the three books of Enoch in Jubilees mentioned above, both 1 Enoch and Jubilees endeavor to show that Enoch's revelations survived the flood because they were passed down to Noah. In a testament-like speech in Jub. 7:38–39, Noah recounts that "Enoch, the father of your father, commanded Methuselah, his son, and Methuselah (commanded) Lamech, his son. And Lamech commanded me everything which his fathers commanded him. And I am commanding you, my sons, just as Enoch commanded his son in the first jubilee."[46] Hence, Noah is faced with the responsibility of preserving the wisdom gleaned from his great-grandfather Enoch. It might be possible (but impossible to prove) that 4Q534–536 is taking up this theme with the reference to the "three books," as well as their transmission to Noah: "And with his father and with his forefathers … Counsel and prudence will be with him and he will know the secrets of man" (4Q534 1 i 7–8).[47]

Given the strong concern in both 1 Enoch and Jubilees for the transmission of Enochic knowledge to his progeny and that these Enochic works seem

---

44. Milik 1976, 66–68. The Enochic status of the third book is debatable. In support of his argument, Milik writes that "The third work, which obviously takes up the 'Book of the Wars of Yahweh'" (Num 21:14) seems to refer to the involvement of the sons of Adam and their daughters (1 En. 6:1) in the struggle between the forces of good and evil, or, in other words, to the visions of Enoch (1 En. 6–19). Refer to the Kitab al-Asaṭir in Ben-Hayyim 1943, 104–25, 174–90; 1944, 71–87, 128.

45. See Greenfield and Stone 1979, 95–98, who doubt Milik's proposal.

46. Translation from Wintermute 1983, 2:71.

47. The books of Enoch as a source rich in wisdom is also attested in 1QapGen xix 25, although in this context Abram is the speaker. He is approached by three men from the nobles of Egypt, who ask Abram about knowledge, wisdom, and truth. In response, Abram "read before them the book of the words of Enoch." While this text is not about Noah, it clearly demonstrates the importance of a book of Enoch as a source of wisdom.

to be alluded to as three different books (Jub. 4:18, 19, 21–22) it is likely that the Enochic trilogy is referred to in 4Q534 1 i 8, in which case the identity of the figure as Noah is strengthened.

2.2.4. Wisdom

That the figure grew in wisdom after reading "three books" is evident, as 4Q534 1 i 8 states that "he will know the secrets of man, and his wisdom shall come to all the people, and he will know the secrets of all the living." While wisdom is not a prominent or explicit characteristic of Noah, other sources do make mention of it. The Genesis Apocryphon, for example, states that, after reaching adulthood, Noah girded his "loins in an appearance of uprightness and wisdom" (vi 4).[48] Wisdom 10:4 implies that Noah was saved from the deluge because of wisdom, although within the context, it is Wisdom, and not Noah, that is the agent: "When the earth was deluged because of him, Wisdom again saved the upright man, steering him with a cheap piece of wood."

The testament given by the unnamed figure in 4Q536 2 ii may also fit within this wisdom-language context. This type of scenario is certainly what we could expect in a text strongly emphasizing the appropriateness of learning wisdom as well as the transmission of knowledge. While column i of 4Q534 is a third-person narrative, 4Q536 2 ii 12 (which overlaps with 4Q534 7 1–6) switches to the first person, as the speaker entreats his audience: "Who will write these words of mine in a book that will not decay, and to keep these words of mine in a scroll (?) that will not fade away (?)."[49] The contents of the everlasting scroll are unknown; however, it is interesting to note a similar setting is found in Jub. 7:20, in which Noah also entreats his sons to follow all ordinances and commandments and to observe righteousness. In 4Q534 7 1, the speaker exhorts his audience also in a manner very befitting of Noah: "Blessed be every man who teaches wise discipline to his sons, and he will not die in the days of wickedness." This testamentary-like setting would certainly

---

48. Philo also attributes wisdom to Noah. *Abraham* 27 states: "For which reason the sacred historian very naturally classes the lover of God and the lover of virtue next in order to him who repents; and this man is in the language of the Hebrews called Noah, but in that of the Greeks, 'rest,' or 'the just man,' both being appellations very well suited to the wise man." See also *Abraham* 31.

49. A similar switch from third to first person also occurs in Jub. 7:26–39. Charles argued that this switch in person reflects a narrative seam between the author's sources and that the source for 7:26–39 was a lost book of Noah (Charles 1902, 61–62).

not be unusual if our unknown figure is Noah, given the theme of transmission of knowledge throughout the Noachic material.[50]

2.2.5. Visions

Related to the wisdom motif is the figure's ability to receive visions. That is, his wisdom is not limited to what he gleaned from the "three books" but is also divine in origin, transmitted by way of visions. 4Q534 1 i 6 states (the last part of the phrase follows Fitzmyer and Puech): "He will be wise and will know … and visions will come to him on his knees." In 4Q536 2 i 8 we read that "he will reveal mysteries as the holy ones," and in line 13 we read that mysteries (or secrets) were transmitted to our figure "concerning the numbers of the remnant." Noah the visionary is a motif also picked up in 1QapGen vi 11, where Noah receives a vision concerning the conduct of the sons of heaven and later reveals his vision (vi 16). Noah is also a visionary in 1 En. 60:1; 65–69 and Jub. 8:18. Of course, that both the figure in 4Q534–536 and Noah had visions does not prove that they are the same person; however, it does give further plausibility to such a hypothesis.

2.2.6. Other Key Words

While much of the narrative context is impossible to reconstruct, 4Q534–536 also contains phrases and motifs that fit well with what we know about Noah, such as "destruction caused by water" (4Q534 1 ii 14), "cities/provinces" (4Q534 1 i 12), "he will be the ninth" (4Q536 2 i 1),[51] "Watchers" (4Q534 1 ii 15), and "remnant" (4Q536 2 i 13).

2.3. 4Q534–536 in Context

Similarities between 4Q534–536 and other Dead Sea Scrolls texts with physiognomic features, such as 4Q186 and 4Q561, have been noted for some time, although no conclusion on the exact relationship between these texts has yet

---

50. The exhortation to record the speaker's own words also fits within a Noachic context, as the "words of Noah" were also transmitted as a specific body of knowledge. See 1QapGen v 29, ALD x 10, Jub. 10:12–13; 21:10. Also, see Dimant 2006, 240, who suggests that "divine wisdom" is atypical of the traditions of Noah and that therefore 4Q534–536 cannot be about Noah.

51. See Puech 2001. This phrase is reconstructed by Puech, and if he is correct, it *might* provide another clue to the identity of the figure. Within Adam's lineage (see Gen 5), it is possible to count Noah as ninth after Adam, although other texts such as 4Q369 count Noah as the tenth from Adam, and 2 Pet 2:5 counts Noah as eighth from Adam.

been reached.[52] All three texts contain similar vocabulary in their physical descriptions, including "hair" (4Q186 1 iii 4; 4Q534 1 i 2; 4Q561 6 4), "teeth" (4Q186 1 iii 3; 4Q534 1 i 3; 4Q561 1 i 3), "legs/thighs" (4Q186 1 ii 5; 1 iii 4; 2 i 5 [שוק]; 4Q534 1 i 3 [ירד]), "hands" (4Q186 1 iii 4; 4Q534 1 i 1), and "birth" (4Q186 1 ii 8; 4Q534 1 i 10). Differences have also been noted particularly in the cryptic text of 4Q186, which combines astrology with physiognomic descriptions to predict the luck and moral character of an individual.[53] Astrological interest seems absent from 4Q534–536, although this cannot be known for certain.[54]

Another major difference, if we agree that 4Q534–536 is about Noah, is that 4Q186 and 4Q561 seem to be treatises on physiognomy (and horoscopy) for practical use in the community, whereas 4Q534–536 incorporates such knowledge to describe a historical figure. A close relationship between the views espoused in the Treatise of the Two Spirits (1QS iii–iv) and the determinism that also underlines physiognomic divination has led some scholars to suggest that physiognomy may have been utilized to determine the moral character of community members, or perhaps new initiates into the community.[55] 4Q186, for example, contains references to specific quantities of "light" and "darkness" (1 ii 7–8; 1 iii 8–9; 2 i 7) that make up a person's moral character, thus enabling a diviner to determine to which camp, either light or dark, the individual belongs. This certainly resonates with what we know about the Treatise of the Two Spirits. While the Treatise does not explicitly discuss physiognomy or astrology, it was written for the purpose of teaching the Sons of Light about the nature (תולדות) of all the children of men (iii 13, 19; iv 15).

In 1953 Gershom Scholem published "The Physiognomy of Rabbi Ishmael," in which he argued that this text and 1QS (iii 13, 19; iv 15) used the term תולדות, based on the phrase ספר תולדות אדם from Gen 5:1, as a technical phrase indicating the moral nature of a person. The Physiognomy of Rabbi Ishmael begins by stating "This is the book of the generations [תולדות] of men to distinguish between the righteous and the wicked" and continues to describe physical features of persons that indicate their righteousness or wickedness. Thus, while scholars have speculated that physiognomy may have

---

52. See Holst and Høgenhaven 2006, 39–42; Albani 1998, 282–92, and the problems discussed there.

53. For example, 4Q186 1 ii 9 records ברגל השור, which is usually interpreted as referring to the zodiac (i.e., "in the foot of Taurus"). This astrological data allows the diviner to predict that עני יהיה ("he will be poor").

54. Is it possible that the concern for the moment of the individual's birth in 4Q535 2 1 ("She wrote down the time of birth") and 4Q535 3 2 ("he at the fifth hour is born at night") also reveals an interest in astrological signs?

55. See Licht 1965, 8–21; A. Lange 1997, 389–90; Alexander 1996a, 385–95.

at some point played a role in determining a person's תולדות mentioned in 1QS iii–iv, in later rabbinic physiognomic literature the connection is made explicit.

Scholem's observation is helpful on two fronts. First, it provides further evidence of the compatibility between the views espoused in the Treatise of the Two Spirits and the determinism underlining physiognomic observation found in three other Qumran documents (4Q186; 4Q534–536; 4Q561). Second, it *might* also provide some basis for understanding why a physiognomic description was included in Noah's birth story. In addition to the fascination with Noah's birth already present during this time, Noah is also mentioned in the תולדות of Adam of Gen 5:1. In this case, as in the Physiognomy of Rabbi Ishmael, what we may have emerging in 4Q534–536 is an interpretative exercise in which the schematized history of Gen 5 is interpreted as a schematization of character types. Noah's exemplary status as a righteous and perfect individual (see also Gen 6:9) would work well in providing a model for recognizing other righteous persons born in the future.[56] Further still, the author of 4Q534–536 may have also been interested in typifying Noah's character to identify those born righteous in a wicked age, the age in which Noah was born and also the same age in which the Qumran community also understood itself to be living.

Just as later Jewish mystics took the word תולדות as a sign to apply physiognomy, so did the author of 4Q534–546, who used it for the interpretation of Noah, as Noah is explicitly part of the תולדות אדם in Gen 5.[57] But in 4Q534–536 the righteousness and future of the individual (Noah) are known, so rather than using physiognomy to determine these things, physiognomic interpretations may have been used simply to reinforce what was already known about Noah. In any event, given the fact that physiognomy is used to predict the future events of an individual, it is possible to argue that 4Q534–536 is also using the birth story, through physiognomic description, to predict Noah's salvific role in God's plan to wipe clean the sins of the Watchers.

---

56. We must concede, however, that this story may not have served such a practical application and that its meaning is limited to the narrative only. If this is the case, given the importance of Noah's priestly character in various Second Temple documents, a physiognomy of Noah would have certainly highlighted his priestly suitability. For an article on the priestly-Noah tradition, see Stone 1999.

57. Gen 5:1 attracted interpretive interest already in the LXX, which translates תולדות אדם as γενέσεως ἀνθρώπων. Here, אדם is not read as a reference to Adam but rather as "humanity" or "humankind." This translation occurs often in the LXX, but this is the only instance where the MT clearly refers to the Adam but is translated as ἀνθρώπων. Similarly, when תולדות is translated as γενέσεως, it always refers to someone's actual genealogy, except in Gen 5:1, where is refers to the genealogy of ἀνθρώπων.

3. Conclusion

This paper has attempted to reevaluate 4Q534–536 to determine the identity of the unknown figure. The paucity of evidence, of course, cautions us from making any certain conclusion. However, while the identity of the figure is difficult, there are a number of thematic features within 4Q534–536 that are also used to describe Noah in other contemporary literature. Moreover, given the community's interest in physiognomy (even if only marginal), and given the interest in Noachic birth traditions within 1 Enoch and Genesis Apocryphon, texts with a close affinity to views espoused in the Dead Sea Scrolls, we can assert with some conviction that the figure is likely Noah. Or, at least it seems that there is nothing that prevents the figure from being identified as Noah. More work, however, is yet to be done on the relationship between 4Q186, 4Q534–536, and 4Q561, which may also yield further insights regarding this elusive character.

The Rebirth of a Book: Noachic Writing in Medieval and Renaissance Europe

Rebecca Scharbach

Medieval and renaissance texts from Europe and the Mediterranean Basin are brimming with references to Noachic knowledge and antediluvian texts. In both Jewish and Christian circles, Noah was depicted as a knower of secrets, a custodian of miraculous objects, and an author of texts. This essay treats two bodies of literature from the period: medieval rabbinic sources and Christian writings from the Renaissance that drew upon those works. The first section of the essay will examine the growth of Noachic traditions inspired by medieval Noah books—medieval compositions that claimed Noachic authorship, such as the Book of Asaph and the Book of Raziel. A second section will survey the types of knowledge and writing that came to be associated with Noah in literature of the period. An exhaustive description of medieval and renaissance references to Noachic wisdom and antediluvian writing would be a book-length project. I have attempted here to provide a representative sample of the available material. A number of sources have been omitted by design; others have been neglected unintentionally. What remains, I hope, is sufficient to capture the richness of the portrait painted of Noah as a transmitter of esoteric knowledge in this period.

Medieval Books Attributed to Noah and Their Reception in Contemporary Literature

The resurgence of the book of Noah tradition in the medieval West derived much of its momentum from the circulation of works billed as rediscovered books of Noah. These texts revived ancient bibliographic tradition about a lost work to furnish pedigrees for contemporary literary productions. The mere act of concretizing ancient book of Noah traditions in this manner lent vital credibility and vigor to the legend. But the contribution of these pieces to the book of Noah legend was not restricted to their resurrection of ancient bibliomythography. In the process of adapting inherited narratives to existing volumes, new facets were added to the received material. Later, these medieval Noah books themselves became the inspiration for new bibliographic traditions concerning the lost work and its cognate literature.

THE BOOK OF ASAPH THE PHYSICIAN

The earliest example of a medieval Noah book is the Book of Asaph the Physician.[1] Although the volume is often cited by medieval authors according to the name of its purported editor, contemporary readers appear to have simultaneously accepted the author of the bibliographic preface at his word when he claimed that "this [volume] is the Book of Remedies ... that was conveyed to Noah on Lubar" (A.1).[2] Hebrew manuscript Munich 231 testifies to this dual vision of the work in a title page identifying the volume as "the Book of Remedies, *called* [by the name of] 'Asaph the Jew'" (emphasis added).[3] Moreover, the bibliographic preface of the work seems to have been the one unchanging

---

1. Some scholars locate the composition of the Book of Asaph at the dawn of the Middle Ages on the basis of internal evidence. (A critical review of the dating question is provided by Melzer 1972, 34–58.) However, the work seems to have come into its own as a literary force only at the turn of the millennium, for the earliest unambiguous citations from the treatise appear in the ninth and tenth centuries. By then, the work is already known in both Jewish and Muslim circles in centers as far flung as Persia (the Persian-Arab medical authority, Rhaze, mentions the medical authority "Asaph the Jew" in a tenth-century text [Melzer 1972, 47]), the Maghreb (a tenth-century Muslim student of Isaac b. Solomon Israeli, Ahmed ibn Al-Gezzar, cites "Asaph b. Berachyahu" on multiple occasions [Steinschneider 1965, 57]), and France (Rabbi Makhir quotes extensively from the historical remarks of the Book of Asaph, including a passage that mentions "Asaph the Jew" by name, in his early ninth-century eschatological treatise, *Abekat Rachel*, composed after his migration to France [Muntner 1957, 34–36]). Nor does the popularity of the work appear to have waned. In the late twelfth and early thirteenth centuries (the last decades before extant manuscript evidence is available), for instance, Rabbi David Kimchi claims to have read a copy of the "Book of Asaph the Physician" in Narbonne (*Commentary to Hosea* 14:8 and 15:15 [Lieber 1984, 38]). Nachmanides is able to quote extensively from the Book of Asaph in Christian Spain (*Torat Ha'adam*, Sha'ar Ha-Gemul 102a), and Rabbi Eliezer b. Nathan cites explanations from a "Book of Healing" by "Asaph the Physician" in Mainz (*Sefer Ha'ezer*, Prague edition, 122 [Melzer 1972, 59]).

2. Unless otherwise stated, I draw my quotations from Melzer's transcription of Munich 231, since his edition provides line numbers and internal pagination of the Hebrew text.

3. Melzer 1972, 92. A copyist moving in rabbinic circles would hardly have used the rather idiosyncratic formula ספר רפואות in its generic meaning, when that particular title formula is already associated with the legendary ספר רפואות hidden away by Hezekiah—a fact that the reception history of the volume will bear out!

facet of an otherwise variable and evolving text.[4] Nor was this brief foray into literary history an incidental addition to an essentially medical volume. Surviving fragments contain additional references to the work's Noachic origins within the body of the text.[5] Despite the diverse shapes the volume took in different centuries and locales, the Book of Asaph the Physician seems to have circulated in all its forms in the guise of an expanded book of Noah.

The contributions of the Book of Asaph the Physician to the book of Noah tradition did not end with invoking the name. The bibliographic myth attributing the Book of Asaph to Noah parallels in essential details the narrative depicting the revelation of a book to Noah in the book of Jubilees (10:1–14).[6] However, the author inserts new explanatory material concerning the composition and reception history of the book of Noah into the basic outlines of the ancient account. Many of these embellishments forward the authorial project of establishing a pedigree for his volume in the most naked way, in as much as they seek to more firmly establish the medical orientation of the Noachic revelation.[7] Yet, in doing so, they simultaneously serve a bibliographic function by accounting for the contents of a lost work. According to our medieval editor, the book of Noah was a comprehensive medical encyclopedia!

Other materials that do not appear in the Jubilees account represent an attempt to contextualize the ancient book revealed to Noah within medieval accounts of literary history.[8] Thus, where the book of Jubilees merely reports that Noah "gave all that he had written to Shem his eldest son" (10:14), the author of the medieval narrative informs the reader that his work is actually copied from a text called "the Book of Shem b. Noah" (A.2)—a name

---

4. Not all of the surviving fragments of the work contain the introductory pages that include the lengthy bibliographic history attributing the book to Noah. However, all extant editions of the introduction—with examples ranging from the thirteenth to the sixteenth centuries—present a uniform bibliographic myth (Muntner 1957, 14–21).

5. Thus, one finds declarations such as, "and so we found ... in the Book of Shem b. Noah, that was given to him by his father," among the brief list of "typical" excerpts collected by Muntner 1957, 156.

6. Whether this material was adapted directly from the book of Jubilees, reached the medieval author by a more circuitous path of transmission, or was developed from an ancient source that also inspired the Jubilees account remains to be definitively determined. (For a brief survey of recent work on the question, see Stone 2006a, 12 n. 27, 13 n. 31.)

7. To cite a single example that will be important to later discussions, the anonymous angel that dictates the book to Noah in Jubilees (Jub. 10:10) is positively identified as Raphael (the angel of healing, according to the meaning of his name) in the medieval text (A.16). A discussion of the other enhancements to the medical orientation of the text is provided by Himmelfarb 1994, 130–31.

8. Although these additions are certainly medieval, I do not mean to comment either way on the path of transmission.

still applied to astrological texts circulating in Jewish circles during that period.[9] The author situates the book of Noah within the structures of a slightly different literary tradition when he identifies his medical work with the legendary Book of Remedies (A.1), which traditional rabbinic literature imagined as a body of illicit healing knowledge hidden away by Hezekiah.[10] A final bibliographic gesture of this type excited sufficient interest to elicit reader participation: each version of the preface includes a unique list of illustrious medical authors dependent on the book of Noah.[11] These limited enhancements of the inherited narrative add a new and significant facet to the book of Noah legend, at once signaling and solving a perceived problem in earlier tales by accounting for the fate of this lost work after its revelation.

Available evidence suggests that the novel bibliographic claims advanced in the preface to the Book of Asaph were quickly absorbed into the existing body of medieval bibliomythography. At the most superficial level, this assimilation is marked by the repetition of the bibliographic assertions put forward by the preface. Thus, Rabbi Shimon b. Tzadok (Germany, thirteenth to fourteenth century) would explicate the talmudic statement that Hezekiah hid the Book of Remedies with the comment,

> Hezekiah hid the Book of Remedies: But from whence did this Book of Remedies come to him? It can be said that when Noah was in the ark there were demons, spirits, and succubi with him and they were injuring him until the majority of them [the people with him in the ark] became ill—also because of the evil spirit. Until an angel came and took one of Noah's sons and brought him to the Garden of Eden and taught him all the remedies in the world. And they wrote those remedies in a book and this is what is called "the Book of Remedies." (Tashbetz Qatan no. 445)[12]

Here the proposal that the lost book of Noah was identical with the lost Book of Remedies—a theory unlikely to have arisen independent of the editorial endeavor to recode a medical encyclopedia as the lost book of Noah—has been accepted by the author of this comment as authentic bibliographic knowledge. Moreover, the extent to which these traditions have entered into the broader discourse is signaled by the fusion of claims advanced by the

---

9. See Leicht 2006, 45–55.

10. See, for instance, m. Pesaḥ. 4:9 and b. Ber. 10b.

11. Munich 231 includes, among others, Hippocrates (C.10), Pedianos Dioskourides (C.11) and Galen (C.13).

12. Unless otherwise stated, rabbinic texts are cited according to the text employed in Bar Ilan University Responsa Project (edition 14). A list of editions is provided by the publishers online at http://www.biu.ac.il/JH/Responsa/books.htm.

Book of Asaph with other bibliographic traditions. For the tradition is not repeated by rote but expanded upon and brought into dialogue with other bibliographic images so that the book in question is now revealed to one of Noah's sons in the garden of Eden and put to paper by the family group. The claims advanced in the preface to the Book of Asaph have been digested to become a single element in a broader discussion.

It was not only the overt bibliographic claims of the Book of Asaph that came to influence the way medieval Jewish authors thought and wrote about these lost works but also the character of the medieval Noah book as a whole. Extant manuscripts of the Book of Asaph cover the full spectrum of medieval medical theory, leaning heavily toward those areas categorized as "magical" by modern scholars, such as the preparation of seasonal amulets. In particular, the volume possessed strong astrological associations.[13] These medical-magical and astrological themes came in time to be attributed to the legendary literary productions associated with the Book of Asaph. Thus, Rabbi Ovadiah of Bertinoro (Italy, fifteenth century) would expand upon a comment of Maimonides with the explanation, "the Book of Healing is a work that teaches about shapes of the stars and talismans, that a certain shape made in a certain period and time heals from a certain illness, and this almost misled humanity into worshipping the stars, therefore he hid it" (commentary on m. Pesaḥ. 4:10).[14] In such cases, the medieval Noah book not only recorded the development of bibliographic tradition but became itself material for new legendary explanations.

THE BOOK OF RAZIEL THE GREAT

The second medieval Noah book is a volume doubly steeped in the book of Noah legend, for the Book of Raziel the Great joins two volumes assert-

---

13. MS Munich 231, for instance, includes instructions for writing an astrological chart for a sick person, a list of dietary restrictions dictated by astrological considerations, and a catalogue of the stars and their properties (Muntner 1957, 14). Similarly, the Florence manuscript (Biblioteca Medicea Laurentia Pluto 1/88.37) includes chapters describing the diseases of the body in terms of the divisions of the astrological year and a treatise on the names of the months in Persian (Muntner 1957, 17). Indeed, the astrological bent of the Asaph material was so strong that the compiler of MS Paris Heb 8/1197 designates the medieval author "Asaph the Astronomer" (Ginzberg 1906b, 1:162). Similar collections of astrological materials had already been ascribed to other biblical figures, such as Ezra (see Stone 1982b).

14. It is difficult to discern whether Bertinoro also accepted the claims to Noachic origins put forward by the volume, since that information is not strictly relevant to the question he answers here—that is, Hezekiah's reasons for hiding the book of healing.

ing a special historical relationship to Noah. The first of these, the Book of Vestments (Sefer Hamalbush), claims a bibliographic history similar to that ascribed to the Book of Adam in the Zohar—a chain tradition in which Noah plays a prominent role. The Book of Secrets (Sefer Harazim) appears as the third volume of most printed editions—sometimes under the name the book of Noah.[15] A late antique composition in its principle parts,[16] the text purports to be one of many esoteric books revealed to Noah.

The two volumes are united by the common assertion that they were revealed by the angel Raziel. The Book of Raziel appears with this double bibliographic myth in the first printed edition of the composition (Amsterdam, 1701). This anthological format is also present in the earliest Hebrew manuscripts of the work—pushing the dual bibliomythography back to the beginning of the seventeenth century. Indeed, at least one of these seventeenth-century manuscripts (BHP MS M 207) formally combines the two traditions by positioning both literary histories together at the beginning of the text to function as a single bibliographic account of the work as a whole.[17]

Whether or not this formal arrangement often obtained, medieval authors also seem to have transmitted the two myths together and interpreted them as single narrative. Thus, one paraphrastic translation of the work into Latin claiming origins in the thirteenth century[18] (Vat. Cod. Reg. Lat. 1300) introduces the text with bibliographic elements taken from both tales. According to this account, the book was revealed to Adam by the angel Raziel (Vestments) after he had repented his sin (Vestments), was inscribed by him on a sapphire stone (Secrets), then passed down through the great men of each generation to Solomon (Secrets).[19] As the reception history of these accounts confirms, many readers in our period seem to have received these two bibliographic traditions as a unit.

The bibliographic account that introduces the Book of Vestments[20] shares its basic outlines with a bibliomythography of ancient books scattered through-

---

15. Blau 1906, 10:335.

16. The reconstructed character of Margaliot's text and the diverse materials from which it was composed invite a certain amount of caution when dating any particular passage (Schiffman and Swartz 1992, 19).

17. A manuscript description is provided by the Bibliotheca Philosophica Hermetica (J. R. Ritman Library) at http://www.ritmanlibrary.nl/c/p/exh/kabb/kab_mheb_01.html.

18. The fifteenth-century manuscript includes a preface dedicating the translation to Alfonso X of Castile (1284). Alejandro García Avilés (1997) argues persuasively that the attribution is genuine.

19. I rely here on the transcription of García Avilés 1997, 29.

20. Long sections of this text have been translated into English by Stone 2006a, 21. A digital reproduction of the first printed edition of 1701 is available through the Jewish

out the text of the Zohar (Spain, thirteenth century). This account states that, when Adam was in the garden of Eden, the angel Raziel brought him a book of holy wisdom (Zohar 1.55b).[21] This book was taken from Adam when he sinned and was exiled from the garden (1.55b, 1.37b). Thereupon, Adam entered the River Gihon and cried in repentance (1.55b).[22] Seeing this, God sent the angel Raphael to return the book to Adam (1.55b). Adam transmitted this book to Seth (1.55b) and then to Noah (1.76a), who applied himself to studying it (1.58b). According to the Zohar, Enoch also received a book "from the place from which the Book of the Generations of Adam came" (1.37b)—and though the book was substantially the same as that which Adam received (1.58b), it was called the book of Enoch because "it was transmitted to him" (1.37b).

The Book of Vestments narrative differs from the Zohar account only in giving Noah a slightly more prominent role in the reception history of this esoteric volume. For according to the Book of Vestments, Noah did not inherit the book directly from Adam but, like Enoch, received the tradition anew through the mediation of the angel Raphael. The organizational logic of this tradition seeks to consolidate disparate accounts of ancient book wisdom into a single chain of transmission—conferring upon esoteric knowledge (the *kabbalah*) a unity of content and reception history that mirrors structurally traditional accounts of oral and written Torah. To achieve this end, a single body of secret knowledge must be repeatedly removed and revealed to new recipients so that it might also be called by their names.[23]

This is not to suggest that the preface to the Book of Vestments adds nothing to the book of Noah tradition. On the contrary, the narrative introduces a series of new images to the existing body of Noah book traditions. It outlines the mechanism by which the book revealed knowledge, for it declares that, when "Noah understood the letters engraved upon it, the spirit of God

---

National Library at http://aleph500.huji.ac.il/nnl/dig/books/bk001329657.html. It is worth noting that the Jellinek's transcription of the prefatory text (Jellinek 1938, 3:156–57) does not conform in all details to the printed edition, although the divergences are trivial.

21. This tradition also appears among the variants to the Book of Secrets (Sefer Harazim) text (Margaliot 1966, 113).

22. Although the image is evocative of apocryphal Adam and Eve literature, a more immediate source is available in Pirqe R. El. 20 (a work upon which the Zohar is more generally dependent.) As in the case of Jub. 10, the problem of identifying the lines of transmission that carried these ancient images to medieval rabbinic sources is beyond the scope of this paper. For a consideration of the problem in general, see Reeves 1999.

23. This peculiarly medieval authorizing technique—which attempts to legitimize literary histories and the current literary creation simultaneously—differs markedly from the continuous genealogies formulated to authenticate apocalyptic literature, such those in 4 Ezra 3:14; 12:35–39, 14; 2 En. 22:11–23; 33:8–12, 47–48 (Stone 1999, 136).

descended upon him [and he acted] with the insight he received from that Holy Name" (3b). In offering this description of the revelation, it simultaneously presents novel information about the form of the ancient book. According to this account, it consisted of the divine name engraved upon a hard material. The Book of Vestments narrative also details the type of knowledge Noah received from this book. In addition to knowledge of the constellations (3b), Noah "learned how to make the ark from it,"[24] it was through "this book that he knew whether it was day or night" when the celestial luminaries were blotted out by the rains, [25] and by means of this book "he learned the food of each and every animal" in the ark (3b).[26] Finally, we are told that "Raphael taught him how to conduct himself according to [its teachings], the nature of its practice, and its sacred acts of purity" [27]—language used elsewhere in the preface to intimate priestly mystical knowledge.[28] Indeed, the text goes on to suggest that this wisdom was subsequently passed from each generation of the

---

24. It is not surprising that the construction of the ark should be considered a miraculous feat. Earlier tales suggest that the ark took 120 years to build (Gen. Rab. 30:7) and that it comprised as many as 900 separate chambers to house hostile species (31:11).

25. As will become apparent in the coming pages, the problem of marking time in the ark was a topic of considerable interest to medieval authors, who claimed that Noah possessed esoteric calendrical knowledge to aid him in the cause. Classical rabbinic sources, in contrast, suggested that the passing of time was marked by the precious stone that lit the ark (the *tzohar*), which dimmed in the daytime and shone brightly during the night (see, e.g.. Gen. Rab. 31:11).

26. The question of how Noah fed the animals in the ark was a problem that exercised the sages of the talmudic period as well. Those sources propose that Noah performed his caretaking duties around the clock—forgoing sleep entirely for the duration of his stay in the ark (Gen. Rab. 31:14). Medieval sources would propose other miraculous solutions to the problem. Pirqe R. El. 23 suggests, for instance, that the angels that escorted each animal into the ark carried the appropriate fodder.

27. אז נתן עליו הספר הקדש הזה ויבינהו כיצד ינהג בו ומה מלאכתו ומה קדושות טהרתו (3b). Interpreting these phrases in light of other occurrences of these terms in the preface renders the passage as follows. ויבינהו כיצד ינהג בו should be read "he taught him how to conduct himself in keeping with [the teachings] of the work (as in ואחר ארבעה דורות עמד חנוך בן ירד השכיל ביראת אלוקים והנהיג עצמו בטהרה והיה רוחץ ומתקדש במים חיים [3b] and מתנהג בו נח הזה הספר בחכמת [3b]). ומה קדושות טהרתו—a phrase that occurs more than once in the preface—may be interpreted, "the nature of its sacred acts of purity" (in keeping with the passage ומה שינהג בו הדרך ... בחלום ... ונגלה מלאכתו וקדושת טהרתו והשכים ... והתחנן ועלה בטהרה והחזיק בשם הטהור ... ויתנהג בו והלך עד שנדמה לקדושי מרום).

28. I take this category from Elior 2005, which I understand to suggest that the ritual, calendrical, and purity related motifs in *merkabah* mysticism are priestly adaptations of Second Temple ceremonial traditions.

priestly line to the next until it reached Aaron (3b).[29] According to the Book of Vestments legend, the holy book thus contained two types of knowledge: secrets that allowed Noah to perform the miraculous feats that built the ark and sustained the inhabitants of the ark through the flood; and ritual knowledge that would be transmitted through the priestly line from one generation to the next. As will become apparent in the coming pages, this account of ancient book culture draws together motifs from a series of contemporary traditions concerning secret knowledge and marvelous objects. Many of these images take on explicit bookish aspects for the first time in the Book of Vestments account.

Although the Book of Secrets is the earlier of the two bibliographic legends from a historical perspective, and even circulated as an independent work in some circles,[30] it was read by many medieval scholars as a continuation of the narrative discussed above, for the Book of Vestments account closes with the revelation of a book to Noah, and the Book of Secrets opens some pages later on the same scene. The contributions of the Book of Secrets to the plot of Noah book mythology are minimal. It states that "many books" were revealed to Noah and that the Book of Secrets copied here is only "the most precious, honored, and difficult of them" (1.29).[31] We are informed that Noah wrote out the book on sapphire stone (1.3),[32] placed it in a golden chest (1.21), and brought it into the ark so that he could use it to calculate the passing time (1.21).[33] Finally, it names King Solomon as the ultimate recipient and master of the secrets contained in the Noah volumes (1.26).[34] The primary contributions of the Book of Secrets to Noah book mythology lie in a detailed description of its contents and powers, for the preface claims that Noah learned many esoteric arts from this work: the secrets of astrology and

---

29. Genealogies including Adam, Enoch, Noah, Shem, Abraham, Isaac, Jacob, Levi, Moses, and Aaron are identified with the priestly tradition in Jubilees (Himmelfarb 2006, 53) and Aramaic Levi (56).

30. For the history of the Book of Secrets as an independent work, see Margaliot 1966.

31. The book of Jubilees may also be understood to suggest that Noah transcribed more than one book (thus VanderKam [2001, 43] renders 10:14, "he gave all the books that he had written to his older son Shem"). For more on this topic, see Stone 2006a, 22 n. 26.

32. Other bookish objects made of sapphire according to the rabbinic tradition include the second set of law tablets carved by Moses (Pirqe R. El. 46) and the staff of Aaron (Exod. Rab. [tenth century] 8.3), which, like the Noah book described in the Book of Vestments tradition, was engraved with the tetragrammaton (Midrash Tehillim 9:1).

33. In this regard, the book of Noah is similar to the *tzohar*, another object carved out of precious stone that marked the passing of time in the ark—in that case, by dimming during the daytime and shining brightly during the night (Gen. Rab. 31:11).

34. For more on Solomon as a master of esoteric knowledge, see Torijano 2002.

its portents (1.7); the art of ascension and the manipulation of heavenly beings (1.7–10); the ability to enslave spirits and demons (1.13); the arts of foretelling the future and dream interpretation (1.12, 1.15–18); and the knowledge necessary to build and supply the ark (1.18–22). Moreover, we are told that when Solomon received the book that Noah had written, he learned to "rule over …all the spirits and the demons that wander the world, and through the wisdom of this book he imprisoned and released [them], and sent out [them] out and brought [them] in" and thus "ruled over everything he desired" (1.26)![35] Whatever the historical provenance of the Book of Secrets account (whether in late antiquity or the early Middle Ages), it functions efficiently as a continuation of the Book of Vestments bibliographic tradition—picking up the story with Noah and continuing the reception history through Solomon. It is in this secondary role that the Book of Secrets indisputably takes its place as a medieval Noah book.

The double bibliographic tradition promoted by the Book of Raziel took on new life in the works of the Solomon cycle, a cluster of Christian magical texts loosely connected to the Book of Raziel tradition. In the bibliographic sections of these works, Solomon's role in the chain of transmission is pushed to the foreground and the book of Noah becomes a study text for that great practitioner. Thus, the Liber Salomonis—a sixteenth-century English reworking[36] of a Latin adaptation of the Book of Raziel—presents a first-person account of Solomon's scholarly pursuits in which the king declares,

> I King Salomon sothely long studyeng in holy words wth vertues and miracles I founde to be while there is fulfilled in eche thing worching trust and will sawe in the books in wch while I studies long found and knowe that Adam and Hermes and Noe and Moyses and many other most wise men had great privityes & virtues in their bookes. (British Library Sloane MS 3826, 48r)[37]

The revelation of a book to Noah is no longer a central bibliographic concern in this account. On the other hand, the existence and virtue of the book of Noah have been confirmed by no less a figure than Solomon himself! Nor were the unique details of the two Raziel traditions entirely forgotten. A

---

35. Solomon appears as a master of demons in late antique pseudepigraphy, such as the Testament of Solomon, and in classical rabbinic literature (see, e.g., b. Giṭ. 68b). However, some have argued that the association may be pushed back as far as the second century B.C.E. (Torijano 2002, 86).

36. British Library MS Sloane 3846 attributes the work to William Parry of Clifford's Inn, who composed it in 1564.

37. As transcribed by Karr 2001.

roughly contemporary Latin composition from this same group of texts, for instance, includes the invocation formula,

> I conjure ye by the name Tetragrammaton Elohim, which expresseth and signifieth the grandeur of so lofty a majesty, that Noah having pronounced it, saved himself, and protected himself with his whole household from the waters of the deluge. (The Key of Solomon 5)

Here the bibliographic assertion that Noah activated the power of the book by pronouncing the letters of the holy name engraved on it has been retained as a bookless tradition of secret knowledge concerning the use of the divine name.

Some authors in this tradition would assess the bibliographic assertions of the Raziel traditions together with the contents of the volumes to which they were attached. Thus, Johann Weyer's (Netherlands, sixteenth century) recoding of the book of Noah legend (cited here in Reginald Scott's 1584 translation into English) seeks to account for both the bibliomythography and the contents of the Book of Secrets.

> There were certeine necromancers that offered sacrifices and burnt offerings unto [Bileth]; and to call him up, they exercised an art, saieng that *Salomon* the wise made it. Which is false: for it was rather *Cham*, the sonne of *Noah*, who after the floud began first to invocate wicked spirits. He invocated *Bileth*, and made an art in his name, and a booke which is knowne to manie mathematicians. There were burnt offerings and sacrifices made, and gifts given, and much wickednes wrought by the exorcists, who mingled therewithall the holie names of God, which in that art are everie where expressed. (Weyer, Pseudomonarchia Daemonum §36; Scott, *Discovery of Witchcraft* 15.2)

The Book of Secrets tradition is read suspiciously here in light of the medieval notion that "the first discoverer of magic was … none other than Cham the son of Noah" (Hugh of Saint Victor[Germany-France, eleventh century], *Didascalicon*, Concerning Magic and Its Parts). The bibliographic tradition that the book of Noah was a volume that gave its owner power over the spirit world is treated as a corruption of the true history in which Ham, the son of Noah, began to invocate wicked spirits in the service of his new art. The contents of the book itself are cited in support for this reinterpretation of the legend on the grounds that the volume is filled with esoteric divine names both Hebrew and foreign (e.g., Helios)[38]—a type of knowledge closely allied

---

38. This is one of the motifs that ties this tradition closely to the Book of Secrets—for while Hermes was a prominent figure in medieval esotericism, Helios appears rarely outside of the Book of Secrets.

with art of adjuration in the mind of the author, for Weyer seems to have inherited the critical views of his teacher, Henry Cornelias Agrippas (Germany-France, fifteenth to sixteenth century), who complained that the "books delivered by Raziel and Raphael" are a collection of "profane observations ... with many unknown names and seals intermixed, that thereby they may terrify and astonish the simple and the ignorant" (*Of Occult Philosophy* 3). In this case, a recipient of the Book of Secrets tradition strives to harmonize the bibliographic claims that the medieval Noah book makes for itself with existing accounts of ancient history by examining the contents of the work.

OTHER MEDIEVAL NOAH BOOKS

Other medieval works were also portrayed as ancient books transmitted by Noah in some traditions. Thus, one late manuscript of Sefer Hayashar (MS Oxford, Bodleian Library, Michael 473/Neubauer 1960)[39] begins,

> The distinguished and wondrous Sefer HaYashar, written by Our Teacher Shmuel, Priest of Righteousness, Head of the Academy, of blessed memory, who received it from the mouth of Rav Huna Bar Sehora, high priest from Africa, he wrote it and vocalized it properly so that there is no fault in it, and Rav Huna copied it from Sefer HaYashar HaGadol of Our Teacher Menachem, Priest of Righteousness, of blessed memory, and it was dedicated and copied while he was there. And this is also the book given to Adam HaRishon when he sinned and the Holy One, blessed be he, banished him from the Garden of Eden, and Adam cried before him, and entreated him, and begged mercy before him, and he sent him this book at the hands of Galitzur the angel, and he gave it to Shem, and to Enoch, and to Methuselah, and to Noah, and to Shem, and to Heber, and to Abraham, and to Isaac, and to Jacob, and to Levi, and to Moses, and to Aharon, and to Phineas, and so each generation transmitted it to the next until it arrived in the hands of Abraham....[40]

The bibliographic preface cited here obviously parallels the introduction to the Book of Raziel in many details. Indeed, medieval traditions identify Galitzur as one of the names given to the angel Raziel.[41] That fact does not negate the possibility that this narrative preserves an independent bibliographic tradition, for most of the antique elements presented in this literary pedigree are

---

39. A seventeenth-century manuscript in Ashkenasic hand (Wandrey 2004, 27).
40. As transcribed in ibid., 200.
41. Thus, for instance, the text that Moses Gaster translated as the Revelation of Moses (B) discusses an "angel Galitzur, surnamed also Raziel" (§6) (Gaster 1893, 590).

already recorded in Pirqe Rabbi Eliezer (Italy/Palestine, ninth century, §§7, 20), a work upon which the author of the Sefer Hayashar is more generally dependent. A survey of individual manuscripts may yet reveal a number of medieval works in this cluster of texts[42] that were purported to have been transmitted by Noah in some textual traditions.

Medieval Noah books adapted an ancient bibliographic myth to furnish a literary pedigree for their contents. In the process of adapting this tradition for a medieval audience, the authors of such works drew additional material into the orbit of the book of Noah legend. Legendary and historical works that had never been associated with Noah were now identified with the lost work. Objects and secrets connected with Noah in contemporary traditions took on explicitly bookish features. Moreover, the medieval Noah books went beyond previous accounts of the primordial work—which claimed to cite passages from this lost book—to portray entire volumes as the product of Noachic authorship. The contents of these pseudepigraphic volumes thus became additional material for the bibliographic myth.

References to Noachic Knowledge in Medieval and Renaissance Literature

With the popularization of the book of Noah tradition in medieval circles, contemporary works began to associate Noah with esoteric knowledge, primordial secrets, and antediluvian writings. Many authors would read hints of Noachic writing into ancient traditions that had survived to the Middle Ages. Rabbinic writers, for instance, would infuse the tradition of an antediluvian priesthood of firstborns with novel images of words and writing. Christian authors would similarly ascribe contemporary qualities of bookishness to the Sethian columns of Josephus—objects that they connected with Noah. Others would associate Noachic writing with his biblical role as a second Adam. Thus, Renaissance scholars would envision Noah as reader and writer of civilizing knowledge.

Noachic Secrets in Medieval Jewish Literature

Most of the Jewish material depicting Noachic secrets associates Noah with priestly knowledge and primordial ceremonial objects. In some of these traditions, Noah is honored incidentally by the revival of the ancient image of an antediluvian priesthood of firstborns. In such cases, Noah is simply identi-

---

42. On the relationship between the Book of Vestments, the Book of Raziel, Sefer HaYashar and other medieval materials, see Wandrey 2004.

fied as one in a series of individuals transmitting primordial knowledge to future generations. Thus, some number Noah among those who were initiated into the "great secret of sacrifice." As Nachmanides (Spain, thirteenth century) writes, "'Cain brought an offering to God from the fruits of the earth,' and 'Abel also brought'—these people understood a great secret concerning sacrifices and offerings, as did Noah" (*Commentary on Genesis* 4:3). Others explicitly refer to a priesthood of firstborns. The Yalkut Shimoni (Germany, thirteenth century) explains, for instance, that "from the beginning of the creation of the world the firstborn used to offer sacrifices and bore the high priesthood. Thus, you find that when Cain killed Abel, it was given to Seth … and Seth gave the high priesthood to Enosh and Enosh to Cainan and so on until Noah" (Sifrei Aggadah on Esther, B1). In these basic descriptions of an antediluvian priesthood, Noah is simply designated as an initiate into the secrets of priestly knowledge.

Noah is assigned a more prominent role in the transmission of certain priestly arts, such as the secret of intercalation.[43] Of course, a number of sources also treat the art of intercalation as a form of esoteric priestly knowledge passed from one generation to the next without differentiating between initiates.[44] Thus, Pirqe Rabbi Eliezer reports that

> the number of the years, the months, the days, the nights, the seasons, the designated times, the equinoxes, the cycles, and the leap years were before the Blessed One and he intercalculated the year and afterwards conveyed them to the First Man in the Garden of Eden, as it is written, this is the calculation of the generations of man, the number through which the generations of humanity are counted, and Eve transmitted to Enoch and he was initiated into the art of intercalculation … and Noah transmitted to Shem who was initiated into the secret of intercalculation and intercalculated the year and was called a priest. (Pirqe. R. El. 7)[45]

---

43. For a political analysis of the secrecy surrounding calendrical knowledge in Jewish circles, see Baron 1952, 8:193–96.

44. Moses Gaster notes that an identical genealogy is provided for the secrets of the calendar in medieval Samaritan chronicles, such as the Samaritan Hebrew Book of Joshua. In these accounts, the secret of calendrical knowledge received from Adam is said to be transmitted by the Samaritan priesthood in perpetuity (Gaster 1925–28, 582).

45. Later sources will read this tradition as referring to a literal book. And indeed, one wonders if the word *sfr* serves a dual purpose here—a pun combining the image of counting and a book. The fact that Eve is named as a link in the transmission of this material would seem to suggest that it was recorded in a form that did not require the purveyor to be initiated into the secret!

Elsewhere, however, Noah is identified as a particularly important figure in the transmission of this secret wisdom because he alone in all of human history was forced to track the calendar without the benefit of astronomical signs. "Noah was in the ark for a full year," according to many traditions, "and he used to calculate the months from the account that the Holy One, blessed be he, gave to Adam HaRishon, and Adam HaRishon transmitted to Noah" (Pesikta Zutra [Germany, eleventh to twelfth century], Gen 7). Indeed, some would designate the practice of calculating full lunar months "the law of Noah in the ark" (Midrash Sechel Tov [Italy, twelfth century], Exod 12). Others would go so far as to suggest that this special knowledge of the calendar was communicated to Noah himself and that he "knew that forty days and forty nights had passed because God revealed this secret to him" directly (Ibn Ezra [Spain-Italy-France, twelfth century], *Commentary on the Torah*, Gen 7:11). In the Middle Ages, priestly knowledge of the calendar thus became a Noachic secret.

Other traditions in this cluster represent the metaphorical mantle of priesthood with literal priestly vestments—sometimes identified with the clothing that God made for Adam and Eve. As Numbers Rabbah (Palestine/Narbonne, twelfth century) tells the tale,

> From the beginning of the creation of the world, Adam Ha-Rishon was the firstborn of the world and when he offered sacrifices ... he wore the garments of the high priesthood ... and the firstborn would continue to use them because Adam gave them to Seth when he died and Seth gave them to Methuselah and when Methuselah died he gave them to Noah and Noah arose and offered a sacrifice.... Then Noah died and gave them to Shem. (Num. Rab. 4:8)

The addition of ritual objects (i.e., the vestments of high priesthood) to the legend is a significant one, for many medieval authors imagined the privileges associated with these articles to be contained within them, such that anyone who could lay hands on the vestments inherited the secrets and powers they represented. One particularly striking tale in this tradition, for instance, envisions Ham subverting the proper chain of transmission for these garments, thereby diverting the miraculous powers associated with them into unworthy channels! Thus, we are told that

> The garment that the Holy One made for Adam ... was with Noah and his sons in the ark. When they left the ark, Ham took it with him and bequeathed it to Nimrod. When he wore them, every beast and animal that saw the writing would fall on its face before him. And human beings thought that it was

because of the strength of his might. Therefore they made him king over them. (Pirqe. R. El. 24)[46]

The importance ascribed to the writing upon the priestly garments in this tale is striking in light of the other objects and books associated with Noah upon which power words and divine names are inscribed. However, the bookishness of the garments in this particular tradition only highlights a notion implicit to all narratives that locate priestly office in an object. Like the ancient volumes of book legend, these ceremonial objects bestowed upon Noah and his fellows had the ability to reveal knowledge and empower their owners.

Other traditions concerning the transmission of priestly articles took on even more pronounced bookish aspects. One priestly object that came to take on a novel relationship to Noah and more pronounced bookish features in the Middle Ages was the rod of Aaron.[47] We are told that "the same staff that was created at dusk on the sixth day was given to Adam Ha-Rishon from the Garden of Eden and Adam passed it on to Enoch and Enoch passed in on to Noah and Noah to Shem" (Pirqe R. El. 39). Whereas early rabbinic traditions had merely mentioned the staff along with other miraculous objects created at dusk on the first Sabbath (m. 'Abot 5:6), medieval accounts identify a line of priestly inheritors (including Noah) who would carry the staff from the moment of creation until the rise of Aaronic priesthood. In addition, medieval accounts bestow several distinctly bookish features on this miraculous object. They report, for instance, that the staff was engraved with "symbols" that could be "read" (Tanna Debe Eliyahu [Babylonia/Palestine/Byzantium/Italy, tenth century], Pirkei Hayeridot 2). More important for a student of Noah traditions, these symbols were sometimes identified as the Tetragrammaton (Midrash Tehillim (Palestine/Italy, eleventh century) 9:1)—the same powerful word inscribed on the Noah book depicted in the Book of Vestments account.[48] Moreover, like the book revealed to Noah in the Book of

---

46. It is interesting to note that the matriarchs frequently function in the line of transmission of these powerful garments without ever accessing the power contained within them. Thus, Aggadat Bereshit 43 relates: "Isaac gave them to Esau, who was the firstborn, but when Isaac saw that his wives were performing idolatrous worship, he took them and deposited them with Rebecca. When Jacob arose and took the birthright from Esau, Rebecca said, 'since Jacob took the birthright, it is proper that he should wear these vestments.'" The power of the garments is alienated from those who wear them in such tales so that wives and other who have access to the garments can also transmit the power they contain.

47. Often conflated in medieval sources with the staff of Moses (Ginzberg 1906a, 1:5).

48. Other sources suggest that the rabbinic acronym for the ten plagues was also engraved upon the rod (Midrash Tanhuma C, Vaera 9).

Secrets narrative, the staff was made of sapphire (Exod. Rab. 8:3). In such traditions, Noah is positively identified as a transmitter of written material connected with the priesthood and its functions.

It was with the composition of the Zohar that the ceremonial wisdom in question was first concretized into a literal book of priestly knowledge and Noah was assigned an even more intimate relationship with the volume. One such account relates that God "gave lofty wisdom to Adam Ha-Rishon … but he attached himself to the evil inclination until the fonts of wisdom were removed from him" so that "later he achieved wisdom through that book."[49] Adam transmitted "this wisdom" directly to "Noah, and he used it to worship the Holy One." Noah then "gave the wisdom to Abraham," who also used it to worship God (Zohar 1.76a). It is not entirely clear from the preceding passage whether the author intends to suggest that the ceremonial wisdom Adam received was transmitted to Noah in its bookish form. The matter is clarified in another episode that expands on Noah's use of the primordial volume. According to this account,

> [Noah] used to hide himself away and exerted himself in the worship of the Master.… And over what did he labor? Over that Book of Adam (which is the Book of Enoch.) He used to apply himself to it in order to worship the Lord … because how else would Noah have known how to offer sacrifices to the Lord? … Rather he found wisdom in it concerning what sustains the world, and he knew that it is maintained by sacrifice and if it were not for sacrifice neither the upper or lower worlds could exist. (Zohar 1.58b)

The centrality of book culture to this second narrative is unequivocal. We are told that Noah could only derive knowledge of sacrificial practice by dedicating himself to the study of this priestly manual.[50] The source of priestly knowledge and capacity is positively located here in the pages of an ancient tome—a volume to which Noah particularly devoted himself.

Not every contemporary rabbinic account of Noachic knowledge imagines Noah as a recipient of priestly knowledge. At least two medieval Jewish traditions ascribe esoteric knowledge to Noah that is not ceremonial in nature. According to the Zohar, the vine that Noah planted after the flood was

---

49. Elsewhere in the Zohar we are informed that the book in question was revealed through the mediation of the angel Raziel (Zohar 1.55b).

50. The third chapter of the medieval Samaritan history, *A Book of Asatir*, also depicts Noah studying a series of ancient books, including the book of Adam. None of these volumes appears to be a book of sacrifice, however, as they are designated the Book of Signs, the Book of Constellations, and the Book of Wars (Stone 2006a, 22). See Jeremy Penner's essay in this volume, "Is 4Q534–536 Really about Noah?"

a shoot from the tree of knowledge that had washed out of Eden. When Noah drank from the fruit of that vine, he repeated the sin of Adam by reveling in forbidden knowledge (Zohar 73a).[51] A second tradition reports that "four keys remained in the hands of the Holy One ... and when they were needed, the Holy One gave them to righteous men.... The key of sustenance he gave to Noah" (Midrash Tanhuma C [Babylonia/Palestine/Italy], Vayetze 16). Whether these keys were conceived as powerful objects or a form of knowledge remains unclear. However, each key granted the possessor unparalleled abilities—allowing Elijah to command the rains, Elisha to cure infertility, Ezekiel to resurrect the dead, and Noah to feed the many inhabitants of the ark.[52] In these latter traditions, Noah's reputation for secret knowledge has moved beyond the boundaries of the priestly realm and been personalized to account for his extraordinary feats and highlight his narrative role as a second Adam.

NOACHIC KNOWLEDGE IN RENAISSANCE CHRISTIAN SOURCES

Accounts of knowledge transmitted to Noah began to appear in Christian sources in the late Middle Ages and multiplied with the advent of the Renaissance. At their most basic, such accounts imagine Noah as an early master of some branch of contemporary knowledge. Most of these tales of intellectual achievement followed the newly translated Muslim astrologer, Albumazar,[53] in portraying Noah as an expert interpreter of the stars. Thus, Pierre D'Ailly (France, fourteenth century) reports that "according to Albumazar ... Noah and his sons ... were knowledgeable astronomers and they first taught the Chaldeans astronomy" (Ymago Mundi 1.280).[54] A related tradition envisions Noah as a "very expert mathematician" who employed his ability to chart

---

51. The building blocks of this tale were already present in earlier literature. Thus, the Jerusalem Targum reports that Noah's vine was a remnant from the garden of Eden but does not identify the plant as the tree of knowledge (Jerusalem Targum, Gen 9:20). Grapes are among the agricultural products identified with the forbidden fruit in early rabbinic traditions (b. Ber. 40a; b. Sanh. 70a), and Genesis Rabbah suggests that Eve gave Adam the forbidden fruit in the form of wine (15:7). The only precursor to the tradition that Noah drank from the tree of knowledge does not appear in rabbinic literature but in Origen (Ginzberg 1909–38 5:190 n. 59), although 3 Baruch also depicts Noah finding a shoot from the tree of life and debating whether or not to plant it (3 Bar. 4).

52. The keys of rain, childbirth, resurrection, and sustenance are also described in the Babylonian Talmud. They are not associated with individuals, in this case, either explicitly or in the prooftexts cited (b. Ta'an. 2a).

53. O'Connor 1956, 120.

54. Cited here according to the translation of O'Connor 1956. For a survey of related sources, see that article.

the skies so that he might appropriately time the expeditions he sent out to repopulate the earth and help them navigate their routes (Guy Le Fèvre de la Boderie [France, sixteenth century], *La Galliade* 1.87–96). Other sources name Noah as a master of the "ancient science" of alchemy, which "Adam learned from God himself" (Gloria Mundi [France, fifteenth century] 1).[55] Some authors move away from the image of Noah as a master of the sciences to claim that the patriarch popularized history and the literary arts. As Richard Lynche (Britain, sixteenth to seventeenth century) explains,

> the Chaldeans generally addicted themselves to letter unto which they were allured and persuaded by Noe, shewing them the use of Historie, and therein the true particulars of the creation of the world until that very time wherein they then lived; which also Noe himself learned and was instructed by his father Lamech, who likewise received his knowledge from his grandfather and the prophet Enoch ... and this Enoch had it by tradition from the father Adam who was possessed therewith by divine instinct and holy inspiration. (Lynche, *An Historical Treatise of the Travels of Noah into Europe*, 1)

In keeping with his biblical role as the father of the current world, Noah is represented in such accounts as a purveyor of civilizing knowledge. This wisdom itself is traced back to primordial origins or divine revelation.

Images of something resembling a Noah book emerge in contemporary Christian literature with a second set of source material. These accounts expand upon the tradition received from Josephus[56] that the children of Seth inscribed their astronomical discoveries upon two pillars designed to survive the coming disasters: one of brick and one of stone (*Ant.* 1.70). Unlike the ancient author, many medieval and renaissance scholars identify Noah as a transmitter and student of these ancient written testimonies. The significance of the knowledge contained in these works also increased in this period as

---

55. Some authors even depict Noah as a possessor of the most highly coveted products of alchemy. Thus, Noah's unusual longevity is associated with his ability to produce the much sought elixir of life (Vincent de Beauvais [France, thirteenth century], *Speculum Naturale*, 82). Similarly, he is said to have built the ark through the powers invested in the mysterious Philosopher's Stone (Paracelsus [Switzerland, fifteenth to sixteenth century], *Commentary on the Revelation of Hermes, Its Various Names*). In the minds of those who repeated such traditions, Noah's possession of these substances was not simply a historical fact but another testimony to his wisdom, for his mastery of these elusive objects indicated that Noah had achieved a perfect understanding and control over matter seldom (if ever) obtained since the advent of historical time.

56. Until the recovery and translation of Josephus himself, the tradition may be traced through authors such as Isidore of Seville, who cite the tale in the name of the ancient author (*Chronicon* 1.5).

the inscriptions on the pillars grew to comprise the entirety of human knowledge in the course of the Middle Ages.[57] Paracelsus (Switzerland, fifteenth to sixteenth century) bears witness to both developments when he explains that

> Adam was the first inventor of arts, because he had knowledge of all things both after the Fall as before. Thence he predicted the world's destruction by water. From this cause, too, it came about that his successors erected two tables of stone, on which they engraved all natural arts in hieroglyphical characters.... Subsequently, Noah found one of these tables under Mount Ararat, after the Deluge.... At length this universal knowledge was divided into several parts, and lessened in its vigor and power. By means of this separation, one man became an astronomer, another a magician, another a cabalist, and a fourth an alchemist. (Paracelsus, *Aura of the Philosophers*, 1).

Noah is identified in this narrative as the redeemer of written material that preserves all of primordial wisdom.

Medieval renderings of the antediluvian columns also translate the bookishness of these monuments into contemporary terms. Thus, an interpolation in John Trevisa's (Britain, fourteenth century) translation of the *Polychronicon* of Ranulf Higden (cited here according to a 1482 edition) suggests

> That tyme men wyste as Adam had sayd / that they shuld be destroyed by fyre or ellys by water Ther for· bookes that they had made by greet trauayl and studye he closed hem in two grete pilers made of marble and of brente Tile / In a pyler of marbel for water and in a pyler of tyle for fyre· For it shold be saued by that maner to helpe of mankynde· Me seyth that the piler of stone escaped the flode and yet is in Siria Gen. (John Trevisa, *Polychronicon* 2.5)

In this loose rendering of the tale, the antediluvian inscriptions, which had already expanded to the measure of many volumes worth of knowledge in the contemporary imagination, are transformed by this medieval translator into a literal library of codices hidden away in structures built of marble and tile!

Medieval and Renaissance literature offers up a rich collection of new images depicting antediluvian books and Noachic knowledge. Many of these motifs are probably pure invention—creative reactions to the rising popularity of the Noah book tradition with the circulation of medieval Noah books. The bulk of medieval lore concerning Noachic knowledge, however, is neither entirely novel nor strictly traditional. Many accounts represent contemporary attempts to harmonize the book of Noah tradition with existing images of

---

57. For more examples of this phenomenon, see Stephens 2005, 70.

ancient book culture and Noachic knowledge. Portions of this apparently novel material may even be entirely traditional—culled from lines of knowledge with which we are unfamiliar. Certainly some of the central themes shaping medieval accounts of Noachic knowledge—such as Noah's membership in a primordial priesthood and the existence of antediluvian columns—are known to possess an ancient pedigree. The important work of distinguishing between vestiges of traditional knowledge and later flights of fancy will be left for another time. For now it must be sufficient to offer an account of the basic outlines of the material to be analyzed.

Part 2: Noah Traditions

NOAH AND THE FLOOD IN THE SEPTUAGINT
Benjamin G. Wright III

The story of Noah and the flood in the Septuagint (LXX) runs essentially from Gen 5:28 with the birth of Noah to the end of Gen 9. Noah and/or the flood are mentioned in several other places in the LXX, but those references do not provide any information that extends beyond what is already in the Masoretic Text (MT). If one were to make a summary statement about the LXX version of the story, one could say that the Greek translator of Genesis strives to render the Hebrew text before him with fidelity and that he does not incorporate developing or existing nonbiblical traditions about Noah into his work.

Robert Hiebert characterizes the Greek translation of Genesis on both lexical and syntactical grounds as "a strict, quantitative representation of its source text,"[1] a description that highlights the translator's isomorphic approach to the process of translation and that warrants the descriptive metaphor "interlinear," as it is used in the *New English Translation of the Septuagint* (NETS).[2] As the term "interlinear" implies, the translator's usual method was to translate at the level of the word or phrase and rarely at the clause or sentence level, resulting in a Greek that is frequently awkward and stilted, even though meaning can be wrung from it. So, to provide just one example of rigid adherence to the word level of the source text, in Gen 9:5 the MT has מיד כל חיה, "from every animal." The LXX translator, here, in fact, working below the word level, renders ἐκ χειρὸς πάντων τῶν θηρίων "from the hand of all the animals." If we ignore the LXX's plural "animals," necessitated by the construal of כל as "all" rather than "every," we see that the translator has divided the initial Hebrew compound preposition into its constituent parts and rendered each

---

1. Hiebert 2007, 1. All translations of the Septuagint are taken from Hiebert's NETS translation. For more on NETS, see the NETS website at ccat.sas.upenn.edu/nets/. Translations of the Hebrew are from the NRSV or are adaptations of the NRSV.

2. Pietersma and Wright 2007, xiii–xx. It is important to emphasize that "interlinear" is a metaphor for the translation process, not a claim that there ever was any physical object that had the Hebrew and Greek in an interlinear relationship.

separately, producing a Greek phrase that looks decidedly odd.³ Yet a translator who worked in this manner, such as the one who rendered Genesis into Greek, did not always produce slavish representations of the Hebrew parent text. All one has to do is to look at the Hebrew and Greek of Genesis synoptically to see that the LXX translator does at times depart from his established patterns; these, of course, are often the most interesting places to study. Even so, it is possible that some of these deviations could reflect the translator's deliberate interpretation of the source text. The presence of exegesis, however, must be demonstrated to be part of the translator's intent at the production stage of the translation (as much as that can be determined), not a factor in its subsequent reception history.⁴ This situation certainly obtains in the LXX of Genesis, in which we find mostly isomorphic representation of the *Vorlage* but also many variations of different kinds, only a few of which, however, could constitute deliberate exegesis of the source.⁵

When we look specifically at the story of the flood in the LXX, we can identify a number of places where the translator nuanced the Hebrew *Vorlage*. Most of these instances represent efforts to clarify or make sense of a text that the translator finds unclear or difficult to understand. Such cases result in a Greek translation that might not map well—grammatically, syntactically, or lexically—onto the Hebrew text, but they do not reflect deliberate exegesis on the translator's part. So, whereas the story of Noah and the flood does not offer the kind of developments of the biblical figure known in other Second Temple Jewish texts, we still find a number of interesting "adjustments," we might say, to the Hebrew biblical text.

At the very beginning of the Noah story, his birth, the translator encounters a difficulty. Since he transliterates the name Noah, he cannot reproduce exactly in Greek the etymological explanation of the MT, which has "And he called his name Noah [נח], saying, 'This one will comfort us [ינחמנו] from our works and from the toil of our hands.'" The Hebrew play is lost in the Greek, "And he named his name Noe [Νωε], saying, 'This one shall give us respite [διαναπαύσει] from our labors and from the pains of our hands.'" Moreover, the Hebrew understands the name to come from the verb נחם "to comfort,"

---

3. The example is taken from Hiebert 2007, 3.

4. For a discussion of this problem with regard to the Septuagint, see Pietersma 2006 and Wright 2008.

5. In what follows, I try to focus on those passages that have implications for the picture of Noah and the flood. There are dozens of small, and for this discussion inconsequential, differences between the MT and the LXX, and I do not treat them here. For a detailed treatment of all of the differences, both large and small, between the MT and the LXX, see Wevers 1993, 72–126. A more general list, without much detailed comment, is given in Lewis 1968, 82–92.

whereas the Greek correctly seems to presuppose a hiphil of the verb נוח. Unfortunately, we cannot know for certain if the translator had a parent text of ינחנו or if he arrived at this etymology on his own.[6]

Genesis 6:1–4 establishes the reasons for God's decision to destroy the earth, and while not directly about Noah, two observations seem worthwhile here. First, in verse 3, the Hebrew has God, due to the illicit mating between the "sons of God" and the "daughters of men," decide to reduce the span of human lifetimes to 120 years: "My spirit shall not abide in humankind [באדם] forever, for they are flesh; their days shall be 120 years." The Greek makes a subtle change: ἐν τοῖς ἀνθρώποις τούτοις, "in *these* men." The use of the demonstrative adjective suggests that, rather than humankind generally, the lifetimes of the illicit offspring will be limited.[7]

Second, the Hebrew of 6:4 refers to two distinct groups: the Nephilim, who "were on the earth in those days"; and the offspring of the sons of God and human women who are called "mighty men [גבורים] that were of old, warriors of renown." The MT is not clear about where the Nephilim came from, who they were, and if they had any relationship with the "mighty men" mentioned later in the verse. The LXX resolves this uncertainty by calling both groups "giants," thereby equating the Nephilim and the mighty men/warriors of the MT. Loren Stuckenbruck observes that the text is ambiguous about how these "giants" contribute to the story of the flood and that there might have been reason to think that some of them survived the flood. In Gen 10:8–11, Nimrod, a postdiluvian descendant of Noah's, is said in the MT to be "the first on earth to become a mighty warrior" (גבר). The LXX translator, apparently connecting Nimrod with the "mighty men" of Gen 6:4, renders "was the first to be a giant on the earth." Later, in Num 13:33, part of Caleb's report to Moses, Caleb says, "There we saw the Nephilim." Again, the LXX translates "giants." In the same chapter, Nephilim get connected with the sons of Anak whom the spies also saw (see 13.22, 33[MT]), and this connection enables broader links between the Nephilim and other groups mentioned in the Bible.[8] Of course, Gen 6:1–4 had a long and fascinating exegetical life in early Judaism, especially in the version found in 1 Enoch.[9] Thus, the translator's collapsing of two separate groups in the MT, Nephilim and "mighty men," into the same group, "giants," seems to reflect broader exegetical traditions known to him that he incorporates into his translation, but still without extensively departing from his usual translation methodology.

---

6. This observation on etymology comes from Wevers 1993, 73–74.
7. Wevers 1993, 77; Lewis 1968, 86.
8. Stuckenbruck 2000, 356–58.
9. For a more extensive study of the myth contained in Gen 6:1–4, see Reed 2005.

When we come to the beginning of the flood narrative proper, the translation exhibits several attempts at clarification, most of which do not substantially alter the Hebrew. Several places merit comment, however. In 6:6, the MT reports that God "repented" that he had made humans and that he was "grieved in his heart." The LXX reduces the anthropopathism of the Hebrew by rendering "then God considered that he had made humankind on the earth, and he thought it over." Later in verse 7, God "repented" in the MT but "became angry" in the LXX, in this case not eliminating any anthropopathism but still masking the statement that God had changed his mind about creating humans, as was made in the MT.[10]

The Greek text of 6:9 describes the now five-hundred-year-old Noah as a righteous (δίκαιος) and perfect man, one who was "well pleasing to God" (τῷ θεῷ εὐρέστησεν Νωε). This Greek maps directly onto the Hebrew את־האלהים התהלך־נח in a quantitative representation, but the Greek verb does not match the Hebrew lexically, even if it does get at the intention of the Hebrew. Here the translator probably harks back to the near context of 5:22, 24, where Enoch is said to have "walked with God" and where the translator uses the identical verb, but this lexical equivalence is more widely characteristic of the Genesis translator (cf. 17:1; 24:40 [both of Abraham]; 48:15 [Abraham and Isaac]). It seems to be a default rendering for him when used in conjunction with God.[11] Verse 11 establishes a verbal contrast between the wrongdoing (ἀδικία) of humankind and the righteous (δίκαιος) man who will save humankind.

After God's command to build the ark and his instructions for doing it, God says to Noah, "And for my part, see, I am going to bring *the flood* [τὸν κατακλυσμόν]." The presence of the article contrasts with the Hebrew, in which God warns that he will cause *a flood*. Apparently by the time of the translator, the story was already well known as the story of *the flood*, and this name is reflected even in the translation.[12] The mention of a "covenant" in 6:18 is the first time the word occurs in the LXX.

After Noah builds the ark, God commands him to enter, and the Hebrew, followed by the Greek, notes that it was in the six-hundredth year of Noah's life that the flood waters began. The Hebrew specifically notes that it was the second month and the seventeenth day when the rain came, but the Greek

---

10. Wevers 1993, 79–80.

11. In only one case is the Hebrew verb not rendered this way in Greek, 13:17, but this verse is not about "walking" with God but "passing through" the land. One could speculate about the reasons for this equivalence. Perhaps the translator wanted to reduce the anthropomorphic implications of "walking with God," or perhaps he was trying to make the Hebrew idiom more transparent to the Greek reader, making it clear why these characters deserved special favor from God.

12. Wevers 1993, 85.

specifies the twenty-seventh day of the second month. Here the Greek translator seems to reveal a penchant for calendrical order. It is important to note, however, that we find no evidence that the translator imports into the Noah story broader controversies about calendar, that is, solar versus lunar, such as we encounter elsewhere in early Judaism.[13] He does know, however, that in 8:14 the earth is dry in the second month and the twenty-seventh day, a year later. He thus alters the initial date so that the period from the beginning of the rains to the earth becoming dry extends for exactly one year rather than a year and ten days.[14]

After the flood waters subside and the ark comes to rest, God commands Noah to leave the ark and, according to the MT, "Bring out with you every living thing that is with you of all flesh—birds and animals and every creeping thing that creeps on the earth—so that they may abound on the earth, and be fruitful, and multiply on the earth." The LXX says essentially the same thing, except for two crucial differences. The translator omits "they may abound," and then he construes the final two verbs as imperatives, not as third-person perfects, as in the MT—a perfectly legitimate way to read the consonantal text.[15] The result, however, is a divine command that mirrors the one given to the first two people in Gen 1:28, "increase and multiply on the earth."[16] The disembarkation of Noah, his family, and all the animals from the ark constitutes a new creative moment, one that will eventuate in a repopulation of the earth with all its various forms of life. The appearance of these same two imperatives just a bit later in 9:1 reemphasizes this second creation, especially since in the LXX the entire command repeats verbatim that given to Adam and Eve in 1:28: "Increase and multiply, and fill the earth and subdue it." The Hebrew, by contrast, says, "Be fruitful and multiply, and fill the earth," and it lacks the final command to subdue the earth. In the LXX Noah has become a new Adam.[17]

After the flood narrative comes the story of Noah's drunkenness. The LXX represents the Hebrew closely. In one place, however, the LXX might be interpreted as being a bit more condemnatory of Noah's behavior than the MT. In 9:24 the Hebrew notes simply that "Noah awoke [ייקץ] from his wine." The LXX, on the other hand, reports that Noah "sobered up" (ἐξένηψεν) from his

---

13. On calendrical issues, see Nadav Sharon and Moshe Tishel's "Distinctive Traditions about Noah and the Flood in Second Temple Jewish Literature" in this volume.
14. Wevers 1993, 93.
15. Ibid., 109.
16. The LXX also interprets the first verb of the pair in Hebrew, פרו "be fruitful," with αὐξάνεσθε "increase."
17. Cf. 4 Ezra 3:10–11.

wine. John William Wevers interprets this verb as indicting Noah's behavior more directly than the MT, but it could just as easily be said that, by using this verb, the translator is playing out the implications of the story as he reads it in the MT.[18] Even if it is not an indictment, however, at the very least the Greek translator, by not using some verb for awakening, makes explicit the Hebrew idiom.

Looking back at the LXX's story of Noah and the flood, given the methodological caveats I noted earlier, we see that the translator has really not taken any great liberties with the Hebrew text. He clarifies, explains a bit, but ultimately tries to give a faithful rendering of the Hebrew text. The real development of the figure of Noah will take place elsewhere in the Jewish literature of the period.

The preserved fragments of Aquila, the so-called Theodotion, and Symmachus do not add much to the discussion. As one might expect, Aquila moves in the direction of an even more rigid representation of the Hebrew text. So, for example, in Aquila's Greek text Noah "walks" with God (περιπατέω), a more literal representation of the Hebrew. He preserves the distinction of the Nephilim and the warriors/heroes of Gen 6:4. In addition, he etymologizes both names, translating Nephilim by ἐπιπίπτοντες, as if the name came from the root נפל, and rendering the word for heroes, גבורים, as δυνατοί. Little remains of Theodotion, and what is available does not reveal much about the translation of the Noah story. Finally, the extant fragments attributed to Symmachus demonstrate the most willingness to try to get at the sense of the Hebrew, and in some cases one might argue for deliberate exegesis. So, for example, the בני־אלהים of 6:4 become in Greek οἱ υἱοὶ τῶν δυναστευόντων, "sons of those who have dominance," a rendering that might reflect an exegetical interpretation. On the other hand, just as in the LXX where the use of "to be well pleasing" to God looks like an attempt to get at the gist of "walking with God," Symmachus's translation, ἐπηκολούθησεν, "he followed," seems to have the same intent.[19]

---

18. Wevers 1993, 124.

19. Lewis 1968, 90–92, labels as "interpretation" several passages attributed to Symmachus that are like this one. But he defines interpretation as "eliminating obscurities, avoiding anthropomorphisms that were offensive to its Greek speaking reader, and at times rendering a different text from the present MT" (92). Indeed, even these three translation strategies are of different orders, and I would hesitate, for instance, to call rendering a text different from MT "interpretation."

Distinctive Traditions about Noah and the Flood in Second Temple Jewish Literature

Nadav Sharon and Moshe Tishel

Introduction

This essay will deal with references to Noah and the flood in the Jewish literature of the Second Temple period and the first centuries following the temple's destruction. It is not our intention to deal directly with the question of the existence of a "book of Noah" or with those sections from 1 Enoch, Jubilees, and other Second Temple literature that are usually attributed to that book,[1] except for times where there might be a connection to a motif found in the literature that we are surveying.

Jack P. Lewis has devoted a whole book to the depiction of Noah and the flood in the Jewish and the Christian literature of antiquity (1968). His main point was that the different authors' *Sitz im Leben* "has determined their treatment of the flood."[2] Lewis's study deals separately with different corpora: Apocrypha and Pseudepigrapha; Philo; Pseudo-Philo; Josephus; the different ancient Greek and Aramaic biblical translations; early Christian literature; rabbinic literature; and later Christian exegesis. However, whereas Lewis concentrates on each of his groups of sources separately and only sometimes comments on shared motifs, our study is thematic. Although we will not deal with all of the sources that Lewis has discussed, we do not intend to summarize the complete retelling of Noah and the flood in any given source but rather to point out the different motifs that are added on to the biblical narrative or derive from biblical exegesis. We will also try to emphasize the sharing of motifs in the different sources, including sources that are peripheral to our main corpus (e.g., Qumran literature, Targumim, rabbinic literature, New Testament). We will consider the different motifs in the narrative order of the Genesis story.

---

1. See the essays in part 1 of this volume by Michael E. Stone, Vered Hillel, and Michael Tuval.
2. Lewis 1968, 2.

Ancient Predictions of the Flood

There is no early prediction or sign of a future flood in the Genesis flood story, but in the literature of the Second Temple period a few texts refer to an ancient prediction of the flood. For example, Josephus mentions Adam's prediction of the coming of the flood:

> to prevent their discoveries from being lost to mankind and perishing before they became known—Adam having predicted a destruction of the universe, at one time by a violent fire and at another by a mighty deluge of water—they erected two pillars, one of brick and the other of stone, and inscribed these discoveries on both; so that, if the pillar of brick disappeared in the deluge, that of stone would remain to teach men what was graven thereon and to inform them that they had also erected one of brick. (*Ant.* 1.70–71)

In the Latin Life of Adam and Eve (hereafter Vita Adam), Eve conveys to her children the angel's prediction of the coming of the flood. Eve tells her children:

> Michael the archangel said to us [i.e., Adam and Eve]: "On account of your conspiracies, our Lord will bring upon your race the wrath of his judgment, first by water, and second by fire...." Make, therefore, tablets of stone, and other tablets of earth, and write on them my whole life and that of your father, which you have heard from us and seen. If he judges our race by water, the tablets of earth will dissolve, but the tablets of stone will endure. If, however, he judges our race by fire, the tablets of stone will be destroyed, but the tablets of earth will be fired. (L.A.E. 49:2–50:2)[3]

Interestingly, both in Josephus's narrative and in the Vita's, this prediction is directly connected to Seth and his children. In the Testament of Adam (and the gnostic Apocalypse of Adam) Adam reveals directly to Seth the prediction of the coming flood (ch. 3).[4]

Destructions by Water and by Fire

In both of the above quoted texts, Josephus's *Antiquities* and the Latin Vita Adam, the predictions concern not merely the coming of a flood of water but rather two future destructions, one by a flood and another by fire.[5]

---

3. Translation from Anderson and Stone 1999, 91E.
4. In Gen. Rab. 23:4, the wives of Lamech predict the coming of the flood.
5. On this theme of destructions by fire and by water, see the very instructive note by

A double destruction by fire and by water is found also in various passages in 1 Enoch. The armies of Azazel (who taught humans how to make swords and foods) will be thrown into a river of fire or into a burning furnace, "and in those days shall punishment come from the Lord of Spirits, and he will open all the chambers of waters that are above the heavens and of the fountains that are beneath the earth" (54:1, 5–7). Later in the narrative, "he [i.e., Enoch] showed me [i.e., Noah] the angels of punishment who are prepared to come and let loose all the powers of the waters" (66); after this comes the second part of the punishment for the sinning angels, which includes rivers of fire (67:4–13).[6]

Philo of Alexandria also speaks of destructions by water and by fire (*Moses* 2.263). However, while in Josephus's *Antiquities* and in the Vita Adam the purpose of the segment is to tell us how knowledge was saved from the antediluvian era despite the flood (see next section), these destructions serve Philo as an explanation of the loss of knowledge. In this passage Philo is explaining why the Israelites had forgotten about the holiness of the Sabbath, and the commandment to observe it, even though it had been holy since before the creation:

> Yet men knew it not, perhaps because by reason of the constant and repeated destructions by water and fire the later generations did not receive from the former the memory of the order and sequence of events in the series of years.[7]

In a dream of one of the giants in the Qumran text Book of the Giants, this double destruction appears as well:

9. ...I watch]ed until tongues of fire from
10. [heaven came down. I watched until the di]rt was covered with all the water, and the fire burned all
11. [the trees of this orchard all around and it did not burn the tree and its shoots on] the earth, whil[e it was

---

Feldman (2004, 24–25 n. 166), which details many more sources, Jewish and non-Jewish, than those dealt with below.

6. See further, end of page 146 below.

7. Philo of Alexandria 1929–68, 6:581. See also Ginzberg 1912. Interestingly, here, as in some other sources that refer to a deluge, Noah is not mentioned. Note also that, unlike other sources, Philo mentions "repeated destructions," which is in line with Plato's *Timaeus* 22c and *Laws* 677a. This conflation of Jewish and Greek traditions, albeit not surprising in Jewish-Hellenistic authors, is interesting in and of itself.

12. [devastated with tongues of fire and water of the delug]e.
(4Q530 [4QEnGiants ar] 2ii 6–12)[8]

In *Alethes Logos*, the second-century pagan Celsus attacks the Jewish claim to special knowledge. By way of example, he derides the Jewish story of the deluge of fire and deluge of water for being copied from the Greeks.[9] This ancient Greek knowledge was already expressed in Plato's *Timaeus*, providing both a mythical and a rational explanation for the catastrophe.[10]

It should be noted that this idea of double destructions by water and by fire is also found in b. Sanh. 108b. However, there it is not found in a prediction of the coming of the flood, but rather it is part of the response of the people to Noah's preaching that they should repent, lest there would be a flood.[11]

This motif is found in 2 Peter as well (3:5–7), but there these two punishments are separated: Noah's flood from the distant past; the other to come in the future. So, too, the Apocalypse of Adam, which is a later, probably gnostic, text, speaks of the flood of water in Noah's time (ch. 3) and of a later destruction by fire (5:10) but does not mention the pillars or tablets containing knowledge.[12]

All of the above passages share the concept of a double destruction, one by fire and one by water, although in some of these sources one of the two destructions is to come in the distant future. The book of 1 Enoch also refers to the flood and to destruction by fire in the end of days. However, there these two destructions are not closely linked. In 106:15 Enoch predicts the coming of the flood when his son, Methuselah, comes to ask him about his miraculous grandson, Noah, just born: "there shall come a great destruction over the whole earth, and there shall be a deluge." Only later, in a second book that Enoch gives Methuselah, does he foresee the throwing of the sinning souls into a fire (108:3–5).[13]

---

8. Translation by Edward M. Cook, in Parry and Tov 2005.

9. "In reality there have been many floods, many conflagrations—those floods in the time of Deucalion and the fire in the time of Phaeton being more recent than the rest" (Celsus 1987, 56).

10. See Plato, *Timaeus* 22c (1929, 33); Celsus 1987, 128 n. 8

11. See also Ginzberg 1912, who claims that the legend of the flood of fire is of Babylonian origin, where it was believed that it would be part of the eschatological judgment.

12. MacRae 1983, 708, dates the Apocalypse to the first to fourth centuries C.E.

13. Note that here, as in 2 Peter and the Apocalypse of Adam mentioned above, Noah is connected only to the destruction by water. Some other texts that refer to the double destructions do not mention Noah at all in relation to them (e.g., Philo, Josephus, Vita Adam, Celsus). See above n. 7.

Preservation of Antediluvian Knowledge

The two sources mentioned above, Josephus and the Vita Adam, mention these predictions of the impending destructions, by water and by fire, in the context of the need to preserve some kind of antediluvian knowledge or wisdom through the cosmic destructions. Both texts offer the same solution: to carve this antediluvian knowledge, or wisdom, on pillars (in Josephus) or on tablets (in the Vita Adam) of stone and of brick or earth, so that the tablet/pillar of stone would endure the flood of water and the tablet/pillar of brick would endure the destruction by fire (*Ant.* 1.70–71; L.A.E. 50:1–2).[14] One major difference between these two sources should be noted: while the knowledge that is to be saved in Josephus is some kind of scientific and astronomical wisdom (*Ant.* 1.69), in the Vita Adam the knowledge is of the biographies of Adam and Eve (50:1).[15]

This theme of the need to preserve some kind of antediluvian knowledge is also present in God's revelation to Enoch in 2 En. 33. However, there are crucial differences between this source and the previous two: (1) Enoch receives the prophecy of the coming flood from God himself, whereas in the previous sources it was predicted by Adam (Josephus) or by Eve, who received the prophecy via an angel (Vita Adam); (2) this source speaks only of a flood of water and does not mention any other destruction (33:12); (3) the knowledge that is to be saved here is already in the form of books and does not need to be carved on tablets or pillars; (4) these are the books of a few of the antediluvian heroes—Adam, Seth, Enosh, Keinan, Mahalalel, Jared, and Enoch (33:10)—not only of Adam and Eve; moreover, at least in the case of the book written by Enoch, it seems that it contains an apocalyptic kind of knowledge[16]—knowledge of the heavens and earth conveyed to Enoch by God himself (33:3); and (5) since the knowledge is already in the form of books, there is need for a different way of preserving it; therefore, these books will be preserved by two of God's angels (33:12).

Jubilees 8:13 also contains an allusion to writings preserved from before the flood by having been carved on rock, as we have seen above in the Vita Adam and in Josephus. There Keinan, the son of Arpachshad,[17] finds writings

---

14. Ginzberg 1912 claims that the legend about the two pillars/tablets is actually a unification of a Babylonian legend (the tablet of brick) and an Egyptian one (the pillar of stone).

15. See van der Horst 2002, 153.

16. The Cologne Mani Codex 48.1–60.12 speaks of apocalypses by Adam, Seth, Enosh, Shem, and Enoch, before speaking of Paul.

17. In the Hebrew Bible, Arpachshad's son is Shelah (Gen 10:24; 11:12), and Keinan is the son of Enosh (Gen 5:9) in the antediluvian era, but in the Septuagint Keinan appears as

that are carved on a rock, but these writings are actually the teachings of the Watchers.

This idea of the preservation of antediluvian knowledge is part of a wide-ranging tendency in the ancient Near East to claim to have access to wisdom from before the flood, that is, to claim antiquity for the knowledge one has.[18] This tendency greatly intensified in the Hellenistic period, when Babylonians and Egyptians were rivaling over the invention of science, particularly astrology, and Jews also joined the debate.[19]

Contrary to the texts mentioned above, as we have already seen, Philo sees in the floods an explanation of the loss of knowledge, an explanation supplied centuries before him by Plato, quoting an old Egyptian priest; not surprisingly, Celsus also sees in the floods and fires an explanation for the loss of knowledge.[20]

Reasons for the Flood

The books of the Apocrypha and Pseudepigrapha provide us with a variety of reasons for the punishment.

1. The Story of the Watchers. The relationship between the flood narrative in Genesis and the fragmentary story of the "sons of God" who took "the daughters of men" as their wives (Gen 6:1–4), which immediately precedes it, is unclear. Although Gen 6:11 and 13 say that the flood is a punishment for חמס (violence), the position of Gen 6:1–4 makes it seem like an introduction to the flood narrative, thus implying that there is a relation of cause and effect between the two. However, it is not explicitly stated that this was the reason for the punishment. Perhaps the editor intended to provide a cause by his positioning of these textual units, although the "original" intent may have been different. Second, nowhere in the flood narrative itself are the Nephilim or "the sons of God" mentioned.[21] It also seems that verse 3 ("Then the Lord

---

the name of both the son of Enosh and of Arpachshad's son (Gen 11:12–13),

18. For a document of Ashurbanipal, king of Assyria in the middle of the seventh century B.C.E., see van der Horst 2002, 139.

19. See the very informative note by Feldman (2004, 24–25 n. 166), as well as van der Horst 2002, who both deal with many more sources, Jewish and non-Jewish, than those mentioned here.

20. "The Greeks of course thought these upheavals ancient since they did not possess records of earlier events, such records being destroyed in the course of floods and conflagrations" (Celsus 1987, 56). Here again it seems that Plato's *Timaeus* was his source (see Plato, *Timaeus* 23a, b). Interestingly, a small fragment of the Book of Giants (2Q26) seems to allude to effacing or erasing of tablets in water. See van der Horst 2002, 148.

21. Skinner 1910, 141.

said, 'My spirit shall not abide in man for ever ... but his days shall be a hundred and twenty years"), which comes immediately after the description of the "sons of God" taking the "daughters of men," is a reaction to the sins of the sons of God, which precede it, and therefore verses 5–7, in which God decides to wipe out all the creatures from the face of the earth, seems to be referring to a different wickedness. Fourth, it is not clear why humankind would be punished for the sins of the sons of God.[22]

Still, a number of texts of the Apocrypha and the Pseudepigrapha see the incident of the Watchers as the main reason for the flood. In 1 Enoch and in Jubilees the immediate cause of the flood is the incident of the Watchers, which is a more complete narrative of the story of the "sons of God" of Gen 6 (1 En. 6–11; 106:13–16; Jub. 5). However, other texts of the Pseudepigrapha and Apocrypha also see the Watchers' story as the primary reason for the flood. This is implied in the Syriac Apocalypse of Baruch (2 Baruch), which is usually dated to the end of the first century–early second century C.E.[23] In an explanation of the vision of the black waters that he had seen, Baruch is told:

> For he [i.e., Adam] became a danger to his own soul: even to the angels became he a danger. For, moreover, at that time when he was created, they enjoyed liberty. And some of them descended, and mingled with the women. And then those who did so were tormented in chains. But the rest of the multitude of the angels, of which there is (no) number, restrained themselves. And those who dwelt on the earth perished together (with them) through the waters of the deluge. (2 Bar. 56:10–16)[24]

The Testament of Naphtali likewise puts the blame for the flood on the Watchers (3:4–5):

> so that you will not become as Sodom which changed the order of its nature. In like manner also the Watchers changed the order of their nature, whom the Lord also cursed at the Flood on their account making the earth uninhabited without inhabitants and fruits.[25]

---

22. Interestingly, Josephus writes about the people's wickedness which started with their abandoning their fathers' customs but connects the sons of God episode to this wickedness (*Ant.* 1.72–74).

23. Stone 1984a, 410.

24. All translations used are from Charles 1913, unless stated otherwise. On the connection between the flood and Adam's sin, see further 4 Ezra 3:9–11 and pages 154–55 below.

25. All translations of the Testaments of the Twelve Patriarchs are by Hollander and Jonge 1985. Regarding the Testaments of the Twelve Patriarchs, it should be taken into

Similarly, we find an allusion to the Watchers tradition in 3 Maccabees. In Simeon the high priest's prayer, he discusses justice and the punishments of the wicked and first mentions the Giants who felt secure due to their might but were destroyed by the flood:

> Thou didst destroy those who aforetime committed iniquity, among whom were giants trusting in their strength and boldness, bringing upon them a boundless flood of water. (2:4)

Although here the Giants are mentioned, not the Watchers,[26] the mention of this tradition in such a text is interesting because of the historical character of this text, which is very different from that of the Testaments of the Twelve Patriarchs, 1 Enoch, and Jubilees.

Other texts place the blame on figures other than the Watchers:

2. Women. In T. Reu. 5, Reuben speaks against women as being evil, tells his sons to stay away from fornication, then adds:

> For thus they bewitched the Watchers before the flood: as these looked at them continually, they lusted after one another, and they conceived the act in their mind, and they changed themselves into the shape of men, and they appeared to them when they were together with their husbands. And they, lusting in their mind after their appearances, bore giants; for the watchers appeared to them as reaching unto heaven.[27] (5:6–7)

Obviously, this author knows the Watchers' story; however, he chooses not only to distance himself from the theologically problematic interpretation that there were actual sexual relations between angels and women[28] but also places the bulk of the blame for the Watchers' transgression on the women instead of the Watchers and implies that their bewitching of the Watchers was the reason for the flood.

---

consideration that, although they include Jewish traditions, in their present form they are Christian (see Hillel 2002, 2–3).

26. Similarly, 3 Bar. 4:10 and Wis 14:6 speak of the destruction of the Giants, not the Watchers, in the flood.

27. This idea, that the thoughts a woman has in her mind or that the things she sees during intercourse influence the kind of child she conceives, also appears in a story about Rabbi Yohanan in b. B. Meṣi'a 84a. There Yohanan says that it is good that women see him when they get out of the *mikveh*, so that they shall have children as beautiful as himself. This idea is also similar to the story of Jacob and Laban and the spotted and speckled sheep and goats (Gen 30:31–31:13). For the continuation of this idea into the Middle Ages and even up until the nineteenth century, see Baumgarten 1997, 10 and n. 27.

28. Lewis 1968, 17.

3. Adam and Eve. As we have seen above, the Vita Adam sees the flood as coming due to Adam and Eve's sin: "Michael the archangel said to us [i.e., Adam and Eve]: 'On account of your conspiracies, our Lord will bring upon your race the wrath of his judgment, first by water, and second by fire'" (49:2–3).

4. Cain. Wisdom of Solomon blames Cain for the coming of the flood. Within its praise of wisdom it says:

> She [i.e., Wisdom] guarded to the end the first-formed father of the world, that was created alone, and delivered him out of his transgression, and gave him strength to get dominion over all things. But when an unrighteous man fell away from her in his anger, he perished himself in the rage wherewith he slew his brother. And when for his cause the earth was drowning with a flood, wisdom again saved it, guiding the righteous man's course by a poor piece of wood. (10:1–4)

This text knows of the tradition connecting the flood with the Watchers and the Giants, as can be seen in 14:6,[29] yet here it explicitly blames Cain, not the Watchers, for the flood.

This motif also appears in the Testament of Benjamin. While telling his children to stay away from the evildoing of Beliar, Benjamin mentions Cain, who did not stay away from it:

> Therefore was also Cain delivered over to seven vengeances by God: for every hundred years the Lord brought one plague upon him; he suffered for two hundred years, and in his nine-hundredth year he was destroyed at the Flood [ἐπὶ τοῦ κατακλυσμοῦ] on account of Abel his righteous brother. (7:3–4)[30]

---

29. "For in the old time also, when proud giants were perishing, the hope of the world, taking refuge on a raft…"

30. Although the words "at the flood" do not appear in some of the manuscripts, they do appear in most, and this is the preferred version in de Jonge's critical edition (1978, 174). In his apparatus he notes that manuscripts e, a, f, and c omit these words. So, too, in the study of the Testaments by Hollander and de Jonge (1985, 433); they have this version alone, and they also point to other texts that have the tradition that Cain died in the flood. Among others, this tradition is found in Eccl. Rab. 6:3. Except for its appearance here, the word κατακλυσμός appears in the Testaments of the Twelve Patriarchs only in T. Reu. 5:6 and T. Naph. 3:5, and in both it refers to the flood.

Although this text does not state explicitly that the flood came due to Cain's sin, it is interesting that the flood is mentioned in connection with Cain, reminiscent of the Wisdom of Solomon.[31]

Noah's Name

The story of Noah in Genesis starts off, of course, with his birth and naming. The choice of name is explained: זה ינחמנו ממעשנו ומעצבון ידינו (RSV: "Out of the ground which the Lord has cursed this one shall bring us relief from our work and from the toil of our hands," 5:29). Philo explains that in Hebrew the name Noah means "rest" (ἀνάπαυσις) or "just" (δίκαιος) in Greek (*Abraham* 27; see also *QG* 1.45). In a different text he plays further with these two explanations: "'Noah' is a sort of cognomen of justice, by participation in which the mind gives us rest from the evil of labours and will give us rest from sorrows and fears" (*QG* 1.87). First Enoch explains the name as follows: "for he will comfort the earth after all the destruction" (107:3); "for he shall be left to you, and he and his sons shall be saved from the destruction" (106:18).

Besides these explanations of the name Noah, Philo also identifies Noah with the Greek flood hero, Deucalion (*Rewards* 23).[32] Interestingly, this is the only such identification in the whole corpus of Jewish-Hellenistic literature.[33] However, this identification is also found in the later gnostic text Apocalypse of Adam (3:8). The pagan Celsus also makes this analogy when he wants to downplay the teaching of Moses.[34]

When Did the Watchers Descend?

In the Genesis narrative, Noah's birth precedes the description of the Watchers' deeds and the wickedness that followed, so it seems that the story of

---

31. T. Adam 3 seems to be conflating this tradition, blaming Cain, with the tradition blaming the women, saying: "a Flood is coming ... because of the daughters of Cain, your [i.e., Seth's] brother, who killed your brother Abel out of passion for your sister Lebuda, since sins had been created through your mother, Eve" (3:5). The tradition that Cain killed Abel out of passion for a sister is found also in rabbinic literature (Gen. Rab. 22:8; Pirqe R. El. 21).

32. See further Geljon, "Philo's Interpretation of Noah," 188 in this volume.

33. Josephus does not use the word κιβωτός, which is the LXX rendering of the word "ark," but rather the word λάρναξ (e.g., *Ant.* 1.77, 78; 20.25), which according to Thackeray (LSJ, 36, n. a.) is the classical word for Deucalion's ark; therefore, it is possible that Josephus is trying to hint at this identification.

34. Celsus 1987, 77.

the Watchers happened during his lifetime. However, some Second Temple sources locate the beginning of the period of wickedness prior to Noah's birth.

For example, 1 Enoch dates the Watchers' descent to the days of Jared (6:6; 106:13), who lived four generations before Noah. Although according to the chronology of Genesis Jared was still living for almost four hundred years of Noah's life,[35] and therefore both the dating of Genesis and that of 1 Enoch are possible, 1 Enoch seems to imply that they descended at the beginning or in the prime of Jared's life, not at a later time, as the author is counting on the wordplay ירד—ירידה (6:6). Jubilees also dates the descent to Jared's days, saying that they were sent to teach humankind to do justice (4:15). In the Jubilees account it is even clearer that this happened before Noah's birth, since Enoch rebukes the Watchers before being taken to heaven (4:22–23),[36] and Enoch, who lived to the age of 365, was not present during the days of Noah. Furthermore, Jub. 4:15 explicitly says that he was named Jared because the Watchers descended in his days. However, along with this "Enochic" tradition, Jubilees also narrates the Genesis tradition, according to which the Watchers began to sin only in the days of Noah (4:33–5:2).

Josephus says that the people continued to believe in God and to act justly until the seventh generation (*Ant.* 1.72). This means that the wickedness began in Enoch's generation, that is, before Noah's lifetime. However, very soon afterward, Josephus says that Noah was "indignant at their conduct" and preached to them (1.74), and this might imply that it indeed continued well into Noah's lifetime. Also, in Sibylline Oracles 1 the wickedness seems to have started long before Noah's life. Noah is placed in the fifth generation (125–126), while the wickedness is said to have started in the preceding generations (73–124).

Noah as an Extraordinary Righteous Man

Genesis 6:9 says: "Noah was a righteous man, blameless in his generation" (cf. 7:1). It is well-known that the rabbis' attitude toward Noah's righteousness is ambivalent: some say that he was truly righteous, others that it was only in his wicked generation that he could have been considered righteous (b. Sanh. 108a). However, in the texts we have examined, we rarely find a similar negative view. On the contrary, there are numerous texts in which Noah is

---

35. Jared begot Enoch when he was 162 years old (Gen 5:18); Enoch begot Methuselah at the age of 65 (5:21); Methuselah begot Lamech when he was 187 (5:25); and Lamech begot Noah when he was 182 years old (5:28). This means that Jared was "only" 596 years old when Noah was born, and he lived to the age of 962 (5:20).

36. See also 4Q203 (4QEnGiants[a] ar) 8.

unambiguously mentioned as being righteous, and these texts continue the theme of Noah's righteousness that is also found in Ezek 14:14, 20.[37]

Noah's unquestionable righteousness is found in the texts we have seen above, Wis 10:4 and 14:6–7. To these we may add apGen (1Q20 [1QapGen ar]) 6:1–2;[38] Jub. 5:19; Josephus, *Ant.* 1.75; Sib. Or. 3.823–825; 2 En. 35:1;[39] 4 Bar. 7:8; Sib. Or. 1.125–127, which emphasizes that "to him God himself spoke…" and thus might be forming a typology with Moses; and Sib. Or. 1.280, which emphasizes that Noah was the "most righteous of men."[40]

This is true also for the book of Ben Sira. In his Praise of the Fathers of Old, ben Sira mentions Noah: "Noah the righteous was found blameless; in the season of destruction he became the continuator; for his sake there was a remnant, And by reason of the covenant with him the flood ceased" (44:17). In 4 Ezra 3:9–11 (end of first century C.E.), Ezra is complaining to God and tells of the judgment that was done in the flood. He first mentions Adam and his sin and the idea that Adam's sin brought death to the world, then goes on to say that all the nations had sinned. He continues:

> But again, in its time thou didst bring the flood upon the earth and the inhabitants of the world and destroy them. And the same fate befell them: as death came upon Adam, so the flood upon them. But thou didst leave one of them, Noah with his household, and all the righteous who have descended from him.[41]

Here Noah's righteousness is not specifically mentioned, but he is the source of righteous descendants.

In this context, it is worth mentioning the connection that is made here between the story of Noah and the flood and the idea that Adam's sin brought death to the world. This connection is also found in 2 Bar. 56 discussed above. On the other hand, another text we noted, Wis 10:1–2, does the exact opposite

---

37. VanderKam 1980, 13–14.

38. These lines refer to his birth. His miraculous birth, which is found in some texts (e.g., 1 En. 106), is itself, of course, evidence of his righteousness. See further "Traditions of the Birth of Noah," by Aryeh Amihay and Daniel Machiela in this volume.

39. What is stated here is that after the flood a righteous man will be left of Enoch's family. One could think that this refers to Noah, but this is not said explicitly. On the other hand, when Noah is mentioned toward the end of the book, it is not said that he was righteous, and the main figure is Melchizedek, not Noah, even though it is not stated explicitly that Melchizedek was righteous either. In general, 2 Enoch downplays Noah's role and brings his brother Nir and Nir's son Melchizedek to the fore. Thus, the role of sacrificing is transferred to them.

40. All translations of Sibylline Oracles are by Collins 1983.

41. Translation by Stone 1990.

and absolves Adam from his sin, saying explicitly that Adam was delivered from his transgression and thus is not held responsible for the coming of sin and death to the world.

Returning to the issue of Noah's righteousness, Noah is mentioned among the patriarchs in Tob 4. In Tobit's moral instruction to his son Tobias, he tells him not to marry a foreign woman:

> Beware, my child, of all whoredom, and take first a wife of the seed of thy fathers, take not a strange wife, which is not of thy father's tribe; for we are the sons of the prophets. Noah, Abraham, Isaac, Jacob, our fathers of old time, remember, my child, that they all took wives of their kinsmen, and were blessed in their children, and their seed shall inherit the land. (4:12)

The fact that Noah is mentioned here together with the righteous patriarchs obviously makes him righteous as well. Furthermore, Noah's being one of the prophets is another proof of his righteousness.[42]

Similarly, in the Testament of Benjamin, when talking about resurrection, Benjamin says: "Then you will see Enoch, Noah and Shem and Abraham and Isaac and Jacob rising on the right hand in gladness" (10:6). The context of this passage, however, implies that it is Christian and thus later.[43]

It is interesting to note that, in almost all of the literature examined here, there is no mention of the one single event in the biblical story of Noah that could be interpreted as a sin or wrongdoing of Noah's. Although Noah's drunkenness and exposure (Gen 9:21) are not explicitly seen as a sin in the biblical narrative, they could easily be interpreted as such.[44] Still, most of the texts dealt with here, including Pseudo-Philo's *Biblical Antiquities*,[45] do not mention this episode at all.[46] In fact, it seems that the episode is only alluded to in three sources: Philo actually interprets this episode in a positive way for Noah: Noah "is said to be drunken, not by drinking wine to excess, but merely

---

42. Another interesting theme that we find here is that Noah married a relative, just like the patriarchs. This idea is not found in Genesis but is known from Jub. 4:33 (on the theme of marriage with relatives, see further Halpern-Amaru 1999, 18–21). Possibly the author of Tobit knew of a similar tradition, or perhaps he assumed that, like the patriarchs, Noah's wife was his relative. In any case, this idea obviously serves the author's interests here to stress his point against marrying foreign women.

43. Hollander and de Jonge 1985, 62.

44. E.g., Gen. Rab. 36:4 (Theodor and Albeck 1996, 338–39).

45. In reference to Noah's righteousness, Pseudo-Philo follows Genesis in saying that Noah "was a righteous man and blameless in his generation" (3:4).

46. Except for the planting of the vine by Noah (Gen 9:20), but not his drunkenness, which is mentioned in 3 Baruch and will be discussed below.

by partaking of wine" (*Q.G.* 2.68). Philo also sees in Noah's being uncovered praise for him "that his nakedness does not (take place) somewhere outside but that he was in his house, concealed by the screen of his house" (2.69).[47] In the book of Jubilees (7:6–10), this episode is mentioned but does not seem to be interpreted in a negative sense. In Josephus (*Ant.* 1.141), however, it does seem to be interpreted as a negative deed ("Drunken, he fell asleep and lay in an indecent state [παρακόσμως] of nudity").

We have already seen (above, p. 152) that Philo explains Noah's name as "just" (δίκαιος). However, we do find in Philo, in *Abraham* 31–37, a view similar to that attributed to some of the rabbis, that Noah could have been considered righteous only in his generation. Here (31) Philo is following the Septuagint rendering of the enigmatic בדרתיו of the MT (Gen 6:9), which has the singular: ἐν τῇ γενεᾷ αὐτοῦ "in his generation," which could lead to the conclusion that he was just only in his generation. Philo allegorically explains the use of the word "man" (ἄνθρωπος), which is used in 6:9 in relation to Noah, as referring to man not in the biological sense but rather in the moral sense: a "man" is one who has "expelled from the soul the untamed and frantic passions and the truly beast-like vices." So, "the unjust is no man…. the follower after righteousness alone is man" (31–35).[48] Philo goes on to say:

> But Moses makes a good point when, after praising him as possessed of all these virtues, he adds that he was perfect in his generation, thus showing that he was not good absolutely but in comparison with the men of that time. For we shall shortly find him mentioning other sages whose virtue was unchallenged, who are not contrasted with the bad, who are adjudged worthy of approval and precedence, not because they were better than their contemporaries but because they possessed a happily-gifted nature and kept it unperverted, who did not have to shun evil courses or indeed come into contact with them at all, but attained pre-eminence in practicing that excellence of words and deeds with which they adorned their lives. (*Abraham* 36–37; see also *Q.G.* 2.45)

Noah as Preacher; The People's Chance to Repent

Doubt might be cast upon Noah's righteousness due to the fact that in the biblical account he did not try to persuade the people of his generation to repent and thus save themselves. But in the texts studied here, no such allegations are

---

47. On Philo's view on Noah's drunkenness, see further Albert Geljon, "Philo's Interpretation of Noah," pp. 189–90 in this volume.

48. See also *Moses* 2.59–60.

raised. On the contrary, some texts actually introduce the theme of Noah as a preacher to his generation.

In Sib. Or. 1.128–130, God commands Noah to preach to the people, so they should repent, and in 150–170 there is a long speech by Noah preaching to the people. He talks about their faithlessness, their bloodthirstiness—wars and murder—and he emphasizes that God sees and knows everything. In 171–172 they respond by mocking Noah and calling him crazy. Then, in 174–198, Noah answers them in a long speech in which he elaborates on their sins and on exactly what will happen in the flood.

Josephus also says Noah preached to his generation (*Ant.* 1.74). Unlike Sib. Or. 1, Josephus says only that Noah tried to convince them to repent and do good deeds; no actual speech is recounted. Babylonian Talmud tractate Sanh. 108a–b also presents some opinions that state that Noah called on the people of his generation to repent. Likewise, 2 Peter knows of "Noah the preacher." He calls Noah "a herald of righteousness" (δικαιοσύνης κήρυκα; 2:5). Interestingly, Noah is here called "the eighth" (ὄγδοος). Some have understood this as referring to his generation: Noah was the eighth preacher.[49] However, Noah was the tenth generation from Adam, and it seems more likely that this is actually a reference to Noah's place among the people coming out of the ark,[50] just like Sib. Or. 1, which refers to Noah as a preacher and emphasizes that he "came out eighth" (280). Thus, this verse may correspond to 1 Pet 3:20, which also refers to eight people who were saved and which might also imply that Noah preached to his generation.[51]

In the earlier 1 Enoch, the task of preaching is given to Enoch, who reproves the Watchers but does not call for repentance (12:4–13:10; see also 4Q203 frag. 8). It seems, therefore, that there was some kind of shift of this motif between Noah and Enoch.[52]

The idea that the people were given a chance to repent is also found in Philo, although there Noah's preaching is not the vehicle. Philo explains the seven days that passed between the entrance to the ark and the beginning of the flood (Gen 7:4, 10) as a time that was intended to give the people a chance to repent (*Q.G.* 2.13). Exactly the same idea is found also in Targum Pseudo-

---

49. Bigg 1978, 276.
50. Reicke 1964, 164–65.
51. Bigg 1978, 276.
52. The affinities of Noah and Enoch are found already in the biblical text, in the similarity of their names and in the fact that they are both said to have walked with God (Gen 5:24; 6:9). This relationship is further elaborated in later texts. For example, Jubilees actually associates the flood with Enoch (4:24). However, this issue is too vast to be dealt with fully in this essay.

Jonathan on Gen 7:4 and 7:10 and in various rabbinic midrashim.[53] Similarly, Philo suggests that the span of 120 years mandated in Gen 6:3 was a time allotted for repentance (*Q.G.* 1.91).[54]

Building the Ark

Most Second Temple sources do not deviate from the Genesis description of the ark (6:14–16). However, whereas Genesis says that the ark had three stories (6:16), both Josephus (*Ant.* 1.77) and Philo (*Moses* 2.60) say that there were four stories, and 2 Enoch has an ambiguous description in God's commandment to Noah: "Make there an ark with … two stories in the middle" (73:1).[55] It is possible that 2 Enoch also knows of the same tradition of four stories, but the passage is not completely clear. Finally, 1 En. 67:2 has a tradition in which angels, not Noah, built the ark.

The Flood

The description of the flood is minimal in Genesis. All that is said is: "all the fountains of the great deep burst forth, and the windows of the heavens were opened. And rain fell upon the earth forty days and forty nights" (7:11–12), followed by further references to the water and their height at different stages (7:17–20, 24), and, finally, at the end of the flood: "the fountains of the deep and the windows of the heavens were closed, the rain from the heavens was restrained" (8:2–3; see also v. 5).

Philo develops the description very dramatically:

> For the great deep rose on high as it had never risen before, and gathering its force rushed through its outlets into the seas of our parts, and the rising tides of these flooded the islands and continents, while in quick succession the streams from the perennial fountains and from the rivers spring-fed or winter-torrents pressed on to join each other and mounted upwards to a vast height. Nor was the air still, for a deep unbroken cloud covered the heaven, and there were monstrous blasts of wind and crashings of thunder and flashings of lightning and downfall of thunderbolts, while the rainstorms dashed down ceaselessly, so that one might think that the different parts of the uni-

---

53. E.g., 'Abot R. Nat. 32. For further references, see Lewis 1968, 130, n. 8.
54. This idea may also be behind Pseudo-Philo's rewriting of Gen 6:3: "'My spirit shall not judge those men forever, because they are flesh, but their years shall be 120.' For them he set the limits of life, but the crimes done by their hands did not cease" (3:2). Cf. 4Q252 1:1–3.
55. Translation from Andersen 1983, 212.

verse were hurrying to be resolved into the single element of water. Until, as in one form it rushed down from above and in another rose up from below, the streams were lifted on high, and thus not only the plains and lowlands were submerged and lost to sight, but even the peaks of the highest mountains. (*Abraham* 42–43)

There is another, less dramatic description in the dream visions of Enoch:

And again I raised mine eyes towards heaven and saw a lofty roof, with seven water torrents thereon, and those torrents flowed with much water ... and behold fountains were opened on the surface.... And the water, the darkness, and mist increased upon it. (1 En. 89:2–4)

Like 1 Enoch, Jubilees also talks of seven ארבת השמים but also of seven fountains: "And the Lord opened seven flood-gates of heaven, and the mouths of the fountains of the great deep, seven mouths in number" (5:24). Similarly, both in 1 Enoch and in Jubilees the draining of the water at the end of the flood is also done with the aid of "the mouths of the abysses" (1 En. 89:7–8; Jub. 5:29). Philo also says that some of the water was drained back to its sources inside the earth:

the water that had covered every land partly disappeared under the heat of the sun, partly subsided into the beds of water torrents and into chasms and the other hollows in the earth. For, as though by God's command, every form of nature, sea, springs and rivers, received back what it had lent as a debt which must be repaid; for each stream subsided into its proper place. (*Moses* 2.63)[56]

The Floating Ark

The Genesis flood narrative barely describes what happens to the ark as it was floating through the flood, just as it does not describe what happened inside the ark. All Genesis says is: "and the waters increased, and bore up the ark, and it rose high above the earth. The waters prevailed and increased greatly upon the earth; and the ark floated on the face of the waters" (7:17–18). However, some later texts elaborated on this point.

We have seen this motif in the passage mentioned earlier from Wisdom of Solomon: "And when for his cause the earth was drowning with a flood, wisdom again saved it, guiding the righteous man's course by a poor piece of wood" (10:4).

---

56. See also 2 Enoch version A 70:8 (*OTP* 1:201–3) and Sib. Or. 1.217–224.

The two themes expressed here, the poor piece of wood that is a ship and that wisdom steers the ships, are elaborated on in Wis 14:1–7, where it is also said that, "for in the old time also, when proud giants were perishing, the hope of the world, taking refuge on a raft, left to the race of men a seed of generations to come, thy hand guiding the helm, for blessed was the wood through which cometh righteousness" (Wis 14:6–7).

This depiction of the floating ark is also found in Sib. Or. 3.823–825: "For when the world was deluged with waters, and a certain single approved man was left floating on the waters in a house of hewn wood." Special attention is given to the floating ark in Sib. Or. 1.225–229: "The wondrous house itself swam on the flood. Battered by many raging waves and swimming under the impact of the winds, it surged terribly. The keel cut immense foam as the rushing waters were moved."

In his praise of the mother who endured the execution of all of her seven sons, the author of the philosophical treatise 4 Maccabees uses a similar depiction of the floating ark to symbolize the mother (15:29–32).

Although this does not seem to derive from any specific nonbiblical Noah tradition, it is interesting that some texts had such an interest in the floating ark. Interestingly, all of these are Jewish-Hellenistic texts.

The Raven and the Dove

In the Genesis narrative, forty days after the water started to withdraw and the peaks of the mountains were seen, Noah sent the raven, which flew back and forth. Next, after an unspecified length of time, he sent the dove, which did not find a dry place and came back to the ark. After another seven days, Noah sent the dove again, and it returned to him with an olive leaf in its mouth. After seven more days he sent the dove once again, and this time it did not return (Gen 8:6–12).

Josephus diminishes the sequence and says that Noah first sent the raven, which came back to him (*Ant.* 1.91), whereas in Genesis it flies back and forth and does not return to Noah.[57] Josephus also speaks of only once that Noah sent the dove, seven days after the raven's return. The dove came back smeared with mud and with an olive branch in its mouth (1.92). The statement that the dove was smeared with mud is extrabiblical, but its source might be Berossus's account of the Babylonian flood narrative.[58] This motif is also found in Sib. Or. 1, which says that the dove "rested herself a little on the damp land" (250). The latter's narrative also corresponds to the Babylonian tradition in other

---

57. Feldman 2004, 33 n. 228.
58. Ibid., 33 n. 230.

details: whereas in Genesis the dove is sent three times after Noah first sent the raven, in Sib. Or. 1 the "black-winged bird" is sent at the end, only after Noah sent two doves (242–256), which is also the sequence of the Babylonian account.[59]

The Sacrifice

Immediately upon exiting the ark, Noah builds an altar and sacrifices on it (Gen 8:20). Jubilees expands a bit on this sacrifice (6:1–3) but also adds another sacrifice not mentioned in Genesis. This second sacrifice is offered when Noah celebrates in a feast the wine produced from the vine that he planted upon exiting the ark. According to Jubilees, Noah acted with his vine according to the law of Lev 19:23–25, waiting for the fifth year in order to use its produce (Jub. 7:1–5).[60] Genesis Apocryphon has the same tradition about Noah waiting until the first day of the fifth year, then holding a feast (12:13–16), and, although the text is broken, it seems that it also speaks of a sacrifice at this feast (12:16–17).

Josephus also adds to the Genesis sacrifice (*Ant.* 1.92) another sacrifice that is offered at a feast after having prepared the wine (1.140). However, Josephus does not speak of the fourth and the fifth years, as does Jubilees, so he does not connect it to the law of Leviticus.

Noah and the Vine

Sometime after exiting the ark, Noah is said to have planted a vine (Gen 9:20) from which he made wine and became drunk. As mentioned above, the episode of Noah's drunkenness and revealing himself in the tent is rarely alluded to in the texts dealt with here. However, the episode of Noah planting the vine has a long and interesting elaboration in the Greek Apocalypse of Baruch (3 Baruch). In this episode Baruch asks the angel to show him which was the tree with which Adam and Eve transgressed; the angel answers that it was the vine, then continues:

> [And I Baruch said, Since also the vine has been the cause of such great evil, and is under judgment of the curse of God, and was the destruction of the first created, how is it now so useful? And the angel said, Thou askest aright. When God caused the deluge upon earth … then the water entered into paradise and destroyed every flower; but it removed wholly without the

---

59. Collins 1983, 1:340 n. t.
60. Cf. 7:35–37.

bounds the shoot of the vine and cast it outside. And when ... Noah came out of the ark, he began to plant of the plants which he found. But he found also the shoot of the vine; and he took it, and was reasoning in himself, What then is it? And I came and spake to him the things concerning it. And he said, Shall I plant it, or what shall I do? Since Adam was destroyed because of it, let me not also meet with the anger of God because of it. And saying these things he prayed that God would reveal to him what he should do concerning it....But God sent his angel Sarasael, and said to him, Arise, Noah, and plant the shoot of the vine, for thus saith the Lord: Its bitterness shall be changed into sweetness, and its curse shall become a blessing, and that which is produced from it shall become the blood of God; and as through it the human race obtained condemnation, so again through Jesus Christ the Immanuel will they receive in Him the upward calling, and the entry into paradise]. Know therefore, O Baruch, that as Adam through this very tree obtained condemnation, and was divested of the glory of God, so also the men who now drink insatiably the wine which is begotten of it, transgress worse than Adam, and are far from the glory of God, and are surrendering themselves to the eternal fire. For (no) good comes through it. For those who drink it to surfeit do these things: neither does a brother pity his brother, nor a father his son, nor children their parents, but from the drinking of wine come all evils, such as murders, adulteries, fornications, perjuries, thefts, and such like. And nothing good is established by it. (4:8–17)

Since there is a direct reference here to Jesus, it is obvious that there is a Christian interpolation into this basically Jewish text,[61] but the question is: What is the extent of this interpolation? Is only the reference to Jesus an interpolation, or is the whole sequence of Noah and the vine (4:9–15) an interpolation, since both the previous and the following verses condemn the vine? H. Maldwyn Hughes is of the opinion that the whole sequence is an interpolation,[62] but the Slavonic version of this passage, which has the whole story of Noah and the vine and is missing the reference to Jesus in verse 15, seems to suggest that only this reference is an interpolation; this is also the opinion of Daniel C. Harlow in his study of 3 Baruch.[63] To this we may add that the verses following the Noah story do not condemn the wine in principle, only excessive drinking of wine. Furthermore, as we shall soon see, some of the traditions that are preserved in this episode are found in Jewish texts.

---

61. Stone 1984a, 411–12.
62. H. M. Hughes 1913, 536. See also Lewis 1978, 22–23.
63. Harlow 1996, 78, 83. In the Slavic version it is 5:8. See also the study of the Slavonic version of 3 Baruch by Gaylord 1983, xlvi, 61 who writes that "the Slavic offers a better version of this verse."

This seems to be an Adamic tradition as well as a Noachic one, thus creating a connection between these two figures.[64] The tradition that the "tree of knowledge" with which Adam and Eve had sinned was the vine recalls the tradition found in 1 En. 32:3–6 and in Apoc. Ab. 23:4–9 that the fruit of the "tree of knowledge" looks like grapes. The tradition itself is also found in b. Sanh. 70a–b and in b. Ber. 40a, and in both places it is also connected to Noah's drunkenness. Interestingly, where Yalqut Shim'oni has this tradition from b. Sanhedrin and b. Berakot, it also has a tradition similar to the one from 3 Baruch about the vine having been cast out of the garden of Eden by the water of the flood: ויטע כרם – מצא גפן שגרופה מגן עדן ואשכלותיה עמה ושתל מפירותיה... (פרשת נח, רמז ס"א), which is also found in Targum Pseudo-Jonathan on Gen 9:20: ואשכח גופנא דמושכיה נהרא מן גינוניתא דעדן ונצביה לכרמא "And he found a vine that had been swept by the river from the garden of Eden, and he planted it as a vineyard."[65]

The Sibyl as Daughter-in-Law of Noah

A very interesting tradition is found at the very end of Sib. Or. 3, which is the oldest of all the Sibylline Oracles.[66] In trying to prove the truthfulness of her oracles, the Sibyl claims: "I was his [Noah's] daughter-in-law and I was of his blood" (827). We may assume that by "of his blood" she means that she is from Noah's family.[67]

According to John J. Collins, an interesting example of this tradition of a connection between Noah and the Sibyl was found in Apamea-Kibotos, that is, a coin depicting the Sibyl and Noah dated to the third century C.E.[68] However, Collins does not state exactly to which coin he is referring, but if he is referring to the coin labeled number 700 in Erwin R. Goodenough's collection of *Jewish Symbols in the Greco-Roman Period*, then there is no actual proof that it is the Sibyl depicted on the coin along with Noah. Noah's name is inscribed on a chest-like ark that is floating on water, and in it are a man and

---

64. On the connection between Adam and Noah and Noah's role as a second Adam, compare Gen 9:1–2 to 1:28. Some Second Temple sources emphasize Noah's role as the father of humanity and compare the two "creations." See 1 En. 10:3; 67:2; Philo, *Moses* 2.62 (compare 4 Macc 15:31) and 65; *Abraham* 46, 56; *Q.G.* 2.47; Sib. Or. 1.269–274. Cf. Orlov 2003, esp. 200–201.

65. See Ginzberg 1938, 167–68. On this episode, see further Orlov 2003.

66. Collins 1984, 365.

67. See above, 155 n. 42, about endogamy.

68. Collins 1983, 331.

a woman. Since the woman's name is not inscribed, it seems likely that she is depicting Noah's wife, not the Sibyl.[69]

Summary

In this survey we have seen a number of extrabiblical traditions about Noah and the flood. Some of these elements are exegetical, or at least derive from the Genesis narrative: the different reasons for the flood, Noah as a righteous man, and so on.

Other elements do not seem to be exegetical but might have been derived from varied external traditions: the ancient predictions of the flood, the floods of water and of fire, the preservation of knowledge from the predeluvian era, Noah's second sacrifice, Noah and the vine, and so forth.

Lewis's thesis that attributes the postbiblical writers' treatment of Noah and the flood to the writers' *Sitz im Leben* is definitely relevant to some of the elements on Noah and the flood in these sources (e.g., Philo's identification of Noah with Deucalion; Jubilees' promotion of its calendar through the flood story, which was not dealt with here). This especially seems to be the case for some of the Jewish-Hellenistic extrabiblical traditions about Noah and the flood that have been examined. As we have shown, it seems that these traditions are, at least in part, an adoption of Greek flood traditions, probably under the influence of Plato. A notable case is that of the preservation of antediluvian knowledge and the associated tradition of destructions by water and by fire. In this case we do not see the influence of a specific writer's *Sitz im Leben* but rather an example of Jewish literature taking part in a much wider trend of the contemporary Near East. At any rate, most of the extrabiblical elements discussed in this study do not seem to stem from any specific *Sitz im Leben*, and the fact that many elements are shared by many different sources proves that often that is not the case. It seems that exegetical problems in the biblical text and some extrabiblical traditions influenced these authors no less, and maybe more, than their *Sitz im Leben*. To this we may add the hypothesis that the abundance of extrabiblical elements that cannot be attributed to any specific *Sitz im Leben*, do not stem from plain exegesis, and are shared by numerous sources may point to the existence of a consolidated extrabiblical Noah tradition, some sort of "Noah book," whether written or oral.

Regardless of our position about these nonbiblical traditions, this survey illustrates the great importance of the figure of Noah and of the story of the

---

69. Goldberg and Goodenough 1953, 119–20. See also Ruth Clements's "A Shelter amid the Flood: Noah's Ark in Early Jewish and Christian Art" in this volume.

flood during the Second Temple Period and in the centuries following the temple's destruction.

THE ROLE OF NOAH AND THE FLOOD IN *JUDEAN ANTIQUITIES* AND *AGAINST APION* BY FLAVIUS JOSEPHUS

Michael Tuval

INTRODUCTION

The purpose of this essay is to contribute to the discussion of the treatment of Noah and the flood in the writings of the first-century C.E. Jewish historian Flavius Josephus. I shall first briefly review Josephus's career and introduce his writings, then discuss the overall character, audience, and purposes of those mentioning Noah and the flood, and finally analyze these passages in light of the preceding discussion.[1] Since Noah in Josephus has recently been the object of two comprehensive treatments by Louis H. Feldman,[2] it seems redundant to rehearse in detail here everything that Josephus wrote on the subject. Instead, I shall discuss the relevant passages in the context of the broader meaning of Josephus's compositions, analyzing the role they play in his presentation of the Judean history and way of life.

JOSEPHUS'S CAREER

As can be gathered from his writings, Josephus was born in 37 C.E. into a priestly family of high status, spent most of his youth in Jerusalem, was appointed commander of Galilee at the beginning of the Great Judean Revolt against Rome in 66 C.E., and was subsequently taken captive by Vespasian. After Vespasian's ascent to the throne in 69 C.E., Josephus was manumitted;

---

1. As will become clear in the course of the following discussion, this paper is greatly indebted to the work of Louis H. Feldman, Steve Mason, and Daniel R. Schwartz. For full references, see the following notes.

2. Feldman 1988a, a revised version of which is reprinted in 1998b, 17–37. See also Feldman 2004, 84–114, and, above all, his commentary ad loc. in 2000, 26–53. Feldman also discusses previous scholarship on Josephus's version of Noah and the flood.

he accompanied Vespasian's son Titus in the course of his military campaign in Judea and after the destruction of Jerusalem sailed with Titus to Rome in 71 C.E. There he was given an imperial pension and accommodation at Vespasian's former residence. As far as we know, Josephus spent the rest of his life in Rome, never returning to his native Judea. The exact date of his death is unknown, but it is reasonable to assume that he died around 100 C.E.[3]

Josephus's Writings

Information concerning Josephus's private life in Rome is sparse and can only be culled from what he chose to write about himself in his writings. These are four in number, in chronological order: *Judean War* (*War*), *Judean Antiquities* (*Ant.*), *Life of Josephus* (*Life*), and *Against Apion* (*Ag. Ap.*).[4] *Judean War* was written in the 70s of the first century C.E. and was definitely completed before 79, the date of Vespasian's death (*Life* 361). It contains seven books and covers the history of Judea between the 70s of the second century B.C.E. and 74 C.E. Out of seven books, fully five deal with the history of the Great Revolt and its aftermath. As it appears from Josephus's own statements in this work, as well as in *Life of Josephus*, the work was supported and approved by Vespasian and Titus themselves.[5] Consequently, in many ways, it is pro-Roman, more specifically pro-Flavian, propaganda. However, it is equally an *apologia* for the people of Judea, for the Judean God, and for Josephus himself.[6]

---

3. For general up-to-date introductions on Josephus, see Attridge 1984; Bilde 1988; Rajak 2002; Mason 2003. An older but still valuable study is Thackeray 1929. On Josephus's development as an historian, see Cohen 1979. On his intellectual development in the course of his literary career, as well as on his presumed interaction with contemporary Jewish groups, see S. Schwartz 1990. On Josephus in the various contexts of Flavian Rome, see the studies in Edmondson, Mason, and Rives 2005.

4. In addition to the studies listed in the previous note, see the introductions to *Judean Antiquities*, *Life of Josephus*, and *Against Apion* in the Brill Josephus Project.

5. The title of the work already signifies that it expresses the Roman point of view on the conflict. Josephus writes that the book was approved by the Caesars (*Life* 361–363; cf. *Ag. Ap.* 1.50–51) and prides himself on the fact that he had an access to the field notes of Vespasian and Titus (*Life* 342, 358). It seems safe to suppose that this approval indicates a measure of support or sponsorship.

6. Throughout *Judean War*, most Judeans are presented as innocent victims of a handful of crazy revolutionary fanatics and the Judean God as disgusted by the horrendous crimes of the latter; God therefore abandons the Judeans in order to fight on the Roman side. Josephus himself is presented as an ideal rebel general, until he realizes his true mission: to serve as God's messenger to the Romans as well as to the Judeans. Thereafter he claimed to have done his best to save Jerusalem from destruction, and after his efforts were not crowned with success, he wrote the most reliable history of the Judean War. On

The remaining three works were largely written and definitely published in the course of the last decade of the first century C.E. As follows from *Ant.* 20.267, *Judean Antiquities* was completed in the thirteenth year of Domitian's rule and the fifty-sixth year of Josephus's own life, that is, 94 C.E. *Judean Antiquities* comprises twenty books and covers the history of the Judeans from the creation of the world until the beginning of the Great Revolt in 66 C.E. The contents, character, and audience of *Judean Antiquities* are discussed below.[7] *Life of Josephus* must have been given its present form shortly afterward, since it is clear both from the concluding statements of *Judean Antiquities* and from its own contents that Josephus intended it as a supplement to *Judean Antiquities*.[8] This one-volume book begins with a brief discussion of Josephus's ancestry and his early years but is mainly occupied with the account of his activities as the commander of the rebel forces in Galilee in the spring and early part of summer 67 C.E. The last seventeen paragraphs of *Life of Josephus* provide some details of Josephus's life between the summer of 67 and the time of writing, that is, the mid-90s of the first century C.E.[9]

Against Apion, comprising two books, appears to be Josephus's last work, and it is different from Josephus's other writings in several ways.[10] Although all of Josephus's works are to a certain degree apologetic,[11] apology is not their primary or declared goal.[12] They are mainly works of historiography. In contrast, even though historiography plays an important role in *Against Apion*, it is first of all an apologetic treatise. Its main goal is to prove to the Greek-speaking world the antiquity of the Judeans and to clear the Judeans of the anti-Semitic charges disseminated by their detractors. The form and purpose of *Against Apion* are discussed below in more detail.[13]

Josephus's self-presentation as the most reliable historian both of the Judean War and of the whole course of Judean history, see *Ag. Ap.* 1.47–56.

7. See Mason 2000; 1998.

8. See *Ant.* 20.262–267; *Life* 1; 430. On *Life of Josephus*, see Mason 2001; Siegert, Schreckenberg, and Vogel 2001; D. R. Schwartz 2008.

9. For a thorough discussion of the relationship between *Judean Antiquities* and *Life of Josephus*, see Mason 2001, xiii–liv. For a detailed comparison of *Judean War* with *Life of Josephus* and a study of their interrelationship, see Cohen 1979.

10. In addition to the comprehensive treatment of Barclay 2006, see Feldman and Levison 1996; Haaland 2006.

11. On the question of "Jewish apologetics" in the Greco-Roman period, see the various assessments in Dalbert 1954; Tcherikover 1956; Georgi, 1986, 83–151; Conzelmann 1992, 135–233; and Feldman 1993.

12. However, see the discussion of the similarity of purposes between *Judean Antiquities* and *Against Apion* below.

13. This analysis is much indebted to Mason 1996.

Josephus mentions Noah (Νῶχος) in *Judean Antiquities* and *Against Apion*, twenty-four times in all. As should be expected, most of the occurrences of the name are in his treatment of the story of the flood in the first book of *Judean Antiquities*.¹⁴ Noah appears twice more in *Judean Antiquities*: in the speech of Moses to the Israelites after his descent from Mount Sinai (*Ant.* 3.87), which has no parallel in the Bible; and in the course of the story of the conversion of the royal house of Adiabene, at the beginning of the last book of *Judean Antiquities*.¹⁵ In *Against Apion*, Noah is mentioned twice in the context of Josephus's discussion of the treatment of the Judean history by non-Greek historians (*Ag. Ap.* 1.130, 131).

Form, Purpose, and Audience of *Judean Antiquities* and *Against Apion*

As has been emphasized a number of times, Josephus was a creative writer firmly rooted in the long tradition of Hellenistic Jewish and wider Near Eastern apologetic historiography of the Greco-Roman period.¹⁶ The main thesis of this essay is that Josephus's treatment of Noah and the flood, both in *Judean Antiquities* and in *Against Apion*, must be read and interpreted primarily in the light of his overarching apologetic concerns and tactics. In other words, even though it is understood that in his treatment of Noah and the flood Josephus used written sources (and, possibly, oral traditions), it is also assumed that he reworked them creatively in order to suit his own purposes and concerns. Therefore, whatever details of his sources he chose to repeat or omit must be seen in the light of his declared or implicit purposes in *Judean Antiquities* and *Against Apion*.¹⁷

---

14. Twenty out of twenty-four references.

15. *Ant.* 20.25. Since it is widely acknowledged that Josephus had a written source for the story of the conversion of Adiabene, the mention of Noah must have been taken by him from there along with all the rest of information. On Josephus's source for the passage, see Schiffman 1987.

16. Sterling 1992. For a thorough discussion of Josephus's tendencies in rewriting the biblical material, see Feldman 1988b, 470–518; 1998a, 14–220 (132–62 on "Josephus as Apologist"); cf. Attridge 1976. For an older but still excellent discussion of Josephus's reinterpretation of biblical history, see Schalit 1944, xi–lxxxii. On parallels between Josephus and rabbinic midrash, see Rappaport 1930.

17. I will not discuss here the question of Josephus's sources apart from the Bible, since it has been recently discussed by Feldman 1998a. His treatment is exhaustive, although I am much more skeptical than Feldman concerning the extent of Josephus's acquaintance with much later rabbinic traditions. On Josephus's sources for Genesis, see Franxman 1979. In any case, even though some of the nonbiblical material in Josephus's story of the flood

Moreover, in the course of the recent discussion of various connections between *Judean Antiquities* and *Against Apion*, it has been emphasized that these two works share a common purpose and were addressed to a more or less similar audience.[18] It has been suggested that *Judean Antiquities* should be viewed as a broad presentation of the Judean constitution and philosophy as a sure way to happiness, addressed to sympathetic Gentiles.[19] *Against Apion*, then, while pursuing the same purpose, takes the discussion of these themes even further, at the same time answering hostile pagan objections to the Judeans and their way of life.[20] In the context of the present essay, it seems that the similar apologetic tendencies exhibited by Josephus's treatment of Noah and the flood in these two works might lend additional support to this hypothesis.

Josephus states the goal of *Judean Antiquities* explicitly in the preface to the work:

> On the whole, one who would wish to read through it would especially learn from this history that those who comply with the will of God and do not venture to transgress laws that have been well enacted succeed in all things beyond belief and that happiness lies before them as a reward from God. But to the extent that they dissociate themselves from the scrupulous observance of these laws the practicable things become impracticable, and whatever seemingly good thing they pursue with zeal turns into irremediable misfortunes.[21]

The ideas that Moses is the ideal law-giver, that the laws of the Judeans are the best of laws on earth, and that their observance brings prosperity and bliss, but their disregard surely leads to divine punishment and downfall, are, without doubt, the leitmotifs of *Judean Antiquities*, which are illustrated explicitly and implicitly by countless examples from history in the course of the narrative.[22] However, it seems that the this passage should be interpreted as a *general* statement concerning Josephus's purposes in writing his twenty

---

was clearly taken from sources other than the Bible, he himself was responsible for the types of materials he eventually chose to use.

18. *Judean Antiquities* and *Against Apion* (as well as *Life of Josephus*) are dedicated to Josephus's literary patron Epaphroditos : *Ant.* 1.8; *Ag. Ap.* 1.1; 2.1; *Life* 430. On Epaphroditos, see most recently Cotton and Eck 2005, 41, 49–52. See further below.

19. Mason 1998.

20. Mason 1996; Haaland 2006.

21. *Ant.* 1.14; all translations of *Judean Antiquities* are by Feldman.

22. Attridge 1976; Mason 1998; 2000.

volumes of *Judean Antiquities* and must be placed in the wider context of his other statements in the preface.

As Josephus reveals in the preface, his intention was to produce a comprehensive account of the multifaceted Judean history for the "Greeks," that is, for the whole Greek-speaking world (*Ant.* 1.5–6). It was a non-Jew, a certain "Epaphroditos, a man who has had a love for every form of culture," who most encouraged and supported him in this undertaking (*Ant.* 1.8). Moreover, Josephus explicitly stated that in this project he considered himself to be continuing the tradition that was initiated by the Judean translators of the Torah into the Greek language, preeminently by "Eleazaros, second to none of the high priests among us."[23]

What was begun by the translators of the Septuagint, Josephus intended to continue. They made the laws of the Judeans, that is, the Pentateuch, available to the Greek-speaking world. Josephus wanted to do the same for the rest of the Judean history, both that which was contained in the sacred writings of his people and that which transpired later, until the beginning of the Great Revolt against Rome. In other words, Josephus mainly intended *Judean Antiquities* for a non-Jewish audience.[24] At the end of the preface he challenged his readers to see for themselves that the Judean laws were the ultimate universal principles and in absolute conformance with nature:

> Our legislator, having shown that God possesses a virtue that is pure, thought that human beings ought to try to participate in it, and he unrelentingly punished those who do not share these thoughts or believe in them. I beseech those who will read my work to examine it in relation to this fundamental view. For if they will look at it thus nothing will appear to them unreasonable or incongruous with the majesty and benevolence of God. For all things have their arrangement in harmony with the nature of the universe. (*Ant.* 1.23–24)

That Josephus himself thought thus seems to be beyond any reasonable doubt.

---

23. *Ant.* 1.9–12. Josephus's long paraphrase of the *Epistle of Aristeas* in *Ant.* 12.12–118 also indicates that he ascribed much importance to that precedent (cf. *Ag. Ap.* 2.45–47). That Josephus might have seen himself as a candidate to the office of "high priest," or even tried to convince the Romans to make him one, was suggested by Chilton 1992, 69–87. That would not be surprising, considering his own high opinion of himself; see *Ant.* 20.263–265: he is one of the "two or three" of those who succeeded to master the Jewish law and, subsequently, were "capable of interpreting the meaning of the Holy Scriptures." See also Tuval forthcoming.

24. However, it is also clear from many passages in *Judean Antiquities* that he often had Jewish readers in mind. In addition to Mason 1998, see Feldman 1998a, 46–50, 132–62, and further references there.

This last quotation is extremely important in the context of the present discussion of Noah and the flood in Josephus. As mentioned above, for Josephus, Judean laws were perfect, universal principles, identical with the laws of nature. The Judean laws embodied virtue, piety, and righteousness. Therefore, he could use the righteous man Noah in order to illustrate his main idea that obedience to God brings happiness, but disobedience—punishment, even though Noah could not have observed specifically Judean laws. As will be apparent from the analysis below, it seems that Josephus was not troubled by the fact that these laws were promulgated long after Noah. Thus, for Josephus, Noah is appropriated as a kind of virtuous proto-Judean, so to speak, who serves to reinforce the importance of following the Judean God's laws.

So, in *Judean Antiquities* Josephus intended to convince his mainly non-Jewish readers that the Judean laws, as contained in the Judean Scriptures, were the best of laws for *all humanity*. The long and illustrious course of Judean history demonstrated this dictum by numerous examples. In this context it is only natural to expect that, when we compare Josephus's account with his sources, we shall discover that he overemphasized certain achievements of the Judeans and played down some of their weaknesses and faults.[25]

As has already been mentioned, *Against Apion* shares a common purpose with *Judean Antiquities*, although it is different in genre. *Against Apion* is a two-volume apologetic treatise, the first part of which (*Ag. Ap.* 1.1–2.144) is devoted mainly to the demonstration of the antiquity of Judeans and to the refutation of various hostile slanders of Judeans, their origins, their legislator Moses, their laws, and their way of life. The second part (2.145–296), while continuing many of the topics discussed previously, shifts from defense to an encomium on the Judean *politeia* and the Judeans' faithfulness to it. It is not surprising, then, that even though the treatment of Noah and the flood in *Against Apion* is much shorter than that in *Judean Antiquities*, they share much in common. In what follows, I shall analyze the passages dealing with Noah and the flood in *Judean Antiquities* and *Against Apion*, then consider their peculiarities in the context of the preceding discussion of the aims and audience of these two compositions.

Even on a cursory reading of *Ant.* 1.63–148, three primary emphases are evident, and these prove to be Josephus's main preoccupations. The first is Josephus's preoccupation with precise chronology, which although present in the biblical narrative does not play such a prominent role in it. The second main subject, totally absent from the Bible, is the emphasis on the non-Jewish witnesses to the account of the flood. The third is the elaboration on the themes of virtue and godliness (and their opposite, lawlessness), with their

---

25. See Feldman 1998a, 74–131; Spilsbury 1998.

corollaries of prosperity and divine favor for the righteous, on the one hand, and divine judgment and the destruction of the wicked, on the other. Even though this third theme at first glance seems to be the most "biblical" of the three, the passage on Noah demonstrates that Josephus was much more concerned with the paradigm than the authors/redactors of Genesis.

One could also add several minor themes developed by Josephus that are either absent from or at least not prominent in his biblical source: the emphasis on the contribution of the biblical heroes to scientific discovery (*Ant.* 1.69–70, 106); the criticism of Greek historiography (*Ant.* 1.121, 129); the "actualization" of *tabula gentium* (*Ant.* 122–138, 143–147); and the issue of prayer as part of the divine service (*Ant.* 1.96–99). The first of these seems to be in line with Josephus's concern—both in *Judean Antiquities* and *Against Apion*—to present the Judeans and their ancestors as creative contributors to human progress, while the second is a prominent feature of Josephus's strategy in answering pagan criticism of Judeans and their way of life. This second topic becomes a key element of *Against Apion*. Ironically, the identification of the various nations that sprang forth from Noah's descendants with the peoples of the contemporary world was taken over by Josephus from the Greek historiographical tradition.[26] The fourth topic should be attributed to Josephus's own religious evolution as a Diaspora Jew; it will be dealt with below in the context of the discussion of Josephus's religious outlook.

Precise Chronology

Josephus's preoccupation with the establishing of precise chronology for the described events is evident throughout the flood passage in *Judean Antiquities*, as well as before and after it. As demonstrated long ago, in his treatment of the chronology of the Noachic passage Josephus follows the Septuagint, which at this point is rather different from the Masoretic Text. In brief, according to the Masoretic version, most of the patriarchs fathered children when they were a hundred years younger than their age according to the LXX. As a result, according to the latter, the flood occurred in *anno mundi* 2262, while according to the Masoretic scheme, it happened in 1656.[27] It has also been suggested that this divergence in favor of a longer chronology might have resulted from a concern to present the world as somewhat older, in line with the contempo-

---

26. See Bickerman 1952 [1985]. On the possible consequences of Josephus's identifications of biblical nations with contemporary peoples for later religious history, see Millar 1993.

27. For a convenient table comparing the two chronological schemes, see Thackeray 1930, 39.

rary Hellenistic-Roman chronographic writing. The question of who initiated the change—the proto-Masoretes or the translators-redactors of the LXX—is of little importance for our argument. The important fact is that Josephus, who was clearly familiar with both text types, in this case opted for the LXX.[28] Indeed, in light of his apologetic aims and methods, it is understandable why he gave his preference to the longer chronology.[29]

Josephus made no secret of the importance of precise chronology for his history. In fact, he stated it clearly a number of times, supplying the reader with additional calculations. Thus, concerning the date of the flood he wrote: "This time was 2,262 years from the birth of Adamos, the first man. The time [ὁ χρόνος] is recorded in the sacred books since the men of that time registered with great accuracy both the births and the deaths of distinguished men" (*Ant.* 1.82). Later, when he introduced Habramos (Abraham), he dated his birth as occurring 992 years after the flood (1.148). Although one could construct an absolute chronology on the basis of the dates given in Genesis, the biblical authors explicitly dated neither the flood relative to the creation of Adam nor the birth of Abraham relative to the flood. Josephus did. A little later, in order to explain his chronological calculations, he exhorted his readers as follows: "And let no one investigate the deaths of the men, for their lives extended to the lives of their sons and the offspring of the latter, but let him examine only their births" (1.88). Again, the Bible did not explicitly exhibit such measure of concern for chronological matters.

The longest apologetic piece concerning the chronology of the early part of biblical history is located in *Ant.* 1.104–108. Since this passage so eloquently illustrates some of Josephus's main concerns in his presentation of Judean history, it is worth quoting in full. In anticipation of his audience's skepticism concerning the incredible longevity of the biblical heroes, he writes:

> But let no one, comparing our present life and the brevity of the years that we live with that of the ancients, think that what is said about them is false, deducing that because now there is no such extension of time in life neither did they reach that length of life. For they were dear to God, having been created by Him, and because of their nourishment, that was more suitable to a longer life, they naturally lived so great a number of years. Furthermore, also, because of their virtue and because it was beneficial for the discoveries that they made in astronomy and geometry, that, indeed, they could not have predicted accurately if they had not lived 600 years, since the great year[30] is

---

28. On Josephus's biblical text, see Feldman 1998a, 23–36, with further references there.
29. On Josephus's predecessors in chronological matters, see Wacholder 1968.
30. On the "great year," see Feldman 2000, 38 n. 260.

completed through so great a period, God granted them a longer life. All those who have written ancient histories among Greeks and barbarians bear witness to my account. For Manetho, who has composed the record of the Egyptians, and Berosos, who composed that that concerns the Chaldaeans, and Mochos and Hestiaios and, in addition to these, the Egyptian Hieronymos, who composed that that concerns the Phoenicians, agree with what I have said. And Hesiod and Hecataios and Hellanicos and Acusilaos and, in addition to these, Ephoros and Nikolaos record that the ancients lived for a thousand years. However, concerning such matters let each one judge as is pleasing to him.[31]

Pagan Witnesses to Judean History

At this point we can proceed to the discussion of the second theme, crucial to Josephus's treatment of the flood and evident both in the above-quoted passage and in *Against Apion*. The fact that Josephus dedicated two passages in *Judean Antiquities* and another one in *Against Apion* to the testimonies of non-Jewish historians demonstrates that it was extremely important for him to place the biblical events into the broader context of general world history and to bring in external witnesses to these events. Of course, there is hardly anything of this sort in the Bible. Here, Josephus's apologetic concerns are most evident. He began by what moderns would call "archaeological witness" concerning the place where Noah's ark came to rest:[32]

> Now the Armenians call this place "Landing Place," for there the ark landed safely, and still today they display its remains. All those who have recorded the histories of the barbarians mention this Flood and the ark, among whom is Berosos the Chaldaean. For he, relating the events connected with the Flood, reports them somewhere in this fashion: "It is said that a certain portion of the boat still exists in Armenia on the mountain of the Cordyaeans and that some people remove and carry off pieces from the bitumen. And people use what they have carried off for talismans." Hieronymos the Egyptian, who composed an ancient history of Phoenicia, and Mnaseas and numerous others mention this. And Nikolaos of Damascus in his ninety-sixth book, reports about these things in these words: "There is above Minyas a great mountain in Armenia called Baris, to that, report has it, many took refuge and were saved at the time of the Flood, and that someone, drifting in an ark, ran ashore upon the mountain peak, and that the remains of the

---

31. On this last clause, which is repeated by Josephus a number of times, see Feldman 2000, 39 n. 271.

32. In this respect, the mention of Noah's ark in *Ant.* 20.25 is similar.

wood were preserved for a long time. And this would be the one of whom Moyses, the lawgiver of the Judeans, wrote."[33]

Although I am aware of the danger of harmonizing, in light of what has been pointed out above concerning the similarity of purpose and tactics between *Judean Antiquities* and *Against Apion*, it seems that the passage about the flood in *Against Apion* may be discussed at this point. Since it exhibits many common features with the two above-quoted passages from *Judean Antiquities*, its analysis can shed additional light on Josephus's politics of writing.

If Josephus's concern to corroborate his account of Judean history by external witnesses was prominent in *Judean Antiquities*, it was definitely paramount in *Against Apion*. In fact, it formed one of his main lines of argument. According to Josephus, one of whose primary purposes in the first part of *Against Apion* was to undermine the reliability of Greek historians and to explain why they did not mention the antiquity of Judeans, one should first of all examine the writings of oriental historians. The histories written by them, claimed Josephus, were in agreement with the Judean version of history and bore witness to the same events. This is the context of his mention of Noah and the flood in *Against Apion*.

> I shall now straightaway describe what is recorded and reported concerning us among the Chaldeans; there is considerable agreement on this as on other points between these sources and our writings. As witness to this stands Berossus, a Chaldean by descent, but well-known to those engaged in learning, since he published for the Greeks works on astronomy and on the subjects of philosophical inquiry among the Chaldeans. Now this Berossus, following the most ancient records, gave an account, like Moses, of the flood and the destruction in it of humankind, and of the ark in which Noah, the founder of our race, was saved when it was carried onto the peaks of the Armenian mountains. Then, listing Noah's descendants and adding their dates, he comes to Naboupolassaros, the king of Babylon and the Chaldeans.[34]

As is widely acknowledged, Josephus did not have direct access to the *Babylonaica* by the Babylonian historian Berossus, to whose account he refers, but rather relied on excerpts from this work made in the first century B.C.E. by Alexander Polyhistor.[35] It should also be mentioned that Berossus's flood hero was not called Noah but Xisuthrus, as is evident from a quotation preserved

---

33. *Ant.* 1.92–95; translation from Feldman 2000, 33–35
34. *Ag. Ap.* 1.128–131; translation in Barclay 2006, 70–81.
35. On Polyhistor, see Freudenthal 1874–75.

by George Syncellus. In other words, Josephus took the liberty not to mention the name supplied by his source but rather created an impression that Berossus actually mentioned the biblical hero by name.[36]

Obedience to God, Keeping the Laws

The third theme prominent in Josephus's passage on Noah and the flood is religious and completely in line with his programmatic statement at the beginning of *Judean Antiquities* quoted above. Josephus promised his readers that by reading his history open-mindedly they would be convinced that those who live righteously and obey the God-given laws, which are identical with the laws of nature (*Ant.* 1.23–24), live happy and blessed lives but that those who break them bring destruction upon themselves. The importance of living according to the (Judean) laws is probably the single most important idea in *Judean Antiquities*.[37] On the one hand, the story of Noah was uniquely suited to serve as an illustration of the principle of the prosperity of the righteous and the destruction of the wicked; on the other hand, Noah was not a proper Judean and lived a long time before the promulgation of the Judean laws. However, if his story is read in the context of Josephus's equation of Judean laws with the laws of nature (which were also established by the same Judean God), then it becomes clear that for Josephus Noah indeed was a follower of "Judean laws."

In order to introduce the story of the flood, Josephus begins by describing the wickedness of humanity at that time. While the Bible only states that "The LORD saw how great was man's wickedness on earth, and how every plan devised by his mind was nothing but evil all the time" (Gen 6:5 NJPS), and mentions the cohabitation of "sons of God" with daughters of men rather neutrally, Josephus used this opportunity to elaborate on the theme of the importance of obeying the customs of the fathers. In addition, he turned Noah into a preacher of righteousness—a detail he could not have found in Genesis:

> And these men for seven generations continued to believe that God was Lord of the universe and to look upon all things with reference to virtue. Then in the course of time they changed from their ancestral habits for the worse, neither offering to God the customary honors nor taking into account justice toward humanity; but, through the things that they did, exhibiting double the zeal for vice that they had formerly shown for virtue, they thereby

---

36. On Berossus and Josephus's use of him, see Barclay 2006, 80–81, notes on *Ag. Ap.* 1.129–131.

37. See Attridge 1976.

incurred the enmity of God for themselves. For many angels of God, consorting with women, fathered children who were insolent and despisers of every good thing because of the confidence that they had in their power. For, according to tradition, they are said to have committed outrages comparable to those said by the Greeks to have been done by giants. Nochos, disgusted with their actions and being displeased with their endeavors, tried to persuade them to improve their attitude and to change their actions.[38] But seeing that they did not give way but were vehemently overpowered by the pleasure of evils, fearing lest they even slay him with his wives and children and those who were dwelling with them, he withdrew from the land.[39]

Another passage in which Josephus returned to this theme is *Ant.* 1.96–103. As was pointed out above, Josephus put into Noah's mouth an eloquent prayer, totally absent from the Bible, that mentioned only his sacrifice. In contrast, in *Judean Antiquities* Noah's prayer is much more important than the sacrifice, and God's favorable response to Noah is said to be to his "supplications," not his sacrifice. This tendency seems to be in line with other passages both in the later writings of Josephus and in other Diaspora Jewish compositions. The Jews of the Greco-Roman Diaspora did not entreat God with sacrifices, which could only be offered in Jerusalem (and by the time Josephus was writing *Judean Antiquities*, not even there); therefore, the sacrificial cult could not have had much day-to-day relevance for them. On the other hand, prayer as an alternative way of worship did.[40]

In answer to Noah's prayer, God promised not to destroy humanity again and explained that "it was not He who had destroyed those who had perished but that they had suffered this punishment because of their own wickedness.... But these outrages that they committed against my piety and virtue forced me to inflict this penalty upon them. But I will cease in the future to punish crimes with such wrath and more especially since you call upon Me" (*Ant.* 1.99–101). In the Bible, God did not speak with Noah at all, but to "his own heart," and his musings followed his smelling of the "pleasant odor" of Noah's sacrifice.

---

38. See the material on Noah as a preacher in Nadav Sharon and Moshe Tishel, "Distinctive Traditions about Noah and the Flood in Second Temple Jewish Literature," in this volume.

39. *Ant.* 1.72–74; translation from Feldman 2000, 26–28.

40. See D. R. Schwartz 1996; 2002; 2004. On Josephus as a Diaspora Jew, see D. R. Schwartz 2007. Cf., however, *Ant.* 1.140, where Noah brings a sacrifice and feasts after harvesting the vine he had planted and making wine. No sacrifice is mentioned in the Bible. It seems that Josephus wanted to provide a more "respectable" context for Noah's getting drunk.

The idea that obedience to God brings happiness but disobedience leads to calamity is repeated immediately after the passage dealing with the flood. Again, nothing of this is in the Bible, but it represents Josephus's own outlook and is in line with the main religious paradigm of *Judean Antiquities*. Speaking of Noah's descendants, Josephus informed his readers that

> When God bade them, because of their large population, to send colonies, in order that they might not engage in civil strife with one another, but cultivating much of the soil they might enjoy its fruits, they did not listen to God owing to their ignorance; and therefore, falling into misfortunes, they came to realize their error. For when they flourished with a multitude of young people, God again advised them to establish a colony. But they, not realizing that their blessings were due to His favor and supposing that their own might was the reason for their prosperity, did not obey. And to this disobedience to God's will they added the suspicion that He was encouraging them with malicious intent to emigrate in order that being scattered they might more easily be assailed.[41]

It should also be borne in mind that another mention of Noah by Josephus, in the speech of Moses after his descent from Mount Sinai, also appears in the context of exhortation to follow God's laws: "God, O Hebrews, just as He also did previously, graciously received me and having prescribed a blessed life for you and a well-ordered constitution, is also coming Himself into the camp" (*Ant.* 3.84). After mentioning Noah, whom God saved from the flood,[42] Moses again encourages the Israelites to follow the laws: "Let them [God's words] be held in reverence by you and let them be more worth fighting for than children and wives. For you will lead a blessed life if you follow them and, enjoying a fruitful earth and a sea that is not stormy and the birth of children begotten in accordance with nature, you will also be terrifying to your enemies" (*Ant.* 3.88). As has already been pointed out, this speech is absent from the Bible and is wholly a Josephan composition.

Conclusion

By way of conclusion, we have seen that Josephus used the story of Noah and the flood, as it appears in his writings, in order to pursue three of his main purposes. Josephus mainly intended *Judean Antiquities* and *Against Apion* for a sympathetic Gentile audience, to whom he desired to prove the reliability of

---

41. *Ant.* 1.110–112; translation from Feldman 2000, 39–40.
42. "[God], on account of Whom Nochos escaped the Flood…—this is the One who graciously bestows these words upon you through me as an interpreter" (*Ant.* 3.87).

the biblical account, the respectability of the Judean tradition, and the excellence of the Judean laws. The story of Noah as presented by Josephus served all of these purposes well. Josephus tried to prove two of the above points by his detailed chronological calculations throughout the passage and by adducing non-Jewish witnesses to the flood story. The third theme—that of living according to the Judean laws—also played a major role in his treatment. As has been discussed above, Josephus promised to prove to his open-minded readers that obedience to the Judean laws brings happiness and blissful life but that failure to follow them causes destruction. As can be seen from his treatment of the story of Noah, he creatively used the biblical narrative to illustrate his main religious idea in *Judean Antiquities*.

Philo's Interpretation of Noah

Albert C. Geljon

The Jewish philosopher and exegete Philo of Alexandria (ca. 15 B.C.E.–ca. 45 C.E.) was a very prolific author whose treatises for the most part offer an interpretation of the Pentateuch. His exegetical writings are usually divided into three main groups.[1] (1) In the Exposition of the Law, Philo presents the Mosaic legislation systematically, offering both a literal and an allegorical reading. These treatises seem to be intended for a broad audience. (2) The Allegorical Commentary is directed to advanced students; in it the Jewish exegete gives a detailed and often complicated exegesis of Genesis in allegorical terms. In this series, Philo's line of thought is often difficult to follow, because, while explaining one verse, Philo quotes another verse, which he then also interprets extensively. Generally Philo regards the biblical figures as different forms of souls that are found in mortals. (3) In *Questions and Answers on Genesis and Exodus*, Philo deals with a biblical verse in the form of formulating a question and giving an answer. He offers both a literal and an allegorical reading. These works have survived only in Armenian translation. In all three series Philo addresses the figure of Noah, and in what follows I treat Philo's presentation on the basis of four important themes.[2]

1. The Righteous and Perfect Noah

In his Exposition of the Law Philo sets out the Mosaic legislation, but he asserts that, before God gave the law to his people, the patriarchs already lived according to the law. At the beginning of *On the Life of Abraham*, Philo explains that the patriarchs are laws endowed with soul and reason, because they lived in accordance with the unwritten law of nature.[3] Philo considers the

---

1. See Morris 1987, 826–54.
2. An overview of Philo's interpretation of Noah and the flood is given by Lewis 1968, 42–73. See also Feldman 1988a.
3. See Martens 1994, 325–26.

patriarchs as types of souls who yearn for virtue (*Abraham* 4–5). He discerns two triads of patriarchs: (1) Enosh, Enoch, and Noah; (2) Abraham, Isaac, and Jacob (*Abraham* 47–48). The second trio is superior to the first, and within each triad there is also a hierarchy or stratification: Noah is more excellent than Enosh and Enoch. Dealing with the first triad, Philo argues that Enosh represents hope, because hope is the first step toward the possession of good things (*Abraham* 7). The Alexandrian exegete bases this interpretation on Gen 4:26 in the LXX translation: "He called his name Enosh; he *hoped* to call on the name of the Lord God."[4] The second place after hope is given to repentance for sins and to improvement. Enoch is a symbol of one who changes from the worse life to the better, for it is written that he was not found because God transferred him (Gen 5:24 LXX). The transference by God implies the change for the better life (*Abraham* 17–18).[5]

Superior to hope and improvement is perfection, which is represented by Noah, since it is written: "Noah, a man righteous and perfect in his generation, was well-pleasing to God" (Gen 6:9). This verse forms the basis for Philo's interpretation of Noah. He is characterized not only as righteous, perfect, and pleasing to God but also as good, wise, holy, and a lover of virtue.[6] However, the epithet par excellence is "righteous."[7] That Noah is perfect means that he acquired all of the virtues and that he, having acquired them, continued to exercise each of them (*Abraham* 34). To be well-pleasing to God is the highest virtue and the summit of happiness (*Unchangeable* 118).[8] Because the righteous Noah follows the right reason (ὀρθὸς λόγος), which is perfect and truly masculine, he fathers male children.[9] The unjust person, whose thoughts are unmanly, fathers female children, and he plants a tree of vice and passions (*Giants* 5; Gen 5:32). Philo usually associates the male gender with reason and virtue, the female with passions and vice.[10] Noah is the tenth descendant from Adam (Gen 5), which shows that, just as ten is the most perfect end of the numbers, so righteousness is perfect and the true end of actions in life

---

4. See *Rewards* 11–14.

5. See *Rewards* 15–21.

6. ἀστεῖος, *Unchangeable* 107; σοφός, *Abraham* 31; τέλειος, *Abraham* 31, 34, 36; *Unchangeable* 118; φιλάρετος, *Abraham* 27, 31; θεοφιλής, *Abraham* 27.

7. δίκαιος, *Alleg. Interp.* 3.78; *Worse* 170; *Posterity* 48, 173, 175; *Giants* 3, 5; *Unchangeable* 118, 140; *Confusion* 105; *Migration* 125; *Heir* 260; *Prelim. Studies* 90; *Abraham* 27, 31.

8. Cf. *QG* 1.97 (discussion of Gen 6:9): righteousness and perfection and being pleasing to God are the greatest virtues.

9. In *Unchangeable* 118 Philo explains that the offspring of the good mind are the virtues mentioned in Genesis: being righteous, perfect, and well-pleasing to God.

10. See, e.g., *Sacrifices* 102–103; *Worse* 28. For Philo's interpretation of male and female, see Baer 1970, 35–54.

(*Prelim. Studies* 90; *Posterity* 173).[11] The Jewish exegete emphasizes Noah's excellent character (καλοκἀγαθία; *Abraham* 35–36) and describes him as most holy (*Virtues* 201). The name Noah means "rest" or "righteous," and these titles are very suitable for a wise man, because there is nothing better than righteousness, the chief among the virtues.[12] Rest indicates that Noah has rest or peace in his mind. He has driven out of his soul all unnatural movements, which are the cause of turmoil and confusion.[13] Such movements are looked for by worthless men, but wise men seek a tranquil and peaceful life (*Abraham* 27). In the Genesis account, Noah's parents and grandparents are not mentioned, only his virtues are listed, and Philo clarifies that this indicates that the wise man does not have a house, family, or country[14] save virtue and virtuous actions (31).[15] Noah is a sage because he has expelled from his soul the untamed passions and the beast-like vices (32).

Because Gen 6:9 says that Noah was perfect in his generation, Philo qualifies Noah's perfection: he is not absolutely good, only in comparison with the men of his time. There are other sages (Abraham, Isaac, Jacob) who were good by nature and excellent in words and deeds without having any contact with evil things. Therefore, the other sages win the first prize and Noah the second prize (37–38).[16] Proof of Noah's excellence is that he was not destroyed in the flood and that after the flood he became the founder of a new race (46).[17]

Other biblical figures are described in the same way as Noah is depicted. Abel, for instance, is a lover of virtue and a man of worth who is placed opposite Cain, the bad man who loves the body and earthly things (*Sacrifices* 1–4; *Worse* 109; *Posterity* 172). Like Noah, Abel oppresses the irrational movements of his soul (*Sacrifices* 45). Moses, who for Philo is the wise man par excellence,

---

11. For the perfection of the number ten, see *Prelim. Studies* 94, 103–105; *Planting* 125.

12. The same interpretation occurs in *Alleg. Interp.* 3.77; *Worse* 121; *Q.G.* 2.45. The translation of "rest" is based on the Hebrew verb נוח "to rest," and Gen 5:29 LXX, where it is written "he [Noah] shall give us rest from our labors and from our sorrows and from the earth that the LORD God has cursed." See Grabbe 1988, 192–93. Because Philo connects the earth with the body and earthly passions, he interprets the phrase "to make rest from the earth" as destroying the passions.

13. See *Worse* 121–122: it is the nature of righteousness to make rest in the place of toil and to destroy grief.

14. In all likelihood, Philo is thinking of God's command to Abraham to leave his land, family, and father's house (Gen 12:1). In *Migration* 2, he explains land as body, family as sense-perception, and father's house as speech.

15. See *Q.G.* 1.97: to the virtuous person, virtue is truly a generation.

16. It is a contest in which virtue is the prize; see *Prelim. Studies* 24.

17. See *Rewards* 22, where Philo explains that Noah received two prizes as a reward for his righteousness: he was saved from the flood and became the beginning of a new generation (cf. *Virtues* 201).

is portrayed in the same way: he bridles the passions, practicing self-restraint and self-control (*Moses* 1.25–26, 154). His own aim is living in accord with the right reason of nature (*Moses* 1.48). Furthermore, Moses fulfills the four functions that the Stoics assign to the wise man: he is king, legislator, priest, and prophet (*Moses* 2.2; *SVF* 3:619).[18]

Describing Noah as virtuous and oppressing the passions, Philo presents him as a Stoic sage. Generally the Stoics place the wise and perfect man in opposition to the worthless man (*SVF* 1:126; 3:661). The sage, being righteous and a man of worth, has reached a state of passionlessness (3:332, 448, 622). Participating in virtue, he acts and lives according to virtue (3:76, 643), and the man who possesses all virtues is perfect (3:76, 299). By way of contrast, the worthless man, being beast-like and wild, acts wickedly without worrying about virtue (3:677, 682). This is the same image as used in Philo's depiction of Noah, whom he also places opposite the worthless man. In the passage on Noah, Philo uses the Stoic definition of passion as an "unnatural movement of the soul" (*Abraham* 27; *SVF* 3:462, 476). According to the Stoic ideal, Noah follows right reason, which can be identified with the divine law (*SVF* 3:560; *Creation* 143).

2. Noah Found Grace with the Lord God

Philo discusses Gen 6:8 in *Unchangeable* 104–116: "Noah found grace [χάρις] with the Lord God."[19] The Jewish exegete explains that Noah, the man of worth, found in all his inquiries as highest truth that all things are a grace or gift of God: earth, water, air, fire, sun, stars, heaven—in a word, all living beings and all plants. God has graciously given the world to the world and its parts to themselves and each other. He gives his boons not because he considers everyone as being worth his grace; rather, he gives his benefits because of his goodness.[20] This goodness is the motive for creating the world (107–108).[21]

In the biblical text it is written that Noah found grace with the Lord God, and Philo explains that "Lord" and "God" are the titles of the two powers of God, of whom the ruling power by which God rules the world is called Lord, whereas God is the name of the creative and beneficial power by which he cre-

---

18. See Geljon 2002, 8–11.
19. The passage is commented on by Winston and Dillon 1983, 330–34.
20. Here Philo interprets the word χαρίς as meaning "free gift," which is the same exegesis of "finding grace" in *Alleg. Interp.* 3.78.
21. Platonic thought, *Tim.* 29d.

ated the world.[22] Philo discerns a difference between Noah and Moses, who is said to have found grace with God himself (Exod 33:17). God shows himself to Moses by himself with nothing else, because Moses possesses the highest wisdom. Noah's wisdom is inferior to and a copy of Moses' wisdom, and therefore he found grace with God's powers, which, being subjected to God, are on a lower ontological level than God himself (109–110).

Philo considers Noah as the good mind who loves God and strives for virtue, and in what follows Philo places Noah in opposition to the mind, which loves the body and the passions and has been sold in slavery to the chief cook. As a eunuch, he has been deprived of all the male and productive parts of the soul, and he does not do good deeds.[23] Such a mind is cast into the prison of passions and finds grace with the chief jailer (111).[24] In the true sense of the word, prisoners are those who are full of folly, incontinence, cowardice, injustice, impiety, and all other plagues. The governor of the prison is the concentration of all vices, and being well-pleasing to him is the greatest penalty (112–113). Philo ends the passage by speaking to the soul and urging him to put away what is well-pleasing to the rulers of the prisons and to strive with all zeal to be pleasing to God. But if one is unable to do so, then one should seek God's powers and become their suppliant until they accept the fidelity of one's service and place one amidst those who are well-pleasing to them, as Noah was well-pleasing (116).

In his discussion of Gen 6:8, Noah is presented as being inferior to Moses, who possesses the highest wisdom. For Philo, Moses is the most eminent philosopher who has both attained the summit of philosophy and received oracles (*Creation* 8). Noah reached only God's powers (Lord and God), but Moses reached God himself. In the same way, in *Abraham* 37–38 Noah is said to win the second prize, whereas other sages win the first prize. But the righteous Noah is also contrasted with the worthless man who, shut in the prison of vices, is led by passions and vices.

---

22. Philo derives θεός from the verb τίθημι, which can mean "to create." For the two powers, see, e.g., *Alleg. Interp.* 1.96, 3.73; *Cherubim* 27; *Sacrifices* 59–60; see Winston 1985, 19–21.

23. Philo here employs the metaphor of begetting virtue. Because a eunuch does not have reproductive organs, he is not able to beget virtue and to do virtuous acts.

24. Philo has Joseph in mind, whom he describes as a eunuch, in contrast with the biblical account, in which Potiphar, the chief caterer, is a eunuch (Gen 39:1).

3. Noah and the Flood

In several places Philo discusses the ark that Noah built on God's command and the flood that took place.[25] In *On the Life of Moses*, Philo retells the story as an example of the punishment of the impious and the honoring of the just (*Moses* 2.59–65). In another passage Philo compares Noah to Deucalion, the figure in Greek mythology who survives the flood (*Rewards* 23), without any critical comments, whereas elsewhere he disapproves of Greek myths (*Prelim. Studies* 61; *Confusion* 2; *Giants* 58). Louis Feldman argues that Philo, in identifying Noah with Deucalion, emphasizes the historicity of the deluge. I have doubts about this view because Philo does not give other external evidence to support the truth of the event.[26]

Explained in an allegorical way, the ark is a symbol of the body, which is the vessel of the soul (*Worse* 170; *Q.G.* 2.1, 19). In the details of the construction of the ark, Philo discovers similarities with the human body. The ark is, for instance, made out of quadrangular beams (Gen 6:14), and most parts of the body are quadrangular (*Q.G.* 2.2). Just as the ark is covered inside and outside with asphalt, which binds things together, so the human body is united outside and inside (*Q.G.* 2.4). Noah coats the ark, that is, the body, with asphalt, and in this way he strengthens the impressions and activities of which the body is the medium. At that moment he is not yet able to understand truth without the body. But after the flood, he can behold things as they really are through the soul alone. By way of contrast, Moses, who is ἀστεῖος from his birth, weeps when he lies in the ark of the body that is covered with asphalt and receives impressions through senses (Exod 2:3, 6). He yearns for a nature without a body (*Confusion* 105–107). Moses realizes that the asphalt does not provide real safety (ἀσφάλεια).

The flood is a cleansing of the soul from wrongdoing. Noah is ordered to bring into the ark seven clean beasts, male and female (Gen 7:2). Philo interprets the seven beasts as the seven parts of the irrational soul: seeing, hearing, smelling, tasting, touching, speaking, and begetting; the eighth part is the mind, the ruling part of the soul.[27] It is characteristic of the wise man to have the irrational parts cleaned, but in the soul of a foolish and worthless man they are polluted (*Worse* 167–173).

---

25. An overview of the interpretation of the story of the flood in Philo, Pseudo-Philo, and Josephus is given by Feldman 2004, 84–114.

26. Feldman 2004, 86.

27. Philo follows the Stoic division of the soul into the ruling part and the seven parts (*SVF* 2:836).

Philo also offers another reading of the flood: it is a symbol of punishment of the soul for its wickedness and misdeeds. The deluge is a throwing of sins and a torrent of injustice in which streams of passions swirled around in the soul (*Confusion* 23–25; cf. *Flight* 192; *Q.G.* 2.9). A great flood arises when the streams of the mind are opened by vices such as madness, folly, desire, and impiety (*Q.G.* 2.18).

4. Noah as a Farmer and a Planter

Genesis 9:20 relates that Noah began to be a farmer, and Philo deals extensively with this fact in *On Agriculture*. At the beginning of this treatise the Jewish exegete argues that there is a great difference between a farmer and a worker on the soil. It is possible to work on the soil without any knowledge, but a farmer is a professional, having knowledge of farming. With skill he cultivates the land and looks after trees and plants (1–7). Having given some examples of good farming—loping, trimming, grafting—Philo moves to a metaphorical use of farming: the husbandry of the soul. It is the task of the mind to reap the fruits of what has been sown or planted. Mature souls are nourished by the instructions in prudence, self-control, and all other virtues. When they have been sown and planted in the mind, they will bring forth beneficial fruits, namely, good and praiseworthy actions. By means of farming, trees of passions and vices are cut down and destroyed (10–11). The righteous man, who is a farmer of the soul, is placed opposite the unjust man, who is a worker on the soil. Cain is an example of a bad man whose occupation is tilling the earth (Gen 4:2). He is also cursed from the earth and shall work the earth with his hand (4:12, 20–21). Philo explains that earth is a symbol of the body, and the worker of the earth pursues bodily pleasures, according to his bodily nature (*Q.G.* 2.66).[28] In the biblical text it is written that Noah *began* to be a farmer, and Philo explains that Noah only began but was not able to go on and lacked the strength to attain the final stage (*Agriculture* 125, 181).

Noah also planted a vineyard, drank the wine, became drunk, and was rendered naked in his house. His youngest son reported his father's nakedness to his brothers (Gen 9:20–22). Philo devotes a whole treatise to *On Planting*, in the first part of which he discusses God's work as a planter and in the second treats the question, which was much discussed in philosophical schools, "Will the wise man get drunk?"[29] Among other things, Philo argues that the verb "to get drunk" (μεθύειν) is derived from "after sacrificing" (μετὰ τὸ θύειν) and

---

28. This interpretation parallels that of Noah as farmer and Cain as worker of the earth in *Worse* 104–111.
29. Seneca reports that Zeno forbade a wise man to get drunk (*Ep.* 83).

that therefore it is fitting for a wise man to become drunk.[30] A worthless man will never perform a sacrificial act (*Planting* 163–164).[31] Drunkenness does not seem to suit the wise man very well, but, wishing to do justice to the biblical text about Noah's behavior, Philo is eager to explain the drunkenness of the wise Noah. He thus argues that a wise man may get drunk.

In the treatise *On Drunkenness*, Philo discusses Moses' views on drunkenness. The Jewish legislator uses wine as a symbol of nakedness, which manifests itself in foolish talking, insensibility, insatiable greediness, and gladness. Noah, having become drunk, was found in this situation (*Drunkenness* 4).[32] Becoming naked means that the soul becomes foolish and senseless, being deprived of virtue. But Noah's foolishness does not reach those outside, but stays in the house, for it is said that "he was rendered naked in his house" (Gen 9:21). When the wise man commits sin, he does not go out, as the worthless man does. The evil of the latter has been spread forth, but that of the former has been contained (*Alleg. Interp.* 2.60).

The soberness to which Noah returns (Gen 9:24) is interpreted as the soberness of the soul, which is very profitable (*Sobriety* 1–5). When Noah becomes sober, he sees what his younger son has done and utters curses. Philo explains that the mind, having become sober, perceives what the young, rebellious wickedness has done (*Sobriety* 30). To become sober is repentance and a recovering as from a disease (*Alleg. Interp.* 2.60).

Conclusion

As noted at the outset, Philo deals with Noah in all three series of writings. In the Exposition of the Law he offers the most literal reading: Noah is described as a righteous person and a wise man. Because of his righteousness, he survives the great flood, which is a punishment of wicked people. In the Allegorical Commentary, Philo gives an allegorical and more complicated exegesis. Noah is not only a historical figure but also a symbol of the good mind that fathers male offspring, that is, the virtues. The flood is allegorically interpreted as a cleansing of the soul. In the *Questions and Answers on Genesis*, Philo combines a literal interpretation with allegorical exegesis. The different series complement each other.

---

30. This etymology occurs in a fragment from Aristotle's *Symposium* (frag. 3 ed. Ross = Athenaeus 40c–d).

31. In *Q.G.* 2.68 Philo writes that Noah does not drink wine to excess but "only drinks some" wine, which always happens to the wise man.

32. I follow Colson's reading of *Drunkenness* 4 (see Philo of Alexandria 1929–68, 3:500).

The most important aspect in Philo's discussion of Noah is his depiction of Noah as a righteous sage and a man of worth who controls his passions. This portrait is based on Gen 6:9, where Noah is called righteous, perfect in his generation, and well-pleasing to God, but Philo furnishes him with the characteristics of a Stoic sage who has driven out the passions or at least controls them. The name Noah means rest, which indicates that Noah has rest in his mind, because he has expelled the passions. Due to his perfection, Noah survives the flood and becomes the founder of a new race. The flood is interpreted as a punishment of the soul for its misdeeds or as a cleansing of wrongdoing. The wise man ought to have a soul cleaned from passions. The flood is also a symbol of the stream of passions and vices that attack the mind. Philo explains that Noah's activities as a farmer (Gen 9:20) consist in cutting down and destroying the trees of passions and vices. Noah, the righteous man, is a farmer of the soul and is contrasted with the unjust Cain, who tills the earth (Gen 4:2) and strives for earthly passions. Noah's perfection is qualified: he is inferior to Moses, the wisest man, who reaches God himself, whereas Noah finds grace with God's powers only. Noah drinks wine, becomes drunk, and is rendered naked in his house (Gen 9:20–21). Being loyal to the biblical text, Philo argues that a wise man may get drunk. Being naked means becoming foolish, but Noah's foolishness is seen only in his house, which is fitting for the wise man. The sin of a wise man has not been spread forth. Thus, Philo plays down Noah's nakedness.

It is evident that Philo offers first and foremost an ethical reading of Noah along the lines of Stoic ethics. Noah nearly becomes a Stoic sage, but Philo believes that this reading of Noah is based on the Pentateuch. There are clear similarities between Mosaic law and Greek philosophy, since the Greek philosophers supposedly learned their theories from Moses, who is more ancient than any Greek philosopher. By describing Noah as a sage, Philo sought to make the biblical figure acceptable for his non-Jewish contemporaries. Philo's interpretation of Noah shows obviously that he was a man of two worlds: the world of Jewish faith, which he inherited from his family; and the world of Greek learning, in which he was profoundly instructed. His reading of Noah is a good example of the Hellenization of a biblical figure.

NOAH IN RABBINIC LITERATURE*

Aryeh Amihay

1. INTRODUCTION

The figure of Noah as it is reflected in rabbinic literature is quite different from the one found in Second Temple literature.[1] In contrast to the central role Noah plays in 1 Enoch, Jubilees, and the Genesis Apocryphon, practically rising to the position of a redeemer, his role in rabbinic literature is not intensified. The rabbis' attitude toward him is ambiguous: he is recognized as the hero of the flood, but at the same time his sins are mentioned.

This change of roles has led some scholars to consider the possibility that there was an anti-Noachic polemic intended to diminish his significance.[2] The main argument of this essay is that there are no signs of a systematic polemic, since the ambiguity regarding Noah also conveys positive attitudes toward his figure.[3] The source of this ambiguity, therefore, is to be found in the bibli-

---

* I am deeply grateful to my friends Moulie Vidas and Nadav Sharon for reading earlier versions of this study and offering insightful and extremely helpful comments. Any remaining errors are my own.

1. On Noah in Second Temple literature, see Bernstein 1999; 2005; Dimant 1998; Feldman 1988a (cf. 1998b, 17-37); 2003; Lewis 1968, 10-81; Segal 2007, 145-67; Stone 1999; VanderKam 1980; 1992a. Note that some of these authors hold a different view regarding Noah in Second Temple literature than the one assumed above. Feldman seems to draw a continuum of Noah's figure between Second Temple times and rabbinic traditions, while Bernstein stresses that the Noah and the flood traditions do not gain a unified treatment in Qumran or in other Second Temple literature (1999, 223).

2. See Kaplan 1931 and, more elaborately, Koltun-Fromm 1997. Baumgarten argues that certain polemical strands can be found as early as the biblical narrative itself. The postdiluvian narrative is intended to ensure that the hero of the flood is not apotheosized as in the Mesopotamian traditions (Baumgarten 1975, 61; cf. Noort 1999, 27-30). For an argument of a very different nature against Noah, see Orlov 2007, 361-96.

3. I have long struggled over the question of the lack of a systematic approach regarding Noah. Should this be ascribed merely to a polysemic tendency of midrash, allowing

cal text and should be ascribed to exegetical techniques and hermeneutical choices rather than to an anti-Noachic ideology.[4] In order to establish this argument, the major sources regarding Noah in rabbinic literature will be discussed, following their chronological order in the biblical narrative.

2. Rabbinic Sources Concerning Noah

2.1. Noah's Birth

Rabbinic sources present only two traditions concerning Noah's birth: a brief comment on him being born circumcised; and more lengthy discussions regarding his name and its explanation (the *midrash-shem*).

Avot de-Rabbi Nathan names Noah as one of the righteous men born circumcised:

> And why does scripture say, *An unblemished and upright man* (Job 1:8)? This is to teach that Job came forth circumcised, for it is said, *And God created Man in his image* (Gen 1:27). Seth too came forth circumcised, for it is said, *And he begot a son in his own likeness, according to his image* (Gen 5:3). Noah too came forth circumcised, for it is said, *He was righteous, flawless in his generation* (Gen 6:9). Shem too came forth circumcised, for it is said, *And Melchizedek, king of Shalem* (Gen 14:18). Jacob too came forth circumcised, for it is said, *And Jacob, a flawless man, who dwelled in tents* (Gen 25:27). Joseph too came forth circumcised, for it is said, *These are the generations of Jacob, Joseph* (Gen 37:2). But it is not improper to say anything but *These are the generations of Jacob, Reuben*? Why then does scripture say *Joseph*? Only [to teach us that] just as Jacob came forth circumcised, so too Joseph came

---

certain verses to be contemporaneously interpreted in opposing ways? As I hope this paper will demonstrate, this issue is of no consequence for the refutation of anti-Noachic polemic in midrash. Even the negative views do not reflect a polemic tone but mainly an adherence to scripture, motivated by value-based decisions. Moreover, on a general note, I may add that the pluralistic nature of midrash seems to be, as recognized by many scholars, the result of many years in the making rather than an inherent trait thereof. See Yadin 2003 for a representation of the views and further bibliography there. See also discussions in Bakhos 2006 (esp. those of Bakhos, Fraade and Yadin); Rubenstein 2005 (esp. those of Boyarin, Elman, Halivni, Rubenstein); Stern 1988; G. Vermes 1973. See most recently and specifically on this topic Fraade 2007.

4. The question of the rabbis' commitment to the literal interpretation of the text is another great methodological issue at point. For a summary of the arguments, see Fraade 1987. In this essay I contend that the motivation is primarily hermeneutical, while at the same time realizing that any exegetical choice embodies and reflects certain values. In this I am following Halbertal's argumentation, applying his method of legal midrash to aggadic midrash. See Halbertal 1997, esp. 15–41, 168–74. Cf. Halivni 1991, 3–79.

forth circumcised. Moses too came forth circumcised, for it is said, *And she saw him that he was good* (Exod 2:2). And what did his mother see that was more handsome and more splendid than anyone else? It was that he came forth circumcised. Wicked Balaam too came forth circumcised for it is said, *The saying of him who hears the words of God* (Num 24:4). Samuel too came forth circumcised, for it is said, *and the boy, Samuel, continued to grow both in stature and in favor* (1 Sam 2:26). David too came forth circumcised, for it is said, *A Miktam of David. Protect me, O God, for I have taken refuge in you* (Ps 16:1). Jeremiah too came forth circumcised, for it is said, *Before I formed you in the belly I knew you, and before you came forth from the womb I consecrated you* (Jer 1:5). Zerubbabel too came forth circumcised, for it is said, *On that day I will take you, O Zerubbabel, my servant, son of Shealtiel, says the Lord* (Hag 2:23).[5]

Three questions rise from this quotation. First, can any link be established between the miraculous birth narratives of Noah found in 1 Enoch, Genesis Apocryphon, and 1Q19 and this citation? Second, what is the scriptural reasoning of this tradition? Finally, what image of Noah is reflected in this tradition, or, in other words, what is the purpose of this tradition?

The fact that Noah is mentioned here within such a diverse group seems to indicate that his being born circumcised is not associated with his role as a semidivine being in the apocryphal birth narratives of Second Temple literature.[6] Noah's outstanding appearance upon birth in 1 En. 106–107 serves to mark him as a prototype of the savior—a role that is more clearly stated in another component of the Enochic literature, namely, the Animal Apocalypse (1 En. 89:1–9).

According to the list in 'Abot de Rabbi Nathan, being born circumcised can indeed signify divinity. This is understood through the prooftext of Adam's creation without the foreskin. The rabbis infer this from Gen 1:27, which states that God created Adam in his image. In other words, the rabbis take for granted that God's image is without a foreskin.[7]

However, though being born circumcised may be a sign of divinity, it is not necessarily so. The fact that wicked Balaam is mentioned as such in the

---

5. 'Abot R. Nat. version A, 2, 50–55. Numbering is based on Becker 2006, 46–48. For translation, I consulted Goldin 1955, 23; Neusner 1997, 22–23.

6. Note that this tradition is completely absent from the shorter version of 'Abot de Rabbi Nathan. In several manuscripts, Samuel does not appear in the list. See Becker 2006, 46–47. On the editions of 'Abot de Rabbi Nathan, see Kister 1998. However, despite the fact that this passage has undergone many changes and expansions, there is no reason to assume that it originally specified Noah alone.

7. This is in line with the concept of the circumcised body being the perfected condition. See further below.

same list testifies to this. In other words, Noah's inclusion in the list does not necessarily mark him as divine, not even as particularly righteous.

The prooftext for Noah's being born circumcised is Gen 6:9: "Noah was a righteous man, flawless [תמים] in his generation."[8] The interpretation of the root תם or תמים to signify circumcision is not exclusive to Noah in this midrash. In fact, it is the point of departure for the midrash when it mentions Job. In addition to Job and Noah, Jacob is also named as being born circumcised for the same reason. To these we should also add Shem/Melchizedek, whose prooftext is him being "King of Shalem," here שלם being read as an adjective, "whole, complete," rather than a proper name, an adjective that is synonymous with תמים (cf. Ps 37:37; Lev 3:1, 6; as well as the standard equivalent in the Aramaic targums for biblical תמים).

The connection between being perfect and circumcision is ideological, in the sense that Jews would not want to consider the divine command of circumcision to be a mutilation of their bodies.[9] The foreskin is therefore considered to be a defect, while circumcision is viewed as the perfected state. Perhaps more important than this is the scriptural basis for this connection.[10] God's appearance to Abraham in Gen 17, where he gives him the command of circumcision, opens with the words: "I am God Almighty [אל שדי], walk before me and be flawless [תמים]." The association of תמים and circumcision is thus an interpretation of Gen 17:1, which takes the introduction of the command to encapsulate what is to follow. The Mishnah makes this explicit in relation to Abraham: "Rabbi says: Great is circumcision, for despite all the religious duties which Abraham our father fulfilled, he was not called 'perfect' until he was circumcised, as it is written, *Walk before me and be flawless* (Gen 17:1)."[11] Genesis Rabbah also makes this point: "God said to Abraham, 'you have no other defect but this foreskin: remove it and the defect will be gone.' Hence, *walk before me and be flawless* (Gen 17:1)."[12]

---

8. Biblical passages are quoted based on the NRSV version and with consultation of Alter 2004. תמים is rendered here as "flawless" to facilitate discussion of Noah having been born circumcised. NRSV and Alter have "blameless" for תמים in Gen 6:9, but the Hebrew might be taken as an adjective modifying the previous adjective, i.e., "completely righteous." On the function of prooftexts, see Boyarin 1990, 22–38.

9. Kalimi 2002 has raised the possibility that this is also framed in the context of a Jewish-Christian polemic. See also Niehoff 2003.

10. On the use of midrash with scripture and the expansion of a narrative that is sometimes based on a single word, see Levinson 2005, 29–101. For a brief English version, see Levinson 2004. See also Fishbane 1998, 9–21; Frenkel 1996, 2:270–303.

11. Ned. 3:11. Translation as quoted in Kalimi 2002, 3. See there for discussion.

12. Gen. Rab. 46:4; translation based on the Soncino edition (Freedman 1939).

In conclusion, Noah's being born circumcised as it appears in 'Abot de Rabbi Nathan does not seem to be related to the role Noah plays in the Enochic literature. If anything, it is a faint echo of a lost tradition.[13] The midrash does not present an effort to deprive Noah of any special characteristics upon birth, nor is it familiar with a larger context in which such characteristics would become more significant. Noah is mentioned as being born circumcised, as are all people who are mentioned as תם or תמים.[14] The midrash probably recognizes him as righteous, since the prooftext provided states that as a fact, but it does not incline to any side regarding the interpretation of "righteous in his generation" (see discussion below).

Noah is given his name in Gen 5:29, where his father prophesies or wishes that "he shall comfort us from our deeds and from the toil of our hands." The explanation of the name is problematic, since "comfort" is derived from the root נחם, whereas Noah's name seems to be derived from the root נוח, which means "rest." This is expressed most clearly in Genesis Rabbah, where Rabbi Yohanan and Resh Lakish agree that either the verb or his name should be altered:

> *He named him Noah saying this one shall comfort us* (Gen 5:29). R. Yohanan said: The name does not correspond to the interpretation [given to it], nor does the interpretation correspond to the name. The text should either have said *This one shall give us rest* [יניחנו] or *He named him Naḥman saying this one shall comfort us* [ינחמנו].[15]

This is followed by a list of etymologies that attempt to establish a connection between the root נוח and the flood narrative in Genesis. Rabbi Yohanan tells a story of all toils rebelling against their craftsmen (the cow against the ploughman, the door against the woodmason, and so forth) and how all rested (i.e., went back to order) after Noah was born. This is related to Lamech's decree (that the son will comfort them of all toils)[16] but also to the flood, reflecting the submission required in order to bring all animals into the ark. Resh Lakish

---

13. I believe that a trace of this tradition in relation to Noah is to be found in 4Q535, where the words נפק שלם ("came out perfect/whole") have been partially preserved (frag. 3, line 2). See Jeremy Penner, "Is 4Q534–536 Really about Noah?" in this volume.

14. Koltun-Fromm 1997, 58 n. 9.

15. Gen. Rab. 25:2. See more on the etymology of Noah's name in Cassuto 1961, 288–89; Lewis 1968, 123; VanderKam 1992a. For the discussion of Noah's name in Philo, see Albert Geljon, "Philo's Interpretation of Noah," in this volume.

16. Cf. this motif also in Targum Pseudo-Jonathan on Gen 5:29: "this one will bring us relief from our work which does not succeed." All English translations of Targum Pseudo-Jonathan are based on Maher 1992.

tells a story of waters flooding tombs and disturbing the peace of the dead. After Noah's birth, these waters ceased. The relation to the flood here is also clear: an unnatural event with water that ceases with Noah's birth. Another tradition relates it to the resting of the ark, as the root נוח is actually used in relation to the ark in Gen 8:4.

One last etymology does not link Noah's name with the root נוח "rest." Instead, it relates Noah's name to the scent of the sacrifice that Noah offered after leaving the ark (Gen 8:21), a word deriving from the same root.[17]

All these traditions share a common concern for the discrepancy between the root of Noah's name and the root of the biblical explanation of the name. In relation to the main question of this essay, it is significant to note that no one uses this to denounce Noah's role as a savior. On the contrary, most of the rabbinic explanations solve the etymological problem of the name while reinforcing this very notion.

2.2. Noah's Righteousness

The question of Noah's righteousness is well known: Was Noah righteous only in comparison to his contemporaneous corrupt generation, a generation so wicked as to be deserving of a flood, or would he be considered righteous in any generation? Although many commentaries base their answer to this question on the word בדרתיו "in his generations" in Gen 6:9, the trigger of this debate probably lies not in an exegetical difficulty of that word but in a wider framework of the Noah narrative. The midrash, therefore, is still exegetical in character, but the commentary does not originate from the word on which it seems to comment,[18] but on the stark contrast between the hero of the flood, the one named righteous in the beginning of the narrative, and the drunken viticulturist at its conclusion. The flood narrative in Genesis bears many similarities to other flood narratives, most strikingly to two Babylonian epics: Atrahasis and the eleventh tablet of the Gilgamesh Epic.[19] Neither of these narratives includes a story similar to the one told in Gen 9 of Noah's drunk-

---

17. On Noah in the tradition of *onomastica sacra*, see Michael E. Stone and Vered Hillel, "Noah in Onomastic Traditions," in this volume.

18. This may be in part due to the fact that some midrashim originate in prior expansions of the biblical narrative, not referring to a specific verse but to a theme. See Fraade 1987, 287–90; Heinemann 1974, 7–88; Levinson 2005, 60–101. For a different view, see Kugel 1983; 1998, 19–29.

19. For relations between the ancient Near Eastern materials and postbiblical traditions, see Baumgarten 1975; van Bekkum 1999; Bhayro 2005; Reeves 1993 (and response by Huggins 1995). For the influence of these narratives on the biblical flood narrative, see Noort 1999; Rendsburg 2007.

enness. This has led many scholars to contend that two ancient figures were merged in Noah's figure as it is found in the Bible: the Babylonian flood hero (whether in the form of Atrahasis or in its transformation, Utnapishtim); and a Phoenician hero who was the discoverer of wine. Although lacking evidence of an equivalent Phoenician hero, this hypothesis seems more than plausible.[20] Note the beginning of the drunkenness narrative in Gen 9:20: "And Noah, the man of the soil, began and planted a vineyard." The exact meaning of the verb "began" in this context is unclear. Perhaps a different verb was there originally that was corrupted or subsequently misunderstood. Maybe it should be read in the context of the flood narrative; that is, this was the first thing he did after leaving the ark. Whatever the meaning of the verb, there can be no doubt that Noah is being introduced here anew: "Noah, the man of the soil," as if the readers do not know who Noah is.

The reasons that led early authors to combine the hero of the flood with the inventor of wine remain obscure. Later generations received these two figures merged into one as a fait accompli. Trying to explain how the story of the most righteous, the one who found favor in the eyes of the Lord, the only one worthy for salvation from the flood, could end in such a manner, they searched for clues in the text:

> *In his generations* (Gen 6:9). R. Judah and R. Nehemiah [disputed]. R. Judah said in his generations he was righteous, had he been in the generation of Moses or in the generation of Samuel he would not have been [considered] righteous.... R. Nehemiah said: if in his generations he was righteous, all the more so in the generation of Moses.[21]

> *These are the generations of Noah: Noah was a righteous man, flawless in his generations* (Gen 6:9). R. Yohanan said: in his generations, but not in other generations [i.e., not by the standards of other generations]. And Resh Lakish said: in his generations, and all the more so in other generations.[22]

Ostensibly, this dispute is solely on the interpretation and the purpose of the expression "in his generations" in Gen 6:9. However, if we ask ourselves what induced Rabbi Judah (later attributed to Rabbi Yohanan) to doubt Noah's righteousness in the first place, I think the best explanation would be the fact that in the biblical narrative Noah is not morally unblemished. The midrash, more than the Hebrew Bible itself, tends to dichotomize the biblical heroes. Either

---

20. See Baumgarten 1975, 58; Driver, 1926, 109; Gunkel 1997, 80; Speiser 1964, 62.
21. Gen. Rab. 30:9. See van Bekkum 1999, 130–31; Koltun-Fromm 1997, 63.
22. b. Sanh. 108a. For translations of Babylonian Talmud, I consulted Neusner 1984–91 and Steinsaltz 1989–99.

they are nothing but good, or they are corrupt to the core.[23] The diverse voices expressed in this wide literature eventually led once more to complex portraits, since any given biblical figure related in rabbinic literature has opposing midrashim concerning him or her.

This is manifested in the dispute quoted above between Rabbis Judah and Nehemiah. Each wants to have Noah go in one clear direction: either a villain (Judah) or a righteous person (Nehemiah). The dispute is not only about the figure of Noah but also regarding the essence of righteousness or the temptation of evil.

The attribution of this dispute in the Babylonian Talmud to the figures of Rabbi Yohanan and Resh Lakish intensifies what is at stake. Resh Lakish, who is said by Rabbi Yohanan to be a bandit who repented and became a rabbi,[24] is acquainted with the world of sin and its temptations. He therefore is the one to present a view that appreciates someone whose self-restraint allows him to overcome those temptations, especially when surrounded by sin and debauchery. Rabbi Yohanan, on the other hand, is an example of the exact opposite. Having been in the world of Torah all his life, he is not easily impressed by someone who has managed to stand out against the background of his contemporaries. To him the story of Noah's drunkenness is a sign that Noah was not that much different from his generation. Rabbi Yohanan presents a rigid view of sin and righteousness: either one is righteous and blameless or one is not. Righteousness remains an ideal that Noah has not achieved. In other words, the debate between Rabbis Judah and Nehemiah in Genesis Rabbah is reframed in the context of the biographies of Rabbi Yohanan and Resh Lakish, fictitious though they may have been, but part of folklore by the time of the Amoraim. By shifting the debate to these figures, the question in dispute becomes epitomized in their characters.[25]

Other midrashim present one or another of these views concerning Noah's righteousness, but not as a dispute. Assembling them, we find the opposing views, but within the text of any given midrash Noah is either the ultimate righteous person or the sinner who was saved only because he was better than everyone else in his generation.

---

23. Rofé 1998, 65–66.
24. b. Giṭ. 47a; b. B. Meṣi'a 84a; y. Ter. 45:4; y. 'Abod. Zar. 41:2.
25. For the relations between Rabbi Yohanan and Resh Lakish and how these served to formulate their halakic personalities, see Boyarin 1993, 212–25; Kalmin 1992, 172. However, see there and in Kalmin 1990 also on the disputed historicity of these stories. For another example of the method presented here of reading midrashic citations of a sage in various sources and noting their inherent coherence, see Boyarin 1986.

Two further examples of discussions about Noah's righteousness can be found in the following midrashim, one from the Babylonian Talmud, the other from Genesis Rabbah:

> *After Noah was five hundred years old* etc. (Gen 5:32). [It is written] *Happy is the man that has not walked* etc. (Ps 1:1). Happy is the man refers to Noah. That has not walked in the counsel of the wicked—R. Judah and R. Nehemiah [differ on this]. R. Judah said: [it means] through three generations: the generation of Enosh, the generation of the Flood and the generation of the separation [of the languages, cf. Gen 11]. R. Nehemiah said: during the generation of the Enosh he was but a child....
>
> But his delight was in the law of the Lord (Ps 1:2) alludes to the seven precepts which he was commanded; *and on his law he meditates* (ibid.) that he inferred one thing from another, arguing, Why did the Holy One, blessed be He, order more clean animals than unclean ones [for the ark]? Is it not that he wants sacrifices offered to Him of the former? Immediately *He took of every clean animal* etc. (Gen 8:20). *He is like a tree planted by streams of water* (Ps 1:3): that the Lord planted him in the ark. *Which yields its fruit in its season* (ibid.) this alludes to Shem; *and whose leaf does not wither* (ibid.) this alludes to Ham; *And in all that he does, he prospers* (ibid.), this alludes to Japheth.[26]

> Rabbi Jeremiah ben Eleazar said, "Only a bit of the praise of someone do they say in his presence, but the whole of it they do not say to his face. Only a bit of the praise in his presence, for it is written, *for you have I seen righteous before me in this generation* (Gen 7:1). The whole of it [i.e., of the praise] not to his face, for it is written, *Noah was a righteous man, flawless in his generations* (Gen 6:9). (b. 'Erub. 18b)

The midrash from Genesis Rabbah is striking in that when it names Noah's sons it does not refer to or hint at the curse of Ham.[27] Noah is likened here to the ideal righteous person of Ps 1 in every way. In tractate b. 'Erubin, the midrash stresses that the Bible names Noah righteous twice, and it is to his merit that the higher praise is not said directly to his face. In neither midrash is there any sign of polemic or that the midrash is aware that others contend that Noah is unrighteous or that it is trying to disprove other views. To the contrary, here Noah's righteousness seems to be taken for granted as a given fact (as it should be, from this point of view, since the Bible states it so explicitly).

---

26. Gen Rab. 26:1. See also Koltun-Fromm 1997, 61–62.
27. Canaan was the one cursed, of course, punished for Ham's deed. See Gen. Rab. 36:7; Speiser 1964, 61–63. For ancient exegesis dealing with this problem, see Aaron 1995; Brooke 1994; and Gero 1980.

The same tendency appears in the opposing view, the one that stresses Noah's sin. In the following two midrashim that tarnish Noah's figure, both from Genesis Rabbah, there is no sign of a polemic. Noah's wickedness, or at least the relativity of his righteousness, is taken to be a fact, again based on the biblical text:

> R. Abahu said, we find that the Holy One, blessed be He, shows mercy to the descendants for the sake of their forbears. But how do we know that the Lord shows mercy to the forbears for the sake of their descendants? Because it says *And Noah found grace* (Gen 6:8), which was for the sake of his offspring [as it is said] *These are the generations of Noah* (Gen 6:9). (Gen. Rab. 29:5)

> R. Berekiah said: Moses was more beloved than Noah. Noah, after having been called *A righteous man* (Gen 6:9) was called *A man of the soil* (Gen 9:20); but Moses, after having been called *An Egyptian man* (Ex 2:19), was called *The man of God* (Deut 33:1). (Gen. Rab. 36:3)

The latter example above enfolds precisely the motivation for this view of Noah. The incongruity between Noah's end and the hero of the flood leads exegetes to stress the fact that he was righteous only in his generation. Since many exegetes agree that the sins of the generation of the flood were sexual sins, the fact that Noah's drunkenness is also associated with a sexual sin places him among his generation.

The first midrash maintains that Noah was not saved in his own right but on account of future generations. Although Shem is not mentioned specifically, we may presume that this refers to Shem, Abraham, and his descendants. In other words, Noah was saved only to make possible the genealogy of the Israelites and eventually the Jewish people. Indeed, such an argument might point to a tendency to reclaim Noah as belonging to Jewish tradition, although this—as will be discussed in the conclusion—remains indecisive.

One last midrash that might refer to Noah's righteousness, before moving along to other aspects of Noah's figure, is found in Genesis Rabbah:

> *These* (Gen 6:9). R. Abbahu said: Wherever "these" [אלה] is written, it dismisses the preceding; "and these" [ואלה] [on the other hand], adds to the preceding. Here that "these" is written, it dismisses the preceding. What does it dismiss? The generation of the Flood. (Gen. Rab. 30:2)

The midrash states that the introduction of the genealogy of Noah signifies a new beginning and a dismissal of all its generation. Where does this place Noah in relation to his generation? In other words, does Rabbi Abbahu's saying agree with Rabbi Yohanan's view of Noah or with the view presented by Resh Lakish? By itself, the saying seems to be ambiguous enough to fit with either reading. Either Noah is set apart from his generation, and thus considered better than them, or Noah is considered a man of his generation, and then this saying should be understood as dismissing Noah as well—and that only after him a new beginning starts. The ambiguity of the midrash remains, but the fact that another midrash, quoted above, has Rabbi Abbahu saying that Noah was saved on account of his progeny probably attests that here, too, Rabbi Abbahu considers Noah to be as sinful as his generation.

Some have tried to argue that the targumic[28] rendering of Gen 6:9 is also a sign of this tendency to depreciate Noah's righteousness. The Hebrew word for righteous is rendered as זכי in Targum Onqelos and זכאי in Targum Pseudo-Jonathan, translated as either "pure" or "innocent."[29] This argument is not decisive, since זכי is a common Aramaic translation for "righteous,"[30] but what is interesting is that Targum Neofiti preserves the Hebrew צדיק. In light of the agreement between Targum Onqelos and Targum Pseudo-Jonathan, it seems that Neofiti's rendering צדיק is an assertion that Noah is righteous and that there is no need to understand the word otherwise in this case. That being said, it should be stressed that there is no reason to consider this to be a disagreement between Neofiti and Pseudo-Jonathan, but rather a reaffirmation of Pseudo-Jonathan's similar view. That Pseudo-Jonathan does not hold a negative view of Noah can be seen from various midrashic expansions in the Noah narrative, none of which bears negative consequences for Noah. Furthermore, Targum Pseudo-Jonathan on Gen 6:9 expands the Hebrew תמים as referring to good deeds: "he was perfect in good works, in his generation" (שלים בעובדין טבין הוה בדרוהי).[31] Therefore, it seems that any ambiguity left in the Hebrew Bible (of which the targumist was probably aware, in light of the midrashim) was annulled in this translation.

In sum, the traditions concerning Noah's righteousness or lack of it seem to be relying above all on the biblical text. No midrash raises the suspicion of an anti-Noachic polemic. The midrashim are not concerned with Noah being pre-Abrahamic or pre-Mosaic, nor do they seem overtly concerned with his appropriation by early Christian traditions as a prototype of Jesus.

---

28. The discussion of Targum in this essay is in view of its role as another strand of rabbinic literature rather than as a genre of its own. It is therefore discussed here for its midrashic qualities rather than as a textual witness. For the problems of date and provenance, see Alexander 1988; Fraade 1992; Kasher 2000; Shinan 1992a. On the Targumim as midrash and their preservation of rabbinic traditions, see Flesher 2005; McNamara 2003; Safrai 2006; Shinan 1992b (cf. Shinan 1994).

29. On translation, see Clarke 1986; Maher 1992.

30. Clarke 1986, 339.

31. Koltun-Fromm 1997, 58 n. 8.

There are certainly some traditions of the Second Temple period that survived in rabbinic literature,[32] but it seems that the context in which Noah's role was intensified in that literature has been neglected or forgotten. In other words, even the rabbis who are critical of Noah do not seem to be concerned with his elevation to a higher level of a priest, a messiah, or an angel. Their main concern, rather, is the two aspects of Noah in the biblical text itself and a reconciliation of this seeming contradiction.

2.3. Noah's Preparations for the Flood

The traditions concerning Noah's preparations for the flood are related to the previous topic, since some of them rely on Noah's righteousness as part of the tradition. Such is the claim in Pirqe Rabbi Eliezer: "Noah said to them: Turn from your ways and evil deeds, so that He bring not upon you the waters of the Flood, and destroy all the seed of the children and men."[33] Noah is portrayed here as a prophet pleading with the people of his generation to repent. Indeed, Noah is called a herald in a passage in Genesis Rabbah:

> *Man* (Gen 6:9). Wherever scripture speaks of "man" [איש], it refers to a righteous man who reproved [his generation]. For during the 120 years Noah planted cedars and cut them down, they asked him, "why [are you doing] this?" and he told them "the Lord of the universe told me that He will bring a Flood on the world." They said to him, "if a flood comes, it will come only on the house of that man" [i.e., on your house alone]. On this it is written *A contemptible brand in the thought of him that is at ease, a thing ready for them whose foot slips* (Job 12:5).
>
> R. Abba said: The Holy one, blessed be He, said, "A single herald stood up for me in the generation of the Flood. This is Noah."
>
> Elsewhere people say "Arouse him, stir him up!" *Contemptible*—because they despised him and called him a contemptible old man. *In the thought of him that is at ease*: this teaches that they were as hard as metal. *A thing ready for them whose foot slips*: two disasters were prepared for them, a disaster from above, and a disaster from below.[34]

Thus Noah is portrayed as preparing his whole life for the flood, not in order to save himself and his family, but rather in order to provoke response, to

---

32. See Nadav Sharon and Moshe Tishel, "Distinctive Traditions about Noah and the Flood in Second Temple Jewish Literature," in this volume.

33. Pirqe R. El. 23. Translation based on Friedlander 1916. On the provenance of Pirqe de Rabbi Eliezer, see Rubenstein 1996.

34. Gen. Rab. 30:7. The midrash is playing here on sound similarities between Hebrew words in Job and its contemporary Aramaic. See Freedman 1939.

instill fear, and to cause people to repent. Several traits in this midrash serve to intensify Noah's prophetic character. First of all, two separate traditions are given of Noah being mocked by his contemporaries. The motif of disbelief in a prophet and rejection of his warnings is widespread in biblical literature and picked up in rabbinic literature as well.[35]

The image of planting the cedar trees is especially interesting in light of the ambivalence concerning Noah's character. The word used here in the midrash derives from the same root describing Noah's plantation of the vineyard in Gen 9:20. The image of Noah as a "man of the earth" served mainly the purposes of those wishing to deride his character. Here it is employed to stress his righteousness. The midrash is claiming that the vineyard was only one of many plantations of Noah. That specific plantation may have led to sin, but its significance is diminished in light of 120 years of planting cedars as part of a campaign to bring his contemporaries to repent. The fact that the contrast to the vineyard is the cedar is also of significance. It serves to strengthen the motif of righteousness, as the righteous are likened to the cedars in the Psalms.[36]

This tradition is also characteristic of the midrashic tendency to intensify and amplify traits of biblical characters. Thus, if the Bible tells of Noah as the hero of the flood, midrash here turns this into a life-long enterprise that Noah was preparing. However, other midrashim do not share this view. While in this midrash Noah is chopping cedar wood for the ark for as long as 120 years, another tradition in Genesis Rabbah has the ark being constructed of itself, or at least assisting Noah in its own construction (אף היא הייתה מסייעת את עצמה).[37] Rabbi Yohanan, in line with his general negative view of Noah, does not say anything of Noah's toil on the construction of the ark, but his comment on Noah's moment of entrance to the ark is telling in this respect, too: "R. Yohanan said: He lacked faith. Had the waters not reached his ankles, he would not have entered the ark."[38] This picture of Noah's hesitation

---

35. Exod 4:1–9; 1 Kgs 22; Jer 37; Amos 7:10–17; Jonah. See D. Marcus 1995.

36. Ps 92:13. Cf. also the imagery of Israel as cedar trees planted by God in Num 24:6. For God as planting cedars, see also Ps 104:16. See Bloch 1995 and, more directly connected to the above discussion, Bhayro 2005, 182. See Ps. 80.

37. Gen. Rab. 31:16. Cf. a later tradition describing the angels collecting the animals for Noah, to spare him the suffering of collecting them himself: Tg. Ps.-J. on Gen 6:20: "From birds according to their kinds, from the animals according to their kinds, from every creeping thing of the earth according to its kind, two of each shall come to you, by an angel that will catch them and bring them to you to keep (them) alive"; cf. Pirqe R. El. 23.

38. Gen. Rab. 32:6. For the purposes of this essay, I tried to present Rabbi Yohanan's view according to the earliest sources possible. However, later midrashim present a similar view of his on Noah. These are either preservations of additional traditions of Rabbi

to enter the ark reflects the same midrashic tendency mentioned above, only with opposite valuation. Whereas one anonymous commentator had Noah preparing for the flood all his life, Rabbi Yohanan wants to denude Noah completely of any righteous activity. Therefore, even the entry into the ark—which could have been portrayed as sheer egotism or fear, devoid of any reverence or piety—is employed by Rabbi Yohanan to draw another aspect of Noah as a sinner: although God informed him explicitly of the flood, he still did not believe it and was hesitant to enter into the ark.

A contending view is offered in another passage from Genesis Rabbah:

> *If the spirit of the ruler rises against you, do not leave your post* (Ecc 10:4). This refers to Noah. Noah said: Just as I entered the ark only with permission, so I will not exit without permission. R. Judah bar Ilai said: Had I been there I would have broken it and gone out, but Noah said I entered with permission, I will exit with permission. *Enter the ark* (Gen 7:1)—*And Noah entered* (Gen 7:7); *Go out of the ark* (Gen 8:16)—*And Noah went out* (Gen 8:18). (Gen. Rab. 34:4)

This tradition stands in direct opposition to Rabbi Yohanan's view, since it corroborates the assumption that Noah deferred his entrance to the ark but justifies it as an act of reverence. The idea that Noah waited for commands from God is based on the fact that such explicit commands are found in the biblical text (Gen 7:1; 8:16). Rabbi Yohanan's view may also be based on the text, though he does not offer any prooftexts. Perhaps none such exists in relation to Noah's motivation in entering the ark, but the idea that the flood had begun before Noah's entrance to the ark can be understood from the text (note especially Gen 7:13, stating that Noah entered the ark "on the very same day" after 7:12 mentioned the rain had been falling for forty days).[39] In either case, Noah eventually does enter the ark, but in Rabbi Yohanan's version the notion of fear and egotism is very evident, devoid of any religious meaning.

Yohanan or the work of a compiler aware of his view, ascribing to him views that would suit those expressed in the earlier midrashim. See, e.g., Goldberg 1977 (repr. in Goldberg 1999, see esp. 73–79).

39. Of course, Gen 7:7 has Noah entering the ark before the beginning of the flood. The incongruity lies in the biblical text due to the different sources the redactor was using for this text. However, the midrashim discussed here already have a stabilized text, and therefore this issue is not discussed in the essay. For a discussion of the sources of the flood narrative, their discernment, and its implication, see see B. J. Schwartz 2007. I thank Baruch Schwartz for sending me an electronic version of his paper, as the book was not yet available for me. For previous discussions, see Driver 1926, 85–112; Gunkel 1997, 60–79, 138–51; Skinner 1910, 147–69; Westermann 1974, 518–614. For an attempt to reconcile the sources, see Wenham 1978. See also Hendel 1995 and the response to it by Rösel 1995.

2.4. Noah during the Flood

Noah's self-interest can also be found in a tradition depicting him helping Og, king of the Bashan, to survive the flood.

> *He blotted out every living thing that was on the face of the ground* (Gen 7:23). Except Noah and those who were with him in the ark, as it is said, *Only Noah was left and those that were with him in the ark* (ibid.), except Og, king of Bashan, who sat down on a piece of wood under the gutter of the ark. He swore to Noah and to his sons that he would be their servant forever. What did Noah do? He bored an aperture in the ark, and he put [through it] his food daily for him, and he also was left, as it is said, *For only Og, king of Bashan, was left of the remnant of the giants* (Deut 3:11). (Pirqe R. El. 23)

Although this midrash does not condemn Noah for helping Og survive the flood, it is notable that Noah is not said to save him out of mercy or compassion, but because Og promised to be his servant forever. This midrash is supposedly interested mainly in accounting for Og's survival of the flood, following Deut 3:11. But considering that Og is said to have campaigned against Israel in their journey from Egypt to Canaan (Num 21:33; Deut 3:1), there is another motif here: blaming Noah for this unnecessary war. If Noah had not saved Og, the Israelites would have been spared this war. The fact that he saved him for his own benefit does not stand in his favor.[40]

Rabbi Yohanan's depiction of Noah's hesitation to enter the ark might reflect another strand of traditions relating to the inconvenience of the stay in the ark, voiced explicitly by Rabbi Ilai above. Since the ark is conceived as the source of rescue and survival, its practicality and convenience are rarely an issue. In this midrash, however, the idea of living with all the animals for the whole duration of the flood is definitely conceived as negative. On God's order in Gen 6:16 to make the ark with "lower, second, and third decks," a tannaitic passage preserved in the Babylonian Talmud comments: "The bottom for dung, the middle for animals, the upper for humans."[41] The Talmud describes the inconvenience of Noah's family as follows:

---

40. This motif resembles that of Haman, whose origins relate him to Agag, king of Amalek, spared by Saul (1 Sam 15). See Amit 2006; Shapira 2004. However, this is not stated explicitly in the midrash as a fault of Noah.

41. b. Sanh. 108b: תנא: תחתיים לזבל, אמצעיים לבהמה, עליונים לאדם. See also Tg. Onq. on Gen 6:16: "make it [with] lower, second, and third *dwelling* compartments" (מדורין ארעאין תנינין ותליתאין תעבדינה). English translations of Onqelos are based on Grossfeld 1988.

> R. Hana bar Bizna told: Eliezer [Abraham's servant] said to Shem, the elder: "It is written *went out of the ark by families* (Gen 8:19). How was it with you?" He said to him: "We had great distress in the ark, an animal whose habit was to be fed by day—we fed by day; one whose habit was to be fed by night—we fed by night. As to the chameleon, father did not know what it ate. One day while he was sitting and cutting a pomegranate, a worm fell out of it, [and the chameleon] ate it. From that point on, he would mash bran for it, when it became maggoty, [the chameleon] ate it." (b. Sanh. 108b)

Not only is the family compelled to live with animals for the whole duration of the flood; they are constantly waiting on them and serving food around the clock to comply with the habits of each animal. A later midrash also has Noah bitten by the lion on one of the feedings (Tanḥ. Noah 14).

Another inconvenience of the time in the ark is a restriction of sexual relations.[42] One clue to the fact that Noah and his sons abstained from sexual relations while in the ark may be found in the fact that, upon leaving the ark, God commands them to be fruitful and multiply (Gen 9:1). This might point to the fact that they were not procreating during the flood. Rabbinic midrash, however, does not cite this verse but finds another source as its prooftext for this tradition. Based on the order of those entering and exiting the ark (Gen 6:18; 8:16), Rabbi Yohanan reaches this conclusion (and again, it is interesting that Rabbi Yohanan, who described Noah's hesitation to enter the ark, is aware of the inconvenience of staying in it):

> And how do we know that they were prohibited [to have sexual intercourse]? For it is written, *And you shall enter the ark, you, your sons, your wife and your sons' wives with you* (Gen 6:18), and it is written [later on], *Go out of the ark, you, your wife, your sons and your sons' wives with you* (Gen 8:16).[43]

This implies that the same number came out as went in, and since intercourse produces children, there was no intercourse. The relation between the flood and themes of sex and sexual sins deserves a study on its own and cannot be dealt here adequately.[44]

---

42. For Syriac traditions of Noah's abstinence, see also Daniel Machiela, "Some Jewish Noah Traditions in Syriac Christian Sources," in this volume. Cf. Koltun-Fromm 1997, 59–61.

43. b. Sanh. 108b. For later Byzantine *piyyutim* that draw on this theme, see van Bekkum 1999, 132–33.

44. Sex is prominently relevant to the flood narrative since the sins that led to the flood were caused by the forbidden copulating of the sons of God with human women (Gen 6:1–4), and the sins themselves are said to be sexual transgressions in various traditions. Furthermore, the fact that Noah's sin upon leaving the ark is somehow related to sex envelops the whole flood narrative in suppressed traditions related to sexual transgression.

One further tradition that is relevant to the discussion of Noah's character is found when Noah intends to send out the raven. The reluctant raven insinuates that Noah is trying to get rid of him since he desires the raven's wife. Noah rebukes him by replying: "I was prohibited regarding what is [usually] permitted, then in what is [always] forbidden, all the more so!"[45] This tradition is adduced in the name of Resh Lakish, who disputed Rabbi Yohanan's view regarding Noah's righteousness. It is interesting, therefore, that the tradition of Noah's abstinence is shared by proponents of both views of Noah's overall character. However, apparently this tradition benefited Resh Lakish's side of the argument, because in the rabbinic mind the ability to practice sexual abstinence was certainly commendable. Although it is not a religious requirement and sexual intercourse is indeed not considered sinful, the ability to be abstinent is a sign of not being promiscuous and therefore of piety.[46]

The exit from the ark raises the same questions as did the entrance to it. Rabbi Ilai's statement that he would not wait an extra second and would break through the ark if it were necessary as soon as he could has been quoted above. Such a vivid expression not only reflects the inconvenience that is associated with the stay in the ark but also praises Noah for his patience. As was the case with traditions of Noah's hesitation to enter, so was the case with his exit. Another tradition corroborates his procrastination in leaving the ark but does not necessarily portray it in a positive light:

> *Go out of the ark* (Gen 8:16). [This may be likened] to an administrator who went away and left someone else in his place. When he came back, he said to him "leave your position" and he was reluctant to leave. He [Noah] said: "Am I to leave and be fruitful and multiply for a [i.e., another] curse?" Until the Holy One, blessed be He, swore to him that he would not bring another flood upon the world, as it is written, *For this is the waters of Noah to me, for as I have sworn that the waters of Noah should no more go over the earth* (Is 54:9). [And he said to him]: Be fruitful and multiply. (Gen. Rab. 34:6)

Noah assumes here a Job-like stance, rebuking God for his destruction, or perhaps like Abraham in Gen 18, negotiating with God on the destruction of Sodom and Gomorrah. The parable of the administrator evokes the notion of a negotiation taking place, but the tone of Noah's words is not clear. He may

---

See Zakovitch 1995, 48–49; Zakovitch and Shinan 2004, 123–28. Cf. Lorberbaum 2004, 403–5.

45. b. Sanh. 108b: במותר לי נאסר לי, בנאסר לי לא כל שכן.

46. Koltun-Fromm 1997, 59–61. For general discussions on this issue, see Boyarin 1993, with special attention on Rabbi Yohanan on pp. 107–22, 138–42; van der Horst 2003; Satlow 2006.

be depressed at realizing the meaning of the destruction of the whole world, rebuking God for the severe punishment, and personally too discouraged to continue with life (this might also be a reflection of the tradition of Noah's abstinence during the flood). Alternatively, he may be bringing the charges for an ulterior purpose, which is the outcome of this negotiation, namely, God's promise never again to inflict a flood on the earth. The second reading, which seems more likely in light of the administrator parable and the outcome of the dialogue, would be less approving of Noah, but then it is surprising that there is no wording in the midrash chastising Noah for insolence against God. Thus the ambiguity of this midrash remains.

2.5. Noah after the Flood: Sacrifice and Drunkenness

There are two important and opposing features regarding Noah's character after leaving the ark. One is the fact that he builds an altar and offers a sacrifice to God; the other is his drunkenness.

The theme of the sacrifice is not developed very much. From the midrashim that do relate to it, it is clear that this tradition posed a problem for the rabbis, since Noah is offering a sacrifice without being a priest and before the laws of sacrifice were given. Later rabbinic literature addresses this problem by relating that a lion bit Noah in the ark, and he was therefore not suitable to offer sacrifices (Tanḥ. Noah 14). According to this midrash, when scripture tells of Noah offering a sacrifice (Gen 8:20), it is actually Noah's son, Shem who is offering the sacrifice in his father's name. For this midrash, the association of Shem with Melchizedek and the fact that Melchizedek was a legitimate priest are both established facts that it does not even stop to make explicit. This problem is stated more explicitly in Pirqe de Rabbi Eliezer, though not in relation to the sacrifice offering but with the secret of the principle of intercalation.[47] The passage is tracing the transmission of the secret knowledge from Adam to Eve to Enoch, who supposedly told it to Noah:[48]

---

47. See Stone 2006a (reprinted in this volume). Earlier rabbinic sources also refer to the intercalation as being a secret, though with no relation to Noah. See b. Roš Haš. 20b; y. Roš Haš. 2:58; b. Ketub. 112a; b. Sanh. 11a. On the latter, see also Rubenstein 2001, 27–28.

48. The manuscripts are corrupt at this point. Some do not specify to whom Enoch passed it on; others say he passed it on directly to Noah. Friedlander suggested in the notes to his translation (1916, 53) that the text read "Methuselah" and that an additional line is lost in which Methuselah passes the secret to Noah. However, in light of connections and similarities between Noah and Enoch (discussed in previous chapters of this book), this is not necessarily the case.

Noah handed on the tradition to Shem, and he was initiated in the principle of intercalation. He intercalated the years and he was called a priest, as it is said *And Melchizedek king of Shalem* (Gen 14:18). And was Shem son of Noah a priest? But because he was the first-born, and because he ministered to his God by day and night, therefore he was called a priest.[49]

Earlier rabbinic literature relates to this problem, and the rabbis offer a play on words, utilizing a similarity of sound between Hebrew "understand" and "build" (ויבן). Genesis 8:20 states that Noah built an altar, and they take it to be that he understood the laws of purity on his own, thus reiterating that Noah did not receive the priestly laws from God but explaining how was it possible for him to offer a sacrifice:

> *Then Noah built an altar to the Lord* (Gen. 8:20). "Built" is written as "understood" [or: perceived]. He said: What is the reason that the Holy One, blessed be He, ordered me to take more clean than unclean animals? Is it not that he wants me to offer a sacrifice from them? Immediately, *He took of every clean animal* etc. (Gen 8:20). (Gen. Rab. 34:9; cf. 26:1)

Targum Pseudo-Jonathan interprets "built" in its literal sense but associates it with an act of rebuilding following the destruction of the flood:

> Then Noah built an altar before the Lord—it is the altar which Adam built at the time he was banished from the garden of Eden and on which he offered an offering, and upon which Cain and Abel offered their offerings. But when the waters of the flood came down it was destroyed. Noah [re]built it and took of all clean animals and of all clean birds, and offered four burnt offerings upon that altar.[50]

The importance of this version does not lie in its interpretation of "built" but rather in its favorable portrayal of Noah after leaving the ark. Even those who portray him as righteous on the outset might want to qualify that in light of narrative that follows after leaving the ark. Here Noah is portrayed as a pious worshiper of God and is connected once more to the beginning of humanity, a connection that emphasizes his important role in history.

This motif is also found in the Pseudo-Jonathan's rendering of Noah's drunkenness. His version of Gen 9:20 reads as follows:

---

49. Pirqe R. El. 8. For further connections between Noah and Melchizedek, see Orlov 2007, 423–39.

50. For translation, see Maher 1992, 43–44.

> Noah began to be a man tilling the earth. And he found a vine that the river had brought from the garden of Eden, and he planted it in order (to have) a vineyard. That same day it sprouted and ripened grapes, and he pressed them.

The fact that the vine comes from the garden of Eden serves to vindicate Noah. This is the best of vines, a vine sent from God, and therefore there is no sin in planting it.[51] Furthermore, while some criticized Noah for choosing to plant a vine as his first action as a "man of the soil,"[52] here it bears no negative connotations. He found the vine that came from the garden of Eden, and the fact that it bore fruit the same day it was planted is also a sign of divine approval. Targum Neofiti does not relate this tradition, but, interestingly, it adds an epithet of righteousness (צדיקא), before narrating the story of the vine.[53]

Noah's drunkenness is also not elaborated extensively in other rabbinic literature. The passage provided above by Rabbi Berekiah (Gen. Rab. 36:3), when discussing his disputed righteousness as a whole, is probably the most direct comment on his character in light of this last event in Gen 9. However, it should be noted that Rabbi Berekiah does not state explicitly that he is relating to the drunkenness episode. This was the reading offered here, based on the epithet "man of the soil" and the association of this epithet with the event.

Other than this passage, there is the widely quoted passage speculating on the nature of Ham's sin:

> Rav and Shmuel [disagreed]. One said he castrated him and the other said he sodomized him. The one who said he castrated him, since he injured him with the fourth, he cursed him by the fourth. And the one who said he sodomized him, learned it from [a comparison of the word] "he saw" [וירא]. Here it is written, *And Ham the father of Canaan saw the nakedness of his father* (Gen 9:22), and there it is written, *and when Shechem son of Hamor saw her* etc. (Gen 34:2). For the one who said that he castrated him, that is the reason he cursed the fourth. But for the one who said he sodomized him, why is the fourth specified? He ought to have cursed him directly [i.e., Ham]! [it is replied]: This and that occurred [i.e., both were cursed]. (b. Sanh. 70a)

---

51. Cf. 3 Bar. 4:8–17 and discussions in Himmelfarb 1993, 91–93; Sharon and Tishel in this volume.

52. See, e.g., Rashi on this verse.

53. Neofiti for Gen 9:20. See Clarke 1986 and McNamara 1992, who suggests that the addition "may be to compensate for the incident about to be narrated" (80). This seems true, of course, but in light of this discussion it seems that it is more a reaffirmation than compensation, stating clearly that even in light of the final story Noah is still considered to be righteous. Neofiti might also be following here the rule that "man" always refers to "a righteous man who reproved." See Gen. Rab. 30:7 (quoted above).

Rav and Shmuel speculate on the nature of Ham's sin, and both agree that it is somehow related to sex. The reason for such an explanation is obvious in light of the Bible's silence on this matter, and considering the fact that it took place when Noah was naked. Another fact upon which both Rav and Shmuel seem to be drawing, although not explicitly stated, is that Noah knew when he awoke what was done to him (Gen 9:24). In other words, whatever the nature of the sin, it has to be something noticeable. By way of contrast, Targum Pseudo-Jonathan says that Noah was told in a dream what was done to him. This is probably because the Targum does not wish the sin to be anything other than what has been already related in the Hebrew Bible, namely, that Ham saw him in his nakedness. The sin is intensified by having Ham tell his brothers in a public place in the street (Tg. Ps-J. on Gen 9:22).[54]

Both Shmuel and Rav also try to solve the question that rises from the text as to why Noah cursed Canaan if Ham performed the sin and to relate their proposed nature of the sin to a measure-for-measure punishment. However, neither solution bears any consequence for Noah's character.[55]

The rabbis' main concern in this story seems to be more the nature of wine rather than the nature of Noah.[56] Wine is portrayed as a cause of sin, and in this connection it is also discussed as the forbidden fruit that Adam and Eve ate. However, it seems as if Noah is not fully responsible for not realizing the dangers of wine. In one midrash God says to Noah: "Noah, should you not have learned from Adam, the first man, that it was only wine that caused him [the expulsion from Eden]?" (b. Sanh. 70a).[57] The tone here is unclear. Is this a reprimand for Noah not learning from Adam's mistake, or is it merely a lament that he did not learn from it? The midrash is inconclusive and there-

---

54. However, note that Targum Psuedo-Jonathan on Gen 9:22 does mention that Ham was the reason that Noah did not have a fourth son. This sentence is left rather obscure without the explanation of Rav. For further discussion of traditions concerning Noah's fourth son, see Gero 1980.

55. For an interesting solution concerning the nature of the sin based on the biblical text, see Bergsma and Hahn 2005. See there also for an overview of solutions offered and further bibliography.

56. For further discussion of the nature of wine in rabbinic literature, see Zellentin 2007, 52–99 (on Noah, see 56–57).

57. Some may wish to suggest that this connection shows that Targum Psuedo-Jonathan (discussed above), when associating the vine with the garden of Eden, was actually using this as a foreshadowing, and therefore the portrayal of the vine in Targum Psuedo-Jonathan is negative, too. This suggestion should be rejected, because there is no sign that the targumist is aware of any connection. After Noah's "fall," so to speak, it does not reiterate the connection of the vine to Eden, and its rendering of Adam's story does not allude to the vine either. Considering the midrashic nature of the Targum, we would expect to find a more explicit expansion, if this were the purpose of claiming the vine was from Eden.

fore remains obscure in relation to the question of Noah's righteousness on this point.

3. Conclusion

A review of rabbinic traditions concerning Noah shows that there is a lack of consistency in their portrayal of Noah. Some rabbis describe him as a righteous man, a man of valor, courage, and piety, while others take him to be a reluctant hero, defiant, and perhaps even an outright sinner. It is my contention that this inconsistency is due to the biblical narrative, itself inconsistent due to various sources and traditions that were brought together.

Quantitatively speaking, there seem to be more midrashim that relate to Noah favorably or neutrally. This is an important factor when asserting that a polemic against Noah was not a major concern for the rabbis. Had they been concerned with Noah's role as a prototype for Jesus or his not being an Israelite (not to mention a pre-Abrahamic and pre-Mosaic hero), we would not expect to have the ambiguity and diversity of opinions of Noah throughout rabbinic literature. The fact that such a significant mass of midrashim speak favorably of Noah weakens the possibility that the rabbis were concerned by an understanding of Noah as prefiguring Jesus or by him being a hero although he is not an Israelite.[58]

Another factor is the fact that even the dicta against him seem strongly tied to the biblical text, not to external traditions. The quantative factor is also easily understood when considering that he is supposed to be the only person God chose to survive the flood. Deriding his character too much might imply a criticism of God.

Noah's figure became prominent in certain circles in Second Temple literature. Attributing divine knowledge to him was a good exegetical move in explaining his offering of a sacrifice. The rise of interest in astronomy gave way to an interest in primordial knowledge that was not given to Moses on Sinai. In this context, Noah and Enoch played a significant role.[59] Within rabbinic Judaism the interest in these issues decreased and eventually disappeared. Moreover, the rabbinic traditions about Noah do not seem aware of these traditions as a whole, even less of their theological and social implications. Even if they were aware of some of the Noah and Enoch traditions of the Second Temple, they generally do not seem to be intimidated by or motivated to contest them.

---

58. Contrast this with the rabbinic treatment of Balaam (Num 22–24). Cf. Braverman 1974; Baskin 1983; Schäfer 2007, 84–92.

59. See Stone 1999.

NOAH AND THE FLOOD IN GNOSTICISM

Sergey Minov

There is a considerable amount of material about Noah and the flood in the writings usually called gnostic.[1] Attention paid by various gnostic writers to this figure fits well into their general interest in the primeval history as it was related in the book of Genesis.[2] One might say that among gnostic interpreters of the book of Genesis the story of Noah was second in popularity only to the story of Adam and Eve. One of the reasons for this popularity was that for many of them the crucial importance of this story lay in the fact that "it is a tradition according to which the creator god had to acknowledge the failure of his creation."[3]

In what follows I will present an overview of how the figure of Noah and the flood were interpreted in various gnostic writings, although the Herculean task of sorting out this at times astonishingly diverse and contradictory material is far from completion. Due to the polythetic character of Gnosticism as a religious phenomenon, it is impossible to give here a comprehensive depiction relevant for gnostic exegesis in all its diverse forms. Nevertheless, a couple of remarks important for understanding gnostic hermeneutics should be made.

However one might like to call the way the gnostics dealt with Scripture—protest exegesis, revisionist reading, hermeneutics of conspiracy, or otherwise—all these characterizations emphasize one of its most fundamental features: the considerable exegetical efforts exerted by those ancient readers who tried to find a way out of the conundrum constituted by their alienation

---

1. Although existence of such a historical entity as "Gnosticism" has been challenged in recent scholarship (see M. A. Williams 1996; King 2003), I shall use this term for the sake of convenience, including in it such distinct movements as Manichaeism and Mandaeism. Even if one refuses to classify these movements as gnostic, one can hardly cast doubt upon their (greater or lesser) indebtedness to the classical gnostic tradition.

2. For a general review of gnostic interpretation of Old Testament, see Pearson 1988b; Luttikhuizen 1997; 2006.

3. Klijn 1981, 219. The scriptural locus meant here is Gen 6:5–7.

from the biblical tradition and, at the same time, their inability or unwillingness to reject this tradition totally. Accordingly, one of the distinguishing features of gnostic approach to Scripture became mythopoesis, when gnostic interpreters did not feel constrained to rewrite the original in agreement with their own peculiar vision of primeval history. Numerous examples of such an attitude to the biblical story of the flood follow.

In what concerns gnostic evaluation of the personality of Noah, there is no unanimity in the gnostic writings, and one can find examples of both positive and negative attitudes toward him. While some aspects of interpretation of the flood and of Noah were inherited by gnostics from their Jewish or Christian matrix, most of the traditions about him that will be considered below are unique to these writings. It should be mentioned from the outset that these writings do not mention "the book of Noah" or, for that matter, any other written or oral medium associated with him.

Unfortunately, not all gnostic texts dealing with Noah and the flood survived. We know, for example, that this topic was explained among other subjects from the book of Genesis by a heavenly revelatory figure in the fragmentary Coptic treatise discovered at Balaiza in Upper Egypt.[4] Nevertheless, the amount of relevant material is still impressive. Most of the texts under discussion were composed between the second and the fourth centuries C.E.

In this necessarily brief overview I will examine only the most important references to Noah and the flood found throughout gnostic sources.[5] For the sake of convenience, I have divided all the relevant sources into the two large groups in accordance with how their authors evaluated this cataclysmic event: positively or negatively. In addition, I will discuss separately those sources that treat the flood in a symbolic or allegorical way, as well as the cluster of traditions dealing with the enigmatic figure of Norea, the rebellious spouse of Noah.

The most popular and most characteristic way in which gnostic writers dealt with the biblical account of the flood is the scenario according to which the catastrophe was initiated by the evil demiurge, that is, the lower deity that created the world. This figure was usually identified with the God of the Old Testament and bore different names in different gnostic traditions.

Thus, according to the teaching of the Ophites as it is reflected in the polemical antignostic treatise of Irenaeus of Lyon (second century C.E.), the name of the demiurge is "Jaldabaoth," and the reason for causing the flood was his disappointment with humanity, which fell short of his expectations:

---

4. For the Coptic text and the English translation, see Kahle 1954, 1:475–76.

5. For a more thorough analysis of the flood in some gnostic sources, see Brakke 2002; Klijn 1981; Luttikhuizen 1999.

Jaldabaoth was angry with men, because they did not worship or honor him. So as their Father and God he sent the deluge on them that he might destroy all together. But even here Wisdom (*Sophia*) opposed him, and those who were with Noah in the ark were saved because of the moisture of light [*propter humectationem illius luminis*] which they had from her.[6]

It is noteworthy that in his inversion of the biblical narrative the gnostic source of Irenaeus combines intertextually the Genesis story of the flood with the tradition about Noah from the Wisdom of Solomon, where the figure of Wisdom appears as a separate agent in the primeval history of humanity and is credited with the salvation of human race from the flood.[7] This might be considered as an example of Jewish influence upon gnostic writers, a phenomenon noted by many scholars.[8]

Accounts of the flood similar to the Ophite version reported by Irenaeus are also found in the genuine gnostic texts discovered in the middle of the twentieth century near Nag Hammadi in Upper Egypt. Thus, a remarkably elaborate retelling of the biblical narrative appears in the Apocryphon of John (NHC II,1; III,1; IV,1; BG 8502,2), a composition that apparently belongs to the so-called "Sethian" branch of Gnosticism.[9] According to this text, the catastrophe was caused by the demiurge "Jaldabaoth," who is characterized as "the Chief Ruler."[10] He resorts to this measure because of his failure to overpower spiritual humanity, yet he is outwitted by the spiritual feminine figure of Pronoia, who being a patron of the spiritual race informed Noah about the coming disaster:

> And he repented for all that had happened through him. He plotted to produce a flood [κατακλυσμός] over all the offspring of man. But the greatness of Providence [πρόνοια], which is the reflection [ἐπίνοια] of the light, instructed Noah and he preached to men. But they did not believe him. It is not as Moses said, "He hid himself in an ark [κιβωτός]," but she sheltered him in a place, not Noah alone but men from the immovable race. They went into a place and sheltered themselves with a luminous cloud. And he (Noah) recognized his lordship and those who were with him in the light which shone upon them, because darkness was falling over everything upon earth.[11]

---

6. *Haer.* 1.30.10; Rousseau and Doutreleau 1979, 2:376–78; trans. Unger 1992, 100.

7. Cf. Wis 10:4.

8. On Jewish background of Gnosticism, see Pearson 1990a; Alexander 1999. On this particular instance, see MacRae 1970.

9. On this branch of Gnosticism, see Schenke 1974; J. D. Turner, 1995; M. A. Williams 2005, as well as a number of relevant articles in Layton 1981.

10. Coptic ⲠⲢⲞⲦⲀⲢⲬⲰⲚ = Greek πρωτάρχων.

11. BG 72:12–73:18; trans. Waldstein and Wisse 1995, 162–64.

It seems that by referring to the waters metaphorically as to the "darkness," the anonymous gnostic author endeavors to go beyond the literal meaning of the biblical story, understanding the flood as a spiritual event. It is also remarkable how he blends the themes peculiar to gnostic mythology, such as the notion of the spiritual race, with the motifs inherited from the earlier Jewish and Christian traditions of exegesis, such as the image of Noah as the preacher of repentance.[12]

In the Apocalypse of Adam (NHC V,5), another composition from Nag Hammadi that exhibits some features typical of Sethian writings, the story of the flood is placed by the author in the narrative framework of a prophetic speech by Adam. Here Adam instructs his son Seth about the events that will take place in the future. Among other things, he tells him about the coming flood in these words:

> For rain-showers of [god] the almighty [παντοκράτωρ] will be poured forth [so that] he might destroy [all] flesh from the earth on account of these things that it seeks after along with [those from] the seed [σπορά] [of] the men to whom passed the life of knowledge [γνῶσις], which came from me [and] Eve, your mother. For they were strangers to him. Afterwards great angels will come on high clouds, who will bring those men into the place where the spirit [of] life dwells.[13]

> [Then] the whole [multitude] of flesh will be left behind in the [waters]. Then god will rest from his wrath. And he will cast his power upon the waters, and [he will] give power to his sons and their wives by means of the ark [κιβωτός] along with [the] animals, whichever he pleased, and the birds of heaven, which he called and released upon the earth. And god will say to Noah—whom the generations will call Deucalion: "Behold, I have protected <you> in the ark along with your wife and your sons and their wives and their animals and the birds of [heaven], which you called [and released upon the earth.] … Therefore I will give the [earth] to you—you and your sons. In kingly fashion you will rule over it—you and your sons. And no seed will come from you of the men who will not stand in my presence in another glory." Then they will become as the cloud of the great light. Those men will come who have been cast from the knowledge of the great aeons and the angels. They will stand before Noah and the aeons. And god will say to Noah: "Why have you departed from what I told you? You have created another generation [γενεά] so that you might scorn my power." Then Noah will say:

---

12. For Jewish sources, see Josephus, *Ant.* 1.74; Sib. Or. 1.147-198; Gen. Rab. 30:7; Eccl. Rab. 9:15; b. Sanh. 108b. For Christian sources, see 2 Pet 2:5; 1 Clem. 7:6; 9:1; Apoc. Paul 50. For other gnostic works, see Concept of Our Great Power (NHC VI,4) 38:25-28.

13. NHC V,5 69:2-71:26; Parrott 1979, 162-67.

"I shall testify before your might that the generation of these men did not come [from me] nor [from] [my sons]."[14]

Here we find a scenario close to that of the Apocryphon of John, when the flood is caused by the demiurge, who acts out of envy by wishing to destroy the spiritual race of gnostics. Remarkably, in distinction from the Apocryphon, where Noah is related to the true God, in the Apocalypse he is depicted as a favorite of the demiurge. According to the version of the Apocalypse, the gnostics were saved from the flood not in the ark but by the angels of the true God, who sheltered them in the special, spiritual place. After the disaster came to an end, they joined Noah and his family, thus causing him to be rebuked by the demiurge. Another noteworthy trait of this composition is that Noah is identified here with Deucalion, the hero of Greek myths about deluge.[15]

Another similar version of the flood is found in a further specimen of Sethian gnostic creativity, the Hypostasis of the Archons (NHC II,4). There the catastrophe is caused by the group of malevolent archons, whose leader is the demiurge Jaldabaoth. In this version of Sethian myth, Noah is associated not with the demiurge but with the God Sabaoth, "the ruler of the forces," who warns him about the flood:

> Then mankind began to multiply and improve. The rulers took counsel with one another and said, "Come, let us cause a deluge [ⲚⲚⲞⲨⲔⲀⲦⲀⲔⲖⲨⲤⲘⲞⲤ] with our hands and obliterate all flesh, from man to beast." But when the ruler of the forces [ⲠⲀⲢⲬⲰⲚ ⲆⲈ ⲚⲚⲆⲨⲚⲀⲘⲒⲤ] came to know of their decision, he said to Noah, "Make yourself an ark [ⲚⲚⲞⲨⲔⲒⲂⲰⲦⲞⲤ] from some wood that does not rot and hide in it—you and your children and the beasts and the birds of heaven from small to large—and set it upon Mount Sir."[16]

A remarkable characteristic of this account is that the site of Noah's ark supposed construction is named "Mount Sir" (ⲠⲦⲞⲞⲨ ⲚⲤⲒⲢ). Connection between this toponym and Noah is peculiar to the Hypostasis and does not appear in other sources. On the one hand, it could be related to the "land of Seiris" (γῆ τὴν Σειρίδα) mentioned by Josephus as the place where the descendants of Seth set the two pillars with the text of Adam's prediction about the

---

14. NHC V,5 70:4–71:26; Parrott 1979, 164–67.

15. See on him Hilhorst 1999.

16. NHC II,4 92:3–15; Layton 1989, 1:246–49. In fact, identification of "the ruler of the forces" with Sabaoth in this passage is not beyond doubt. While Layton and Luttikhuizen (2006, 104) follow this line, some scholars claim that this description corresponds better with the figure of Jaldabaoth; see Bullard 1970, 94–95; Gilhus 1985, 83–84.

coming destructions of universe by fire and by water.[17] On the other hand, it resembles closely the Mount "Seir" (MT שׂעיר; LXX Σηιρ) known from the Bible and located in the region of Edom, that is, south of the Dead Sea.[18] For the time being, the exact genesis of this exegetical tradition seems to be hard to establish.

Further on in his account of Noah, the author introduces another remarkable exegetical tradition according to which the process of the ark's building was hindered due to the intervention of Norea, a feminine figure who destroyed the ark built by Noah for the first time, because he refused to let her in. I shall discuss Norea at greater length below.

In another Sethian composition, the Gospel of the Egyptians (NHC III,2; IV,2), the flood again is understood as an episode in the war waged by the forces of evil against the spiritual race of gnostics. Here we find the figure of Seth, who prophesies about the flood that will happen as one of the several perils to be brought by the devil and his powers upon the world in their war against "the great, incorruptible race" from the seed of Seth:

> And [the] flood [κατακλυσμός] will [come] as an [example (τύπος) for] [the] consummation of the aeon, [and it will come] into the world [κόσμος] [because of this] race [γενεά].[19]

The idea of the flood as a weapon used by the evil demiurge against the spiritual race appears also in the Paraphrase of Shem (NHC VII,1), a gnostic text of unclear affiliation whose mythological system is rather unique. The anonymous author describes the catastrophe in the following way:

> And in order that that his plan might become idle, he sent a demon that the plan of her wickedness might be proclaimed, (namely) that he cause a flood [κατακλυσμός], and he destroy your race [γενεά], in order to take the light and to take away from faith.[20]

> For before the flood [κατακλυσμός] came from the winds and the demons, <evil> came to men. But yet, in order that the power [δύναμις] which is in tower [πύργος] might be brought forth, and might rest upon the earth, the Nature [φύσις], which has been disturbed, wanted to harm the seed [σπέρμα]

---

17. Josephus, *Ant.* 1.71; Thackeray 1930, 32–33. Perhaps, the reference is to "Seria," a land close to India and identified by some scholars as China; for a discussion of this toponym, see Reinink 1975.

18. Cf. Gen 14:6; Deut 1:2; 2:1–5; 33:2; Josh 24:4; Ezek 35:2–3, 7, 15.

19. NHC IV,2 72:10–73:6 (NHC III,2 61:1–22); trans. Böhlig and Wisse 1975, 134–36. See also the editors' comments on the passage (188–89).

20. NHC VII,1 25:7–15; Pearson 1996, 76–77.

which will be upon the earth after the flood. Demons were sent to them, and a deviation of the winds, and a burden of the angels, and a fear of the prophet, a condemnation of speech, that I may teach you, O Shem, from what blindness your race [γενεά] is saved.[21]

The syntax of the Coptic text of this passage is rather difficult, and it is hard to determine exactly which mythological figure is responsible for causing the flood,[22] but there is no doubt that the flood is aimed against the spiritual race of Shem. Thus, we meet here again the basic structure of the flood story that appears in a number of texts that belong to the Sethian branch of Gnosticism. Michel Roberge claimed that the Paraphrase of Shem drew its inspiration from Sethian as well as from Valentinian gnostic traditions,[23] so it seems reasonable to suggest that its author reworked earlier (Sethian?) gnostic traditions about the flood and accommodated them to his highly idiosyncratic version of gnostic myth.

As we have seen, the earliest evidence connecting the flood with the evil demiurge comes from the work of Irenaeus, who ascribes it to the Ophites. Later, such an approach to the flood figures most prominently in the texts associated with Sethian Gnosticism, and there may have existed some continuity between these two heterodox movements. Indeed, some ancient sources do speak about close relationship between the two. Thus, Theodoret of Cyr identifies Irenaeus's Ophites with "Sethians, whom some call Ophians or Ophites."[24] Similarity of the flood accounts in these two traditions lends plausibility to Tuomas Rasimus's suggestion that "the relationship between the Sethian and Ophite forms of Gnosticism can be explained in terms of a rewriting of Ophite materials by 'Seth-honoring' persons."[25]

Finally, it should be noted that outside the classical gnostic texts a similar notion of the flood to be an instrument of the evil forces is found occasionally in Manichaeism. Thus, Theodoret of Cyr (fifth century C.E.), while describing Mani and his teaching, relates that in the confrontation between God (Light) and Matter (Darkness) the latter had at her disposal such a weapon against the former as "water to bring upon a flood" (Greek ὕδωρ, ἵνα κατακλυσμὸν ἐπενέγκῃ).[26] The image of the "overwhelming waters" (Syriac ܡܝܐ ܓܢܒܐ), that belong to the realm of Darkness, also appears in the version of the Manichaean

---

21. NHC VII,1 28:5–22; Pearson 1996, 82–85.
22. Cf. Sevrin 1975, who notes that "ce passage est particulièrement confus" (77 n. 52).
23. See Roberge 2000, 114.
24. Theodoret, Haer. 1.14 (PG 83:364C): Οἱ δὲ Σηθιανοὶ, οὓς Ὀφιανοὺς ἢ Ὀφίτας τινὲς ὀνομάζουσιν.
25. Rasimus 2005, 262–63.
26. Haer. 1.26; PG 83:377C; trans. Pásztori-Kupán 2006, 205.

myth retold by Severus of Antioch (sixth century C.E.) in an anti-Manichaean homily.[27] According to John Reeves, this passage reflects the well-known gnostic idea about the flood as the work of the malevolent demiurge.[28]

While in most of the mythological systems considered above the flood is introduced as a negative event, understood to be an attempt to destroy the spiritual race by the evil forces, a number of gnostic traditions presented it in a positive light, following the logic of the biblical account. In almost all of these cases the flood is connected with the famous episode of the "sons of God" coming to the "daughters of men" (Gen 6:1–4). In the sequence of biblical narrative, this bizarre liaison is followed immediately by God's decision to cause the deluge. As a result, many ancient exegetes, including some gnostics, who understood the "sons of God" to be angels, considered this forbidden liaison to be the main reason behind the disaster. The flood was regarded as the divine punishment for the sin of transgression of the established boundaries that separate the different orders of being.

For example, we find this connection affirmed in a brief but unambiguous passage in the Valentinian Exposition (NHC XI,2), an anonymous composition from Nag Hammadi whose author thought the biblical "sons of God" to be angels:

> Therefore the angels lusted after the daughters of men and came down to flesh so that God would cause a flood [κατακλυσμός]. And he almost regretted that he had created the world [κόσμος].[29]

Moreover, the flood is understood as a positive event also in one version of Sethian Gnosticism. Thus, according to the Latin heresiographical treatise *Against All Heresies* it was caused by the "Mother," the "power above all powers," who initiated the spiritual race of gnostics by creating Seth, while her opponents, the archons, created Cain and Abel. Her main reason for bringing this calamity upon the earth was to destroy the evil offspring of angels and men that posed a threat to the spiritual race of Seth:

> For they say that there wicked minglings [*permixtiones*] of angels and men, and therefore that power, which as we said they call Mother [*matrem*], brought about the flood for punishment, so that that seed of mingling might be taken away and only this seed which was pure [*semen, quod esset purum*] might be kept intact.

---

27. *Homily* 123; Brière 1960, 166.
28. Reeves 1992, 182 n. 43.
29. NHC XI,2 38:34–39; Hedrick 1990, 138–39.

However, the "Mother" did not succeed in carrying out her plan completely, for she was tricked by the archons, who managed to smuggle some descendants of the evil seed into the ark:

> But they who created beings from the earlier seed secretly and surreptitiously, without the knowledge of that power which they call Mother, sent the seed of Ham with those eight souls in the ark, so that the seed of malice [*semen malitiae*] might not perish but be preserved with the rest and after the flood return to earth and grow, as an example to the others, and spread out and fill and occupy the whole earth.[30]

Again, the fall of the angels is understood to be the reason for the flood in the Concept of Our Great Power (NHC VI,4), a gnostic composition of unclear provenance and ideological affiliation. In the mythological system of this work, the figure of the Old Testament God, an analogue of the figure of demiurge in other gnostic systems, is not evil at all. Rather, he is empowered by the supreme authority of the "Great Power" to watch over the created world and to sustain it.[31] When the angels corrupt themselves with the daughters of men, it is not he but the water itself, personified as "the father of the flesh," that brings the end of the first aeon, "the aeon of the flesh," by the means of deluge:

> For when they (i.e., the angels) had been defiled and gone in unto the flesh, even the father of the flesh, the water, took his own vengeance. For when he (i.e., the OT God) had found Noah pious [εὐσεβής] and worthy,—the Father of the flesh having also subdued the angels—he (Noah), for his part, preached piety [εὐσέβεια] for 120 years and no one heeded him. But he (Noah) had made a wooden ark [κιβωτός], and the man whom he (i.e., the OT God) had found went into it, and (then) the Flood [κατακλυσμός] came. And thus Noah was preserved, and his sons. For if no ark had been made for humankind to enter, the water of the Flood would not have come; thus he (i.e., the OT God) purposed and resolved to rescue the gods and angels, and the <great> powers of all of them and their wantonness and (mis)behaviour, by removing them likewise from the world and maintaining them in lasting habitations [διαμονή]. And the way of the flesh perished; the work of the Power alone stood firm.[32]

---

30. Pseudo-Tertullian, *Adv. Omn. Haer.* 2.8–9; Kroymann 1906, 218; trans. Grant 2003, 89.

31. Cf. NHC VI,4 37:12–23.

32. NHC VI,4 38:17–39:15; trans. F. E. Williams 2001, 7. Cf. also 40:31–41:2 and 43:17–22 (ibid., 9, 13). For a detailed commentary on this story, see ibid., 75–84.

A noteworthy feature of this version of the flood is the prominent role played by the water as an independent agent, whose aversion to the sexual transgression initiates the cataclysm. According to Francis Williams, it could be explained by the author's indebtedness to the Encratite tradition, where particular stress was laid upon the sacrament of baptism and observance of sexual abstinence in its aftermath.[33]

An additional example of the connection between Gen 6:1–4 and the flood having been made explicit comes from the system of Justin the Gnostic (second century C.E.). He built a syncretistic mythological system that is distinct from what one might call the "classic gnostic myth." In it he combines God's decision to destroy the world in Gen 6:7 with the preceding resolution to shorten the span of human life to 120 years in Gen 6:3. Justin integrates these verses into his myth by putting them into the mouth of "Elohim," the second unbegotten principle of the universe, who turns to the "Good One," the first unbegotten principle, with the following request: "Lord, let me destroy the universe which I made; for my spirit is imprisoned among men and I wish to take it back."[34]

A positive evaluation of the flood is also found in the Hermetic tractate Asclepius (NHC VI,8). In distinction from the majority of gnostic systems, in this Hermetic work the demiurge is presented as a benevolent figure. Accordingly, the flood, while placed within the framework of the Stoic myth of recurring cosmic catastrophe and restoration, is understood by the author as an episode in the demiurge's struggle against the world's evil:

> And when these things had happened, O Asclepius, then the Lord, the Father and god from the only first (God), god the creator [δημιουργός], when he looked upon the things that happened, established his design, which is good, against the disorder. He took away error and cut off evil. Sometimes he submerged it in a great flood, at other times he burned it in a searing fire.[35]

Finally, the treatment of the flood in Mandaean tradition should be mentioned here. The relevant material appears in the Right Ginza, where we find a retelling of the biblical narrative, close enough to the original storyline:

---

33. F. E. Williams 2001, 76.
34. Hippolytus, *Haer.* 5.26.17–18: ὁ δὲ πατὴρ λέγει πρὸς τὸν ἀγαθόν· ἔασόν με, κύριε, καταστρέψαι τὸν κόσμον ὃν πεποίηκα· τὸ πνεῦμα γάρ μου ἐνδέδεται εἰς τοὺς ἀνθρώπους, καὶ θέλω αὐτὸ ἀπολαβεῖν; Marcovich 1986, 204; trans. Grant 1961, 97. On this aspect of Justin's mythological system, see Marcovich 1988, 105–6.
35. NHC VI,8 73:23–34; Parrott 1979, 431–33.

Then, when there were still eight thousand years left of the years [of Mars, and hence of the world], there came a call to Nu of the Ark, and spoke to him thus: "Build an ark." So Nu had carpenters come who could do the work properly, cut cedars of Harran and [the so-called] female cedars of Lebanon and built for three hundred years. He put the ark together so that it measured 300 cubits in length, 50 cubits in width, and 30 cubits in height. Then Nu took two of each species, male and female, and led them into the ark. Then for 42 days and 42 nights the higher waters from the heavens and the lower waters from the earth came, submerged the mountains and submerged the high places. Thus all the world was destroyed by water.

The ark floated on the water for eleven months. After eleven months there was calm and the ark went lower and stopped on Mount Qardun. Then Nu understood in his soul that there was calm in the world. Nu then sent out the crow and [thus] spoke to him: "Go, see if there is calm in the world." The crow went out and found a corpse; he ate of it and forgot what Nu had commanded him to do. So Nu, after that, sent out the dove and [thus] spoke to her: "Go, see if there is calm in the world, and where the crow is that I sent out before you."

Then the dove went out and found the crow that was standing over a corpse and eating it. She saw the olive tree, on Mount Qardun, whose leaves had sprung up out of the water. The dove gathered [a little branch] and brought [it] to Nu, so that he could know in his soul that calm had descended. Thus Nu cursed the crow and blessed the dove.

Then the age of the world was guarded by Šum the son of Nu, and by his wife Nhuraita, from whom the world was again reawakened.[36]

A noteworthy feature of this version of the flood is that its author makes use of the story about the raven feeding on a corpse. This tradition originated, most probably, in a Greek-speaking milieu, since its exegetical rationale is to provide an explanation for the raven's nonreturn to the ark after it was sent by Noah to examine whether the waters of the flood ceased. This element of the flood story is absent from the Hebrew text, but it does appear in the Septuagint.[37] The exegetical motif is not unique to the Right Ginza, since it is attested in a number of earlier Jewish and Christian sources.[38]

The sources that we have seen until now approach the story of the flood in what one might call a "historiosophic" way of reading of the biblical narrative, whether inverting it or not. In addition to these texts, representing the main-

---

36. Right Ginza 18; trans. Lupieri 2002, 201–2.
37. LXX of Gen 8:7: καὶ ἀπέστειλεν τὸν κόρακα τοῦ ἰδεῖν εἰ κεκόπακεν τὸ ὕδωρ καὶ ἐξελθὼν οὐχ ὑπέστρεψεν ἕως τοῦ ξηρανθῆναι τὸ ὕδωρ ἀπὸ τῆς γῆς.
38. Cf. Pirqe R. El. 23; Augustine, *Faust.* 12.20; Sulpitius Severus, *Chronicle* 1.3.

stream line in the gnostic approach to the biblical story of Noah, there are also several examples when some of its constitutive elements are interpreted in a figurative way—symbolic or allegorical.

Thus, we find occasionally cases of the ark being interpreted allegorically. For instance, the mythological system of Marcosians, one of the offshoots of Valentinian Gnosticism, resorts to such hermeneutics. According to the summary of their doctrine made by Irenaeus (*Haer.* 1.18.3-4), the numbers that appear in the biblical story are significant and have their correspondence in the spiritual world of Aeons. Consequently, the number of individuals that were preserved in the ark (Gen 7:13) points at the Ogdoad, that is, the eight Aeons emanated from the primeval Monad. Furthermore, the 30 cubits of the ark's height (Gen 6:15) serve as an allegory of the Triacontad, the thirty Aeons that emanated from the Ogdoad.

An additional example of Noah's ark being interpreted allegorically comes from Manichaean sources, where it was employed as a symbol for the community of believers, as in the Coptic Manichaean Psalms, where Noah's ark appears as a symbol of the Manichaean Church:

> Lo, the ship has put in for you, Noah is aboard, he steers.
> The ship is the commandment [ἐντολή], Noah is the Mind [νοῦς] of Light.
> Embark your merchandise, sail with the dew of the wind.[39]

> The] Commandment [ἐντολή] was knowledge, the Commandment was a Church. ...
> It was a tree, it was a ship, it [was] ...
> It was a tree in the desert, it was an ark [? κιβωτός] in the flood [κατακλυσμός].[40]

The author of these hymns seems to be playing upon the double meaning of the Greek word for "ark" (κιβωτός), from which Coptic ⲔⲒⲂⲰⲦⲞⲤ is derived, that was used in LXX to translate both the ark of Noah (Hebrew תבה) and the ark of the covenant (ארון).[41]

A similar intertextual juxtaposition of the two symbols—the ark of the covenant and the one of Noah—is found in the Gospel of Philip (NHC II,3). The author of this Valentinian composition makes use of typological exegesis, while putting the imagery of the ark and the flood into the eschatological perspective of final "restoration:"

> The bridal chamber [ⲠⲔⲞⲒⲦⲰⲚ], however, remains hidden. It is the holy

---

39. Trans. Allberry 1938, 157, lines 19–21.
40. Ibid., 1938, 177, lines 1–11.
41. See on this Helderman 1997, 137–47.

in the holy. The veil at first concealed how God controlled the creation, but when the veil is rent and the things inside are revealed, this house will be left desolate, or rather will be [destroyed]. And the whole (inferior) godhead will flee [from] here but not into the holies [of the] holies, for it will not be able to mix with the unmixed [light] and the [flawless] fullness, but will be under the wings of the cross [and under] its arms. This ark [ⲧⲉⲉⲓϭⲓⲃⲱⲧⲟⲥ] will be [their] salvation when the flood of water [ⲡⲕⲁⲧⲁⲕⲗⲩⲥⲙⲟⲥ ⲙ̄ⲙⲟⲟⲩ] surges over them.[42]

An intriguing detail of this latter-days scenario is that we are presented with two distinct groups of people: those of the priesthood, who shall enter the ultimate mystery of the "bridal chamber"; and, inferior to them, the followers of the lower divinity, who shall seek salvation "under the wings of the cross."[43] Unfortunately, the author of the Gospel of Philip prefers to remain elusive and does not provide his readers with a key that would allow us to decode his message and get a clearer understanding of the kind of groups to which he refers. However, it seems plausible to suggest that he projects into the eschatological perspective the difference between the two groups, namely, between the spiritual and psychic races of humankind, that appears in many gnostic interpretations of the flood. Albeit in a cryptic form, he describes two different scenarios of behavior in the eschatological future that shall separate between the gnostic Christians and the ordinary believers.

In addition to that, there is one example of what one might call a "critical" approach to our story. It is reported by Origen that Apelles (second century C.E.), a disciple of Marcion and one of the earliest exegetes of Genesis, criticized the biblical narrative of the flood following the lines of ancient rational exegesis. The main difficulty for him was the inadequate size of Noah's ark that obviously could not accommodate all the species of animals as well as necessary amount of provisions for them:

> In no way could it have been accomplished that in so short a time so many kinds of animals and their foods, which were to last for a whole year, should be taken abroad. For when two by two the unclean animals, that is, two male and two female of each—this is what the repeated word means—led into the ark, how could the space described be made big enough to take even four elephants alone? It is clear that the story is false; but if this is so, it is clear that this writing is not from God.[44]

---

42. NHC II,3 84:21–85:1; Layton 1989, 1:211. On this passage, see also Helderman 1997, 134–37.

43. See M. L. Turner 1996, 202–03.

44. *Hom. Gen.* 2.2; trans. Grant 2003, 81.

This approach to the biblical text, although rarely found, fits well the general inclination of gnostic exegetes to disregard the text's literal aspect in the pursuit of its historiosophic or spiritual meanings, which were more important to them. A good illustration of this tendency comes from the letter that Manichaean Secundinus sent to Augustine. There he reproaches his former co-religionist among other things for having "gone over to the Jewish tribes with their barbaric customs," meaning Augustine's joining the Catholic church, and asks him with a note of irony:

> Or had you set yourself to count the number of Amorites (Josh 10:5) or the pancarpus in Noah's ark [*an pancarpum in arca Noe conspicere disposueras*]? I know that you have always hated these things, I know that you have always loved great things, that quit the earth and seek the heavens, that mortify the body and give life to the soul. So who is it that has suddenly changed you?[45]

The most ridiculous activity that Augustine's Manichean correspondent could imagine for an exegete to be engaged in is to count the living things "of all sorts" (*pancarpus*) in the ark.[46] Although clearly exaggerated for the sake of rhetoric, this remarkable argument shows us how a typical gnostic reader of Scripture would express his aversion to its literal sense, considering its investigation to be the lot of barbarous Jews, blind to the higher dimensions of the inspired text.

Norea

As a final point of my overview, I shall consider briefly one of the masterpieces of gnostic mythopoesis: the exegetical tradition where Noah is opposed by his rebellious wife.

This mysterious feminine figure appears through a wide array of gnostic and nongnostic sources with considerable variation in the spelling of her name: Norea, Noraia, Noria, Nora, Nuraita, Nhuraita, Horaia, Orea, Oraia.[47] As it was noted by Bentley Layton, there are two basic strands in the development of gnostic traditions concerned with this figure.[48] In one group of texts she appears as the wife of Seth.[49] In another, which is of the direct relevance for us, she figures primarily as the wife of Noah.

---

45. Zycha 1891–92, 2:896–97; trans. Gardner and Lieu 2004, 138–39.
46. On the meaning of this rare Latin word, see Lewis and Short 1879, 1296.
47. For a comprehensive discussion of the subject, see Stichel 1979.
48. Layton 1974, 366–67.
49. Cf. Irenaeus, *Haer.* 1.30.9; Epiphanius, *Pan.* 3.39.5.2–3.

The *Panarion*, a heresiographical treatise written by Epiphanius of Salamis (fourth century C.E.), is one of the earliest sources in which we meet this personage. In the chapter dealing with "gnostics" (or "Borborites"), he retells disparagingly the story about how the wife of Noah, whose name was "Noria," was forbidden by her husband to enter the ark. Taking revenge on him, she set the ship on fire three consequent times, thus causing a significant delay in its construction:

> The gnostics, who are closely associated with this Nicolaus, ... propose some further names for nonsense to us, and forge books of nonsense. One they call "Noria" [Νωρίαν τινὰ βίβλον καλοῦντες], and mix falsehood with truth by their alteration of the Greeks' legendary recital and imagining from the meaning the Greek superstition really has. For they say that this Noria is Noah's wife. But their aim in calling her Noria is to make their own alteration, with foreign names, of what the Greek recited in Greek, and thus make an impression on their dupes so that they will translate Pyrrha's name too, and name her Noria. Now, since "nura" [νοῦρα] means "fire" [πῦρ] in Aramaic, not ancient Hebrew—the ancient Hebrew for "fire" is "'esh" [ἠσάθ]—it follows that they are making an ignorant, unskilled use of this name. Noah's wife was neither the Greeks' Pyrrha nor the gnostics' mythical Noria, but Barthenos. (And for that matter, the Greeks say that the wife of Deucalion was named Pyrrha.)
>
> Then, once again presenting us with mime like Philiston's, they suggest the reason why Noria was not allowed to join Noah in the ark, though she would often have liked to. The archon who made the world, they say, wanted to destroy her in the flood with all the rest. But they say that she laid siege to the ark and burned it, a first and a second time, and a third. And this is why Noah's own ark took many years to build—it was burned often by Noria.
>
> For Noah was obedient to the archon, they say, but Noria revealed the powers on high and Barbelo, the scion of powers—the opposite of the archon, as the other powers are. And she intimated that what has been taken from the Mother on high by the archons who made the world, and the others with him—gods, demons and angels—must be gathered from the power in bodies, through the male and female emissions.[50]

As we have already seen in the writings associated with Sethian Gnosticism, the gnostic source used by Epiphanius understood the flood to be directed against the spiritual race whose chief representative here is Norea. Noah is associated with the evil demiurge as, for example, in the Apocalypse of Adam.

Noteworthy is Epiphanius's mention of the gnostic book named after Norea, which cannot be discarded as a fruit of his fantasy. In fact, we have

---

50. *Pan.* 2.26.1.3–9; Holl 1915, 275–76; trans. F. E. Williams 1994, 82–83.

firm evidence that books ascribed to this figure did exist and circulate among gnostics. Thus, in the anonymous gnostic treatise On the Origins of the World (NHC II,5) from Nag Hammadi, it is stated that one can find the names of the seven female powers of chaos "in the first Book of Noraia" (ϨⲚ ⲦϢⲞⲢⲠ ⲚⲂⲒⲂⲖⲞⲤ ⲚⲚⲰⲢⲀⲒⲀⲤ).[51] Norea appears also as the main protagonist in a short gnostic prose hymn from Nag Hammadi known as the Thought of Norea (NHC IX,2).[52] This composition presents the reader with an expanded form of Norea's plea to the Father of All for deliverance from the power of the archons that is found also in the Hypostasis of the Archons, to which this work seems to be closely related.[53] However, no connection with Noah or the flood seems to be implied by the author of the Thought.

From the Hypostasis of the Archons, a Sethian writing from Nag Hammadi already discussed briefly above, one can see that Epiphanius did not make up the story about Norea. Rather, he used a genuine gnostic story about Noah and his unruly wife as his source. The author of the Hypostasis introduces Norea as the daughter of Eve, a virgin whose mission in the world is to assist spiritual humanity:

> Again Eve became pregnant, and she bore [Norea]. And she said. "He has begotten on [me a] virgin as an assistance [ⲚⲞⲨⲠⲀⲢⲐⲈⲚⲞⲤ ⲚⲂⲞⲎⲐⲈⲒⲀ] [for] many generation of mankind." She is the virgin whom the forces did not defile.[54]

The assisting function of Norea further comes to the fore in the account of Noah and the flood. Here she tries to board the ark built by Noah, but he refuses to let her in. As a result, Norea burns the ship down. After that, the evil archons intervene and try to seduce her, but she escapes them by turning for help to the highest God, serving thus as a paradigm for how a gnostic should face demonic attacks:

---

51. NHC II,5 102:10–11 (§18); Layton 1989, 2:38–39. A couple of lines further on, the author again refers to this composition, although in a slightly different form, as "the first Account of Oraia" (ϨⲚ ⲠϢⲞⲢⲠ ⲚⲖⲞⲄⲞⲤ ⲚⲰⲢⲀⲒⲀⲤ; 102:24–25 [§20]). The editor of NHC II,5 holds both variants "Noraia" and "Oraia" as equally possible.

52. NHC IX,2; for the Coptic text with an English translation, see Pearson 1981, 87–99. The title of this composition is modern. It was given to it by its editor Birger Pearson in accordance with the phrase "the thought of Norea" (ⲦⲚⲞⲎⲤⲒⲤ ⲚⲚⲞⲢⲈⲀ) that occurs at the end of the tractate (29:3; ibid, 98–99).

53. The exact nature of relationship between these two texts is unclear. Pearson (1981, 89–90) suggests a possibility of the Thought of Norea being dependent upon of the sources of the Hypostasis of the Archons.

54. NHC II,4 91:34–92:3; Layton 1989, 1:246–47.

Then Orea [ⲰⲢⲈⲀ] came to him wanting to board the ark. And when he would not let her, she blew upon the ark and caused it to be consumed by fire. Again he made the ark, for a second time.

The rulers went to meet her intending to lead her astray. Their supreme chief said to her, "Your mother Eve came to us." But Norea [ⲚⲰⲢⲈⲀ] turned to them and said to them, "It is you who are the rulers of the darkness; you are accursed. And you did not know my mother; instead it was your female counterpart that you knew. For I am not your descendant; rather it is from the world above that I am come."

The arrogant ruler turned, with all his might, [and] his countenance came to be like (a) black ...; he said to her presumptuously, "You must render service to us, [as did] also your mother Eve; for I have been given...."

But Norea turned, with the might of ...; and in a loud voice [she] cried out [up to] the holy one, the God of entirety, "Rescue me from the rulers of unrighteousness and save me from their clutches—forthwith!" The <great> angel came down from the heavens and said to her, "Why are you crying up to God? Why do you act so boldly towards the holy spirit?" Norea said, "Who are you?" The rulers of unrighteousness had withdrawn from her. He said, "It is I who am Eleleth, sagacity, the great angel, who stands in the presence of the holy spirit. I have been sent to speak with you and save you from the grasp of the lawless. And I shall teach you about your root.[55]

Norea's interference with Noah's ark-building emphasizes that true salvation comes through reception of the spiritual "help," not through the works of the Jewish God "Sabaoth," who in the mythological scheme of the Hypostasis of the Archons occupies position halfway between evil and good.[56]

Although there are significant differences between the two versions of Norea's story, the one narrated by Epiphanius and the one found in the Hypostasis of the Archons, their basic plot is bascially the same. In both of them Norea appears as an enemy of the archons, and in both her husband's refusal to let her board the ark results in burning the ship.[57] In order to make sense of

---

55. NHC II,4 92:14–93:14; Layton 1989, 1:248–51.

56. See Layton 1976, 62, 99.

57. On the conflict between Norea and the archons in the Hypostasis of the Archons, see also McGuire 1988, who undertakes literary analysis of the text, reading it through the lenses of Ricouerian hermeneutics, and argues that this confrontation reflects tension "between two modes of power, each of which has a distinctly sexual and social force" (241). According to McGuire, the Hypostasis "challenges its readers to identify with the 'children of Norea,' to inherit the promise, and to resist and rename those powers that would claim falsely to rule in their world" (258). In a similar vein, Karen L. King claims, while analyzing the story from the standpoint of feminist hermeneutics, that it "shows that already in antiquity the Genesis narrative could be read as a story about powerful female spirituality, not as proof of women's natural inferiority" (1994, 66).

the discrepancies as well as similarities between these two traditions, it seems reasonable to suggest that both Epiphanius's gnostics and the author of the Hypostasis borrowed the story about Norea from a common source, while adapting it to their own needs. Accordingly, one may safely deduce from this that already by the third century C.E. there existed a gnostic exegetical tradition about Noah's wife named Norea, who rebelled against her husband and burned down the ark.

In addition to these two main sources on Norea as Noah's wife, a similar tradition is attested in the Mandaean Right Ginza, where she bears the name "Nuraita":

> When twenty-five ages (generations) pass, the world will be destroyed by water. Mankind will be separated from their bodies through a separation caused by water. For it has been written down for that age that the bodies have to die by water and the souls ascend to the light, except for Nu (Noah), the man, and Nuraita, his wife, and Šum (Shem), Iam (?) and Iapit (Japheth), the sons of Nu, who will be saved from death by water. From them the world again has to be reawakened.[58]

Like the Mandaean flood account quoted above, this passage seems to be devoid of any significant features typical of subversive rewriting of the canonical story of the flood by the majority of gnostic exegetes of Genesis.

The unusual character of Norea has drawn considerable scholarly attention, and much ink has been spilled over the possible etymology of her name.[59] The earliest attempt to interpret her name was made by Epiphanius himself, who tried to play the linguistic card in order to expose his rivals as ignoramuses. He related the name to the Aramaic "fire" (נורא), while suggesting that gnostics derived it from the figure of Deucalion's wife Pyrrha (Greek Πύρρα), whose personal name in Greek resembles the word for "fire" (πῦρ). Reasonable enough, this interpretation did not enjoy much popularity among modern scholars, so that further attempts to clarify the name were made. Thus, there are some scholars who argued in favor of another Semitic etymology for the name "Norea," deriving it from the Hebrew word for "maiden" (נערה).[60] Some understood it to be a form of the Egyptian personal name "Orea" and regarded it as connected with the uraeus, the fire-breathing snake of Egyptian mythology.[61]

---

58. Right Ginza 2.1.121; trans. Lupieri 2002, 200.

59. Among the most important contributions on Norea, one should mention Gilhus 1985, 77–95; Pearson 1977; 1988a; Stichel 1979, 54–88; Stroumsa 1984, 53–61.

60. See Bousset 1907, 14. For more references to scholars who accept this etymology, see Pearson 1988a, 266 n. 5.

61. See Bullard 1970, 95–98.

An ingenious solution of the riddle of Norea's name and origins has been suggested by Birger Pearson. He argued that it goes ultimately back to the name of the biblical Na'amah (Hebrew נעמה "pleasing, lovely"), the sister of Tubal-cain (Gen 4:22), whose name in the Greek milieu was at one point rendered by a Greek equivalent of her name as "Horaia" (Greek Ὡραία "beautiful, pleasing"), and from this name the mixed form "Norea" (Νωρία) was subsequently derived.[62] According to Pearson, in the ancient Jewish exegesis Na'amah functioned as the main female protagonist in the story about seduction of the "sons of God" by the "daughters of men."[63] Subsequently, this originally Jewish exegetical tradition was picked up by gnostics and reinterpreted "in a typically gnostic hermeneutical inversion."[64]

Persuasive as it may sound, Pearson's theory of Norea's origins can hardly be accepted without taking into consideration some aspects of the problem that he ignored. For example, the way in which Pearson discards the Aramaic etymology of Norea's name suggested by Epiphanius without any serious reason is unconvincing.[65] As a matter of fact, this possibility should be given serious weight in any future attempt to understand this figure.

Thus, so far no good argument has been proposed as to why the etymology of Norea's name based on Aramaic "fire" (נורא) should be discarded as secondary. This option seems even more attractive when one takes into consideration the note made by Ian Gilhus that "when Norea burns the ark, she performs a function which lies inherent in her name."[66] In view of that, one cannot resolve the problem of Norea's name while disconnecting it from the role she plays in the story of her conflict with Noah. The situation is complicated further by the fact that alongside this etymology there is a possibility of another closely related explanation of Norea's name, which is based on the Aramaic word for "light" (נוהרא). There is a solid linguistic basis for this etymology, since pronunciation of this word was very close to the name of Norea as, for example, it could be seen from Jewish Palestinian Aramaic, where it appears as nôhrâ (נוהרה).[67] Furthermore, it is strengthened by the intimate

---

62. See Pearson 1977, 146–50.
63. Ibid., 147–49. His thesis has been strengthened by Stroumsa 1984, 56–57, who introduced new evidence into the discussion, namely, the Midrash of Shemhazai and Azael. Recently, Manolis Papoutsakis has argued that reaction against the negative description of Na'amah as a seductress of the "sons of God" can be found in Jewish exegetical tradition already during the Second Temple period, namely, in 1 Enoch. See Papoutsakis 2004, 35–36.
64. Pearson 1988a, 266.
65. Pearson 1977, 146.
66. Gilhus 1985, 89.
67. See Sokoloff 1992, 342.

connection forged by the author of the Hypostasis of the Archons between the notion of "light" and the narrative function of Norea in this composition.[68] Finally, this etymology seems to be even more plausible in light of the fact that one finds that several texts from Nag Hammadi contain Aramaic wordplays, including the Hypostasis.[69] I propose that the story of Norea is based upon a rather sophisticated wordplay that involves both Aramaic "light" and "fire," when the same figure can both pour spiritual light upon the faithful gnostics and show her fiery and wrathful side to the supporters of the demiurge. In addition to that, the existence of the two basic variants of spelling for Noah's wife name (Norea and Orea), which presents a challenge for scholars looking for its ultimate etymology, could be a witness to a Hebrew wordplay taking place besides the Aramaic one.[70]

In addition to these etymological considerations, one must take into account, while discussing the genesis of the image of Norea in Gnosticism, that there existed a number of similar feminine personages in various gnostic systems whose features or functions might have influenced the author of the Hypostasis or Epiphanius's gnostics.

These include the luminous feminine figure from the Apocryphon of John who informs Noah about the demiurge's plan to cause the flood.[71] Another possibility is the second person in the basic gnostic triad of Father, Mother, and Son. Often she bears the name of "Sophia," that is, Wisdom, but sometimes she is named differently, as in the Thought of Norea, where she is referred to as "Ennoia of the Light."[72]

Another possible "relative" of Norea is the "Virgin of Light" (ⲦⲠⲀⲢⲐⲈⲚⲞⲤ ⲘⲠⲞⲨⲀⲒⲚⲈ), one of the central feminine images in Manichaean mythology.[73] This figure comes closest to the image of Norea in the Acts of Archelaus (fourth

---

68. Cf. NHC II,4 96:17–28; see on this Gilhus 1985, 89–91.

69. Cf. the way its author plays upon the name of Eve in 89:17–32, making allusions to "serpent" (Aramaic חויא) and to the verb "to instruct" (Aramaic חוא); see on this Pearson 1990b, 41–46. Among other Aramaisms in this work, one should mention such personal names of demonic powers as "Samael," "Saklas" (on these, see Bullard 1970, 52–53, 108–9), and "Yaldabaoth" himself (see Black 1983).

70. See Gilhus 1985, 89, who speaks about a possible Hebrew etymology for the name Orea, the one based on the Hebrew word for "light" (אור).

71. She has slightly different names in the various versions of this work: "the greatness of Providence, which is the Reflection of the light" (ⲦⲘⲚⲦⲚⲞϬ ⲘⲠⲢⲞⲚⲞⲒⲀ ⲈⲦⲈ ⲦⲈⲠⲈⲒⲚⲞⲒⲀ ⲘⲠⲞⲨⲞⲒⲚ), BG 72,17–19; "the greatness of the light of Providence" (ⲦⲘⲚⲦⲚⲞϬ ⲘⲠⲞⲨⲞⲈⲒⲚ ⲚⲦⲈ ⲦⲠⲢⲞⲚⲞⲒⲀ), NHC 29, 1–2; trans. Waldstein and Wisse 1995, 162–63.

72. NHC IX,2 27:11–12; Pearson 1981, 94–95.

73. See Pearson 1977, 145–46; 1988a, 271. For more on this figure, see van Lindt 1992, 170–75; M. Vermes 2001, 51 n. 58.

century C.E.), where she is described as "a beautiful [ὡραία] and well-dressed virgin, of great elegance," who opposes the evil archons.[74] One should not forget also that in Syriac, the primary language of Mani's teaching as well as of the earliest Manichaean mission, she was known as ܒܬܘܠܬ ܢܘܗܪܐ.[75] Furthermore, it is noteworthy that in some texts the Virgin of Light is associated with the moon, which in Manichaean myth is one of the two "Ships of Light" (the other "Ship of Light" being the sun).[76] This image, in its turn, seems to be at least in one case associated with Noah, who in one Coptic Manichaean psalm is presented as an impersonation of the "Mind of Light" (ⲠⲚⲞⲨⲤ ⲚⲞⲨⲀⲒⲚⲈ), a member of the mythological triad including also Jesus the Splendor and the Virgin of Light:

> Lo, the ship has put in for you, Noah is aboard, he steers.
> The ship is the commandment [ἐντολή], Noah is the Mind [νοῦς] of Light.
> Embark your merchandise, sail with the dew of the wind.[77]

For the time being, it appears that the problem of the origins of Norea's name cannot be resolved unambiguously in favor of one of the already suggested hypotheses. The main reason is the fragmentary character of our evidence and impossibility at the present state of research of stratifying the vast array of traditions under consideration with satisfactory precision. More fruitful seems to be an approach that would not try to reduce the large number of traditions associated with Norea to a single line of development but take as a starting point a possibility of their parallel growth with different centers of crystallization.

I shall conclude this brief outline of gnostic traditions about Norea by taking a short glimpse at its *Nachleben*.

---

74. Hegemonius, *Acta Archelai* 9.1: *Virgo quaedam decora et exornata, elegans valde* (Beeson 1906, 13; trans. M. Vermes 2001, 51). In the Greek fragment of the Acts quoted by Epiphanius she is called παρθένος τις ὡραία κεκοσμημένη (*Pan.* 66.27.1; Holl 1931, 60).

75. Ephrem, *Discourses to Hypatius* 3; ed. Mitchell 1912–21, 1:67, line 19.

76. Cf. Kephalaia 3 (24:16–20); 29 (82:32–83:1).

77. Trans. Allberry 1938, 157, lines 19–21. On the "Mind of Light," see van Lindt 1992, 154–69. Association of this figure of Manichaean mythology with Noah is unique to this source. Van Lindt suggests that the author of the hymn relied upon an earlier gnostic tradition in this case (168; see also 120 for additional remarks on this particular passage). It should be also taken into consideration that "The Psalms of the Wanderers" (ψαλμοὶ Σαρακωτῶν), where this notion appears, seems to be one of the oldest parts of the Coptic Manichaean collection of hymns and might reflect an earlier Syriac stratum in the development of Manichaean tradition.

A fascinating case of how the figure of Norea moved full circle back into the Jewish milieu is found in a medieval Jewish magical composition from the Cairo Genizah.[78] In this text, an Aramaic spell against impotence, "Niriyah, Noah's bride" (נִירִיה כלת נח), appears as a malevolent figure who invented magic spells and, thus, brought sin and corruption into the world and against whom God's help is invoked (col. 1c, lines 35–37). Reimund Leicht, who has compared this text with the story about Norea in the Hypostasis of the Archons, comes to the conclusion that it should be regarded as a tendentious and polemically aimed inversion of the gnostic myth that, in an ironic way, applies to the latter its own subversive method of reading biblical stories.[79]

Finally, Joseph Dan has suggested, developing Gershom Scholem's ideas, that the figure of the "daughter of light" in Sefer ha-Bahir, an early medieval Jewish mystical composition, might possibly be related to Norea.[80] There seem to be also some repercussions of the figure of Norea in Islamic traditions about antediluvian heroes.[81] Yet, all this diverse material is in need of further investigation in order to clarify the exact nature of relationship between these traditions and the extraordinary feminine gnostic figure from late antiquity.

---

78. T.-S. K 1.162. First published, with a German translation, by Schäfer and Shaked 1999, nos. 61, 65–88. The relevant section has been reproduced, with an English translation and thorough discussion, by Leicht 2000.

79. Leicht 2000, 137–40.

80. See Dan 1987, 138–39, where he reflects upon Scholem's ideas expressed in Scholem 1987, 94–96.

81. See Wasserstrom 1994, 97–99.

Some Jewish Noah Traditions in Syriac Christian Sources

Daniel A. Machiela

1. Introduction

Extrabiblical traditions about Noah often took on their own life within the sundry streams of ancient biblical interpretation, as the essays in this volume amply demonstrate. This life, however, was commonly breathed into the raw material of earlier traditions, transmitted orally or through written media. The Syriac-speaking Christian community undoubtedly produced some of the most creative and prolific exegetes of late antiquity—a *collegium* whose interpretative vibrancy is increasingly brought to light with the ongoing publication of previously inaccessible manuscripts. A striking aspect of ancient Syriac exegesis is the great extent to which it interacts with, and is indebted to, earlier and contemporaneous Jewish biblical interpretation, as Sebastian Brock and others have shown.[1] The goal of the present essay is to shed further light on this relationship.

2. Survey of Motifs

The format of this study does not allow for a comprehensive treatment of Syriac portrayals of Noah, and it should be stated at the outset that sources postdating the fifth to seventh centuries C.E. often largely repeat those preceding them.[2] The aim is rather to focus on a small sample of Noah motifs, as presented in Syriac sources, that seem to be influenced in some manner by

---

1. See the seminal survey of Brock 1979. Other pertinent studies include those of Hidal 1974 and Kronholm 1978. Despite these contributions, this area remains in need of extensive study.

2. There are, of course, exceptions to any rule. One might note in particular the magisterial *Chronicle* of Michael the Syrian (thirteenth century), or the anomalous *Chronicle to the Year of Christ* 1234, both of which are discussed more fully below.

Jewish exegesis. In the following pages I will present and discuss four such cases.

2.1. Abstinence on the Ark

One extrabiblical component of Syriac portrayals of Noah is his sexual abstinence (along with his family and the animals) before and during his time aboard the ark. Our first Syriac attestation of this motif is in Aphrahat (fourth century c.e.), who took every opportunity to demonstrate the ܬܡܝܡܘܬܐ (lit. "innocence" or "perfection") of Noah, which included sexual continence.[3] One of Aphrahat's clearest statements on the matter occurs in his *Demonstration* 13:5–6 on the Sabbath:

> Noah was five hundred years old when God spoke with him and said, "I have seen that you are righteous and innocent [ܬܡܝܡ] before me in this generation" (Gen 6:9). And insofar as his innocence is made manifest for us, it was in this matter; that when he saw that the generation of Seth mingled with the household of Cain, which was cursed, he resolved that he would not take a wife and would not father children, lest they mingle with the household of Cain, the cursed seed, and render themselves accursed.[4]

Shortly after this, the Persian sage continues:

> And when [Noah's] three sons had been born he began to make the ark. He kept close watch over his sons, that they might not take wives until the time when they entered into the ark, lest they produce children who would pervert their way and because their sinful conduct may not be forgiven in light of the future retribution to take place.[5]

Aphrahat clearly believed that one of Noah's most noble and righteous characteristics was his eschewal of marriage and intercourse in view of the wicked and calamitous times in which he lived. The best thing he could do was to take care not to add to this lethal situation through procreation. While Aphrahat is the first Syrian known to explicitly discuss Noah's sexual abstinence, the trait

---

3. See his *Demonstrations* 3, 13, and 18 in Parisot 1894. Cf. Koltun-Fromm 1997, 57–71. For a more detailed treatment of celibacy and marriage in the Syriac tradition, and the tracing of this motif to Jewish sources in the Adam and Eve narrative, see Anderson 1989.
4. Parisot 1894, 550.
5. Ibid., 555.

may be implied by earlier Eastern fathers such as Theophilus of Antioch (late second century C.E.).[6]

Ephrem the Syrian, a younger contemporary of Aphrahat (ca. 306–373 C.E.), was also intensely interested in this aspect of Noah and used the word ܩܕܝܫܘܬܐ (lit. "holiness") as a technical term to speak of Noah's sexual abstinence on the ark.[7] In his *Commentary on Genesis* 6.12, Ephrem wrote:

> And God said to Noah, "Go out, you and your wife, your sons and your sons' wives" (Gen 8:16). Those whom God had caused to come in singly, to observe sexual abstinence [ܩܕܝܫܘܬܐ] on the ark, he caused to leave in couples, in order to multiply and be fruitful in creation. He also said concerning the animals which observed sexual abstinence [ܩܕܝܫܘܬܐ] in the ark, "Take out with you every animal that was with you … and let them give birth on the earth and be fruitful and multiply on it" (Gen 8:17–18).

And again in his first *Nisibene Hymn* we read:

> Noah overcame the waves of lust, which in his generation had drowned the sons of Seth. Because his flesh revolted against the daughters of Cain, his chariot rode on the surface of the waves. Because women defiled him not, he coupled the beasts, whereof in the ark he joined together all pairs in the yoke of wedlock.

Both Aphrahat and Ephrem highly prized and encouraged the ideal of celibacy in their own religious and social milieu, and this undoubtedly fueled their enthusiasm to confer the trait upon Noah. The motif is also found in the *Cave of Treasures* (ca. third to sixth centuries. C.E.), which, although attributed to Ephrem, seems to have taken its final shape at a later period.[8]

Syrian Christians, however, were not the first to suggest Noah's abstinence. Already in the early first century C.E. Philo of Alexandria, in his *Q.G.* 2.49, noted that Noah and his family practiced abstinence on the ark.

> When they [Noah and his family] went in [to the ark] the sons are mentioned together with their father and the daughters-in-law together with their mother-in-law (Gen 7:7). But when they went out it was as married

---

6. See his *Ad Autolyctum* 3.19.

7. See especially the following quotes from his *Commentary on Genesis* 6.12 and his *Nisibene Hymn* 1.4. Cf. Brock 1992, 133–34; Anderson 1989, 122. For Ephrem's commentary, see Mathews and Amar 1994. A translation of the *Nisibine Hymns* may be found in McVey 1989.

8. For the text and an English translation, see Budge 1927, 98–99. See also Ri 1987. A version of the Syriac (and Arabic) text may be found in the early edition of Bezold 1888.

couples, the father together with his wife and then several sons, each with his wife (Gen 8:18). For he [probably Moses] wishes through deeds rather than words to teach his disciples what is right for them to do. Accordingly, he said nothing by way of vocal explanation to the effect that those who went in should abstain from intercourse with their wives, and that when they went out they should sow seed in accordance with nature. This (he indicated) by the order (of words), and not by exclaiming and crying aloud, "After so great a destruction of all those who were on the earth, do not indulge in luxury, for this is neither fitting nor lawful. It is enough for you to receive the honor of life. But to go to bed with your wives is the part of those seeking and desiring sensual satisfaction." For these it was fitting to sympathize with wretched humanity, as being kin to it. And at the same time they were watching for something unseen that might be impending, lest evil might overtake them at some time. But in addition to this it would have been inept for them now, while the living were perishing, to beget those who were not (yet) in existence, and to be snared and flooded at an unreasonable hour with sensual pleasure. But after (the flood) had ceased and come to an end, and they had been saved from evil, he again instructed them through the order (of their leaving the ark) to hasten to procreate.[9]

Here Philo suggested at least two reasons for Noah and his family refraining from intercourse on the ark: (1) it simply would not be acceptable ("neither fitting nor lawful") to partake of enjoyment in such close proximity to the catastrophic human death and destruction accompanying the flood;[10] and (2) the inhabitants of the ark were afraid that some other terrible event may occur and that "evil might overtake them."[11] A third reason is given—that it would be unseemly to father children while people are dying outside—but this is simply another way of restating the first reason. These explanations (especially the second) seem to posit that divine retribution would have resulted from sexual activity on the ark, thereby destroying utterly what little hope was left for humanity.

A variety of rabbinic sources follow the same interpretation as Philo, although many postdate the comments of Ephrem. Among the earliest examples is Gen. Rab. 34:7 (ca. early fifth century C.E.):[12]

---

9. My text is a slightly updated form of R. Marcus's (1961, 129–30) translation from the Armenian.

10. The absurdity of such conduct has been made poignantly in recent times by Najib Mahfouz (1991) in his short story "At the Bus Stop."

11. A similar concern is expressed in Josephus, *Ant.* 1.3.7; Gen. Rab. 34:6; and Midrash Hagadol 1.165.

12. See also b. Sanh. 108b; y. Ta'anit 1.64d; Tanḥuma (Buber) 1.42–43; Tanḥuma Noah

"You and your wife, etc." (Gen 8:16). Rav Yehudah son of Simon and Rav Hanan in the name of Rav Shm'uel son of Rav Yizhak (say), "As soon as Noah entered the ark he kept himself from being fruitful and multiplying. Thus it is written 'Enter the ark, you and your sons' (Gen 6:18) by yourself, 'and your wife and sons' wives' by themselves. However, when he left he allowed himself, since it is written 'Go out from the ark, you and your wife, and so forth.'"

Other accounts added several exceptions to the noble continence of the majority of humans and animals, as in Midrash Tanḥuma: "Ham, the progenitor of the Canaanites, was one of the three beings who indulged in intercourse while on the ark. Those who did so were Ham, the dog, and the raven."[13] In these sources, as in Philo, we find a parallel to Ephrem's assumption that sexual abstention was observed while on the ark, but what of Aphrahat's additional notion of similar conduct *before* the flood? This, too, is reflected in some (albeit fewer) Jewish sources, such as Tanḥuma and Sefer Hayashar.[14]

While it is likely that Syrian Christian exegetes were influenced by their Jewish counterparts, some parts of their explanations of Noah's sexual continence are characteristically Syrian. For example, Aphrahat's reasoning is based on the standard Syriac interpretation of Gen 6:1–2, in which the "sons of God" were understood to be the Sethites, while the "daughters of men" represented the descendants of Cain.[15]

2.2. Noah's Drunken Dream

In Gen 9:20–23 we read of Noah planting a vineyard, getting drunk on the wine that it had produced, then lying exposed in his tent. This sets the scene for Ham's transgression of entering and seeing his father's nakedness, after which Noah awakes, somehow knows what Ham had done, and proceeds to curse Ham's son Canaan (rather than Ham himself). The idiosyncrasies of this passage have provided fertile exegetical soil for centuries of commentators, Jewish and Christian alike. One question addressed intermittently was *how* Noah could have known what happened to him while he was sleeping. A rare

---

11–12; Pirqe R. El. 23; Midrash Hagadol 1.165. Cf. Ginzberg 1909–38, 1:166; 5:188 n. 54. On dating, see Strack and Stemberger 1992, 279.

13. See the edition of Berman 1996, 65. For more on this topic, see pp. 208–9 in Aryeh Amihay, "Noah in Rabbinic Literature," in this volume.

14. Tanḥuma (Buber) 1.25–26 and Yashar Noah, 14a–14b. Cf. Ginzberg 1909–38, 1:159; 5:179 n. 30. The translation is my own.

15. The same interpretation surfaces in Jewish sources at a later time (e.g., Pirqe de Rabbi Eliezer and The Chronicle of Jerahmeel). Cf. Ginzberg 1909–38, 5:172 n. 14. For the same approach in Byzantine Christian works, see Adler 1989, 113–16, 137–38, 209–210.

answer to this question is shared by a handful of Jewish and Syriac sources: that Noah was informed of present and future events by way of a dream while asleep. The Palestinian Targum Pseudo-Jonathan to Gen 9:24 reads: ואיתער נח מן חמריה וידע באשתעות חלמא ית דעבד ליה חם בריה ("And Noah awoke from his wine, and he knew *through the narration of a dream* what his son Ham had done to him").[16] The same explanation appears to lie behind the Genesis Apocryphon from Qumran Cave 1, a very early interpretation of Genesis (ca. second century B.C.E.).[17] In columns 13–15 of the scroll, Noah is the recipient of an extensive symbolic dream vision in which he learns (among other things) of the future conduct of his descendants (thereby also addressing why he would curse Canaan and not Ham).[18] Despite the scroll's fragmentary state, the narrative locus of this dream seems quite clearly to be Noah's wine-induced slumber.

An explanation very similar to that in Pseudo-Jonathan is found in the Syriac commentary tradition. An anonymous *Commentary on Genesis-Exodus 9:32* states: ܘܢܘܚ ܝܕܥ ܟܠ ܡܕܡ ܕܥܒܕ ܠܗ ܒܪܗ ܙܥܘܪܐ ܒܝܕ ܓܠܝܢܐ ܐܠܗܝܐ ܕܗܘܐ ܠܗ ܒܚܙܘܐ ("And Noah knew all that his young(est) son did to him by way of a divine vision that [came] to him as a dream").[19] Isho'dad of Merv's ninth-century C.E. *Commentary on the Old Testament*, which appears to have depended heavily on the *Commentary on Genesis-Exodus 9:32*, contains the same statement.[20] The rarity of this particular tradition makes it very likely that the Syrians received knowledge of it either from Jewish written sources or oral transmission.[21]

2.3. Noah as Founder of a City

The Genesis Apocryphon and the book of Jubilees (ca. 170–150 B.C.E.)[22] preserve an unusual tradition according to which Noah and his sons built cities

---

16. See Clarke 1984, 10.

17. The date of this scroll has been debated for some time. For a summary of the issues and argument for the dating mentioned above, see my Ph.D. dissertation (Machiela 2007, 301–13), completed under James C. VanderKam, now published as Machiela 2009.

18. For more on the dream and its setting, see Machiela 2007, 193–221.

19. Van Rompay 1986, 63 [Syriac], 81 [trans.].

20. Vosté and van den Eynde 1950–55, 128 [Syriac], 138 [trans.].

21. One possibility of how this may have occurred was proposed recently by Boyarin 2004, 26. He suggests that there may have been what he terms "chained communion or communication" between various Jewish and Christian groups in antiquity, whereby specially situated persons within one group may act as a link to others with which the group would not normally associate itself.

22. See VanderKam 1989, 2:v–vi.

(or a single city) at the foot of Mount Lubar after leaving the ark.[23] Like so many of the traditions shared by these two texts, the foundation stories bear a general resemblance to each other but are not the same. In Jub. 7:13–17 we discover that three cities are built following Noah's planting of his vineyard and Ham's shameful viewing of his drunken father, one city by each of Noah's sons. It is Ham who initiates the process, having departed from his father in protest of his son Canaan being cursed. Noah and Shem unsurprisingly dwell together. The names of the cities are also given: Ham founds Neelatamauk, Japheth Adataneses, and Shem Sedeqatelebab, each (wisely) naming the town after his wife.[24] Finally, in Jub. 7:35 Noah again enjoins his sons, "You will now go and build yourselves cities," attesting to the importance of this motif in Jubilees and perhaps pointing forward to the Tower of Babel episode. In the Genesis Apocryphon the description is much shorter, with Noah stating simply, "we built a ci[ty] for the devastation on the earth was great."[25] Some significant discrepancies with Jubilees are found in the Apocryphon's portrayal of Noah and his sons building the city *together* and the placement of the building project *before* Noah planted his vineyard, rather than as a result of it. A third witness to this tradition among the Dead Sea Scrolls is 4Q244 frag. 8, although its text is very fragmentary.

The foundation of a city following the flood is also ascribed to Noah and his sons in a handful of Syriac sources. In the *Cave of Treasures*, for example, we read that Noah and his sons "built a city and called the name thereof Themânôn [lit. 'Eight'], after the name of the eight souls who had gone forth from the Ark."[26] A longer Greek recension of the later (and originally Syriac) Apocalypse of Pseudo-Methodius quotes this tradition.[27] Solomon of Basrah's *Book of the Bee* (ca. 1222 C.E.), which also drew liberally from the *Cave of Treasures*, contains a similar statement and adds that "it is today the seat of

---

23. From a history of religions perspective this is not altogether surprising, since the heroes and king-deities of Greek and Mesopotamian mythology were often associated with the founding of cities.

24. Names and quotations found in Jubilees are taken from VanderKam 1989.

25. 1QapGen (1Q20) 12.8–9. The full statement reads, "After this, I went down to the base of the mountain, my sons and I, and we built a ci[ty] for the devastation on the earth was great." The words "we built a ci[ty]" (‏[יני]מֿ אנינבו‎) has been read differently in earlier editions of the scroll (cf. Fitzmyer 2004, 86–87, 159) and is based on my own examinations of the photographs. Further details are provided in Machiela 2007, 153. Of course, the partially reconstructed "a ci[ty]" could technically also be "ci[ties]," as in Jubilees, but this seems to be abnegated by the verb "we built."

26. Budge 1927, 116. Ri 1987, 249. On the modern identification of this toponym, see Hoffmann 1880, 174.

27. See Lolos 1976, 56.

a bishopric in the province of Sûbâ."[28] As in the Genesis Apocryphon, these texts portray a communal construction project and place this event before Noah planted his vineyard. Brock has already pointed out that Ephrem's significantly earlier *Commentary on Genesis* (7.1–2) may presuppose this same tradition, since Ham runs out "into the city street" (ܪܒܐܣܘ) to tell his brothers about his father's nakedness.[29] The presence of a street seems to assume that a city was built by Noah and his sons before the vineyard was planted. As Stone has noted elsewhere in this volume, the same tradition is attested in Armenian sources and the apocryphal Epistle of Titus.[30]

2.4. THE DIVISION OF THE EARTH AMONG NOAH'S SONS AND GRANDSONS

Our final example is another extrabiblical tradition shared by the Genesis Apocryphon and Jubilees: Noah's postflood division of the earth among his three sons, which in both texts corresponds to the so-called Table of Nations from Gen 10.[31] Although the two accounts exhibit significant differences, both 1QapGen 16–17 and Jub. 8:11–9:15 describe a two-stage partition of the habitable earth (*oikoumene*). In the first stage, Noah assigns each son a continent: Japheth receives Europe, Shem Asia, and Ham Libya (i.e., modern Africa). It is quite clear that the major borders (e.g., the Tina and Gihon Rivers) and descriptive toponyms employed are indebted to a classical Hellenistic conception of geography sometimes referred to as the "Ionian" world map (*mappa mundi*), so named for its development in the province of Ionia, in western Asia Minor.[32]

In the second stage, each son divides his inherited portion among his own sons. Although the Genesis Apocryphon is fragmentary, it is relatively certain that both accounts include an added narrative component in which Ham's son Canaan refuses to migrate to his allotted land. Instead, he defiantly breaks his solemn oath and occupies the land intended for Arpachshad, that is, the biblical land of Canaan. While the Genesis Apocryphon places this event before the earth's division (in the dream mentioned above),[33] in Jubilees we are

---

28. See the text and translation of Budge 1886, 32. I am indebted to Professor Stone for pointing out an Armenian tradition in the work of Moses of Choren that may be related to this "city-building" aspect of Noah and his sons. See Thomson 1978, 77–81.

29. Brock 1979, 219.

30. See pp. 311–12, 315–16.

31. For further treatment of this motif in Jubilees, see VanderKam 1994, 46–69; Scott 1997a, 295–323; 1997b, 368–81; 2002. For the Genesis Apocryphon, see Machiela 2008; 2007, 220–84; and Eshel 2007, 111–31.

32. Cf. Alexander 1982; Machiela 2007, 174–81.

33. See Machiela 2008.

informed afterwards. For both authors, this addition ingeniously resolves a number of interpretative conundrums in the Hexateuch, such as the bewildering curse of Canaan rather than Ham in Gen 9:25 and the seemingly callous commands of God to wipe out the native tribes of Canaan in Deuteronomy and Joshua. A part of this story's purpose, it seems, is to make clear that both actions are well-merited. Although Jubilees and the Genesis Apocryphon are the only sources containing this tradition in its entirety, its influence may be detected in a surprising array of other Jewish and non-Jewish sources, such as Sib. Or. 3:110–155,[34] the Pseudo-Clementine *Recognitions* 1.30.2–31.2,[35] the Samaritan Asaṭir 4,[36] the rabbinic Midrash Haggadah on Gen 12:6,[37] Epiphanius of Salamis's *Panarion* 66.83.3–85.7,[38] the Sethian gnostic Apocalypse of Adam 72.15–74.26,[39] and even the Russian Primary Chronicle, written in Kiev in 1113.[40] In a number of these sources the original apologetic intent of the motif has been lost.

It is among Syriac exegetes, however, that the tradition of Noah's division of the earth seems to gain the strongest foothold, reflecting a vibrant interest in material associated with the Table of Nations. We may begin by citing the incredibly learned Jacob of Edessa (ca. 640–708 C.E.), who, while fielding a question regarding the patriarch Abraham from a Stylite named John of Lathrippa, draws from the tradition in order to provide the appropriate background for his answer. Below I provide a first translation into English of the pertinent Syriac passage:[41]

---

34. Collins dates this section of the third oracle to 160–150 B.C.E. and locates it in Egypt, perhaps Leontopolis (against the traditional proposal of Alexandria). For further details and Collins's translation, see Collins 1983, 354–57, 364–65.

35. Jones 1995, 56–58. Cf. Scott 2002, 97–125.

36. Gaster 1927, 228–36

37. See the Hebrew edition of Buber 1893–94, part 1, 27. Cf. Himmelfarb 1994, 115–41.

38. See the translation of F. E. Williams 1994, 302–3. The *Panarion* was written between 374 and 377 C.E.

39. The best edition is that of Morard 1985, 35–39. Or see Hendrick 1980, 236–39. For an English translation only, see MacRae 1983, 714; or MacRae and Parrott 1990, 277–86.

40. Cross and Sherbowitz-Wetzor 1953, 1–2. This is a chronicle of Russian history that begins by situating ancient Rus in the apportionment of Japheth. The Japheth section is elaborated in a unique way in this chronicle, paying special attention to the Baltic (then called the Varangian) regions. Because the focus is on a portion of Japheth's territory, there is no reference to Canaan's misdeed, as in the other examples.

41. The Syriac only may be found in W. Wright 1867, 430–60. At the beginning of the twentieth century, a French translation was published in Nau 1905, 197–208, 258–82. My translation is based on Wright's Syriac text and the manuscript in which the letter is found. This is bound in volume Add. 12,172 of the British Library. I express my deep thanks to

I begin for you from here: during his lifetime Noah divided the entire habitable earth among his three sons: Shem, Ham, and Japheth. To each of them he gave a portion and an allotment of the earth to settle, and for his sons [to inherit], and he placed a curse on whoever was headstrong and entered into the allotment of his brother. He also blessed Shem and Japheth, saying "God will increase Japheth and will dwell in the tent of Shem" [Gen 9:27]. And he sent forth a curse against Canaan, the son of Ham, as if on account of an incident of his being naked, but in reality because in the future he would transgress against his command and against the precept on account of the allotment of their inheritance, and would enter into the inheritance of his brothers.

This, then, is the land that God promised to the descendants of Abraham; it had been given by Noah to Shem. For this reason he both blessed him and said to him that he would dwell in the tent of Shem. Then each one of these also divided his portion among his sons. It was at that time that Peleg son of Eber was born, just as it is narrated in the holy writing of Moses [Gen 10:25]. They also set down curses against anyone who would enter into the inheritance of his brothers. The land of Palestine, which God promised to Abraham, fell into the allotment (comprised of) the entire land that stretches from the Euphrates and to the west, up to the sea; and from the mountain called Amanus, which separates Syria from Cilicia, up to the entrances of Egypt. To Lud, son of Shem, the one who has a city in the region of Palestine named after him up to the present,[42] and to Hul and Aus, the sons of Aram, firstborn son of Shem; to these this land was given out of the second allotment, which Shem divided among his sons.

It is because of this that, after the division of languages in Babel and the overturning of the tower that foolishly they had built, all peoples were henceforth divided from one another, each one going its own way. Each one picked up forthwith and set out to journey to the land of inheritance that had fallen to it. But when the sons of Canaan realized that they were Hamites and that their brothers were (placed) in Egypt and Cush, it being the land that fell to the sons of Ham, and they then saw the goodness of that land belonging to Shem, which is from Mount Amanus up to Palestine (that is, to the land of Syria and Phoenecia, and the entire seacoast), and to Lebanon and Senir and Hermon—the regions of the sources of the rivers—they yearned greatly to live in them. They also saw the weakness of its leaders, who were not up to the challenge, and once again their own might, and they knew that they would be able to overpower these (inhabitants) and settle in it. They brazenly

---

Dr. Joseph Amar, who offered many suggestions while reading together and read a proof of the translation.

42. Modern Lod. For the toponymic history of this city, see J. J. Schwartz 1991. The fact that Lud and Lod are easily associated may have given Jacob sufficient cause to make this emendation to the standard layout of the Revised Table.

took control and stayed in that land, and held sway over it, thereby treading the commandments of their ancestors underfoot and rebelling against the curse of Noah, their common forefather, and of his three sons: Shem, Ham, and Japheth.

But when God—who knows all things before they occur, just as it is written, "there is nothing which exists that is hidden from him, or escapes his notice" [cf. Sir 42:20], who searches the hearts and emotions of everyone, who knows the mind of a man and sees the thoughts within it, even considering and observing all of those impulses that have yet to be conceived in it in the future—looked and saw all the sons of Shem, he could not see among any of them a peaceable or pure heart, or an inclination toward the word of knowledge like the mind of Abraham, son of Terah the Chaldean. Neither the sons of Elam, nor the sons of Asshur, not even the sons of Lud or of Aram who were living in that land apportioned to Shem with those rebellious sons of Canaan. Not even those belonging to the Chaldeans, the sons of Arpachshad. Because of this, God chose Abraham for himself from all the sons of Shem. He determined that he would inherit the land seized by those rebels, the sons of Canaan, when they waged war and laid waste to it, so that his seed might dwell in it, and that God might establish him in it, just as Noah had said in his blessing. This is the reason God chose Abraham.

It is clear that Jacob takes this tradition as authoritative and must have received it (either directly or indirectly) from Jewish sources.[43] Some significant changes have been made vis-à-vis the earlier Jewish texts, such as the assignment of the land of Palestine to the Ludites and Arameans (including Hul and Aus) rather than to Arpachshad. It is probable that Jacob or another Syrian had his own reasons for doing this, since Aram was considered the ancestor of the Syrians. In any event, the basic twofold structure is clearly the same as in the Genesis Apocryphon and Jubilees, although the actual geographic descriptions of each allotment are not provided.

The Syriac Chronicle to the Year of Christ 1234, which at points resembles Jubilees closely enough to be considered versional evidence by Tisserant and VanderKam, preserves only the first division of the earth by Noah to his

---

43. Elsewhere in the letter he explicitly invokes Jewish sources, such as in his later statement about Moses: "Written accounts that have come down from the Jews also clearly manifest that writing existed before Moses—and these are not fraudulent—which also speak about Moses; that his father Amram taught him writing and Hebrew books along with the writing of the Egyptians when he was still a young man in the house of Pharaoh. So also from this we are able to say that there truly were writing and books before the time of Moses." For a Jewish tradition resembling this one, see ALD 13:4 and its explanation in Greenfield, Stone, and Eshel 2004, 102–3, 208.

three sons.[44] As in Jubilees, Shem receives the "center of the earth" (cf. Jub. 8:12), and it is clear that in both the chronicle and Jubilees the same general geographic area is discussed. However, the chronicle chooses its own way to describe Shem's allotment by noting some of its borders and the major regions encompassed within them. The list of countries, which includes Palestine, Arabia, Phoenecia, Syria, Mesopotamia, Hyrcania,[45] Asshur, Sanir, Babylon, Persia, and northern India, is made up both of lands mentioned in Jubilees and of those that are not. The lands not mentioned in Jubilees possess names that appear somewhat updated, yet differ from the contemporary terms used by other Christian chroniclers.

The account of Ham's portion resembles Jub. 8:22–23 much more closely, listing the same sites in similar order and direction. The same is true of Japheth's territory (Jub. 8:25–29), including his "five large islands," although here the chronicle's version is slightly further abridged. As in Jub. 8:30, the "first" division concludes with a summary of the climates of each son's allotment.

Later in the chronicle we read about the transgression of Canaan's sons in a statement very similar to Jub. 10:29,[46] to which the chronicler adds the parenthetical comment, "[t]he land of Palestine belonged to the sons of Joktan, the grandsons of Ham [error for Shem]." This aside is curious, since it is from the line of Joktan's brother Peleg that Abraham and the Israelites eventually issue.[47] Following the description of the misdeed of Canaan's sons we learn that "they transgressed the command of Noah, and inherited the curse that befell them through prophecy."[48] Although the chronicle does not contain Noah's imposition of oaths against the transgression of boundaries (cf. Jub. 9:14–15; 10:30–32), it clearly depends on such vows having been made. In addition, the transgression is linked to Noah's prophetic curse of Canaan in Gen 9:25.

The great Christian chronicler Michael the Syrian (ca. 1126–1199) also tells of the earth's division in his chronicle, following Noah and his sons alighting from the ark.[49] He writes, "then Noah divided the earth among his

---

44. See Tisserant 1921; VanderKam 1989, 1:xiii. The full Syriac text may be found in Chabot 1953.

45. An area south of the Caspian Sea and north of Media and Parthia.

46. The chronicle substitutes the toponym Palestine for Jubilees' Lebanon.

47. I.e., both Jacob of Edessa and the chronicle assign this land to descendants of Shem who are *not* direct ancestors of Abraham. This is a significant departure from Jewish sources and their original apologetic intent.

48. Chabot 1953, 48.2–4 [Syriac].

49. Book 2, chs. 1–2. The Syriac text and a French translation may be found in Chabot 1899–1924, 1:14–19 (trans.), 4:7–9 (Syriac). A thirteenth-century Armenian epitome was translated into French earlier by Langlois 1868.

sons, placing curses on any who would transgress his brother's border. The division of Shem was as follows…" (7.14–17).[50] So begins the now-familiar first, schematic description of the allotment of each son (7.16–20). While it is clear that the basic tradition cited is that of the much earlier Jewish sources, by Michael's time (late twelfth century C.E.) the geographic terms had undergone extensive revision at the hands of those in the Greco-Byzantine and Syrian chronographic schools, which incorporated and updated similar aspects of the Jewish tradition (e.g., Hippolytus of Rome,[51] George Synkellos,[52] George the Monk [Hamartolos],[53] and George Cedrenus[54]). Michael also added other conventional items, such as lists of descendants following the earth's first division and of the cardinal directions with which each son was associated (Shem with the east, Japheth the north, and Ham the south). As in other Christian chronicles, Japheth, Shem, and Ham are associated with the Tigris, Euphrates, and Nile Rivers, respectively.[55] The opening and closing lines of this section, however, exhibit close affinities with the descriptions in Jubilees and the Genesis Apocryphon.

After a genealogical aside concerning the line of Shem, which serves as a narrative bridge to reach the time of Peleg, we read that "in the 120th year of Peleg the earth was divided a second time by the children of Shem and the other sons of Noah" (8.24–25).[56] This begins yet another geographic description, in which Shem's descendents are said to receive as an inheritance (ܢܝܪܘܬܬܐ; cf. 1QapGen 16.12) the "entire center of the habitable earth" (cf. Jub. 8:12), while Ham's sons acquire the entire south (8.35–9.10), and Japheth the remaining northern regions (9.10–20). Although the toponyms used to describe the suballotments are those expected in Christian chronicles, the second division closely resembles the accounts of Jubilees and the Genesis Apocryphon in content, language, and the formulaic introduction to each

---

50. Translation from the Syriac is my own. All page and line numbers refer to the Syriac text (Chabot 1899–1924, vol. 4) in the main column at the center of the folio.

51. The best Greek edition of his chronicle, with critical apparatus and notes, is found in Helm and Bauer 1955, 10–43.

52. See Adler and Tuffin 2002, 62–71. Synkellos died in the opening years of the ninth century C.E. and spent most of his life between monasteries in Palestine and his charge as *synkellos* (private secretary) under patriarch Tarasaios (784–806) in Constantinople.

53. See de Boor 1978, 1:55.4–57.9.

54. See Bekker 1838–39, 1:23.17–26.14.

55. A helpful analysis of all of the confusing elements comprising the division of the earth tradition in Michael's chronicle, and numerous other Syriac sources, has been published by Witakowski 1993.

56. As in Gen 10:25 and many Jewish sources dependent on it, this division (נִפְלְגָה הָאָרֶץ) is a wordplay on the name Peleg (פֶּלֶג).

son's inheritance. Like other chronicles, however, the general borders given by Michael do not fit the following descriptions of the lands that fall within them. For example, the sons of Ham are said to inhabit the entire southern region, yet we are later surprised to find that they own much of Asia Minor as well (as in Gen 10). It is clear that the now centuries-long process of transmission has produced some idiosyncrasies within these later accounts.

Final evidence that Michael relied on the Jewish "division of the earth" tradition comes during his telling of the Tower of Babel incident. Here he mentioned, as an aside, that the Lord confused the language of those in the land of Shinar because "they trampled on the law [ܢܡܘܣܐ], raged against the commandment [ܦܘܩܕܢܐ], and did not observe the assigned limit [ܬܚܘܡܐ] of righteous Noah and his division of the earth" (9.26–28). This is an unusual explanation for the confusion of tongues, but one obviously drawing on the transgression of Canaan originally accompanying Noah's division of the earth. Indeed, the story of Canaan's misdeed, much as it is found in the Chronicle to the Year of Christ 1234 and Jubilees, is written in small print in the right margin of the late sixteenth-century manuscript on which Chabot's edition is based.[57] In summary, Michael presents significant portions of the much earlier Jewish tradition about Noah, but these are intermingled with numerous later accretions that have often displaced and confused the "original" material. Witakowski has helpfully observed that many of these changes grew out of the intended function of the "universal chronicle," which was to demonstrate the sovereignty of God over all of history and humanity.[58] This, of course, encompassed every known people and locale, and the tradition, therefore, necessarily expanded with ethnographic knowledge.

3. Conclusion

The handful of links between Jewish and Syriac treatments of Noah presented above could, no doubt, be augmented appreciably. However, they are sufficient to demonstrate that both traditions shared a distinctive approach to the biblical text, as well as a number of specific interpretations regarding Noah. This is not surprising when we consider that a significant number of Syriac Christians were very likely Jewish converts and that there appears to have been interaction between Jewish and Christian scholars and laity in urban

---

57. Lines 47–62 in the Syriac (p. 9). For an engaging history of the manuscript and its publication, see Weltecke 1997.

58. Witakowski 1993, 652–53.

centers such as Edessa.[59] Examples such as those above lend credence to such connections.

Although the many elements distinguishing Syriac Christian understandings of Noah from their Jewish counterparts cannot be fully discussed here, I will conclude by suggesting two factors that played a major role in how Genesis (and the Hebrew Scriptures in general) was read by the Syrians: christocentrism and ethnocentrism.[60] Regarding the first, we should take care to distinguish christocentrism (with reference to Jesus of Nazareth) from messianism, since association of Noah with messianic and eschatological expectations is present in some Jewish readings of Noah and the flood in Genesis—especially those that focus on Noah's astounding birth or the flood's role in judging evildoers.[61] However, a distinctive feature of Syriac Christian exegesis is the strong typological parallel of Noah, the ark, and the flood with Jesus, the church, and Christ's final judgment, respectively. Another such tradition is that the ark traveled in the four cardinal directions to mark the shape of a cross over the face of the inundated earth, advocated by Ephrem and the *Cave of Treasures*. To be certain, this correlation is not always as strong as in the writings of Ephrem, Jacob of Serug (fifth to sixth century), or Theodore Bar Koni (late eighth century), but it is very often present in some form.

As for ethnocentrism, many Syrian exegetes saw their own heritage reflected at many junctures in Scripture, especially in the early chapters of Genesis, centered as they were on Mesopotamia. We may refer to the opinion of Jacob of Edessa and others, cited above, that the Levantine lands fell to Aram and his descendants rather than Arpachshad, as in Jewish sources, or the widespread argument—linked to the Tower of Babel episode—that Syriac

---

59. On this topic in general, see the articles of Brock 1979; Drijvers 1985; 1992. Both articles have been republished in Drijvers 1994. See also Gafni 1981, esp. 571. One story of Jewish conversion, albeit embellished in some details, is found in the History of Rabban Bar-'Idta, published by Budge 1902, 172 [Syriac], 261–62 [trans.]. An impressive familiarity with Jewish sources and traditions is exhibited throughout Jacob of Edessa's thirteenth letter to John the Stylite, mentioned above.

60. It is, of course, a gross oversimplification to tacitly refer to either "side" as a monolithic group, both in terms of the many distinctions within each and the sometimes fuzzy border between "Jews" and "Christians." The problematization of these areas by Daniel Boyarin, Judith Lieu, and others certainly deserves to be taken into account and are duly noted. Still, the two factors noted here seem to represent a significant divergence from Jewish interpretation for the majority of Syriac Christian exegetes.

61. On Noah's birth, see Aryeh Amihay and Daniel Machiela, "Traditions of the Birth of Noah," in this volume. Association of the flood with the eschatological judgment is found in 1 Enoch, the Genesis Apocryphon, the Sybilline Oracles, and other texts.

(not Hebrew) was the primordial tongue.[62] Regarding the Table of Nations, there is the strong Syriac proclivity to view Nimrod favorably (in contrast to the widely negative Jewish view), probably because he was the founder of famous Mesopotamian cities, which the Syrians happily linked to a number of their own cultural centers. Perhaps the identification of the ark's landing with Mount Qardo (i.e., Gordyene) in Mesopotamia should be included here also, although this tradition surfaces in Targum Pseudo-Jonathan as well.[63]

One final, broad observation may be made in connection with a development in Jewish sources. The earliest Jewish sources appear to have been very keen on Noah and his role as an exemplary model of righteousness. This is especially true in the Genesis Apocryphon, but it also comes through in the Sybilline Oracles and 1 Enoch. In later rabbinic texts, however, there is a noticeable cooling. Here Noah is of a decidedly mixed character, typically to be judged righteous only within the context of "his generation" (Gen 6:9).[64] Consequently, Noah intermittently becomes an example of how *not* to behave. Syriac scholars tended to follow the former path, opting to depict the patriarch as a wholly righteous model of faith. This may well be tied to the Christian adoption of Noah as a type of Christ noted above. Thus, while the Syrians held on to many of the same interpretations of individual words or passages as the rabbis, their overall portrait matched better the intertestamental Jewish representation of the famed flood hero.

---

62. On this point Jacob of Edessa (in his thirteenth letter to John the Stylite, referenced above) breaks rank with his compatriots.

63. Again, see further the essay by Stone in this volume, pp. 309–12.

64. See Amihay, "Noah in Rabbinic Literature," in this volume.

The Literary Presentation of Noah in the Qur'ān

Erica Martin

1. Introduction

The following pages consider the literary shape of Noah in the Muslim Scripture. The first challenge facing my project is the abundance of Noahic material in the Qur'ān. There seem to be many different Noahs with varying stories. I will focus primarily on the Noah story found in sūras 11 *Hūd* and 71 *Nūh* for reasons outlined below. I also consider five other qur'ānic presentations of the Noah story, found in sūras 7, 10, 23, 26, and 54.[1]

The second challenge facing my project is ascertaining the relationship between Noah stories in the seven sūras listed above and their surrounding material. These stories occur in groups of *Straflegenden*, or punishment stories. Punishment stories describe communities who reject a divinely sent messenger from among their own people. The Noah stories cannot be fully addressed without examining their participation and paradigmatic use in this distinctive qur'ānic phenomenon.[2]

2. The Qur'ānic Noah

In this there is a sign, but most of them do not believe.[3]

The present discussion offers observations about differences and similarities in the shape of the Noah story each time it is presented in the Qur'ān, then explores connections between the presentations in terms of plot structure and verbatim repetition.

---

1. Noah appears in twenty-nine sūras (chapters) of the Qur'ān. Frequently his name is simply mentioned in lists of prophets prior to Muhammad. My focus is on the seven sūras that recount some portion of the Noah story.

2. See Welch 2000, who analyzes the forms of qur'ānic punishment stories and the distinction between punishment stories and prophetic legends.

3. Q 26.121. All translations are my own.

The name "Noah" is mentioned repeatedly in the Qur'ān, usually in lists of prophets.[4] Four out of the seven qur'ānic Noah accounts explicitly state that Noah is sent by God,[5] and all seven agree that Noah's audience consisted of his own people.[6] In five accounts, Noah suffers derision from his community, alternately being charged with idiocy, possession, lying, or just being a man who could not possibly convey a divine message.[7] Three accounts stress that Noah asks no reward for his efforts,[8] and in all versions he is ultimately rejected.[9] Noah's deliverance in a ship or ark is attested in six sūras,[10] and six sūras agree that other people were drowned.[11]

In table 1 I divide each of the qur'ānic presentations of the Noah story into story elements to determine which facets are shared by the greatest number of presentations and which facets are the isolated concern of one or two sūras.

TABLE 1: STRUCTURE OF THE NOAH STORY IN THE SELECTED SŪRAS

Story Elements	Sūra 7. 59–64	Sūra 10. 71–74	Sūra 11. 25–49	Sūra 23. 23–31	Sūra 26. 105–122	Sūra 54. 9–17	Sūra 71. 1–25
commission/warning	X		X	X	X		X
Noah argues with the people	X	X	X	X	X	X	
Noah complains to God				X	X	X	X
warn no more			X	X			
ship-building instructions			X	X			

---

4. This essay compares and contrasts Noah stories in sūras 7, 10, 11, 23, 26, 54, and 71.
5. Sent by God: Q 7.59; 11.25; 23.23; and 71.1.
6. His own people: Q 7.59; 10.71; 11.26; 23.23; 26.105; 54.9; and 71.3.
7. Idiocy: Q 7.60–61; possession: Q 54.9; 23.25; lying: Q 11.27; "just a man": Q 11.27; 23.24.
8. No reward: Q 10.27; 11.29; and 26.109.
9. Rejected: explicitly in Q 7.64; 10.73; 11.32; 26.117; and 54.9. The rejection is implicit in Q 23.24–25 and 71.5–24.
10. Delivered in a ship or ark: Q 7.64; 10.73; 11.37, 41–43, 48; 23.27; 26.119; and 54.13.
11. Others drowned: Q 7.64; 10.73; 11.43; 23.27; 26.120; and 71.25.

Noah builds			X				
the flood begins			X			X	
some are saved			X		X	X	
the drowned ones/son	X	X	X		X		X
the flood ceases			X				X
disembarkation orders			X				
the moral		X	X	X	X	X	

Given the evidence offered above, it is clear some elements are "standard," appearing in more sūras than others.[12] The most ubiquitous element, appearing in six of the seven sūras, is "Noah argues with the people." The elements I titled "commission/warning," "the drowned ones/son," and "the moral" each appear in five of the seven sūras. Four of the seven sūras contain the element "Noah complains to God."

Table 1 shows that sūra 11, *Hūd*, contains the story elements "Noah builds" and "disembarkation orders." These elements are not found in any of the other presentations, perhaps indicating that they are late and optional embellishments. *Hūd*'s version of the story element "Noah argues with the people" is the most extensive.[13] While the element "the drowned ones/son" is present in five of the seven versions, only *Hūd* contains the story of Noah's drowned son, rather than speaking briefly and generically of the "drowned ones." *Hūd*, then, presents the most developed version of the qur'ānic Noah story.

The fullness of the version found in *Hūd* is matched only by the extensive treatment given to the story element "Noah complains to God" in sūra 71, *Nūh*. The three other story elements present in *Nūh*, "commission/warning," "the drowned ones/son," and "the flood ceases," receive perfunctory treatment. Their inclusion provides the story frame to relate Noah's complaint, which represents the bulk of *Nūh*. "Noah Complains to God" is the only story

---

12. For convenience, I have shaded these "standard" elements in table 1.

13. The story element "Noah argues with the people" continues for nine long verses in sūra 11 (11.27–35), compared to three verses in sūra 7 (7.60–63), two in sūra 10 (10.71–72), two in 23 (23.24–25), six in 26 (26.111–116), and one in sūra 54 (54.9).

element *absent* from *Hūd*, but its absence disrupts the logical flow of the sūra. Although no complaint to God is made, in 11.37b God instructs Noah, "Do not speak to me about those who do wrong, [for] they will indeed be drowned."

Sūras *Hūd* and *Nūh* contain similar disruptions to the logical flow of events at the end of the flood. *Hūd* portrays Noah attempting to intercede with God for the life of his son, and *Nūh* portrays Noah asking God to destroy the unfaithful and to preserve the believers, including his own parents. Curiously, in both sūras this intercession/condemnation occurs after the audience has already been notified that the flood is over, its damage done.

The flood ends:
11.44 It was said, "Oh earth, swallow your water, and oh sky, leave off your water. And the matter ended, and it rested on Judi, and it was said, "Away with the wrongdoing people!"

71.25 Because of their sins they were drowned, they were made to enter the fire, they found no one, aside from God, to help.

Intercession/condemnation:
11.45 And Noah called upon his Lord. He said, "My Lord, surely my son is of my family, and surely your promise is true, for you are the most just of judges!"
11.46 He said, "Oh Noah, indeed he is not of your family, for he does unjust deeds. Do not ask me about that which you have no knowledge. I admonish you so that you will not be among the ignorant ones."
11.47 He said, "My Lord, I do seek refuge with you, lest I ask you about that which I have no knowledge. Unless you forgive me and have mercy on me, I will be among the lost."

71.26 And Noah said, "Oh my Lord! Do not leave any of the unbelievers upon on earth!
71.27 "If you leave them, they will mislead your servants, and they will bear none but sinning unbelieving ones.
71.28 "Oh my Lord! Forgive me, my parents, and the one who enters my house in faith, and the believing men and the believing women: and do not add to the wrongdoers anything but destruction!"

Noah disembarks:
11.48 It was said, "Oh Noah! Descend in peace with blessings from Us, upon you and upon some of the people from you. But (as for) some

(End of sūra 71)

of the people, we will let them live (for a while), then the painful punishment from us will befall them.

These observations suggest that *Hūd* and *Nūh* may once have been a unified literary presentation of the Noah story.

The highly developed flood story found in *Hūd* is not independent of those found in the other sūras. There is substantial duplication of material between *Hūd*, Sūra 23 *Al-Mu'minūn*, and Sūra 26 *Al-Shu'arā*. Notably, *Al-Mu'minūn* and *Al-Shu'arā* are rarely congruent. If *Hūd* is the latest, most amplified version, it may have combined material from the other sūras to form its new, embellished account. The following table demonstrates instances of parallelism.[14]

Sūra 23 *Al-Mu'minūn*	Sūra 11 *Hūd*	Sūra 26 *Al-Shu'arā*
23.24a And the leaders of those who disbelieved among his people said, "He is none other than flesh like ourselves,	11.27a And the leaders of those who disbelieved among his people said, "We don't see that you are anything but flesh like ourselves,	
	11.27b and we don't see that any [people] follow you, except the one that are lowly in our opinion. We don't see that you have more favor than us, rather, we think that you are liars!"	26.111 They said: "Shall we believe in you, but the contemptible follow you?
	11.29 And [he said], "Oh, my people, I don't ask you for money for it [this message], in-	26.109 And I do not ask you for a reward for it, my reward is with the Lord of Worlds.

---

14. Because the verses do not occur in the same order in each sūra, the incidences of parallelism are arranged according to the order of sūra 11.

		26.114 "I will not drive away believers."
	deed, my reward is only with God. I will not drive away those who believe, indeed, they will encounter their Lord, but I see that you are an ignorant people."	
23.27a So We revealed to him,	11.36 It was revealed to Noah, "[None] of your people will believe except those who believed already. Do not grieve about what they do.	
"Build a ship before our eyes and by our inspiration, 23.27c and do not speak to me about those who do wrong, [for] they will indeed be drowned." 23.27b and when Our command was issued, the oven gushed forth, and We said, "Enter into it (the ship) two of every kind, a pair, and your family, except the one among you against whom the word was already sent out....	11.37 "Build a ship before our eyes and by our inspiration, and do not speak to me about those who do wrong, [for] they will indeed be drowned." 11.40 Until, behold! Our command was issued, and the oven gushed forth, and We said, "Carry into it (the ship) two of every kind, a pair, and your family, except the one against whom the word was already sent out, and those who believe. But those who believe with him were but a few.	

There is internal disagreement in *Hūd* regarding the origin of the floodwaters. In line 40 the floodwaters originate in the (singular) "oven." In line 44

God orders both the earth and sky to cease emitting water, "Oh earth, swallow your water, and oh sky, leave off your water." The only other description of the beginning of the flood in the Qur'ān is provided in sūra 54, *Al-Qamar*, lines 11–12, wherein both the earth and sky are given as sources of the deluge,

> We opened the gates of heaven with water pouring out,
> cracked open the earth in springs,
> so the water met according to the decree.

A final observation regarding the version of the Noah story presented in *Hūd* concerns the accusation of forgery in verse 35, which breaks the flow of the story.

> 32. They said, "Oh Noah, you have already argued with us, and you extend our argument. Bring to us what you promise us, if you are right!"
> 33. He said, "Indeed God will bring it to you if he wills. You cannot do anything about it!
> 34. "I want to advise you, but my advice will not profit you if God wants to lead you astray. He is your Lord; to him is your return!"
> 35. Or do they say, "He forged it?" Say, "If I forged it, then my crime is on me! I am free of what you charge me"!
> 36. It was revealed to Noah, "[None] of your people will believe except those who believed already. Do not grieve about what they do."

The exact words "they may say, 'He forged it!'" were used with regard to Muhammad's own preaching in 11.13, to which Muhammad is instructed to reply, "Bring ten forged sūras like it, and call upon whom you are able, other than God, if you are right." The abrupt shift away from Noah's argument with the people, then back to it following "Or do they say, 'He forged it?'" suggests that this verse was inserted to make the parallelism between Muhammad and Noah's work as "warners" more explicit.

To determine the literary shape of Noah in the Qur'ān, I have addressed commonalities between the qur'ānic Noah stories, describing shared details and story elements. I then determined a "standard" story shape for the Noah/flood tale in the Qur'ān and discussed the sūra that best represents that story shape. However, variations and contradictions in each sūra's presentation of the Noah story need to be addressed as well. Two of the seven sūras make a distinction between Noah's "people" and the "chiefs of the unbelievers among his people," who are identified as the real culprits.[15] In one version, the community threatens to stone him, in another Noah is driven out of their

---

15. Chiefs of the unbelievers referred to in Q 11.27 and 38; 23.24.

company, and a third version seems to envision a judicial setting where the people might "sentence" him.[16] As previously mentioned, Noah's message is rejected for different reasons in different sūras, either because his audience thinks he is an idiot, possessed, a liar, or "just a man."[17] In two of the sūras, Noah's followers are directly maligned as "lowly."[18] Finally, although six sūras announce the drowning of the unbelievers, only one sūra adds that they were made to enter the "Fire of Punishment."[19]

3. Survey of the Sūras That Relate Portions of the Noah story

3.1. Sūrat al-Qamar (Q 54)

Sūra 54, titled *Al-Qamar*, "The Moon," is 55 verses in length. The first line of the sūra, the source of its title, hurtles the reader into the drama of the eschatological moment: "The hour has come, the moon has split apart."

The sūra is divided into three sections. The introduction (54.1–8) is eschatological; the middle section (54.9–42) contains brief versions of the punishment stories of Noah, 'Ād, Thamūd, Lot, and Pharaoh, which serve as an object lesson for Muhammad's contemporaries in the third and final section (54.43–55). The verses are short and poetically beautiful.

Although the first and last sections of *Al-Qamar* contain arguments coinciding with the polemics of other sūras, these verses do not present the material in a manner designed to convince unbelievers. The messages expressed are resignation to others' unbelief and assurance that on the last day believers will be vindicated before those who rejected them. Noah's story is summed up in five lines:

> Before them, the people of Noah rejected, they rejected Our servant and said, "A madman!" and he was driven away.
> So he called to his Lord, "I am defeated, so help me!"
> We opened the gates of heaven with water pouring out,
> cracked open the earth in springs,
> so the water met according to the decree.
> We carried him in an object of board and joiner,
> She floats under our eyes, as a reward to the rejected ones.
> And we have left it as a sign, so are there any who remember? (Q 54.9–15)

---

16. Noah is threatened with stoning in Q 26.116, being driven out in Q 54.9 and he urges them to pass their sentence upon him in Q 10.71.
17. See note 24.
18. Followers as "lowly" in Q 11.27 and 23.111.
19. Fire of Punishment in Q 71.25.

'Ād and Thamūd's prophets, identified in other versions of the punishment stories as Hūd and Salih, go unnamed in this version. Rather than narrating the punishment-stories, *Al-Qamar* evokes them in order to summon the two statements (sometimes in modified form), which occur after each story.

> How was my punishment and my warning!
> And we have made the Qur'ān easy to remember, so are there any who remember? (Q 54.21–22)

The repeated exclamation, "How was my punishment and my warning!" is not a threat in the present context but a cry of victory: awaited justification for the believers. The sūra has an antiphonal quality; the repeated question "are there any who remember?" hangs in the air like an invitation for the audience to respond, "We do!"

3.2. SŪRAT AL-SHU'ARĀ (Q 26)

Sūra 26, titled *Al-Shu'arā*, "The Poets," is 227 verses in length. I divide *Al-Shu'arā* into three major sections: an introduction asserting that a new revelation has come (26.1–9); a long narrative section containing prior revelations, including stories about Moses, Abraham, Noah, Hūd, Salih, Lot, and Shu'aib (26.10–191); and a conclusion interpreting the implications of the narrative section for the sūra's audience (26.192–227).

The narrative material relating to Moses and Abraham (26.10–104) presents extended, detailed prophetic stories quite different from the brief and cryptic punishment stories that follow. Whereas sūras *Al-A'rāf* (Q 7) and *Hūd* (Q 11) relate the stories of the prophets chronologically (a mythic chronology with Noah appearing first, Abraham in the middle with Lot and nonbiblical prophets, and Moses last), only in *Al-Shu'arā* are the Moses and Abraham stories prefixed. This gives the impression *Al-Shu'arā* has joined two different bodies of prophetic stories to accomplish its purpose.[20]

Despite the perceptible seam in *Al-Shu'arā*, each prophetic story is playfully connected to the next via keywords and images that unite the stories and spill into the conclusion, recapitulating the overarching message of the sūra. A few examples suffice to demonstrate the "keyword" linkages between the prophetic stories.

The popular qur'ānic presentation of Moses' confrontation with the sorcerers of Pharaoh in *Al-Shu'arā* stresses the adoptive familial connection

---

20. Welch (2000, 79–82) illustrates that the prophetic stories in *Al-Shu'arā* do not share the schematic form of the punishment stories that follow.

between Moses and Pharaoh, saying, "(Pharaoh) said, 'Didn't we raise you among us as a child? And you stayed among us years of your life?'" (Q 26.18). As the children of Israel leave Egypt, a difficult passage in *Al-Shu'arā* notes, "So We expelled them from gardens and springs" (Q 26.57). After delivering the fleeing children of Israel, God states, "Indeed, in this is a sign, but most of them do not believe." "Then We drowned [أَغْرَقْنَا] the others. And indeed your Lord is He, the Powerful, the Merciful" (Q 26.66–68). Each of these elements—familial connection to the destroyed people, gardens and springs, drowning, and signs—are taken up in the following prophetic stories.

Abraham's story begins by invoking the familial connection, "And recite to them Abraham's story. Behold, he said to his father and his people, 'What do you worship'" (26.69–70), which is later reinforced by Abraham's prayer, "And forgive my father, indeed he was among those astray" (Q 26.86). Although technically the word "garden" is present in Abraham's story, "Make me one of the inheritors of the Garden of Bliss" (Q 26.85), this expression may be accidental rather than indicative of the connective editorial activity I attempt to demonstrate. The closing is an exact duplication of the closing of Moses' story. "Indeed, in this is a sign, but most of them do not believe. And indeed your Lord is He, the Powerful, the Merciful" (Q 26.103–104).

The punishment stories of Noah, Hūd, Salih, Lot, and Shu'aib in *Al-Shu'arā* are formulaic, bearing nearly identical opening and closing statements. The opening statement reads:

> _____ rejected the messengers. Behold, their brother _____ said to them, "Won't you fear? I am trustworthy messenger for you, so fear God, and obey me. And I do not ask of you any reward regarding it (the message), indeed my reward is only with the Lord of the Worlds."[21]

The closing statements are as follows:

> Indeed, in this is a sign, but most of them do not believe. And indeed your Lord is He, the Powerful, the Merciful.[22]

The story of each prophet reinforces the ideas of familial connection and sign. The Noah story, depicting the drowning of the unbelievers, uses the word أَغْرَقْنَا ("we drowned"), creating a connection with the drowning mentioned in the

---

21. The parallel passages are Noah: Q 26.105–109; Hud: Q 26.123–127; Salih: Q 26.141–145; Lot: Q 26.160–164; and Shu'aib: Q 26.176–180.

22. The parallel passages are Noah: Q 26.121–122; Hud: Q 26.139b–140; Salih: Q 26.158b–159; Lot: Q 26.174–175; and Shu'aib: Q 26.190–191.

story of Moses (Q 26.66; 26.120). The retellings of the Hūd and Salih stories invoke the image of جَنَّاتٍ وَعُيُونٍ, "gardens and springs," further linking this second body of prophetic material to the first (Q 26.134; 26.147).

Reading the second block of prophetic stories together, each prophet is depicted as criticizing his people regarding a specific social issue, which taken cumulatively, as the parallel form of the stories encourages, creates a formidable list of injustices. The people of Noah despise the misfortunate. The people of Hūd abuse their power. Salih's community is a people of plenty who refuse to share the bounty of their land even with a single camel. The charge of homosexuality is leveled against the people of Lot, and Shu'aib's brethren are dishonest businessmen.

The conclusion of *Al-Shu'arā* asserts the validity of all previous stories and the truth of the current prophet's admonition, warning that those who ignore his teaching should expect the destruction that befell so many wicked communities in the past. Unbelief and polytheism are the crimes of his people. It again invokes the family motif, saying, "warn your nearest relatives..." (Q 26.214). The sign invoked in this portion of the sūra, interestingly enough, is that "the learned of the children of Israel knew it," that is, recognized the preceding verses as revelation, thus verifying the prophet's connection to the divine (Q 26.197).

Reference to the prophets' "brotherhood" is idiomatic. However, the way the familial connection motif is invoked in the preceding and following material causes it to stand out in the present context and assists in unifying the sūra. "Drowning" and "gardens and springs" become key words tying together the bodies of prophetic material in the narrative section.

Al-Shu'arā represents two separate bodies of prophetic material artfully joined and given a new context by bracketing them with an introduction and conclusion to validate the authority and message of a new prophet. The sūra is polemical, and its polemics are directed to unbelievers who nevertheless identify with the biblical stories to the extent they are challenged to verify Muhammad's prophethood through them. The rhetoric in *Al-Shu'arā* carries none of the venomous images of torture and death for unbelievers such as those seen in sūra 23, to follow. *Al-Shu'arā* depicts the prophet as dejected, not angry, with unbelievers. Here he rather gently invites the audience to believe, presenting the equation of new prophecy with previously known prophecy as logical and praiseworthy.

3.3. SŪRAT NŪH (Q 71)

Sūra 71, titled *Nūh*, "Noah," is 27 verses in length. As previously mentioned, *Nūh* presents a small portion of the Noah story, which in this sūra alone is not structured as a punishment story.[23] The story element titled "Noah complains to God" (Q 71.5–24) is framed by perfunctory opening and closing statements. Noah's commission is summed up in one verse (Q 71.1), and his warning to the people extends over two verses:

> He said, "Oh my people, I am a clear warner for you that you should worship God, fear Him, and obey me." (Q 71.2–3)

The order وَاتَّقُوهُ وَأَطِيعُونِ "fear Him and obey me," in 71.3 is an important refrain in sūra 26, where the fuller statement فَاتَّقُوا اللَّهَ وَأَطِيعُونِ, "fear God and obey me," is repeated eight times.

The complaint element in *Nūh*, lines 5–24, has little to do with the story of Noah and everything to do with conflicts in Muhammad's ministry to the Quraish as depicted in the traditional literature. The prophet, be it Noah or Muhammad, urges his people to abandon worship of other gods, but the people cling to gods named Wadd, Suwa', Yaguth, Ya'uq, and Nasr. This detail is absent from all other presentations of the Noah story in the Qur'ān. The prophet asserts that he has spoken to the people both publicly and privately, arguing from the wonder of the created world to urge them to repent.

The final three lines of *Nūh* represent an addition to the complaint element that breaks the narrative flow of the story. They present a prayer by Noah to blot out the unbelievers after the reader has already been informed they have been drowned. These final lines also betray the audience for whom the sūra is intended, at least in its canonical form.

> And Noah said, "Oh my Lord! Do not leave any of the unbelievers on earth! If you leave them, they will mislead your servants, and they will bear none but sinning unbelieving ones. Oh my Lord! Forgive me, my parents, and the one who enters my house in faith, and the believing men and the believing women: and do not add to the wrongdoers anything but destruction!" (Q 71.26–28)

This sūra is directed to believers and is concerned with the problem of attrition. The object of the prophet's distress is not the fate of the "sinning unbelieving ones" but anxiety that their continuing presence and unbelief will weaken the commitment of believers and "mislead thy devotees." The polemic of this sūra is directed internally, as exhortation to individuals within the group.

---

23. Welch 2000, 89.

3.4. SŪRAT AL-MU'MINŪN (Q 23)

Sūra 23, titled *Al-Mu'minūn*, "The Believers," is 118 verses long. *Al-Mu'minūn* contains a two-part introduction, the first section reading like a creed, consisting of short, terse lines stating a list of correct behaviors, including charity, avoidance of gossip, sexual continence, honesty in business relationships, and prayer (Q 23.1–11). A succinct statement of cosmology and anthropology follows. After explaining the human life cycle, the afterlife, the organization of the heavens, and the fruitfulness of the earth, it invokes the image of "a tree coming out of Mount Sinai" (Q 23.20). The closing lines, almost as an aside, marvel at the usefulness of cattle and الفلك (ships), foreshadowing the Noah story.

Following the introduction, *Al-Mu'minūn* presents a review of history beginning with the story of Noah, then moves to the story of an unnamed prophet. It alludes to other unnamed prophets but provides no details of their stories. A punishment story featuring Moses and Aaron follows, and one line is allotted to the "son of Mary," who, along with his mother, is called a sign.

The key word الفلك "ship" connects Noah's story to the proceeding material. In contrast to *Al-Shu'arā*, the prophets are not called "brothers" of their people. The prophetic stories in this sūra are short and thinly told, but each stresses the charge leveled by the prophet's community that he is "just a man," and the community accuses the prophet of "falsehood."[24] Only in the story of Noah does the community add that there must be بِهِ جِنَّةٌ (a jinn in him)—that he is possessed.

After the prophetic stories, *Al-Mu'minūn* returns to the present in a long and winding discussion of the merits of belief and the perils of disbelief, at several points returning to the short creed-like commandments of the introduction. Wonder is expressed that unbelievers fail to recognize or deny the prophet, saying بِهِ جِنَّةٌ (that he is possessed), a charge linking this section to the preceeding Noah story. This portion of the sūra also contains a striking series of questions and answers, reading like debate preparation for conflicts with unbelievers, including the assertion, "God has begotten no son, nor is there any god along with him" (Q 23.81–94).

The sūra closes with disturbing images of the afterlife, the sinners aflame, their faces burned and distorted. On behalf of the believers, the sūra indulges in a bit of mockery, "But you made them [the object of] ridicule, so much

---

24. The accusation that the prophet is "just a man" is found of Noah in Q 23.25, of the unnamed prophet in Q 23.33, and of Moses and Aaron in Q 23.47. A charge of falsehood is raised against Noah in Q 23.26, against the unnamed prophet in Q 23.39, and against Moses and Aaron in Q 23.48.

that they made you forget my message while you were laughing at them!" (Q 23.110). The implication is clearly the same sentiment expressed in *Hūd*, when Noah is building the ark: "And every time the leaders from this people passed, they mocked him. He said, 'If you mock us, we will mock you, as you mocked!'" (Q 11.38). A final exaltation of God provides the conclusion.

Al-Mu'minūn is not as tightly organized as the previous sūras, but some attempt is made to create connections between the components. *Al-Mu'minūn* is far more interested in mocking unbelievers than in proselytizing, and its target audience is those who have already accepted the message. They are vindicated by the ridicule directed at the unbelievers.

3.5. SŪRAT HŪD (Q 11)

Sūra 11, titled *Hūd*, is 123 verses in length. Substantial portions of *Hūd* are discussed above. The two-part introduction first invites the audience to believe and repent (Q 11.1–4). The perils of disbelief are then contrasted with rewards of faith, the difference between them likened to the difference between the blind and deaf and those who can see and hear (11.5–24).

Hūd fully relates punishment stories featuring Noah, Hūd, Salih, and Shu'aib. The tale of Abraham's angelic visitation is a lead-in to the prophetic story featuring Lot, and the story of Moses and Pharaoh is briefly invoked but not recounted. The expansive amplification of the Noah story is not mirrored in the other prophetic and punishment-stories, but as a whole the style remains fuller than in many other sūras. Key-word connections between prophetic stories are absent.

Punishment stories featuring the three Arab prophets—Hūd, Salih, and Shu'aib—are structurally linked by the statement "We saved ____ and those who believed with him"[25] and the closing imprecation بُعْدًا, which may be rendered in English as "away with," as in, "Away with Ad the people of Hūd!" (Q 11.60). Neither Noah nor Lot receives this full closing formula, revealing schematic differences between prophetic stories and true punishment stories. The curse بُعْدًا appears in the Noah story at the end of the flood; unity between these sets of material is achieved through intercalation of materials, alternating between biblical and Arab figures as examples.[26] Perhaps the "but

---

25. Of Hud: Q 11.58; of Salih: Q 11.66; of Shu'aib: Q 11.94.
26. 11.44. Whereas Welch, employing form criticism, feels that the alternation between prophetic stories and punishment stories "weakens their dramatic and rhetorical effects" (2000, 92), in my literary reading the overall rhetorical effect of interweaving the stories creates a powerfully unified sūra that brings a litany of examples to bear in its case for continued belief.

we saved..." element of the concluding formula was assumed in the stories of Noah and Lot, as both escaped with all but one member of their families.[27]

The conclusion discusses God's reasons for inflicting punishment upon communities in the manner described in the prophetic narratives. Whereas we have seen the prophetic stories utilized in previous sūras to authenticate the prophet's message, *Hūd* employs them as encouragement:

> All We tell you from the stories of the messengers, with it We strengthen your heart. In this the truth has come to you and an admonition and a reminder for the believers. (11.120)

Hūd is directed to believers, as indicated by the repeated reminder "we saved ____ and those who believed with him" (absent from the other versions) and the explicit message of encouragement in Q 11.120. It is a paraenetic call to correct belief, reminding the audience of what they already know to be true by invoking foundational prophetic stories.

3.6. SŪRAT YŪNUS (Q 10)

Sūra 10, titled *Yūnus*, "Jonah," is 209 verses in length. *Yūnus* immediately addresses the perception of Muhammad as "just a man," a charge that haunts Muhammad and the prophets of old in many sūras. *Yūnus* beseeches its audience to praise God, invoking the wonder of creation and describing eventual punishment or reward for those who reject or accept this demand. Rather than detailing the careers of past prophets and drawing a corollary to Muhammad, *Yūnus* begins with an extended apology for the veracity of Muhammad's prophethood and message before adducing the careers of prior prophets as supporting evidence.

This sūra reads more like a public address than those surveyed thus far, with the command قُل "Say!" punctuating the initial discussion seventeen times before line 70. In an effective bit of oratory, *Yūnus* supplies argumentation from the perspectives of both the unbelievers and Muhammad (they say X, so you say Y). Each question/statement attributed to unbelievers sets up the correct response perfectly. Interestingly, the audience is addressed as "mankind" (يَا أَيُّهَا النَّاسُ) rather than "children of Adam" (يَا بَنِي آدَمَ), the appellation given in sūra 7.

Stories of the Arab prophets are absent from *Yūnus*. It briefly tells the story of Noah, mentioning in passing that many other messengers have been

---

27. Of interest here is that in Q 66.10 Noah and Lot are both said to have had unbelieving wives who were destroyed.

sent. *Yūnus* then turns to Moses' conflict with the sorcerers of Pharaoh and the Red Sea crossing. Pharaoh's sorcerers do not repent when they witness Moses' superior powers, as they did in sūra 26. Instead, about to be overcome by the sea, *Pharaoh* submits to the will of God, declaring, "I believe that there is no God except the one the children of Israel believe in, and I am among those who submit" (Q 10.90b).

The prophet Jonah, who provides the sūra's title, receives only one verse, but this small report presents a problem:

> If only there had been a town that believed so that its faith would have profited it, aside from the people of Jonah! When they believed, we removed from them the punishment of disgrace in the life of the world, and allowed them enjoyment for a time. (Q 10.98)

Muhammad, or the audience, is instructed to verify the stories of past prophets revealed in the sūra with biblicist informants: "If you are in doubt about what We revealed to you, then ask those who have been reading the book before you. The truth has indeed come to you from your Lord, so do not be among the doubters" (Q 10.94). However, one wonders if a biblicist audience would readily assent to the notion that Jonah was sent to his own people, not a foreign populace, or that Pharaoh repented and submitted to God.

The audience of *Yūnus* consists of nonbelievers. The question-and-answer style of the opening verses is an effective polemical tool, addressing the audience's reservations on the speaker's terms.

3.7. Sūrat al-Aʿrāf (Q 7)

Sūra 7, titled *Al-Aʿrāf*, "The Heights," is 206 verses in length. Beginning with a review of the many communities that have been destroyed for their sins, *Al-Aʿrāf* appeals to the image of the scales of judgment to motivate its audience. Words of accusation throughout the sūra are spoken in the second person, often coupled with chastising statements. Example of these include, "Little do you remember! Little do you give thanks!" (Q 7.3, 10).

After accusatory opening statements, *Al-Aʿrāf* relates the story of Iblis's (Satan's) refusal to prostrate himself before Adam, expulsion from heaven, and temptation of Adam (and his wife) in the garden. This tale is immediately directed against the sūra's audience, "Oh children of Adam! Do not let Satan tempt you in the same way he had your parents expelled from the garden!" (Q 7.27). The audience in this sūra is not "mankind," as in sūra 10, but "children of Adam." Although these may seem to be synonymous, *Al-Aʿrāf* connects the "children of Adam" explicitly with the communities of Noah, Hūd, Salih, Lot,

Shuʿaib, and Moses, as if each is a distinct generation in the genealogy of the same group.

The sūra stresses that each prophet was sent to his own people, which may explain Abraham's conspicuous absence. Moses' story is not limited to the contest with Pharoah's sorcerers (who, incidentally, convert to Moses' God on the spot) and crossing of the sea. Unlike the other sūras under investigation, Al-Aʿrāf discusses Moses' effort to turn his *own people* away from polytheism, relating the story of the golden calf. While Moses receives the tablets from God, his people create an image to worship from their jewelry. Although Moses is outraged by their infidelity to God, Al-Aʿrāf denies that he impiously broke the first tablets of the law. In a rather humorous allusion to the biblical story, God gives Moses the tablets with the following instruction, *"hold these firmly*, and instruct your people to hold to what is best in them" (Q 7.145). When Moses discovers the calf image among the people, the Qurʾān states:

> And when Moses returned to his people, angry and grieved, he said, "You have done evil in my place while I was gone. Did you hasten (to bring on) the decree of your Lord?" and he put down the tablets and seized his brother by the head, dragging him toward himself. (Q 7.150a)

After Moses rectifies the situation, we read: "When the anger of Moses was subsided, *he took up the tablets*: in the writing thereon was guidance and Mercy for such as fear their Lord" (Q 7.154a).

Al-Aʿrāf is a vast polemic argument directed to an unbelieving biblicist audience, revealing possible sectarian tensions between the speaker and the addressees. The focus of the sūra is Muhammad's continuity with biblical prophets and tradition.

4. Noah in Muslim Interpretation

Having presented my assessment of the literary shape of the qurʾānic Noah story, I now turn to the story of Noah as presented in writings of three major Qurʾān interpreters—al-Ṭabarī (224–5 A.H./839 C.E.–310 A.H./923 C.E.); al-Qurṭubī (ca. 600 A.H./1200 C.E.–671 A.H./1273 C.E.); and Ibn Kathīr (ca. 700 A.H./1300 C.E.–774 A.H./1373 C.E.)—to determine how these writers understood Noah in the Qurʾān.[28] I have two specific objectives with regard to these interpreters. First, I examine al-Ṭabarī's *Taʾrīkh al-rusul wa al-mulūk* (*The History of the Messengers and the Kings*) and Ibn Kathīr's *Qiṣaṣ al-anbiyāʾ* (*Stories*

---

28. Dates for al-Ṭabarī and Ibn Kathīr are taken from van Donzel, 1998, vols. 3 and 10; al-Qurṭubī from www.tafseercomparison.org.

of the Prophets) to determine the impact of variation and contradiction in the qur'ānic Noah story on the way these authors relate the flood narrative. Following this, I turn to two classic works of *tafsīr* (exegesis), al-Ṭabarī's *Jāmiʿ al-bayān fī tafsīr al-Qurʾān* and al-Qurṭubī's *al-Jāmiʿ li-aḥkām al-Qurʾān*, to revisit problematic verses in *Hūd*'s presentation of the Noah story and benefit from the exegetical insight of these interpreters.

Al-Ṭabarī was one of the earliest and most prominent Muslim historians and exegetes. *Taʾrīkh al-rusul wa al-mulūk* is a history stretching from the creation of the world to A.H. 915. In the treatment of the Noah story in this history, the reader finds Ṭabarī has interwoven *Isrāʾīliyyāt*, sources derived from the Bible and Jewish folklore, with the qur'ānic Noah material. The addition of *Isrāʾīliyyāt* enables the author to deal at length with characters and questions not addressed in the Qurʾān, such as Noah's father Lamech, Noah's age at different stages of the story, the construction and dimensions of the ark, the organization of people and animals aboard during the journey, the identity of the drowned son, and the extent of the flooded area.

Ṭabarī deals with variation and contradiction in the qur'ānic Noah story using selection and harmonization.[29] Qur'ānic quotations are interspersed throughout Ṭabarī's narrative, but sources for these quotations are limited to sūras *Hūd*, *Nūḥ*, and *Al-Qamar*. This selectivity limits the number of variants at play and reduces the need to struggle with incongruities. The compatibility of the versions of the Noah story presented in sūras *Hūd* and *Nūḥ* is discussed above. Ṭabarī draws heavily on the amplified Noah story presented in these two sūras and supplements the accounts with three details found in *Sūrat Al-Qamar*: the charge that Noah was مَجْنُون (crazy), the simultaneous gushing forth of water from both the heavens and the earth, and the assertion that Noah was saved as "a reward to one who had been rejected."[30] These details, while absent from sūras *Hūd* and *Nūḥ*, harmonize easily in Ṭabarī's overall rendition of the Noah story.

Writing nearly 450 years later, Ibn Kathīr is widely celebrated as a master of *ḥadīth* (traditions relating to the words and deeds of Muhammad) and *tafsīr*. *Qiṣaṣ al-anbiyāʾ* is closely related to his renowned *tafsīr*, organized by prophet, in rough chronological order.[31]

Ibn Kathīr's solution to qur'ānic variance and contradiction in *Qiṣaṣ al-anbiyāʾ* is full harmonization. He writes, "We have already spoken about all of these passages in our interpretation [*tafsīr*]. We will relate the meaning of the story through the group of them from all of these places, and from

---

29. Ṭabarī 1965.
30. See 54.9, 11 and 13 respectively.
31. Wheeler 2002, 7.

the traditions and sayings."[32] *Qiṣaṣ al-anbiyā'* records each reference to Noah in the Qur'ān side by side and then offers supplementary information found in *hadīth* and *Israiliyyat*. There is no indication that variation between the accounts, such as the distinction between Noah's "people" and the "chiefs of the unbelievers among his people," the reasons for the community's rejection (idiocy, possession, lying, that he is "just a man," or that he has lowly followers), or the actual threat posed to Noah by his community (stoning, expulsion, sentencing) are in any way incongruent.[33]

Al-Qurṭubī, writing between the lifetimes of al-Ṭabarī and Ibn Kathīr, produced the twenty-volume *al-Jāmi' li-aḥkām al-Qur'ān*, which concentrates on the extrapolation of legal rulings from the Qur'ān but simultaneously provides exegesis of verses, comments on difficult words and stylistic considerations, and relates *hadīth*.[34]

Turning to al-Ṭabarī's *Jāmi' al-bayān fī tafsīr al-Qur'ān* and al-Qurṭubī's *al-Jāmi' li-aḥkām al-Qur'ān*, I revisit some points of interest in *Hūd*'s presentation of the Noah story, discussed above.

11.35. Or, do they say, "He forged it?"

Above I offer the observation this verse breaks the narrative flow of the Noah story in *Hūd* and suggest this verse was inserted to emphasize the parallelism between Muhammad and Noah's work as warners. Qurṭubī understands the subject "he" as Noah and the forged object "it" as "the revelation and the message."[35] Ṭabarī, however, glosses the verse, making reference to Muhammad, "Or, do the associators (polytheists) from your people say 'Muhammad made up this Qur'ān'?" and adds, in a footnote, Muhammad's story breaks through into Noah's in this verse.[36]

11.40. The oven gushed forth…

Of particular interest is the description of the beginning of the flood in Q 23.27 and 11.40. Although most English translations of the Qur'ān render the verse, "and the fountains of the earth gushed forth," the Arabic text reads, وَفَارَ التَّنُّورُ, the *oven* gushed forth.[37] Arabic dictionaries give both "oven" and "fountain" as possible translations for التَّنُّور; however, the latter translation may

---

32. Ibn Kathīr 1968, 82.
33. See page 264 above.
34. There are brief articles on al-Qurṭubī and his *tafsīr* at www.tafseercomparison.org.
35. Qurṭubī 1967, 9:29.
36. Ṭabarī 1969, 375.
37. See تَنُّورٍ as both "oven" and "fountain" in Lane 1863–93. "Oven" only in Cowan 1979.

be based on the use of the word in the context of these verses. The root associated with the word is probably *n-w-r*, relating to fire.³⁸ Ṭabarī understands the word التَّنُّور as "oven" rather than "fountain," specifically a "bread oven," stoked hot by the arrival of the punishment. He recognizes that some interpreters understand the oven to be an expression indicating the face of the earth on the strength of the parallel flood account in *Sūrat Al-Qamar*, stating, "We cracked open the earth in springs." ³⁹

Qurṭubī notes the word is not of Arabic origin. He knows the two explanations of التَّنُّور given by Ṭabarī and offers several others, including interpretations stating it was a bread-baking oven that once belonged to Eve and became Noah's, the place where the waters met around the ship, daybreak, the highest point on the earth, or a fountain. Qurṭubī also cites *Sūrat Al-Qamar* as supporting evidence.⁴⁰

11.42–43, 45–46. It (the ark) sailed with them among waves like mountains. And Noah called to his son, for he was isolated, "Oh my son, embark with us and do not be among the drowned!" He (the son) said, "I will seek refuge on a mountain that will save me from the water." He (Noah) said, "Today there is no rescuer from the command of God, except on whom he has mercy." And the water passed between them, and he was among the drowned…. And Noah called upon his Lord, he said, "My Lord, surely my son is of my family, and surely your promise is true, for you are the most just of judges." He (God) said, "Oh Noah, indeed he is not of your family, for he does unjust deeds. Do not ask me about that which you have no knowledge. I admonish you so that you will not be among the ignorant."

The drowned son is a peculiarity unique to *Hūd*'s presentation of the Noah story. There is no reference to this event elsewhere in the Qur'ān. Although the son remains unnamed in the verses above, early exegetical tradition sought to identify this elusive yet dramatic character. In his *tafsīr*, Ṭabarī glosses the phrase "And Noah called to his son" with "And Noah called to his son Yam."⁴¹ In *Ta'rīkh* he elaborates, offering a second name for the son:

> And it is said that before the flood Noah had two sons who both died. One of them was called Canaan, and he was the one who drowned in the flood. The other of the two was called Eber. He died before the flood.⁴²

---

38. The Syriac dictionary renders "oven" as the only translation (Margoliouth 1903).
39. Ṭabarī 1969, 376, Q 54.12.
40. Qurṭubī 1967, 9:33.
41. Ibid.
42. Ṭabarī 1965, 199.

Ṭabarī mentions Shem, Ham, and Japeth and the racial divisions of their offspring, then returns to the drowned son, saying, "Canaan, he was the one who drowned, and the Arabs call him Yam."[43]

Qurṭubī's *tafsīr* agrees, "*He* was an unbeliever, and his name was Canaan, and it is said that his name was Yam," but also entertains grammatical speculation that the drowned person was "her son," meaning the son of Noah's wife, but not Noah's own.[44] This is consistent with the qur'ānic tradition regarding the wickedness of Noah's wife:

> God sets forth the wife of Noah and the wife of Lot as an example to the unbelievers. They were under (the authority of) two of our righteous servants, but they betrayed them, so they (the husbands) did not assist them before God. And it was said, "Enter the Fire along with (those that) enter!" (Q 66.10)

In *Qiṣaṣ*, Ibn Kathīr is similarly inclined to highlight the link between the sinful son and sinful mother.

> As for the wife of Noah, she was the mother of all his sons, and they were Shem and Japeth and Ham and Yam—the People of the Book call him Canaan, and he is the one that was drowned—and Eber, who died before the flood. And it is said that she was drowned with the (ones) drowned, for she was an unbeliever, among the ones against whom the word had gone forth.[45]

On the strength of the qur'ānic quotation "My Lord, surely my son is of my family," all three Muslim exegetes surveyed eventually agree that the drowned son was truly Noah's. None of these sensitive readers seems troubled that Noah's intercession occurs after the flood ends, shedding doubt on my assertion this disrupts the logical flow of events. In Ṭabarī's *tafsīr*, Noah's outburst seems less an intercessory supplication for the life of the son and more a cry of grief and request for explanation.

5. Conclusion

The style of the Qur'ān is notoriously allusive and elliptical, requiring a knowledgeable audience to supply missing details.[46] Economy of style enables

---

43. Ibid.
44. Qurṭubī 1967, 9:38.
45. Ibn Kathīr 1968, 100.
46. "A distinctly referential, as contrasted with expository, style characterizes the

the Qur'ān to focus on its message without diluting the urgency of prophetic utterance by pausing to review traditions presumed to be shared.

Announcing itself as divine revelation, qur'ānic disclosure is doubly spare, allowing for multiple levels of meaning through "an arresting starkness of foreground, an enormous freight of background."[47] This permits the renewal of signification essential for ongoing interpretation. It is little wonder that qur'ānic referentiality generated a growing demand for *Israiliyyat* (explanatory biblicist lore) in the centuries following its revelation, as it was encountered by audiences who did not possess the required extratextual competencies.

The story of Noah is no exception to this qur'ānic rule. Although it is retold in seven sūras throughout the Qur'ān, abundance of attention to Noah does not result in abundance of detail. Only one sūra, *Hūd*, describes the building of the ark. In the other six versions, the existence of Noah's ship is simply a given, fulfilling an unspoken expectation. We learn nothing of Noah's genealogy or the exigencies of life on the ark—two topics of great interest for later Muslim interpretation.[48] Instead, the details of Noah's story are subordinated to the purpose for which it is employed, either validation of Muhammad's message or exhortation for believers to persist in the face of oppression.[49]

Definition of the literary shape of Noah in the Qur'ān requires assessment of similarities, differences, and contradictions among the seven presentations of his story. I demonstrate above that the highly developed version presented in *Hūd*, possibly supplemented by the amplified "complaint element" in *Nūh*, emerges as the dominant story shape. This assertion gains considerable support from the treatment of the Noah story in al-Ṭabarī's *Ta'rīkh al-rusul wa al-Mulūk*, which conflates the details of *Hūd* and *Nūh* into a unified account.

Having identified the dominant story shape, subordinate versions must be either harmonized or ignored. The above investigation of Muslim exegesis of the Noah story demonstrates that this decision is particular to the individual:

Quranic treatment of most of what I have alluded to as the schemata of revelation, exhibited there as components of earlier established literary types" (Wansbrough 1977), 1.

47. Alter 1981, 17. Alter writes this description of certain biblical narratives in a discussion of Erich Auerbach's description of biblical narrative as purposely spare and "fraught with background," a jointly literary and theological device. See Auerbach 1957.

48. For instance, in Ṭabarī's *Ta'rīkh*.

49. "In salvation history the role of scripture, I have suggested, was polemical.... It was by recourse to a number of exegetical devices that Muslim scripture was adapted to the several needs of a new confessional community. Of those devices haggadic exegesis employed the greatest number whose function could be described as 'prognostic', that is, designed to adapt the *topoi* of Biblical salvation history to the mission of the Arabian prophet" (Wansbrough 1978, 89).

whereas Ibn Kathīr preferres full harmonization in *Qiṣaṣ al-anbiyāʾ*, al-Ṭabarī's *Taʾrīkh* limits the harmonized material and disregards other versions.

Whether variant details are reconciled or ignored, multiple inclusions of the Noah story have a cumulative effect. The qurʾānic *Straflegenden* and prophetic stories are not neutral retellings but are crafted to convey particular messages; repetition of these stories strengthens the audience's assent to the intended perspective. The audience is then pressed to authenticate Muhammad's authority and message on the basis of its congruence with prior prophets as the Qurʾān portrays them.

A Shelter amid the Flood: Noah's Ark in Early Jewish and Christian Art

Ruth Clements

The story of Noah provided fertile ground not only for the literary imaginations of early Jews and Christians but for their artistic imaginations as well. In the context of a collection of essays on the interpretation of the Noah story in mostly literary contexts, an investigation of artistic representations of Noah potentially may provide a *non*textually bound window onto how this and other biblical narratives were received and were held to have meaning in early Jewish/Christian culture.

Before proceeding, however, a few methodological reflections are in order. A guiding underlying assumption in most studies of literary texts that interpret biblical stories is that such interpretations have the Bible's base text (with all its linguistic detail) to some extent in view. In other words, we tend to assume that interpreting texts respond to, and are responsible to, a biblical text as their "control." This can be seen in the kinds of questions we ask; traditionally, biblical expansions or "rewritings" have been seen first and foremost in terms of how they "fill in" the biblical narrative or work out textual contradictions or other problems, rather than in terms of the cultural product or message that they present.[1]

Jocelyn Penny Small, in discussing the relationship between classical Greek texts and artistic production, has pointed out the extent to which the transmission and reception of literature in ancient Greek culture was *disassociated* from any written text. Small notes that cultural dissemination of the "classics" took place in largely oral and aural venues of recitation and performance. She argues that the *imaginary* life of classic narratives is often formed by the nexus of memory and culture, not text or diction and culture—so that images (e.g., scenes from Homer, on vase paintings) often contain or repeat

---

1. See, e.g., for a by now classic statement, Kugel 1983.

scenes that do not exist in any text—because the artists were synthesizing from memory and imagination, not exegeting text.[2]

I suggest that we have to envision at least a partly analogous situation for the relationship between the biblical text and early Jewish and Christian art. We know from the practice of ancient biblical translation and from the evidence of the Qumran scrolls that the study of biblical *texts*—and even the composition of various kinds of textual interpretation—was an important part of the Jewish culture out of which early Christianity and its Jewish contemporaries emerged. However, we know, too, that for the bulk of Jewish and early Christian populations, the primary venue for conveying and receiving the teachings of the Torah was listening to readings and oral expositions in communal settings. In addition, the evidence of Qumran and other early Bible manuscripts presents *no* concrete evidence of a practice of biblical text illustration before the late fifth century, whereas the earliest artistic representations of biblical scenes begin to evolve two centuries or more before that. In early Jewish and Christian contexts, then, the earliest biblical art emerges to serve other purposes than enhancing or elucidating a biblical text.

For the present investigation, Small's insights have a more particular application as well. Most important, we are reminded that there is not a straight line from text—biblical or otherwise—to picture. In "reading" biblical art, of course, we may find indications of extrabiblical interpretive traditions and may thus be able to trace their cultural durability. In fact, extrabiblical

---

2. Small 2003. Most relevant to the discussion of biblically based art, Small takes issue with the influential position of Kurt Weitzmann, who argued that Christian and Jewish monumental art had its origins in biblical text illustration; he posited an ancient tradition of illustrated Septuagint manuscripts (scrolls), modeled on the classical Greek practice of illustrating epic tales (see, e.g., his *Illustrations in Roll and Codex* [1947]). Small reminds us that the earliest extant *classical* illustrated texts date only from the second century c.e. at the earliest and that we cannot with certainty push the phenomenon back several centuries. Neither do the Judean Desert finds give any hint of a text-illustration tradition. It should be noted that Weitzmann's position was early criticized on other grounds. See, e.g., Gutmann 1966, 39, who cites research on the classical cycles demonstrating that the later illustrated cycles were not of necessity based on an earlier illustrated manuscript tradition; see further Gutmann 1983. Gutmann also notes the possibility that, like ancient pagan artists, the creators of Dura Europos and other Jewish monumental art might have been working with pattern books (that is, not based on manuscript illustration but themselves developed for plastic arts), drawings, or even other paintings (Gutmann 1966, 40 n. 18). The entire discussion is complicated by the fact that students of early illuminated biblical manuscripts, the earliest examples of which date to no earlier than the fifth century (see further below), tend to argue for manuscript archetypes originating in the third century. The salient point is that, from any of these three perspectives, it is not prudent to argue for a tradition of text illustration *prior* to the third century.

details may appear in illustrations within biblical manuscripts themselves, to elucidate the biblical text;[3] this should indicate to us something of the richly complex cultural context of interpretive traditions *outside* the (biblical) text within which biblical narratives were heard or read and understood.[4] Early Jewish and Christian art was not interpreting biblical *texts* but telling *stories* about those texts—and the stories told had to do with the particular significance of the biblical narratives in the lives of particular communities.

These things having been said, I want to first discuss two early images of Noah and see what they can tell us about cultural readings (not exegetical interpretations) of the flood narrative. I will then trace more briefly some iconographic interpretations of the Noah story in Jewish and Christian monumental and manuscript contexts.

1. Noah's Box: The Earliest Images of the תבה

The earliest representation of Noah we have is a coin that was first struck in the reign of Septimius Severus (192–211 c.e.), that is, sometime before the earliest set of paintings at Dura Europos (see fig. 1).[5] There are five extant representatives of this coin type, struck throughout the first half of the third century. It may be that they were struck at the accession of each of the emperors; the last one extant is from the reign of Trebonianus Gallus (251–253).[6] The

---

3. A good example from the standpoint of Noah art is the widely seen graphic detail of the raven feeding on a drowned corpse (Pirqe R. El. 23; see the discussion of this exegetical development in Sergey Minov, "Noah and the Flood in Gnosticism," in this volume), which appears not only in the wall mosaics of the church of San Marco in Venice but also in (for example) the Byzantine Octateuch Noah cycle (I discuss both of these below; for a fuller discussion of this detail, see Gutmann 1977). The fifth-century Ashburnham Pentateuch features scribal glosses to the illustrations, noting such features as the location of Ararat (in Armenia; again, see discussion of this manuscript below). See also more generally Bernabò 2001.

4. Nira Stone (1999) has explored the implications of this extrabiblical dynamic in early Christian Gospel illustration, vis-à-vis the Christian apocryphal literature.

5. 246 c.e. Note that there is no extant identified painting of Noah in an ark at Dura Europos. This is in keeping with the presumed focus of the Dura Europos paintings on the narrative history of the people of Israel (that is, beginning with Abraham). See Kessler 1990, 153–64.

6. Recent articles on these coins include Kindler 1971; Meshorer 1981. Tameanko 2000 brings together drawings of all five examples (also posted on the website of the American Israel Numismatic Association: http://www.amerisrael.com/article_noahs_ark.html). A detailed discussion of the coins, setting them in the context of other literary and nonliterary evidence for the Apamean Jewish community, is found in Trebilco 1991, 86–95. The notes to his discussion give a very thorough review of the scholarly debates concerning

Fig. 1. Bronze coin of Apameia, 27 millimeters in diameter, reign of Septimius Severus, 192–211 C.E. From Walter Lowrie, *Monuments of the Early Church* (New York: Macmillan, 1906), 237, fig. 79.

coins come from Apamea Kibotos, in Asia Minor. They present a two-scene narrative—a couple in a chest that is floating on the water and a couple out of the chest on dry land, with raised right hands.[7] The narrative action moves from right to left, which has been associated with "le sens de l'écriture sémitique," implying that the designer of the coin was Jewish.[8] The chest is labeled Νωε, and, in fact, at least two other iconographic features locate us in the Genesis story: a large bird perched on the top of the ark (the raven); and another flying toward the ark with a branch in its beak (the dove). Another feature is more puzzling from a biblical point of view: the ark is basically a two-person box, and there is no attempt to convey a sense that anyone (human or animal) was rescued besides Noah and his wife. The question may be asked, not only where this nonliterary Noah comes from, but how he came to be there at all. A look at the wider cultural context for this coin may help us out.

---

the coins from the late nineteenth century on. See also for the earlier critical discussion Kreitzer 1999, and see nn. 20 and 22 below.

7. The technique of representing multiple narrative scenes in an artistic composition is often seen in ancient monumental art (especially sarcophagi; Trebilco 1991, 87). More significantly, perhaps, the two-scene narrative technique bears a striking similarity to that found in some of the illustrations of Dura, which likewise represent progressive action by positioning the same characters at different narrative moments. Thus, the *technique* of representation certainly links the coins with the Dura style and sets them off from pagan coins of the same era. See Grabar 1951, 12–13.

8. Grabar 1951, 11–12. It is probable that the Apamean Jewish community, like its contemporaries in other cities of Asia Minor, used a Greek translation of the Scriptures; see the discussion in Trebilco 1991, 67–68, 74–77, on the use of the LXX in nearby Acmonia. This probability makes the question of narrative direction of the scenes on the coins even more intriguing and the supposed influence of Semitic writing less convincing.

Apamea Kibotos was founded by Antiochus I, below the older trade city of Celaenae, close to the source of the Marsyas River.[9] Antiochus III brought a large contingent of Persian Jews to the area circa 205 B.C.E.; according to Josephus, they were given considerable autonomy and self-governance privileges (Josephus, *Ant.* 12.3.4). Because of its location, Apamea was a thriving trade city, and the Jews became a prominent part of its economic and civic life. Strabo is the first writer who refers to the city as Apamea Cibotos, "as it is called" (Strabo, *Geography* 12.8.13). One theory for the origin of the nickname is that, since the city was at the crux of important trade routes, the κιβωτοί (chests) in which goods were transported came to stand for the city itself, as an indication of its economic importance. An Apamean coin from the time of Hadrian shows the local god Marsyas (associated with the river) lying in the mouth of a cave; above it are five chests and the inscription ΑΠΑΜΕΩΝ ΜΑΡΣΥΑΣ ΚΙΒΟΤΟΙ. Two other similar coins have only one or two chests.[10] Clearly, these coins link the river and the city's economic importance, which suggests that the nickname derives from the city's geographical and socioeconomic situation.[11]

Phrygia was no stranger to local flood stories. Paul Trebilco outlines at least four such legends, three of which might be seen to have some bearing on the present question. The story of King Nannakos, who was given an oracle predicting that all human beings would die in Deucalion's flood, is associated with the city of Iconium.[12] Plutarch retells a flood story involving King Midas and his son, which is actually set at Celaenae.[13] Finally, the story of Philemon and Baucis (found in Ovid's *Metamorphoses*) relates the rescue of a couple who walk up a hill out of range of the flood waters. It is certainly plausible, as Trebilco suggests, that the Jews who came to Apamea under Antiochus III found a local tradition of a great flood, which they then reinterpreted as

---

9. For the history of Apamea as drawn from the classical sources, see Ramsay 1897, 396–450.

10. See Trebilco 1991, 90–91 and the notes thereto for a description of these coins and references.

11. One long-standing opinion holds that the nickname derived from the Jewish Noah tradition, cited, for example, by Grabar 1951. Grabar does not mention the pagan Kibotos coins, however. For a listing of other scholars who have held to the "Jewish influence" theory, see Trebilco 1991, 222 n. 6.

12. In the aftermath of the flood, the king was instructed to make clay figures (*eikones*) to repopulate the earth, from which event the city is said to have gotten its name. Suidas, Zenobius, and Stephanus of Byzantium all recount this story. Cf. the discussion in Trebilco 1991, 88–89.

13. Plutarch, *Parallel Lives* 5. Trebilco (1991, 90) relates the growth of this legend to local geography, where earthquakes caused the creation of lakes.

Noah's deluge. Κιβωτός (box or chest) is the Septuagint's translation for the Hebrew תבה, Noah's (and baby Moses') vehicle.[14] It would be but a small leap to make an association between the biblical story, local tradition, and the city's nickname and characteristic iconography.

Sibylline Oracles 1.321–325 reflects the tradition that Mount Ararat was in the mountains above Apamea, at the source of the Marsyas River.[15] Sextus Julius Africanus, writing at the same time that the coins were being issued, mentions the landing of Noah's ark on Ararat, "which we know to be in Parthia; but some say is in Kelainai of Phrygia." Always a stickler for accuracy, Africanus lets us know that he has "seen both places."[16] The note implies that in Africanus's day, the "landing place" at Apamea was a known spot for public pilgrimage.

The coin series itself seems to have been sponsored in some way by the Jewish community. At least one of the city officials referred to on the coins has a clearly, though not necessarily exclusively, Jewish name (Alexander).[17] The coin was most likely struck to bring the community to the emperor's eye through allusion to its local claim to legendary fame.[18] A long-standing theory

---

14. See the appendix to this essay.

15. This tradition is taken as an indication of the Phrygian provenance of the Jewish substratum of Sibylline Oracles books 1–2; cf. Collins 1983, 332. Collins leans toward a dating of the Jewish stratum of these books between 30 C.E. and the destruction of the temple, and of the Christian redaction no later than 150 C.E. (331–32). This dating lends weight to the proposition that the Apamean community was drawing on a venerable and to some extent well-known connection with their city when they had the coins struck.

16. Fragment from the *Chronography*, preserved in the *Chronicon* of George Syncellus (§22). Translation from Adler and Tuffin 2002, 30.

17. Note that this Alexander is named "high priest" of the city (like similar city officials named on other coins). Trebilco (1991, 222 n. 14) argues that this is evidence against his Jewishness and that use of the title by a Jew would have implied apostasy and separation from the Jewish community. This is not necessarily the case, however; as Trebilco himself notes elsewhere, Jews were permitted to hold local public office and exempted from duties that would conflict with their religion (1991, 173–83; and see the following note).

18. Septimius Severus has a mixed reputation on Jewish questions, to say the least. The *Historia Augusta* relates that he made an edict forbidding conversion to both Judaism and Christianity. Linder mentions the report in *Historia Augusta* but does not have a record of the actual law; he interprets the "edict" as a law dating back to Antoninus Pius and reissued in 202, which permitted Jews (and *only* Jews) to be circumcised (1987, 99–101). On the other hand, he does report a law or series of laws, jointly passed by Septimius Severus and his son and successor Caracalla, permitting Jews to hold public office and requiring them to take part only in those liturgies (public observances) that did not conflict with their religion (103–6, 110–13). Linder infers that the offices had previously been closed to Jews, at least from the time of Hadrian. If this is the case, our coins, featuring Jewish city officials, might originally have been struck in gratitude to the emperor for the reinstatement of these

holds that the Noah coins, along with the other picturesque local Apamean coins portraying local (pagan) religious legends, had their original model in a depiction of local legends found on a painted stoa or other public building or monument in the city itself.[19] Such decorated public structures were not uncommon in the ancient world, though we have no physical evidence for such in ancient Apamea. If this were in fact the case, however, it would mean that the community's own version of the flood legend was accepted by their pagan neighbors as a facet of the city's public persona and distinctive image within its wider cultural context.

It has been suggested that the narrative model for these coins is the well-known but not "local" story of young Deucalion and Pyrrha—who weathered their flood in a chest.[20] A support for this suggestion is the frequent linking of Deucalion's flood with that of Noah in both Jewish and early Christian literary contexts.[21] The drawback is that I have been unable to find that such an iconographic model actually exists among the artistic remnants preserved for us.[22] The most that can be said is to note, following Joseph Fink, that Greco-Roman mythology preserved other legends of figures rescued in chests, along with their iconography.[23] In any event, when the Apamean community commissioned these coins, they drew on a pagan iconography that would be understandable to the main target of their message—the emperor and his beneficence—but they labeled the image so that no one would be in

---

civil privileges (or in acknowledgement of the Jews' willingness to assume the financial obligations associated with them).

19. See first Ramsay 1897; Trebilco 1991, 87–88 and notes gives the pedigree of this proposal. Grabar (1951, 12) sets out the other elements of this conception: (1) the Jews of Apamea had material remains of the ark that they venerated and displayed as proof of their claim; and (2) the city's nickname came from the association with Noah's κιβωτός. I have not found evidence in primary sources that supports (1), and, as we have seen, the city's nickname may plausibly have resulted from its economic importance.

20. For an extensive discussion of the "Deucalion connection," see Kreitzer 1999, 253–54. Starting in the seventeenth century, a dominant scholarly assumption was that Deucalion and Pyrrha provided the narrative model for the coins. One possible corollary of this position was that it would have been Gentile God-fearers in public office who commissioned the coins. So Reinach 1903, 62–63, quoted in Kreitzer 1999, 255–56.

21. For example, Philo, *Rewards* 23; Justin, *Apology* 2.7.2. Theophilus of Antioch, Origen, and others felt compelled to argue *against* such a linkage. See the discussion of the literary sources in Kreitzer 1999, 236–39.

22. The discussion referred to by Kreitzer (n. 20 above) seems to have revolved around literary themes in the Deucalion myth, not actual artistic models. Rutgers (2000, 93–95) states (in discussing early Christian Noah representations) that such a model exists but does not document the statement.

23. See Fink 1955, 5–17, and discussion below.

any doubt about the specificity of its content to their own sacred narrative and their own community's local claim to fame.

This is especially interesting in view of the literary context of controversy around the Noah story at about this time; issues such as the size of the ark and the fit of all those animals were critical flashpoints in both Christian and Jewish circles.[24] Apamea's Noah in a box seems serenely unconscious of controversy over size and fit—we have the smallest size and fit possible and no animals. Similarly, the biblical account focuses on Noah alone, Noah and his sons, or Noah, his sons, and their wives all together; this scene couples Noah with his wife alone, which is very romantic but not based in the literary source.[25] This pairing was early taken as a link with the narrative and imagery of the Deucalion story.[26]

The second image I want to consider is the Noah of the early Christian catacombs. As on the Noah coins, the ark is represented as a chest, sometimes with legs, sometimes without. Noah stands within, arms lifted up in a gesture of prayer, sometimes toward the bird flying above him (see fig. 2). In contrast to the coins, Noah is invariably alone. This iconography appears to be universal for the catacombs. It is certainly possible to see the image as deriving in some way from the type represented by the Noah coins.[27]

---

24. The flood story seems to have figured prominently among Marcionites, for example, through the second and third centuries, as one textual target illustrating the literary improbability of the biblical narrative (how could a container of this projected size house even two of the largest animals, like elephants?). When Origen, in the mid-third century, refutes this criticism as formulated by the Marcionite Apelles, he draws on rabbinic traditions that he has learned—which in their turn testify to a similar kind of textual polemic going on in at least some Jewish circles (Origen, *Hom. Gen.* 2.1–2).

25. As a number of scholars have pointed out, the presence of Noah's wife is itself a bit of an anomaly. The biblical account either singles out Noah alone or speaks of his extended family (sons alone or sons and wives) but does not focus on Noah and wife as a couple (Jub. 4:33 gives her a name, Emzara, but no dramatic role beyond that). One literary current that focuses on Noah's wife in her own right is Valentinian Gnosticism—she is called Norea in a few texts—but this does not seem a likely source for the current image, due to both cultural and narrative improbability: in the gnostic texts Noah and wife are more adversaries than partners, as represented here.

26. So first Falconieri 1668, who also significantly interpreted the raised right hands of the second pair as drawing on the narrative moment when Deucalion and Pyrrha, in response to the goddess Themis's command, throw rocks over their shoulders, which then become the new race of human beings. Kreitzer 1999, 259 discusses Falconieri's monograph.

27. So Grabar 1951, 13. Fink (1955, 9) implies that the coins themselves represent a "pre-Christian" (his word) iconographic synthesis, equally available to the catacomb designers.

Fig. 2. Figure of Noah in ark, tomb of Petrus and Marcellinus (first half of fourth century). From Josef Wilpert, *Die Malereien der Katakomben Roms* (Freiburg im Breisgau: Herder, 1903), fig. 186.

Josef Fink observes that the catacomb figure combines the classical figure of the *orans* with that of the classical icon of rescue in a chest.[28] In classical art, the *orans* is a female figure, arms extended in prayer. The catacomb paintings represent the first application of this figure to males, specifically to biblical heroes (Noah, Daniel, Abraham, the three youths in the fiery furnace).[29] The figure is traditionally seen in its early Christian contexts as giving thanks for salvation or perhaps as praying for the salvation of those interred in the catacombs.[30]

Accepting the general tenor of the previous discussion in this case as well, I will leave aside trying to decide the question of the particular origin of the image and look instead at the significance of the choice of this image for the catacombs and its meaning within this new context.

First, the design and construction of catacombs for a particular group is a statement (like a synagogue or other specially constructed building) that the

---

28. A number of non-flood-related pagan myths involve the punishment of being cast into the sea in a chest, which then preserves the lives of the occupants. The best known are the stories of Danae and the infant Perseus and Tenes and his sister Hemithea. See Fink 1955, 7–8 on pagan themes and iconography, with accompanying plates 2–3.

29. Following the discussion of Fink 1955, 5–7.

30. So Wilpert 1891; Wilpert suggested that the many "free" (that is, not integrated into iconographic biblical scenes) female *orans* figures in the catacombs represent the souls of the deceased interceding for their friends on earth. It is possible that the biblical *orans* shares this function as well. See the discussion in Hassett 1911.

group has culturally "arrived"—it bespeaks the expectation of continuity in a given social setting.[31] Paul Corbey Finney argues that those responsible for the earliest Christian catacombs in Rome were a solidly established group but not necessarily the wealthiest; they chose less expensive design alternatives from the available pagan pattern books. It is probably more important to see the artistic narrative underlying the catacomb Noah as (like that of the Noah coins) the pagan rescue in a chest from flood waters, "baptized" in this case to a complex of Christian and biblical resignifications.[32]

An additional characteristic of catacomb art is that most biblical stories are conveyed through the solitary figure and/or the iconographic single frozen scene.[33] Thus, Daniel among the lions, Abraham and Isaac at the moment of sacrifice, and the three youths in the fiery furnace are pictured, like Noah, at the narrative moment of crisis, often in the *orans* stance and often in juxtaposition with one another.

I have suggested elsewhere that the juxtaposition of these figures complicates the "salvation" reading of each individually.[34] I would merely like to recall here that the narrative moment alluded to in the Noah iconography is while the flood waters are still high—at the moment when the promise of future exit from the ark is recognized because of the leaves the bird brings back—just as Daniel gives thanks while still among the lions and the three youths while still in the furnace. A literary reading that helps to fill out this cultural context is 4 Maccabees, where Daniel, Isaac, and the three youths are held up as models for the seven martyred sons (e.g., 16:20–21) and where Noah provides the model to enable the mother herself to endure the deaths of her sons and to withstand "the storms that assail religion" (4 Macc 15:31–32).[35]

---

31. See the discussion of Finney 1994, ch. 6, "The Earliest Christian Art," 146–230, on the social and economic contours of the construction of the earliest Christian catacombs in Rome.

32. Finney stresses the point that the use of pagan imagery in the catacomb context should not be taken as an indication of some sort of syncretistic combination of pagan and biblical beliefs. Instead, those early commissioners of Christian catacomb art should be seen as voting with their pocketbooks—choosing among the available (pagan) artistic products to convey ideas not at all like the perceptions these images would produce in the pagan viewer.

33. That is, in contrast to the narrative sequences found both at Dura and on the Noah coins. The best known exception to this statement is the iconography of the story of Jonah, which, although indeed focusing on one figure, is often represented through multiple scenes. The story of Susanna is also usually represented through two narrative moments (conviction/vindication).

34. In Clements 2006. These ideas are also developed in Clements forthcoming.

35. I would argue that the same model is implicit in the early encomium on Eleazar, who "steered the ship of religion over the sea of the emotions, (2) and though buffeted by

In other words, the Noah of the catacombs and his compatriots, in contrast, it seems, to a general consensus on art-historical readings of this complex, bore at least a double signification for the people who chose and adapted it: indeed, the praying biblical heroes represented hope in future salvation, but also and in company with this, they put forth a model of endurance for those facing persecution and martyrdom.[36] In later catacomb art and on Christian sarcophagi, which date primarily from the fourth century C.E. and on, both the image of Noah alone in a chest and the association with one or more of the other "martyr" heroes persists, perpetuating Noah as a model of endurance of persecution into the age when present persecution ceased to define Christian identity.

Considering these two early Noahs, then, a reading that moves between texts, icon, and context has complicated both the strictly exegetical picture and the iconographic picture. We have seen that the situation of Jews and/or Christians vis-à-vis the pagan powers that controlled their cultural contexts activated two very different early "readings" of the story of Noah, expressed in two not *dis*similar iconographies. In Apamea, the coins present a bold public statement of proud presence to the non-Jewish cultural context. In the catacombs, a very similar image makes a private statement of fortitude *against* the powers and principalities.

2. Monumental Noah

In contrast to the "freeze-frame" iconography of the coins and the catacombs, Noah begins to receive a more expanded narrative treatment in synagogue and church decorative art of the fifth century and on. The second part of this essay will highlight a few aspects of that expansion.

Two extant synagogue floor mosaics, both dating from the fifth to sixth centuries C.E., feature the Noah story.[37] One, from Gerasa, Jordan, consists of a long, oblong central panel with a border, partially preserved. The panel

---

the stormings of the tyrant and overwhelmed by the mighty waves of tortures, (3) in no way did he turn the rudder of religion until he sailed into the haven of immortal victory" (4 Macc 7:1–3).

36. Bear in mind, too, that the icons of Isaac, Daniel, and the three youths present the most common forms of Christian martyrdom before the "Peace" of Constantine: beheading, beasts, and burning; it is little wonder that they are so persistently present in the pre-Constantinian catacombs.

37. An additional mosaic that *may* feature Noah has recently been unearthed by a Hebrew University team at Khirbet Wadi Hamam in the Galilee's Arbel National Park (see http://www.sciencedaily.com/releases/2007/11/071121100831.htm). This mosaic features carpenters working on a monumental structure, identification uncertain (but the ark is

contains three rows of animals (birds, larger beasts, and smaller animals); the border appears to have only larger animals and birds. In the upper left corner are visible a bird with a branch in its beak and two men's heads, labeled (in Greek) "Ham" and "Japheth." The animals in the main panel are all proceeding toward the right; it is very likely that the large missing piece of the mosaic on the lower left had some type of representation of the ark. Rachel Hachlili surmises that the "realistic" style in which the animals were rendered had its source in a pattern book.[38] The key element from our point of view is the expansiveness of the setting; although we do not know what this ark looked like, the focus of the action is now on its surroundings, on the figures coming out as much as the figure within. The synagogue floor at Mopsuestia also fills the expansive floor space with animals.[39] There are seemingly no human figures, but the ark itself is an open, empty chest—with legs—in the center of the synagogue floor.

A twelfth-century floor mosaic from a church in Otranto, Italy, bears interesting similarities to the Mopsuestia floor, in particular. This mosaic is part of a larger design that includes the signs of the zodiac and other briefer allusions to biblical stories, such as those of Adam and Eve, Cain and Abel.[40] The Noah story is portrayed in two scenes, occurring about halfway down the length of the composition (following twelve medallions with the signs of the zodiac). Latin inscriptions frame the scenes off from what precedes and follows; the two Noah scenes are separated from each other by the trunk of a tree that runs the length of the mosaic. The left frame features Noah, kneeling facing the left edge, from which the hand of God protrudes in a gesture of command.[41] The rest of the frame is taken up with the building of the ark (by Noah's sons? there are five young men in the picture), complete with a crosscut saw. Below the building scene is a line of bucolic figures squeezing grapes and making wine (one is labeled *Noe*; the others are again presumably his sons), and below that is a monumental scene of the building of the Tower

---

one possibility). The mosaic is still being restored, so it has been left out of consideration in this discussion.

38. Hachlili 1996, 119.

39. It has now become a debated point whether the Mopsuestia basilica functioned as a Jewish or a Christian building. See Hachlili 1996, 181 n. 48, who refers to Avi-Yonah 1981; see also Eid 2003.

40. For a discussion of the iconography and plates, including a view of the full floor, see Haug 1977.

41. This method of portraying God's direct interaction with human beings is a Jewish iconographical element, used at Dura Europos and elsewhere, and persisting in Christian iconography, in scenes such as, for example, the binding of Isaac and the giving of the Torah, as well as in representations of God's command to Noah to build the ark.

of Babel. The right-hand frame shows the ark as a box on legs, and here again the artist has filled the floor space with animals. In contrast to the other mosaics, however, this ark is filled with people: Noah and two sons emerge from the top of the chest/ark; a son and one of the wives are pictured in the open doors in the side of the ark. Noah's hands are outstretched to the returning dove with olive branch, while further to the right the raven munches on a corpse, making for an interesting conflation of pre- and postdebarkation scenes. The exiting animals spill over the frame of the scene and continue down the lower half of the mosaic, becoming more fantastical as they go. At the bottom of the picture, Alexander the Great is pictured enthroned between two griffins.[42]

Interestingly, whether this is a function of genre, theology, or the physical possibilities of floor design, all three of these floor mosaics share a focus on release from the ark and life following the flood; the raging waters are out of the picture.

The construction of monumental Christian basilicas allowed the production of elaborate wall or ceiling mosaics utilizing biblical or other themes.[43] An interesting series of ceiling mosaics detailing the flood story is located in the Basilica of San Marco in Venice. The mosaics date from the first half of the thirteenth century, although they are based on an older archetype, the Noah cycle found in the Cotton Genesis (see discussion below). The cycle begins with a three-scene sequence: Noah hears God's command; Noah speaks with another person; carpenters use medieval-era tools to build the ark (Noah's conversation partner appears to be the foreman). Thereafter the story continues in separately framed scenes: getting the animals onto the ark (a big chest with a roof); the rain and those killed in the flood; sending out the dove; getting it back; the rainbow; the sacrifice; and a final three-scene sequence of Noah harvesting grapes and lying drunk, with the three sons waiting outside. Text above the images frames the story they tell.

Interestingly, "extrabiblical" details inform the pictures. Again, in the scene where Noah sends out the dove, the raven feeds nearby on a floating

---

42. Haug (1977, 25–26) notes that Noah's son Ham is the biblical ancestor of Babel and suggests that this part of the mosaic sets a "third world," the world of God's creation and covenant represented in the church (in turn represented iconographically by the ark) over against the world empires of Babylon and Alexander. Even more remarkable is the appearance of the labeled figure of King Arthur at the top of the mosaic. For a discussion of the political context and implications of this iconography, see Haug 1977, 93–95.

43. The best-preserved early structure is the church of San Vitale in Ravenna, Italy, completed in the mid-sixth century. It does not include Noah among its biblical subjects, however. A number of other later structures include Noah scenes in fresco, mosaic, or reliefs (wood or stone). An exhaustive treatment of the rich artistic heritage would require a book in itself and is not attempted here.

cadaver.⁴⁴ As in the Otranto mosaic, God's act of commanding Noah is represented artistically by an extended heavenly hand.

The "Old Testament" narratives represented at San Marco (Adam, Noah, Abraham, Joseph, Moses) are located in the narthex, which location makes its own kind of theological statement. Originally, the narthex, although part of the church *building*, was not considered part of the church proper. This was the place where those not yet baptized (catechumens) were required to wait, while they prepared themselves for entry into the community of the faithful. So here, the "Old Testament" images are styled as preparatory to the "New."

3. The Turn to Text: Illuminated Manuscripts

The mosaics of San Marco, which wear their texts on their sleeves, provide a good lead-in to the discussion of Noah's appearance in illuminated manuscripts. The first extant illuminated biblical manuscripts that we have date to no earlier than the fifth century C.E. The two to which I will give particular attention are those called commonly the Cotton Genesis and the Ashburnham Pentateuch.⁴⁵

The Cotton Genesis, so called because it formed a part of the collection of Sir Robert Cotton from the early seventeenth century, was a lavishly illustrated codex of the Greek Genesis dating from the fifth century, possibly produced in Alexandria.⁴⁶ It featured about 340 pages of miniatures. Most of the manuscript was destroyed in a fire in the Ashburnham House library, in 1731; today there are fragments or drawings of 134 pages.⁴⁷ The remaining fragments have been linked to the mosaics of San Marco, and, however the codex got to Venice, it seems to have remained there long enough to have provided a model for the cathedral mosaics.⁴⁸ Kurt Weitzmann and Herbert Kessler used the fragments and the correspondences with Venice and related Genesis cycles to propose a reconstruction of the codex.⁴⁹

---

44. See n. 3 above.
45. Again, I make no attempt to offer an exhaustive account of illuminated Noahs. The following treatment only highlights a few salient features of various manuscript traditions.
46. For the critical reconstruction and edition of the manuscript and its artwork, see Weitzmann and Kessler 1986.
47. Drawings were made of a few of the pages in 1622 by Daniel Rabel, soon after Cotton purchased the manuscript. After the fire, George Vertue made and exhibited water-color copies of some of the sixty leaves that were then in the possession of the Library.
48. Weitzmann and Kessler 1986, 6–7, 16–29.
49. See Weitzmann and Kessler 1986, "Introduction," 8–16, on their method and on the families of manuscripts and other art related to the Cotton Genesis and the San Marco mosaics.

According to that reconstruction, twenty-two folios of the original contained miniatures relating to Noah and the flood.[50] Two of these scenes were full-page size: the building of the ark and the command to enter the ark. Several pages had two scenes, with or without accompanying text; most had one fairly good-sized scene. The paintings always come after the text they are meant to illustrate. Here, for the first time, the picture is intended to elucidate the text. One technique by which this occurs might be called "narrative expansion," that is, elaborating on a scene that is told much more tersely in the text. A good example of this is the scene of the building of the ark, which, as we can deduce from the deployment of this scene in St. Mark's, was replete with the realia of shipbuilding.[51]

The Latin Ashburnham Pentateuch[52] was traditionally dated to the sixth or seventh century but has recently been located in the fifth century.[53] Of the manuscript's more than two hundred conjectured original folios and perhaps sixty-nine miniatures, 143 folios with nineteen miniatures now survive. Bezalel Narkiss, the miniatures' most recent editor, has shown that they are built on both Syrian and Roman iconographic traditions; he posits a third-century Syrian Jewish biblical manuscript as one of the predecessors and models used by the Christian artist of the Ashburnham.[54]

The full manuscript apparently contained a series of three full-page miniatures of Noah-related scenes. The two extant miniatures represent the flood, on the one hand (f. 9r; fig. 3), and multiple events connected with leaving the ark, on the other (f. 10v; fig. 4). It is plausible that the first page contained a similar grouping of preflood events (e.g., the command to build the ark, the building itself, entering the ark).

Numerous extratextual details make these two miniatures extremely interesting in terms of tracing the play of interpretive traditions. The first miniature consists of the closed ark as an oval chest on legs. The windows and door are fastened with bars across the outside, in keeping with the biblical statement that God shut Noah and company in the ark (Gen 7:16); the captions note, "Here is the flood of waters.... Here is Noah shut in...." The flood

---

50. Of these pages, we have fragments of six with the remnants of illustrations.

51. Weitzmann holds that this, in turn, was based on a stock iconography for Daedalus as craftsman and artificer (in Weitzmann and Kessler 1986, 39–40).

52. It was housed in the Library of Tours until 1842, when it was stolen. In 1847 it was bought by the Earl of Ashburnham. It was returned to Paris in 1888 and is now in the National Library there.

53. See the discussion and critical edition by Bezalel Narkiss 2007, 435–40. The English section of his commentary runs from 297–490.

54. Narkiss 2007, 327–28, and see n. 55 below.

Fig. 3. Noah's ark amid the flood. Note the giants among the victims. From the Ashburnham Pentateuch (seventh or fifth century). Bibliothèque Nationale de France (Nouv. Acq. Lat. 2334), f. 9r. Used by permission.

waters surrounding the ark are replete with victims: humans, animals, and two very obvious giants. Narkiss notes the traditions found both in Jubilees (7:20–26) and in Pirqe R. El. 22 that the flood waters rose high enough to kill the giants.[55] This is not to suggest a dependence on either literary source but to note the persistence of the tradition in the predecessor manuscripts of the Ashburnham.

---

55. Ibid., 341. A significant proportion of illustrative details and/or labels in the manuscript share traditions with Pirqe Rabbi Eliezer in particular, according to Narkiss (390–91). He posits a basic "Jewish Aramaic" manuscript layer, a "Greco-Syrian" (Christian) layer, and an "Ambrosean" (Latin Christian) layer to the drawings and interpretations featured in the Ashburnham (389, 400–401).

Fig. 4. After the flood (multiple scene frame). From the Ashburnham Pentateuch (seventh or fifth century). Bibliothèque Nationale de France (Nouv. Acq. Lat. 2334), f. 10v. Used by permission.

The next miniature combines a number of different narrative moments. From the three windows on the second level of the ark we see Noah twice sending out the raven and receiving back the dove with an olive branch in its beak. The ark rests upon mountains that at the top of the miniature are labeled the "mountains of Armenia," to represent the actual landing. The top of the ark is open, and all eight human inhabitants are looking out of the top.[56] Noah

---

56. Note the contrast between this feature and the earliest "Noah in a box." The iconography begins to change in the fourth century to include the remainder of the ark's inhabitants (Narkiss 2007, 344). This is in keeping with 1 Pet 3:20, which stresses the group of eight who were saved and which is at the root of a Christian Noah baptismal typology.

is glancing up to the right, where a rainbow breaks the frame and the hand of God emerges from a cloud in a gesture of promise. Males and females are grouped separately here, as happens also in a different scene at the exit door two levels down, where the humans prepare to disembark. Outside the ark, the animals are seen leaving in pairs.

In the lower left-hand corner, Noah is offering his sacrifice after the flood. In a very interesting move, the sacrifice has become a baptismal Eucharist.[57] The flat stone altar holds three chalices, reminiscent of the baptismal custom of third-century Syria and Rome, where newly baptized persons were given water, wine, and honey to drink.[58] Interestingly, however, the caption for this scene pulls us back into the text (lest the iconography confuse)—but with a surprising twist: "Here is Noah where he sacrifices from all cattle and every bird in the world."[59]

In general, the captions for each scene in the Ashburnam Pentateuch further elucidate both the text and the message of the pictures. Sometimes they give extra narrative or historical information, as in the label locating the ark in Armenia; sometimes they point to or elucidate the theological interpretation of the narrative, as does the label on the flood scene noted above, pointing to Noah's perfect protection by God and, like 1 Pet 3:20–21, moving us toward the understanding of the Noah story as a type for baptism.[60]

Lavish illustration cycles similar to that of the Cotton Genesis are also seen in other contexts. The Vienna Genesis, a sixth-century production prob-

---

57. Narkiss 2007, 345.

58. Ibid., 342. He attributes this to the Syrian Christian layer (395–97, see n. 55 above). He notes among other literary parallels Ephrem Syrus's *Hymn* 2, which juxtaposes animal sacrifices to the (bloodless) Eucharist. Narkiss states that the three-cup custom came "later" to Rome. However, the *Apostolic Tradition* of Hippolytus of Rome, plausibly dated to the beginning of the third century, also speaks of three cups in the baptismal liturgy: mixed wine, milk mixed with honey, and water alone, "for a sign of the laver," to show that the inner as well as the outer person may be cleansed (section 23; critical edition Dix [and Chadwick] 1992). Chadwick notes the generally early (late second to early third century) provenance of this liturgy, as well as its connections with Syrian practice ("Preface to the Second Edition," d–i).

59. *Ex omni pecore et ex omni ave mundi.* The text is closest to the LXX and clearly does not reflect the Hebrew Bible's version of events, which limits the sacrifices to every "clean" bird and animal. The caption may be pointing the reader to a typology of this sacrifice as pointing to the universal significance of the covenant between Christ and the church. A similar significance is read at Exod 24:4–9, the feast of Moses and the elders on the mountain (Narkiss 2007, 344–45).

60. On this nearly ubiquitous Christian typological reading of the flood narrative, see, e.g., Lewis 1968.

ably from Syria,[61] also has a longer cycle, with some affinities to the Cotton manuscript, but these seem to be related to shared artistic conventions rather than a common model.[62] In their representations of the ark, for example, they differ strikingly. The Cotton ark seems to have been a simple, if large, chest (see, e.g., panel 32v); the Vienna ark was a more complex three-tiered affair.

The Byzantine Octateuchs, produced in Constantinople in the eleventh and twelfth centuries, also reproduce an extensive cycle of illustrations.[63] Although the iconographic style is distinctively Byzantine, we meet a number of motifs and compositional features known from other contexts: the hand of God; a building scene; a chest-like ark (which in early scenes has a rounded bottom but from the flood on is pictured as flat-bottomed); the detail of the raven feeding on a cadaver. In these last two details particularly the Octateuch cycle resembles the San Marco mosaics. Both before and after the flood, the ark is several times portrayed open at the top with its human inhabitants looking out. In contrast to the composition of both Ashburnham and Otranto, Noah's wife is by his side, although the other wives and husbands stand separately.

Other differences and perhaps innovations occur in the expansive Octateuch context. Occasionally captions add extra information, as when the sons of God wedding the daughters of men (Gen 6:4) are labeled as the progeny of Seth and Cain, respectively.[64] One interesting artistic move occurs in the illustration of the humans and animals entering the ark, where the humans are portrayed within and the animals distributed around the outside in a "carpet" effect, reminiscent of the earlier floor mosaics. One scene that is not found in the other cycles we have examined is a scene of Noah and his sons *dismantling* the ark after the flood. The scene answers the exegetical question of how Noah found wood usable for the postinundation sacrifice; one perhaps

---

61. Of a projected ninety-six folios with two illustrations each, we have twenty-four folios, each with an illustration at the bottom. Many of the illustrations contain multiple scenes, like the Ashburnham Pentateuch. The critical edition is by Wellesz 1960.

62. Both manuscripts, for example share the convention of using the hand of God to portray God's role in the biblical narrative—except in the illustration of the creation, where God is anthropomorphic. See Weitzmann and Kessler 1986. N.B.—this stylistic innovation for the creation story is probably related to Gen 1:26–27, where the first human is said to be made in the image of God.

63. Critical edition, Weitzmann and Bernabò 1999. The Octateuchs survive in four primary manuscripts, reproducing essentially the same cycles of illustrations and text layout; the four are edited synoptically by Weitzmann and Bernabò.

64. This tradition is found in a number of places, e.g., Pirqe R. El. 21–22; the Syriac *Cave of Treasures* (ca. sixth century but containing earlier traditions) 17. See Adler 1989.

unlooked-for implication is that relics of the "true ark"—whether in Phrygia or Armenia—were less than likely to have lasted a long time.

From the ninth century and forward, we see Noah in other types of manuscript contexts as well. One earlier manuscript, dating from the mid-sixth century but extant at the earliest in a ninth-century copy, is the *Christianikē Topographia* by the Alexandrian Cosmas Indicopleustes. This combination of geography, chronology, and travelogue was written, interestingly, to polemicize against the "pagan" notion that the earth was spherical and to develop the concept that the earth and heavens together take the form of a large chest with a curved lid (!). The author's biblical model for this cosmos, however, is not Noah's chest, but the biblical tabernacle.[65] He does illustrate Noah's chest, however, as a three-tiered affair with sloping sides, which he says floated half in and half out of the water; its purpose was to bring Noah and his family across the sea from the world of Paradise into our own world.

Other manuscripts preserve the tone of the biblical cycles. The sermons of Gregory Nazianzus were issued in Byzantium in the ninth century, in an illustrated manuscript featuring a number of Genesis miniatures.[66] Noah's ark as depicted here is a three-tiered affair similar to that found in the Vienna Genesis. From the twelfth century or so and forward, we also have numbers of illustrated Psalters (on the Christian side) and Haggadot (on the Jewish side). Often two Noah scenes were presented. The building of the ark and the drunkenness of Noah are favorites; these are combined, for example, in the Golden Haggadah (Catalonia, early fourteenth century). The twelfth-century Winchester Psalter puts together the building scene with a second frame of the ark afloat amid corpses, dove returning and raven feeding on cadaver (which *could* be a giant's head). The thirteenth-century St. Louis Psalter pairs a similar flood scene with Noah's drunkenness.

Out of the context of illustrating Genesis, Noah iconography begins to recapture some of its earlier, leaner representational character. In the Lire Abbey Psalter (Latin; late thirteenth–early fourteenth century), in the incipit to Ps 1 (*Beatus vir*) the B is decorated with a medallion of the sacrifice of Isaac above a medallion of Noah alone in the ark, on the water, receiving the dove. Noah and dove have once again become emblematic of the Noah story, and

---

65. *Christian Topography*, book 2.
66. See Bibliothèque Nationale de France, MS grec 510. From the eleventh century on, the sermons for festivals were published in illustrated manuscripts. The miniatures in these, however, seem to have utilized different miniature cycles and models. See Galavaris 1969, 134–35; cf. 51, 68.

it is interesting that in both this and in other similar contexts, Noah is again paired with his erstwhile companion of the catacombs, Isaac.[67]

One final example, the thirteenth-century *North French Miscellany*,[68] illustrates, like the Noah coins from Apamea, the way that iconography may cross cultural contexts in order to make a statement of community identity. The *Miscellany* features a full-page medallion of the solo Noah in the ark, in the midst of the waters, with raven perched and dove returning. The ark itself, though, of brick and stucco, red-roofed, is an unmistakable and unshakeable building. The *Miscellany* itself took shape in the aftermath of a massacre and martyrdom of Jews at Metz in 1278. In a number of ways, the iconography of the miniatures here included, painted in Christian artisans' workshops (albeit perhaps by some Jewish artisans),[69] using Christian iconographic models, nevertheless succeeds in articulating a stand against the church and its secular agents: the governments of Louis IX and his son and successor, Philip III.[70] In this case, I want to suggest, a Christian iconographic model meant to convey the theme of shelter in the church from the besetting storms of life has transmuted into a symbol of shelter and protection from the waves of political persecution in thirteenth-century France.

In this admittedly incomplete sketch, we have, on the one hand, noted intersections, biblical and otherwise, between text and art; we have also noted

---

67. As also in the Winchester Psalter. In these instances, too, the positioning of Isaac (kneeling to be beheaded by Abraham) reverts to catacomb iconography.

68. Facsimile edition with critical essays in Salter, Salter, and Schonfeld 2003. On the general iconographic provenance(s) of the miniatures, see ch. 7 in vol. 2.

69. So Sed-Rajna 1982, 18, who suggests that the creators of these miniatures were Jewish artists working within the confines of Christian workshops.

70. For example, a series of four miniatures (on ff. 524r–527v) represent in turn: Queen Esther before King Ahasuerus (Esth 8:3); Moses praying with Aharon and Hur during the battle with Amalek (Exod 17); Samuel beheading Agag (1 Sam 15:32–33); and Mordechai's triumph over Haman (Esth 6:11). Taken together, the four pictures represent the three biblical moments of challenge to and triumph over Amalek (Exod 17), which is at the root of the annual Purim celebration (*contra* Sed-Rajna 1982, 19, who seems to miss the Amalek connection). The second picture in the series represents Moses with raised arms but folded hands, Aaron and Hur supporting his elbows. As Daniel Sperber (1995) points out, this iconography avoids portraying Moses with hands outstretched in the form of a cross, which fits in with rabbinic polemic against praying with outstretched hands. However, the iconography itself was created in a French Christian workshop; the same representation appears in the St. Louis Psalter (f. 34), painted before 1270. Here in the *Miscellany*, the Christian iconography plays a double polemic role, first in standing against the image of the cross, and second in helping articulate the artistic message that Amalek (the church) will ultimately be defeated.

the transfer of artistic motifs between external culture and biblical culture, between Jewish and Christian contexts, between nontextual and textual settings. I began and ended this essay with three instances of how minority communities interpreted the Noah story artistically through the lens of and to meet the exigencies of social and political circumstances. The salient feature shared by all three is the image of Noah protected in the ark from the raging elements without—a telling indication of the meaning of this story for diverse communities of readers under stress.

Appendix: Labeling the תבה[71]

In the earliest Greek version of the story of Deucalion and Pyrrha, the young couple rides out the storm in a λάρναξ, an older Greek term for "chest."[72] The same term appears in the story of Perseus and Danae,[73] as well as in a number of stories found in Pausanias concerned with hiding and rescue.[74] First-century C.E. grammarians gloss that same term (as found in Homer) with the more current κιβωτός.[75]

In the Hebrew Bible, both Noah's vehicle and that of the infant Moses are called a תבה. The primary meaning of the Hebrew term is "chest"; it is used exclusively in the Bible for the two chests that weather the water. Other arks or chests, particularly the ark of the covenant, are designated by the term ארון. It is suggestive, at the very least, that the Hebrew biblical tradition preserves a distinctive term for hiding or rescue from water accomplished in a chest.

The LXX erases this distinction: both types of chests are labeled κιβωτός. Paul Trebilco suggests that the LXX's choice of terms is intended "precisely to distinguish the story from the Greek myth of Deucalion."[76] Philo follows the LXX, using the same term for both. In at least one context (*Q.G.* 2:4), he brings the two κιβωτοι together, where Noah's chest designates the body, covered with pitch, immured in the things of this world, and the ark of the covenant represents the world that is perceptible only to the intellect.[77] Interestingly,

---

71. For a careful linguistic study of biblical "ark language," see Loewe 2001.
72. Apollodorus, *Bibliotheca* 1.7.2.
73. Apollodorus, *Bibliotheca* 2.4.1; cf. also Strabo, *Geography* 10.5.10.
74. E.g., Pausanias, *Description of Greece* 3.24.1; 10.14.1.
75. Aristonicus of Alexandria (fl. turn of the era), *Scolia on Iliad* 18.413; Appolonius of Alexandria (end of first century C.E.), *Homeric Lexicon*.
76. Trebilco 1991, 224 n. 35. For a more extensive discussion of the implications of the Septuagint's translation choices, see Harl 1987.
77. In those contexts where Noah's κιβωτός is in view, the chest/body has a protecting function, preserving virtues along with passions. The word λάρναξ occurs only once in Philo (according to the *TLG*), at *Migration* 16, in connection with the bones of Joseph. The

Josephus, although obviously having the biblical account in mind, uses the older λάρναξ throughout his rendition of the Noah story (*Ant.* 1.72–108). The ark of the covenant appears consistently as the biblical κιβωτός. Although he does not mention Deucalion in his account of Noah's flood, by using the older term, Josephus evokes the classical tales of chests upon the water, subtly subsuming the Greek accounts under the rubric of the biblical one and reinstating the Hebrew Bible's special distinction for chests used for rescue from or through water.

It is quite plausible, then, that early Jewish and Christian iconography of Noah, like Josephus, draws indirectly on the Bible's own link between Noah's rescue vehicle and those of flood stories from other cultures.

---

term denotes a coffin or bone box in which "some people" "bury" the parts of the self that serve the body, to consign them to oblivion.

Part 3: Miscellaneous Noah Texts and Traditions

Noah in Onomastic Traditions

Vered Hillel and Michael E. Stone

1. The first etymology of Noah's name is to be found in Gen 5:29, which reads: ויקרא את שמו נח לאמר זה ינחמנו "and he named him Noah, saying, 'This one will provide us relief (comfort us)....'" Here we may have a *popular* etymology from the root נחמ, yet this is not the root of Hebrew נח "Noah," which is apparently נוח, meaning "to rest," and this tension was the cause of much exegetical concern in postbiblical sources. Thus, despite the biblical etymology "provide relief, comfort," many entries listed below show an unanimity in giving an etymology of Noah as "rest." As Wutz points out, this derives from Hebrew נוח,[1] from which Armenian "cessation" also comes. A further confusion with נוע (Greek Νωε and Νωα) sometimes leads to Noah being assigned the meaning "movement." This etymology results from the inability of Greek to represent Hebrew laryngeals; as a result, both נוח and נוע look the same in Greek transliteration. Another meaning, "righteous," is derived exegetically from the biblical verse נח איש צדיק, "Noah was a righteous man" (Gen 6:9), and does not have any obvious linguistic etymological basis.[2] This is found in Philo and Ambrose, see below.

2. Jub. 4:28 is based on the root נחמ. The verse is derived from Gen 5:29: "He called his name Noah, saying, 'This one *will comfort* me for my trouble and all my work, and for the ground which the Lord hath cursed.'"

3. In the story of the birth of Noah in 1 Enoch, Enoch tells Methuselah: "And now make known to thy son Lamech that he who has been born is in truth his son, and call his name Noah, for he shall be left to you, and he and his sons shall be saved from the destruction" (1 En. 106:18). Presumably "he shall be left to you" is taken as a name midrash of Noah, perhaps deriving also from

---

1. Wutz 1915, 584.
2. The name in the Bible is discussed in some detail in Kikawada and Bailey 1992.

נוח. Perhaps the same explanation of Noah lies behind 4 Ezra 3:11: "Nevertheless one of them thou didst spare—Noah with his household."

4. Theophilus of Antioch, usually dated to the late second century, is one of the earliest witnesses to the etymology "rest," which dominates the onomastic tradition as it is presented below.[3] He declares (book 3; ch. 19): "Noah, which Hebrew word means 'rest.'"[4] The same is found in later patristic authors such as Ephraim the Syrian (fourth century c.e.; *Nisibene Hymns* 1.10), who says, "Noah was refreshed in rest, that his dwelling-place should give rest according to his name."[5]

5. Here we add some brief notes on rabbinic traditions, not aspiring to be exhaustive. A late source says that Methuselah named his grandson Noah because the earth was placated, while Lamech called him Menachem (Sefer Hayashar, Bereshit 13b). This is a play on the explanation in Scripture that Noah "will console us" (ינחמנו). Thus both interpretations of Noah as "rest" and מנחם are accounted for. This double tradition is based on the disjunction noted above between the root of "Noah" and the root of ינחמנו, "will provide us relief (comfort us)." Genesis Rabbah 25:2 develops this crux a little differently, stating that the name does not correspond to the interpretation and vice versa. The struggle over the name midrash gave rise to several explanations. For example, in Gen. Rab. 25:2 Noah is called the one "that caused rest" because (1) the animals' rebellion against humans that began with Adam's sin ended during the time of Noah; (2) the earth rested from the flood waters; (3) the heavenly bodies enjoyed rest during the time of the flood; and (4) the ark rested after the waters subsided.[6] Genesis Rabbah 33:3 adds another interpretation: Noah signifies the pleasant one because his sacrifice was pleasant to God.[7] This surely reflects yet another Hebrew root, נחח "to give a pleasant odor."

6. In Franz X. Wutz's work we find the following etymologies.[8]

Page 686: Greek Lists, Unedited Manuscripts to Vaticanum primum$_3$, Vaticanum primum$_4$, and Vaticanum primum$_5$

---

3. Coxe 1989, 116.
4. This name midrash appears in a letter that refutes the Greek flood story of Deucalion and Phyrra and confirms Noah as the true hero.
5. Stopford 1983, 163.
6. Cf. Gen. Rab. 33:3.
7. See also Aryeh Amihay, "Noah in Rabbinic Literature," in this volume.
8. Wutz 1915.

Νῶε. ἀνάπαυσις.   Noah.   rest.

Page 710: Greek Lists, Unedited Manuscripts to Vaticanum primum$_2$
Νῶε. ἀνάπαυσις.   Noah.   rest.

Page 727: Suppl. Grec 919, 11$_v$ (13. saec.) – Suppl.13
329 Νῶε. ἀνάπαυσις.   Noah.   rest.

Page 737: Philo, *Alleg. Interp.* 3.24, 102; *Abraham* 5
Νῶε. ἀνάπαυσις ἤ δίκαιος.   Noah.   rest or righteous.

Page 737: Philo, *Worse* 111 (W.); *Posterity* 48; *Agriculture* 2
Νῶε. δίκαιος.   Noah.   righteous.

Page 746: Excerpts from Origen
Νῶε. δικαιοσύνη.   Noah.   righteousness.

Page 749: Lactantius's Lists
Noe. requies.   Noah.   rest.

Page 769: Ambrose, *Parad.* 3.19 (277,20 Sch); *Noe* 1.2 (413,16 Sch)
Noe. iustus, requies.   Noah.   righteous, rest.

Page 813: Syriac Onomastica (Wutz's retroversion)
Νῶε. ἀνάπαυσις.   Noah.   rest.

Page 821: Syriac list in BM 860,29 (Add. 12154); ninth century (Wutz's retroversion)
Νῶε. ἀνάπαυσις.   Noah.   rest

On page 842, Wutz discusses a Syriac list that has Νωc. ταπcινωσις., i.c., Noah. humiliation.

Page 924: Armenian Ona I
Նոյ. հանգիստ կ. արդար   Noah.   rest or righteous.

Page 982: Armenian Ona II
Նոյ. դադարումն կ. հանգիստ   Noah   cessation or rest

Pages 1007, 1009, 1013: Ethiopic Onomastica (Wutz's retroversion)
Νῶε. ἀνάπαυσις.   Noah.   rest.

7. In *Names of the Patriarchs*[9] we find:
    Նոյ. հանգիստ　　　　　　　Noah.　　　rest.

8. In Armenian Ona V (line 380)[10] we find:
    Նոյ. դադարումն կամ հանգիստ　Noah.　　cessation or rest

---

9. Stone 1982a, 164.
10. Stone 1981, 150–51.

Mount Ararat and the Ark
Michael E. Stone

The identification of the "mountains of Ararat" (Gen 9:4) has naturally been of considerable interest. In present times, explorers and travelers, particularly those of a theologically conservative orientation, have argued over the identification of the mountain, and claims have been made about the existence of remains of a wooden structure, sometimes identified as the ark, on various mountains, even supposedly visible from space. We shall not even start to refer the reader to the extensive literature on these "identifications"; a search of the Internet will suffice to provide much information about it.

In a significant and intriguing book, Norman Cohn traced the interplay in Enlightenment times of the literal belief in the flood and the ark and the growing understanding of geology and palaeontology, including fossils.[1] This tension came to a peak in the mid-nineteenth century, and it continues today in conflicting claims about "creationism" and evolution.[2] The present volume must remain limited, however, to the perceptions of these events by ancient Judaism, early Christianity, and allied traditions, at which time, on the whole, the biblical account was taken for granted. Considerable uncertainty surrounded the identification of the "mountains of Ararat," and, at the same time, writers also steeped in the classical tradition knew the Greek flood story of Deucalion and Pyrrha as well as the Mesopotamian flood story.

Here my purpose is not to give an exhaustive study of these traditions in antiquity, which would involve intercultural detective work, on the one hand, and exhaustive literary investigations, on the other. I have resolved to use as a key the verses in the Hebrew Bible generally thought to apply to Mount Ararat (as it is inaccurately called) and present some cases of their interpretation by the ancient biblical translations and early biblical retellings.

---

1. Cohn 1996.
2. Compare, for example, the discussion in the nineteenth century of Adam's navel, so well presented by Stephen Gould 1985, esp. 99–103.

Mount Masis, traditionally Mount Ararat, in historical Armenia. Note the double peak.

Ararat in the Bible and Its Translations

Genesis 8:4

The biblical text reads: ותנח התבה בחודש השביעי בשבעה עשר יום לחודש על הרי אררט, "And the ark rested in the seventh month on the seventeenth day of the month on the mountains of Ararat." Armenian traditions and many modern ones simply identify the mountains of Ararat of the Bible with the Greater Masis, the highest peak (5,165 m) of a two-peaked mountain in historical Armenia.[3] As we shall see, the situation in late antiquity was more complicated.[4]

The Septuagint translation, of third century B.C.E., translates ἐπὶ τὰ ὄρη τὰ Ἀραράτ, "on the mountains, Ararat," transliterating the name of the mountain. This adds no information to the text of the Hebrew Bible, and its translators expressed no widely accepted geographical identification for "mountains of Ararat." In the Hexaplaric tradition οἱ λ′ (οἱ λοιποί reliqui) read ἀρμ[ενίας], "of Armenia," showing a connection of the mountains of Ararat with Armenia, though it identifies specifically neither the mountain, nor "Armenia." This

---

3. See, for example, Mellink 1962, 1:194–95. He stresses the Ararat-Urartu connection, and regards the connection with 'modern Mount Ararat' to "preserve the name in a restricted sense." The connection with Urartu is certain, but the identification with modern Mt. Ararat is simplistic, and see the discussions by Hewsen and Garsoïan, cited in notes 7 and 8 below.

4. See See Hakobyan, Melikʻ-Baxšyan, and Barsełyan 1991, 704.

connection is also to be found in the writings of the pagan rhetor Apollonius Molon, of the first century B.C.E. He is quoted as saying that "the man who survived the flood left Armenia, with his sons, having been expelled from his native place by the inhabitants of the land. Having traversed the intermediate country, he came to the mountainous part of Syria, which is desolate."[5] It is clear, then, that, in the first century B.C.E. in the Hellenistic world and, we may assume, in the Jewish Hellenistic world, the mountains of Ararat were thought to be in Armenia.

Their more specific identification, as I have noted, raises problems. Early in the Christian era, the Aramaic biblical translation of Onqelos reads על טורי קרדו "on the mountains of Qardo," that is, Gordyene. The same is found in Targum Neofiti, which has the spelling "Qardon." There is reason to think that in such matters Targum Onqelos reflects a Babylonian tradition.[6] This name is also found in certain Hexaplaric witnesses that attribute the reading καρδι to "to hebraikon" and "hē syrē." Thus all these witnesses identify the mountains of Ararat with Qardu, that is, with Korduk‛ or Gordyene, and, therefore, with southern mountains of present-day Kurdistan. This identification was old in Armenian tradition as well. In the fifth century, P‛awstos (3.10) knows the name Sararat, although some have considered this a misreading of *i leṙins Araratay* as *i leṙin Sararatay* (i.e., "on the mountains of Ararat" is misread as "on the mountain of Sararat").[7] One wonders about both these suggestions, whether it is likely that a well-known name from the Bible would be corrupted, by whatever textual process, to an otherwise unattested form. In his *Historical Atlas* Hewsen marks a mountain named Sararad (with a variant Ararad) on his map 110 E4, but this, he informs us, is based on P‛awstos.[8] Garsoïan would interpret the variant הוררט "Hūrarat" of Qumran 1QIsa^a to Isa 37:38 as showing, quite indubitably, that the biblical reference is to Urartu, presumably because of the long ū or ō in the first syllable.[9] In *Q.G.* 31 and 32, Philo does not mention the name of the mountain. Josephus (*Ant.* 1.90) speaks of "a certain mountain in Armenia." In an interesting tradition, in sec-

---

5. See M. Stern 1974, 1.150. Stern notes that "the Babylonian tradition, which was contaminated with the Jewish account in the Hellenistic period, records that many people were saved on Mount Ararat" (ibid., 151).

6. References to Mt. Qardu are also found in Syriac sources.

7. Or an inadvertent error. See the important discussion by Nina Garsoïan 1989, 252–53.

8. Hewsen 2001. See his discussion on p. 15. In fact, the issue is more complex, and there is some evidence, not discussed here, for the existence of a Mount Sararat.

9. See Garsoïan 1989, 252. The *hē* remains unexplained and the variant ה/א is not less difficult that that of ā/ū. This reading also occurs in 4Q252CommGen A 1,10 and 4Q196 Tobit^a ar 2,4 (Ararat).

tion 92, Josephus says, "However, the Armenians call this place Ἀποβατήριον The Place of Descent; for the ark being saved in that place, its remains are shown there by the inhabitants to this day." Professor Hewsen has remarked on the striking similarity of this information with the Armenian tradition identifying Naxiǰevan as the place of descent (*Nax* = "first" and *iǰ* = "descent," so the place of the first descent from the ark). This, so he says, "sounds like a folk etymology for Nakhichevan, whose modern name is derived from an earlier Nakhjawan, apparently from the same folk etymology.[10] This identification may actually be very old and may have been made by Jews in the old Armenian capitals (Armavir, Artashat) from which Mount Ararat is clearly visible."[11] If Hewsen's view is accepted, and it is only hypothetical, then the connection of the "mountains of Ararat" with Masis might be rather old.

It is hard to know precisely what the tradition preserved by Josephus in the name of Nicolaus of Damascus witnesses:

> There is a great mountain in Armenia, over Minyas, called Baris, upon which it is reported that many who fled at the time of the Deluge were saved; and that one who was carried in an ark came on shore upon the top of it; and that the remains of the timber were a great while preserved. This might be the man about whom Moses, the legislator of the Jews wrote. (*Ant.* 1.95, citing Nicolaus of Damascus book 96)[12]

That the mountain of the flood is in Armenia is clear in the writing of this pre-Christian, pagan author from Syria, but exactly where in Armenia is not specific. We can make no suggestion as to the origins of the name Baris.

Josephus cites yet another tradition, from Berossus, who says: "It is said there is still some part of this ship in Armenia, at the mountain of the Cordyaeans; and that some people carry off pieces of the bitumen, which they take away, and use chiefly as amulets for the averting of mischiefs" (*Ant.* 1.93).[13] This identification of the "mountains of Ararat" with Gordyene connects with that of Targum Onqelos and the Hexaplaric *reliqui*, and its attribution to Ber-

---

10. Naxǰavan, an older name of Naxiǰevan, is connected with Noah's descent from the ark; see Hakobyan, Melikʻ-Baxšyan, and Barsełyan 1991, 951. There is another village called Naxǰavan, and, according to Armenian tradition, in that village of Naxǰavan is the tomb of Noah's wife (ibid., 956). On this tradition, see Stone 1996a, 122. On the name of Noah's wife, see ibid., 91 and 96, and in the present volume, 228–36.

11. Personal communication from Robert Hewsen, 25 April 2005.

12. On Nicolaus of Damascus, see Wacholder 1962. See M. Stern 1974, 1:236–37. Much later, within two pages, Georgius Syncellus identifies it as in both Phrygia (§22) and Armenia (§23): see Adler and Tuffin 2002, 30–31.

13. See M. Stern 1974, 1:56, 58.

ossus may confirm its Babylonian origin. Gordyene is easily available from Mesopotamia.

In Jub. 5:28 we read the following: "Noah planted vines on the mountain on which the ark had rested, named Lubar, one of the Ararat Mountains," and the same name recurs in Jub. 7:1, 17 and 10:15. The name Lubar is also mentioned in the extract from Jubilees found in the Book of Asaf the Physician.[14] Independent additional witness to it is in other texts from Qumran, namely, 1Q20 (1QGenesis Apocryphon) 12:13, 4Q244 (4Q pseudo-Daniel[b]) frag. 8:3, and 6Q8 (6QGiants) f26:1. We have found no other reflexes of the name Lubar, but it clearly was the name of the mountain of Ararat upon which the ark rested according to one pre-Christian Jewish tradition and had other connections with Noah.

In the Palestinian (Jerusalem) Targum, which stems from the early Christian period and from the Land of Israel, we read the following translation of Gen 8:4:

> And the ark rested in the seventh month, that is the month of Nisan, on the seventeenth day, on the mountains of Qardon [קרדון]. The name of one mountain was Qardiniya [קרדניא] and the name of the other mountain was Arminiya [ארמניא]. And there the city of Arminiya [ארמניא] was built, in the eastern land.

The mention of two mountains in connection with the ark, which explains the plural in the biblical text, is conflated here with the tradition of Qardo-Gordyene. The text does know a second tradition relating the second mountain to Armenia, which is distinguished from Gordyene. However, it is not clear that earlier, in Hellenistic times, such a distinction was preserved, and there is confusion about which territory the name "Armenia" designates. Targum Yerushalmi likely reflects a later geographical tradition. The identification of Mount Arminiya is not clear, and it could be a second (unidentified) mountain of Gordyene or, conceivably, a mountain further north, that is, Masis. The building of a city called Arminiya after the descent from the ark is not mentioned in the Bible but is known in the Armenian sources, as is discussed above.[15] Josephus knows the place name Apobaterion but does not mention

---

14. See pp. 15, 114–15 in this volume.

15. For alternative Noah traditions, see Moses of Xorēn 1.6; P'awstos's traditions were mentioned above, nn. 6 and 8. *Encyclopedia Judaica* (1:474) remarks that Targum Yerushalmi is presenting a later geographical situation than that of the Jewish Hellenistic sources. In my opinion, it is overlaying the Jewish Hellenistic sources with a later geographical reality. See also Lewis 1968, 98. On cities built after disembarking from the ark, see Daniel Machiela, "Some Jewish Noah Traditions in Syriac Christian Sources," in this volume.

a city name. This may be taken to mean that in Palestine, in approximately the mid-first millennium, Armenia was understood to be farther north, and something of the geographical realities of Armenia (i.e., the two-peaked Masis mountain) was known, as well as the Armenian tradition that Noah built a city when he came forth from the ark. This would bespeak a direct familiarity with the Armenian Christian tradition and might also be one of the very first pieces of evidence hinting at an identification of Masis as the mountains of Ararat of the Hebrew Bible.

ISAIAH 37:38

The Hebrew text reads: ויהי הוא משתחוה בית נסרך אלהיו אדרמלך ושראצר בניו הכהו בחרב והמה נמלטו ארץ אררט וימלך אסר־חדן בנו תחתיו, "While he was worshiping in the temple of his god Nisroch, he was struck down with the sword by his sons Adrammelech and Sarezer. They fled to the land of Ararat, and his son Esarhaddon succeeded him as king." For this verse the Septuagint has καὶ ἐν τῷ αὐτὸν προσκυνεῖν ἐν τῷ οἴκῳ Νασαραχ τὸν παταχρον αὐτοῦ Ἀδραμελεχ καὶ Σαρασαρ οἱ υἱοὶ αὐτοῦ ἐπάταξαν αὐτὸν μαχαιραῖς, αὐτοὶ δὲ διεσώθησαν εἰς Ἀρμενίαν καὶ ἐβασίλευσεν Ασορδαν ὁ υἱὸς αὐτοῦ ἀντ᾽ αὐτοῦ.

Here the Septuagint, which in Genesis simply represented "Ararat" by a transliteration, translates it "Armenia." The translations of Genesis and Isaiah, of course, are not by a single translator, but the Greek of the Torah was very influential. Targum Isaiah, however, reads ואינון אשתזבו לארעא קרדו, "and they took refuge in the land of Qardo," reflecting the same tradition as the Palestinian Targum of Genesis.

The Hebrew of the parallel in 2 Kgs 19:37 is identical, and the Greek is very similar, except that for "Armenia" it reads the transliteration "Ararat." The Aramaic Targum of 2 Kings reads the same as the Targum Isaiah at this point. There is no hint of the tradition of two mountains found in the Palestinian Targum of Gen 8:4. Referring to the same tradition, the book of Tobit reads τὰ ὄρη Αραρατ, "the mountains of Ararat." In 4Q196, the Aramaic of Tobit, we find *ṭûrē Ararat* (frag. 2.4). As noted above, Lubar is the name of the mountain elsewhere in 1QGenesis Apocryphon.[16]

3. JEREMIAH 51:27

The third occurrence of the name "Ararat" in the Hebrew Bible is in Jer 51:27. This verse includes "the kingdom of Ararat" in a list of nations. Again we seek

---

16. See above p. 311.

to evaluate the understanding of these names in the Second Temple period and later.

שאו נס בארץ
תקעו שופר בגוים
קדשו עליה גוים
השמיעו עליה ממלכות
אררט מני ואשכנז
פקדו עליה טפסר
העלו־סוס כילק סמר

> Raise a standard on earth,
>   Sound a horn among the nations,
> Appoint nations against her,
>   Assemble kingdoms against her
>   —Ararat, Minni, and Ashkenaz—
> Designate a marshal against her,
>   Bring up horses like swarming locusts! (JPS)

In the Septuagint we read:

ἄρατε σημεῖον ἐπὶ τῇ γῇ σαλπίσατε ἐν ἔθνεσιν σάλπιγγι
ἁγιάσατε ἐπ' αὐτὴν ἔθνη παραγγείλατε ἐπ' αὐτὴν βασιλείαις
Αραρατ παρ' ἐμοῦ καὶ τοῖς Ασχαναζαίοις ἐπιστήσατε ἐπ' αὐτὴν
βελοστάσεις ἀναβιβάσατε ἐπ' αὐτὴν ἵππον ὡς ἀκρίδων πλῆθος

This translation raises a series of interesting text-critical issues that lie beyond our discussion. Crucial for the present enquiry is the list of nations. In English, based on the Hebrew, we read, "Ararat, Minni, and Ashkenaz." It is commonly accepted that Ashkenaz is the Scythians. For example, according to *Interpreters Dictionary of the Bible*, "the association of Ararat, Minni, Ashkenaz and Medes (Jer. 51:27–28) recalls the military situation of the early sixth century B.C., when Urartu, Manneans, Scythians, and Medes were all active preceding the fall of Babylon."[17] The Greek, however, transliterates the first and third terms Αραρατ and τοῖς Ἀσχαναζαίοις, giving a gentilic form for Ashkenaz, that is, Ashkenazians. The Greek translator rendered Hebrew מני,

---

17. Mellink 1962, 1:194. Minni seem to be the Manneans, a people associated in the Assyrian inscriptions with the Urarteans, whose territory was South of Lake Van (Gelb 1962).

which occurs only here in the Bible, not as an ethnic or even a place name but as a form of the preposition in "from," so reading "from me," so παρ' ἐμοῦ. In the Targum we find, once more, an intriguing tradition: מלכות קרדו משרית הורמיני הדיב "kingdom of the land of Qardo (Ararat), the dwelling place of Hūrmînî (*corresponding to* Minni), Adiabene (*corresponding to* Ashkenaz)." Moreover, מני taken by some sources to mean "from," appears as הורמיני "Hormini," an alternative form of Harmînê or Hārmînē. This place name occurs in Targum Amos 4:3 and Targum Micah 7:12.[18] The Targum undoubtedly partly at least reflects a later political situation than that of the biblical books. The suggestion has been raised that this form should be related to the name "Armenia," and this is made more plausible by Targum Micah 7:12, which translates "great Hūrmînî." This, Jastrow suggests, might translate Armenia Maior.[19] In Amos 4:3 we find in Hebrew והשלכתנה ההרמונה. This is translated by NRSV as "and you shall be flung out into Harmon," while JPS translates "And flung on the refuse heap." There is clearly a linguistic problem here in the word ההרמונה, which is listed by BDB with the notation "meaning dubious." The Greek gives ὁ ὄρος τοῦ Ῥεμμαν, "the mountain of Rhemman," which is based on separating the word into הר "mountain" and רמונה. Intriguingly, the Targum separates this word into two parts but then translates the first part and then the whole word, producing *ṭûrē harmînî*, "mountains of Harmînî." This evokes Gen 8:4, "mountains of Ararat." I conclude from these two readings that Ha/ūrmînî is used by Targum to the Prophets to refer to Armenia. This is, fairly obviously, a wordplay, but its repeated use shows the importance of Armenia in the early Christian period and even its geographical referent.

Appendix

1. The Ark in Apamea

In the essay on art, the particular connection of Noah's ark with Apamea may be observed (see pp. 277–99 above). The chronographic tradition connects this with the location of Mount Ararat in Pisidia, which it preserved alongside the Armenian identification. An example is provided by Sextus Julius Africanus, cited by George Syncellus and John Malalas: "But when the water

---

18. The Hebrew, according to the vast majority of authorities, should be translated "from," deriving from the preposition מן "from."
19. Jastrow 1950, 1:368.

receded, the ark came to rest on the mountains of Ararat, which we know to be in Parthia, but some say it is Kelainai in Phrygia."[20]

The sixth-century Byzantine chronographer John Malalas says in book 1.4:

> After the flood had ceased and the waters had abated, the ark was found to have settled on the mountains of Ararat in the province of Pisidia, whose metropolis is Apamaea. Its timbers are there to the present day, as Pergamos the Pamphylian has written. Josephos and Eusebios Pamphyliou and other chroniclers have stated that the mountains of Ararat are near Armenia, between the Parthians, the Armenians and the Adiabenoi, and the ark settled there.[21]

2. Concerning a City Built after Exit from Ark

Here I adduce several lesser-known traditions about a city built after the exit from the ark. This section makes no claim to being exhaustive but simply to record some material I have encountered in the course of my research. The one tradition that is shared by these sources, and which is quite striking, is the idea that Noah or (one of) his sons built a city after he left the ark.

(a) D. de Bruyne 1925, 37.47–72, gives this fragment, from page 290 of his eighth-century manuscript.[22]

> Uel propinquam sororem fas esse non alienam sicut fili noe post transactum cataclysmum respexerunt / 290 / sibi loca in qua aedificarent sibi civitates, nuncupantes eas in nomine uxorum suarum, quorum similitudinem et isti iugati consumant.

> So it is not lawful for a closely related sister to be a stranger/estranged, just as the sons of Noah, after the passing of the flood, sought out places for themselves in which they built cities for themselves, naming them in the name of their wives, whose (the sons) likeness also those having been bound together might destroy.[23]

(b) According to the Hebrew Bible, a city was built by Cain (Gen 4:17) and another by the men of the generation of the Tower of Babel (Gen 11:4).

---

20. See Adler and Tuffin 2002, 30 = §22.
21. Jeffreys, Jeffreys, and Scott 1986, 4.
22. See the note on p. 67 of de Bruyne 1925.
23. T. A. Bergren has assisted with the translation of this passage, which has a number of grammatical difficulties in it. He is not entirely sure of all details.

The city in Gen 4:17 is named after the Cainite Enoch, but not after his wife. In addition, Ninveh and three other cities are mentioned as built by Ham's descendant Nimrod (Gen 10:10–11). None of these cities seems to fit with the tradition that Noah or his sons built a city when they left the ark.

3. Palestinian Targum Genesis 8:4

Another tradition about the city built after leaving the ark is given above, according to the Palestinian Targum to Gen 8:4, which says, "The name of one mountain was Qardiniya, and the name of another mountain was Arminiya. And there the city of Arminiya was built, in the eastern land."

4. Jubilees 7:16

This tradition about city-building is more ancient, however, and Jub. 7:16 reads: "And Shem dwelt with his father Noah, and he built a city close to his father on the mountain, and he too called its name after the name of his wife Sedeqetelebab." This contains the detail included in the apocryphal Epistle of Titus, in which the city was named by the name of the builder's wife (see above).

5. Armenian Apocryphal Traditions

In an Armenian apocryphal retelling of the early history of humankind, we read that the mountain upon which the ark rested was Masis. "55 And Noah, after receiving God's blessing, descended the mountain and dwelt in Agori. 56 When his seed multiplied, they went down to Ijevan and 57 they filled the first dwelling [nax ijevan], and in such a way they filled the earth. 58 And the name of the place was called Naxijevan, and that is Noah's tomb. 59 Such it is until today."[24] Here biblical events are connected with Armenian geography; Armenian names are used, and onomastic aetiologies are invoked. Thus the name Իջևան Ijevan is connected with the Armenian word իջանել "to descend," that is, "place of descent," and with օթևան "lodgings," while Naxijevan, a different place, is understood as "dwelling of the first descent." Moreover, the place of their initial descent is identified as a site in Armenia called Agoři, at the foot of Mount Ararat. They moved to Naxijevan, which is actually a city. So, although the building of a city is not mentioned explicitly, a city is said to be the place of Noah's dwelling on leaving the ark.

---

24. Lipscomb 1990, 205.

BIBLIOGRAPHY

Aaron, David H. 1995. Early Rabbinic Exegesis on Noah's Son Ham and the So-Called "Hamitic Myth." *JAAR* 63:721–59.

Abegg, Martin G., and Craig A. Evans. 1998. Messianic Passages in the Dead Sea Scrolls. Pages 191–203 in *Qumran-Messianism: Studies on the Messianic Expectations in the Dead Sea Scrolls*. Edited by James H. Charlesworth, Hermann Lichtenberger, and Gerbern S. Oegema. Tübingen: Mohr Siebeck.

Adler, William. 1989. *Time Immemorial: Archaic History and Its Sources in Christian Chronography from Julius Africanus to George Syncellus*. Dumbarton Oaks Studies 26. Washington, D.C.: Dumbarton Oaks Research Library and Collection.

Adler, William, and Paul Tuffin. 2002. *The Chronography of George Synkellos: A Byzantine Chronicle of Universal History from the Creation*. Oxford: Oxford University Press.

Albani, Matthias. 1998. Horoscopes in the Qumran Scrolls. Pages 279–330 in vol. 2 of *The Dead Sea Scrolls after Fifty Years: A Comprehensive Assessment*. Edited by Peter W. Flint and James C. VanderKam. Leiden: Brill.

Alexander, Philip S. 1982. Notes on the "Imago Mundi" of the Book of Jubilees. *JJS* 33:197–213.

———. 1988. Jewish Aramaic Translations of Hebrew Scriptures. Pages 217–53 in *Mikra: Text, Translation, Reading and Interpretation of the Bible in Ancient Judaism and Early Christianity*. Edited by Martin J. Mulder. CRINT 2.1. Assen: Van Gorcum; Philadelphia: Fortress.

———. 1990. Jewish Elements in Gnosticism and the Development of Gnostic Self-Definition. Pages 124–35 in *Gnosticism, Judaism, and Egyptian Christianity*. Minneapolis: Fortress, 1990.

———. 1996a. Physiognomy, Initiation, and Rank in the Qumran Community. Pages 385–94 in vol. 1 of *Geschichte—Tradition—Reflexion: Festschrift für Martin Hengel zum 70. Geburtstag*. Edited by Hubert Cancik, Hermann Lichtenberger, and Peter Schäfer. Tübingen: Mohr Siebeck.

———. 1996b. The Song of Songs as Historical Allegory: Notes on the Development of an Exegetical Tradition. Pages 14–29 in *Targumic and Cognate Studies: Essays in Honour of Martin McNamara*. JSOTSup 230. Edited by Kevin J. Cathcart and Michael Maher. Sheffield: Sheffield Academic Press.

———. 1999. Jewish Elements in Gnosticism and Magic *c*. CE 70–*c*. CE 270. Pages 1052–78 in vol. 3 of *The Cambridge History of Judaism: The Early Roman Period*.

Edited by William Horbury, William D. Davies, and John Sturdy. Cambridge: Cambridge University Press.

———. 2002. The Enochic Literature and the Bible: Intertextuality and Its Implications. Pages 57–69 in *The Bible as Book: The Hebrew Bible and the Judaean Desert Discoveries.* Edited by Edward D. Herbert and Emanuel Tov. London: British Library; New Castle, Del.: Oak Knoll.

———. 2006. *The Mystical Texts.* LSTS 61. London: T&T Clark.

Allberry, Charles R. C., ed. 1938. *A Manichaean Psalm-Book, Part II.* Manichaean Manuscripts in the Chester Beatty Collection 2. Stuttgart: Kohlhammer.

Alter, Robert. 1981. *The Art of Biblical Narrative.* New York: Basic Books.

———. 2004. *The Five Books of Moses: A Translation with Commentary.* New York: Norton.

Amit, Yairah. 2006. The Saul Polemic in the Persian Period. Pages 647–61 in *Judah and the Judeans in the Persian Period.* Edited by Oded Lipschits and Manfred Oeming. Winona Lake, Ind.: Eisenbrauns.

Andersen, Francis I. 1983. 2 (Slavonic Apocalypse of) Enoch. *OTP* 1:91–213.

Anderson, Gary A. 1989. Celibacy or Consummation in the Garden? Reflections on Early Jewish and Christian Interpretations of the Garden of Eden. *HTR* 82:121–48.

Anderson, Gary A., and Michael E. Stone. 1999. *A Synopsis of the Books of Adam and Eve.* 2nd ed. SBLEJL 17. Atlanta: Scholars Press.

Anderson, Janice Capel. 1985. Double and Triple Stories, the Implied Reader, and Redundancy in Matthew. *Semeia* 31:71–89.

Attridge, Harold W. 1976. *The Interpretation of Biblical History in the 'Antiquitates Judaicae' of Flavius Josephus.* Missoula, Mont.: Scholars Press.

———, 1984. Josephus and His Works. Pages 185–232 in Stone 1984b.

Auerbach, Erich. 1957. *Mimesis: The Representation of Reality in Western Literature.* Translated by W. Trask. Garden City, N.Y.: Doubleday.

Avigad, Nahman, and Yigael Yadin. 1956. *A Genesis Apocryphon: A Scroll from the Wilderness of Judaea.* Jerusalem: Magnes and Heikhal Ha-Sefer. [Hebrew and English]

Avi-Yonah, Michael. 1981. The Mosaic of Mopsuestia—Church or Synagogue? Pages 186–90 in *Ancient Synagogues Revealed.* Edited by Lee I. Levine. Jerusalem: Israel Exploration Society.

Baer, Richard A. 1970. *Philo's Use of the Categories Male and Female.* ALGHJ 3. Leiden: Brill.

Bailey, Lloyd R. 1989. *Noah—The Person and the Story in History and Tradition.* Studies on Personalities of the Old Testament. Columbia: South Carolina University Press.

Bakhos, Carol, ed. 2006. *Current Trends in the Study of Midrash.* JSJSup 106. Leiden: Brill.

Barclay, John M. G. 2006. *Flavius Josephus, Against Apion: Translation and Commentary.* Leiden: Brill.

Baron, Salo Wittmayer. 1952. *A Social and Religious History of the Jews.* New York: Columbia University Press.

Barthélemy, Dominique, and J. T. Milik. 1955. *Qumran Cave 1*. DJD 1. Oxford: Clarendon.
Barton, John. 1992. Source Criticism (OT). *ABD* 6:162–65.
Baskin, Judith R. 1983. *Pharaoh's Counsellors: Job, Jethro, and Balaam in Rabbinic and Patristic Tradition*. BJS 47. Chico, Calif.: Scholars Press.
Baumgarten, Albert I. 1975. Myth and Midrash: Genesis 9:20–29. Pages 55–71 in *Judaism before 70*. Vol. 3 of *Christianity, Judaism and Other Greco-Roman Cults—Studies for Morton Smith at Sixty*. Edited by Jacob Neusner. SJLA 12. Leiden: Brill.
———. 1997. *The Flourishing of Jewish Sects in the Maccabean Era: An Interpretation*. JSJSup 55. Leiden: Brill.
Baxter, Wayne. 2006. Noachic Traditions and the Book of Noah. *JSP* 15:179–94.
Becker, Hans-Jürgen, ed. 2006. *Avot de-Rabbi Natan: Synoptische Edition beider Versionen*. Tübingen: Mohr Siebeck.
Beeson, Charles H. 1906. *Acta Archelai*. GCS 16. Leipzig: Hinrichs.
Bekker, Immanuel. 1838–39. *Georgius Cedrenus, Historiarum Compendium*. 2 vols. Bonn: Weber.
Bekkum, Wout J. van. 1999. The Lesson of the Flood: מבול in Rabbinic Tradition. Pages 124–33 in García Martínez and Luttikhuizen 1999.
Bell, Richard. 1937–39. *The Qur'an Translated, with a Critical Re-arrangement of the Surahs*. Edinburgh: T&T Clark.
Ben-Ḥayyim, Zeev. 1943. The Book of Asaṭir. *Tarbiz* 14:104–25, 174–90.
———. 1944. The Book of Asaṭir. *Tarbiz* 15:71–87, 128.
Bergsma, John S., and Scott Walker Hahn. 2005. Noah's Nakedness and the Curse on Canaan (Genesis 9:20–27). *JBL* 124:25–40.
Berman, Samuel A. 1996. *Midrash Tanhuma-Yelammedenu*. Hoboken, N.J.: Ktav.
Bernabò, Massimo. 2001. *Pseudepigraphical Images in Early Art*. North Richmond Hills, Tex.: BIBAL.
Bernstein, Moshe J. 1996. Re-arrangement, Anticipation and Harmonization as Exegetical Features in the Genesis Apocryphon. *DSD* 3:37–57.
———. 1998. Pentateuchal Interpretation at Qumran. Pages 128–59 in *The Dead Sea Scrolls after Fifty Years: A Comprehensive Assessment*. Edited by Peter W. Flint and James C. VanderKam. Leiden: Brill.
———. 1999. Noah and the Flood at Qumran. Pages 199–231 in *The Provo International Conference on the Dead Sea Scrolls: Technological Innovations, New Texts and Reformulated Issues*. Edited by Donald W. Parry and Eugene Ulrich. STDJ 30. Leiden: Brill.
———. 2005. From the Watchers to the Flood: Story and Exegesis in the Early Columns of the *Genesis Apocryphon*. Pages 39–63 in *Reworking the Bible: Apocryphal and Related Texts at Qumran*. Edited by Esther G. Chazon, Devorah Dimant, and Ruth Clements. STDJ 58. Leiden: Brill.
Berthelot, Katell. 2006. 4QMMT et la question du canon de la Bible hébraïque. Pages 1–15 in *From 4QMMT to Resurrection: Mélanges qumraniens en homage à Émile Puech*. Edited by Florentino García Martínez, Annette Steudel, and Eibert Tigchelaar. Leiden: Brill.

Beyer, Klaus. 1984. *Die aramäischen Texte vom Toten Meer samt den Inschriften aus Palästina, dem Testament Levis aus der Kairo Genisa, der Fastenrolle und den alten talmudischen Zitaten.* Göttingen: Vandenhoeck & Ruprecht.

———. 1994. *Die aramäischen Texte vom Toten Meer samt den Inschriften aus Palästina, dem Testament Levis aus der Kairo Genisa, der Fastenrolle und den alten talmudischen Zitaten: Ergänzungsband.* Göttingen: Vandenhoeck & Ruprecht.

———. 2004. *Die aramäischen Texte vom Toten Meer samt den Inschriften aus Palästina, dem Testament Levis aus der Kairo Genisa, der Fastenrolle un den alten talmudischen Zitanen: Band 2.* Göttingen: Vandenhoeck & Ruprecht.

Bezold, Carl. 1888. *Die Schatzhöhle.* 2 vols. Leipzig: Hinrichs.

Bhayro, Siam. 2005. *The Shemihazah and Asael Narrative of 1 Enoch 6–11: Introduction, Text, Translation and Commentary with Reference to Ancient Near Eastern and Biblical Antecedents.* AOAT 322. Münster: Ugarit-Verlag.

———. 2006. Noah's Library: Sources for 1 Enoch 6–11. *JSP* 15:163–77.

Bickerman, Elias J. 1952 [1985]. Origines Gentium. *CP* 47:65–81. Reprinted as pages 401–17 in idem, *Religions and Politics in the Hellenistic and Roman Periods.* Edited by Emilio Gabba and Morton Smith. Como: Edzioni New Press.

Bigg, Charles. 1978. *A Critical and Exegetical Commentary on the Epistles of St. Peter and St. Jude.* ICC. Edinburgh: T&T Clark.

Bilde, Per. 1988. *Flavius Josephus between Jerusalem and Rome.* JSPSup 2. Sheffield: JSOT Press.

Bitzer, Lloyd F. 1968. The Rhetorical Situation. *Philosophy and Rhetoric* 1/1:1–14.

Black, Matthew. 1978. "The Two Witnesses" of Revelation 11.3f in Jewish and Christian Apocalyptic Tradition. Pages 227–37 in *Donum gentilicium.* Edited by Ernst Bammel, C. K. Barrett, and W. D. Davies. Oxford: Clarendon.

———. 1983. An Aramaic Etymology for Jaldabaoth? Pages 46–68 in *The New Testament and Gnosis: Essays in Honour of Robert McL. Wilson.* Edited by A. H. B. Logan and A. J. M. Wedderburn. Edinburgh: T&T Clark.

———. 1985. *The Book of Enoch or 1 Enoch.* SVTP 7. Leiden: Brill.

Blau, Ludwig. 1906. Raziel, Book of. Page 335 in vol. 10 of *Jewish Encyclopedia.* New York: Funk & Wagnalls.

Bloch, Ariel A. 1995. The Cedar and the Palm Tree: A Paired Male-Female Symbol in Hebrew and Aramaic. Pages 13–17 in *Solving Riddles and Untying Knots: Biblical, Epigraphic and Semitic Studies in Honor of Jonas C. Greenfield.* Edited by Ziony Zevit, Seymour Gitin, and Michael Sokoloff. Winona Lake, Ind.: Eisenbrauns.

Boccaccini, Gabriele, ed. 2005. *Enoch and Qumran Origins: New Light on a Forgotten Connection.* Grand Rapids: Eerdmans.

———, ed. 2007. *Enoch and the Messiah Son of Man: Revisiting the Book of Parables.* Grand Rapids: Eerdmans.

Böhlig, Alexander, and Frederik W. Wisse, eds. 1975. *Nag Hammadi Codices III,2 and IV,2: The Gospel of the Egyptians.* NHS 4. Leiden: Brill.

Boor, Carl de, ed. 1978. *Georgius Monachus, Chronicon.* 2 vols. Bibliotheca Scriptorum Graecorum et Romanorum Teubneriana. Stuttgart: Teubner.

Bousset, Wilhelm. 1907. *Hauptprobleme der Gnosis.* FRLANT 10. Göttingen: Vandenhoeck & Ruprecht.

Boussett, Wilhelm, and Hugo Gressmann. 1966. *Die Religion des Judentums im spät-hellenistischen Zeitalter*. Handbuch zum N.T. 21. Tübingen: Mohr Siebeck.

Boyarin, Daniel. 1986. Voices in the Text: Midrash and the Inner Tension of Biblical Narrative. *RB* 93:581–97.

———. 1990. *Intertextuality and the Reading of Midrash*. Bloomington: Indiana University Press.

———. 1993. *Carnal Israel: Reading Sex in Talmudic Culture*. New Historicism: Studies in Cultural Poetics 25. Berkeley and Los Angeles: University of California Press.

———. 2004. *Border Lines: The Partition of Judeo-Christianity*. Philadelphia: University of Pennsylvania Press.

Brakke, David. 2002. The Seed of Seth at the Flood: Biblical Interpretation and Gnostic Theological Reflection. Pages 41–62 in *Reading in Christian Communities: Essays on Interpretation in the Early Church*. Edited by Charles A. Bobertz and David Brakke. Christianity and Judaism in Antiquity 14. Notre Dame, Ind.: University of Notre Dame Press.

Braverman, Jay. 1974. Balaam in Rabbinic and Early Christian Tradition. Pages 41–50 in *Joshua Finkel Festschrift*. Edited by Sidney B. Hoenig and Leon D. Stitskin. New York: Yeshiva University Press.

Brenner, Athalya. 1982a. *Colour Terms in the Old Testament*. JSOTSup 21. Sheffield: JSOT Press.

———. 1982b. "My Lover Is Radiant and Ruddy": Song of Songs 5:10–11 [Hebrew]. *Beit Miqra* 27:168–73.

Brière, Maurice, ed. 1960. *Les homiliae cathedralis de Sévère d'Antioche: Introduction générale a toutes les homélies*. PO 29.1. Paris: Firmin-Didot.

Brock, Sebastian P. 1979. Jewish Traditions in Syriac Sources. *JSS* 30:212–32.

———. 1992. *The Luminous Eye*. Cistercian Studies Series 124. Kalamazoo, Mich.: Cistercian Publications.

Brooke, George J. 1994. The Thematic Content of 4Q252. *JQR* 85:33–59.

Brown, Raymond. 1966–70. *The Gospel according to John*. AB 29–29A. 2 vols. New York: Doubleday.

Brownlee, William H. 1986. *Ezekiel 1–19*. WBC 28. Waco, Tex.: Word.

Bruyne, Domitien de. 1925. Epistula Titi discipuli Pauli de dispositione sanctimonii. *Revue Bénédictine* 37:47–72.

Buber, Solomon. 1893–94. *Midrash Aggadah*. 2 vols in 1. Vienna: Avraham Phanta. Repr., Jerusalem: Haktav Institute, 1996.

Budge, E. A. Wallis. 1886. *The Book of the Bee*. Oxford: Clarendon. Repr., Piscataway, N.J.: Gorgias, 2006.

———. 1902. *The Histories of Rabban Hormizd the Persian and Rabban Bar Bar-'Idta*. 2 vols. London: Luac & Co. Repr., Gorgias Historical Texts 4–5. Piscataway, N.J.: Gorgias, 2003.

———. 1927. *The Book of the Cave of Treasures*. London: Religious Tract Society.

Bullard, Roger A., ed. 1970. *The Hypostasis of the Archons: The Coptic Text with Translation and Commentary*. Patristische Texte und Studien 10. Berlin: de Gruyter.

Burton, John. 1977. *The Collection of the Qur'an*. Cambridge: Cambridge University Press.

Cameron, Ron, and Arthur J. Dewey, trans. 1979. *The Cologne Mani Codex (P. Colon. Inv. Nr. 4780): Concerning the Origin of His Body.* SBLTT 15. Missoula, Mont.: Scholars Press.
Caquot, André. 1991. 4QMess ar 1 i 8–11. *RevQ* 15:145–55.
Carmignac, Jean. 1965. Les horoscopes de Qumran. *RevQ* 5:199–217.
Casey, Maurice. 1976. The Use of the Term "Son of Man" in the Similitudes of Enoch. *JSJ* 7:11–27.
Cassuto, Umberto. 1961. *A Commentary on the Book of Genesis. Part 1: From Adam to Noah, Genesis I–VI 8.* Translated by Israel Abrahams. Jerusalem: Magnes.
Celsus. 1987. *On the True Doctrine, A Discourse against the Christians.* Translated by R. Joseph Hoffman. Oxford: Oxford University Press.
Chabot, Jean-Baptiste. 1899–1924. *Chronique de Michel le Syrien, Patriarche Jacobite d'Antioche:1166–1199.* 5 vols. Paris: LeRoux. Repr., 1963.
———. 1953. *Scriptores Syri 36: Chronicon ad annum Christi 1234 pertinens 1.* CSCO 81. Leuven: Durbecq.
Charles, R. H., ed. 1893. *The Book of Enoch translated from Professor Dillmann's Ethiopic Text.* Oxford: Clarendon.
———. 1902. *The Book of Jubilees or Little Genesis.* London: Macmillan.
———. 1906. *The Ethiopic Version of the Book of Enoch.* Anecdota Oxoniensa, Semitic Series 11. Oxford: Clarendon.
———. 1908. *The Testaments of the Twelve Patriarchs.* London: Adam & Charles Black.
———. 1912. *The Book of Enoch or 1 Enoch.* Oxford: Clarendon.
———. 1913. *The Apocrypha and Pseudepigrapha of the Old Testament in English.* Oxford: Clarendon.
Charlesworth, James H. 2002. A Rare Consensus among Enoch Specialists: The Date of the Earliest Enoch Books. *Henoch* 24:225–34.
Chazon, Esther G., and Michael E. Stone. 1999. *Pseudepigraphic Perspectives: The Apocrypha and Pseudepigrapha in Light of the Dead Sea Scrolls; Proceedings of the International Symposium of the Orion Center for the Study of the Dead Sea Scrolls and Associated Literature, 12–14 January, 1997.* STDJ 31. Leiden: Brill.
Chilton, Bruce. 1992. *The Temple of Jesus.* University Park: Pennsylvania State University Press.
Clarke, Ernest G. 1984. *Targum Pseudo-Jonathan of the Pentateuch: Text and Concordance.* Hoboken, N.J.: Ktav.
———. 1986. Noah: גבר צדיק or גבר זכי. Pages 337–45 in *Salvación en la palabra: Targum, Derash, Berith: En memoria del profesor Alejandro Díez Macho.* Edited Domingo Muñoz León. Madrid: Ediciones Cristiandad.
Clements, Ruth. 2006. Intertext, Outertext, Context: Early Jewish and Christian Artistic Representations of the Sacrifice of Isaac. Paper presented at the Society of Biblical Literature Annual Meeting, Washington, D.C., 20 November.
———. Forthcoming. The Parallel Lives of Early Jewish/Christian Text and Art. In *New Approaches to the Study of Biblical Interpretation in the Second Temple Period and in Early Christianity: Proceedings of the Eleventh Orion Center International Symposium, June 18–21, 2007.* Leiden: Brill.

Cohen, Shaye J. D. 1979. *Josephus in Galilee and Rome: His Vita and Development as a Historian*. Columbia Studies in the Classical Tradition 8. Leiden: Brill.
Cohn, Norman. 1996. *Noah's Flood: The Genesis Story in Western Thought*. New Haven: Yale University Press.
Collins, John J. 1980. The Heavenly Representative: The Son of Man in the Similitudes of Enoch. Pages 119–24 in *Ideal Figures in Ancient Judaism*. Edited by George W. E. Nickelsburg and John J. Collins. SBLSCS 12. Chico, Calif.: Scholars Press, 1980.
———. 1982. Apocalyptic Technique: Setting and Function in the Book of Watchers. *CBQ* 44:91–111.
———. 1983. Sibylline Oracles. *OTP* 1:317–472.
———. 1984. The Sibylline Oracles. Pages 357–81 in Stone 1984b.
———. 1986. *The Testamentary Literature in Recent Scholarship*. Atlanta: Scholars Press; Philadelphia: Fortress.
———. 1992. The Son of Man in First-Century Judaism. *NTS* 38:448–66.
———. 1993. *Daniel*. Hermeneia. Minneapolis: Fortress.
———. 1997. *Apocalypticism in the Dead Sea Scrolls*. London: Routledge.
———. 1998. *Apocalyptic Imagination: An Introduction to Jewish Apocalyptic Literature*. 2nd ed. Grand Rapids: Eerdmans.
Conzelmann, Hans. 1992. *Gentiles, Jews, Christians: Polemics and Apologetics in the Greco-Roman Era*. Translated by M. Eugene Boring. Minneapolis: Fortress.
Cotton, Hannah M., and Werner Eck. 2005. Josephus' Roman Audience: Josephus and Roman Elites. Pages 37–52 in Edmondson, Mason, and Rives 2005.
Cowan, J. Milton, ed. 1979. *The Hans Wehr Dictionary of Modern Written Arabic*. Ithaca, N.Y.: Cornell University Press.
Cowley, Roger W. 1988. *Ethiopian Biblical Interpretation: A Study in Exegetical Tradition and Hermeneutics*. University of Cambridge Oriental Publications 38. Cambridge: Cambridge University Press.
Coxe, A. Cleveland, ed. 1989. *Fathers of the Second Century*. ANF 2. Grand Rapids: Eerdmans.
Cross, Samuel H., and Olgerd P. Sherbowitz-Wetzor, trans. and eds. 1953. *The Russian Primary Chronicle: Laurentian Text*. Mediaeval Academy of America 60. Cambridge, Mass.: Mediaeval Academy of America.
Dalbert, Peter. 1954. *Die Theologie der hellenistisch-jüdischen Missionsliteratur unter Ausschluss von Philo und Josephus*. Hamburg-Volksdorf: Reich.
Dan, Joseph. 1987. *Gershom Scholem and the Mystical Dimension of Jewish History*. Modern Jewish Masters Series 2. New York: New York University Press.
Davidson, Maxwell J. 1992. *Angels at Qumran. A Comparative Study of 1 Enoch 1–36, 72–108 and Sectarian Writings from Qumran*. JSPSup 11. Sheffield: JSOT Press.
Davies, W. D., and Dale C. Allison. 1988. *A Critical and Exegetical Commentary on the Gospel according to Saint Matthew*. ICC. Edinburgh: T&T Clark.
Davila, James. 1998. 4QMess Ar (4Q534) and Merkavah Mysticism. *DSD* 5:367–81.
Dillmann, August. 1853. *Das Buch Henoch*. Leipzig: Vogel.
Dimant, Devorah. 1974. The Fallen Angels in the Dead Sea Scrolls and in the Apocryphal and Pseudepigrapic Books Related to Them [Hebrew]. Ph.D. diss., Jerusalem.

———. 1998. Noah in Early Jewish Literature. Pages 123–50 in *Biblical Figures outside of the Bible*. Edited by Michael E. Stone and Theodore A. Bergren. Harrisburg, Pa.: Trinity Press International.

———. 2002. 1 Enoch 6–11: A Fragment of a Parabiblical Work. *JJS* 53:223–37.

———. 2006. Two "Scientific" Fictions: The So-Called *Book of Noah* and the Alleged Quotation of *Jubilees* in CD 16:3–4. Pages 230–49 in *Studies in the Hebrew Bible, Qumran, and the Septuagint Presented to Eugene Ulrich*. Edited by Peter W. Flint, Emanuel Tov, and James C. VanderKam. Leiden: Brill.

DiTommaso, Lorenzo. 2001. *A Bibliography of Pseudepigrapha Research 1850–1999*. JSPSup 39. Sheffield: Sheffield Academic Press.

———. 2005. 4QPseudo-Daniel[a–b] (4Q243–4Q244) and the Book of Daniel. *DSD* 12:101–33.

Dix, Gregory. 1992. *The Treatise on the Apostolic Tradition of St. Hippolytus of Rome*. London: SPCK, 1937, 1968. Reissued with corrections, preface, and bibliography by Henry Chandwick: London: Alban; Ridgfield, Conn.: Morehouse, 1992.

Donzel, Emeri J. van, ed. 1998. *The Encyclopaedia of Islam, New Edition*. Leiden: Brill.

Drijvers, Hans J. W. 1985. Jews and Christians at Edessa. *JJS* 36:88–102.

———. 1992. Syrian Christianity and Judaism. Pages 124–37 in *The Jews among Pagans and Christians in the Roman Empire*. Edited by Judith Lieu, John A. North, and Tessa Rajak. London: Routledge.

———. 1994. *History and Religion in Late Antique Syria*. Variorum Collected Studies 464. Aldershot, U.K.: Variorum.

Driver, Samuel R. 1926. *The Book of Genesis*. Revised and enlarged edition. London: Methuen.

Edmondson, Jonathan, Steve Mason, and James Rives, eds. 2005. *Flavius Josephus and Flavian Rome*. Oxford: Oxford University Press.

Eichrodt, Walther. 1970. *Ezekiel: A Commentary*. Translated by Cosslett Quin. OTL. London: SCM.

Eid, Volker. 2003. Rettende Arche–rettende Kirche: Ein frühchristliches Mosaik im kilikischen Mopsuhestia. *Bibel und Kirche* 58:43–45.

Elior, Rachel. 2005. *The Three Temples: On the Emergence of Jewish Mysticism in Late Antiquity*. Oxford: Littman Library of Jewish Civilization.

Eshel, Esther. 2003. Apotropaic Prayers in the Second Temple Period. Pages 69–88 in *Liturgical Perspectives: Prayer and Poetry in Light of the Dead Sea Scrolls*. Edited by Esther G. Chazon. STDJ 48. Leiden: Brill.

———. 2007. The *Imago Mundi* of the *Genesis Apocryphon*. Pages 113–31 in *Heavenly Tablets: Interpretation, Identity and Tradition in Ancient Judaism*. Edited by Lynn R. LiDonnici and Andrea Lieber. JSJSup 119. Leiden: Brill

———. 2009. "The Dream Visions in the Noah Story of the Genesis Apocryphon and Related Texts." Pages 119–32 in *Prophecy after the Prophets? The Contribution of the Dead Sea Scrolls to the Understanding of Biblical and Extra-biblical Prophecy*. Edited by Armin Lange and Kristin De Troyer. Leuven: Peeters.

Fabricius, Johann Albert. 1713. *Codex Pseudepigraphus Veteris Testamenti*. Hamburg: Liebezeit.

Falconieri, Ottavio. 1668. *Dissertatio de numo Apamensi Deucalioni diluvii typum exhibente*. Rome.
Falk, Daniel K. 2007. *The Parabiblical Texts: Strategies for Extending the Scriptures among the Dead Sea Scrolls*. Companion to the Qumran Scrolls 8; LSTS 63. London: T&T Clark.
Feldman, Louis H. 1988a. Josephus' Portrait of Noah and Its Parallels in Philo, Pseudo-Philo's *Biblical Antiquities*, and Rabbinic Midrashim. *PAAJR* 55:31–57.
———. 1988b. Use, Authority and Exegesis of Mikra in the Writings of Josephus. Pages 455–518 in *Mikra: Text, Translation, Reading and Interpretation of the Bible in Ancient Judaism and Early Christianity*. Edited by Martin J. Mulder. CRINT 2.1. Assen: Van Gorcum; Philadelphia: Fortress.
———. 1993. *Jew and Gentile in the Ancient World: Attitudes and Interactions from Alexander to Justinian*. Princeton: Princeton University Press.
———. 1998a. *Josephus's Interpretation of the Bible*. Berkeley and Los Angeles: University of California Press.
———. 1998b. *Studies in Josephus' Rewritten Bible*. JSJSup 58. Leiden: Brill.
———, ed. 2000. *Flavius Josephus, Judean Antiquities 1–4: Translation and Commentary*. Leiden: Brill.
———. 2002. Philo's View of Moses' Birth and Upbringing. *CBQ* 64:258–81.
———. 2003. Questions about the Great Flood, as Viewed by Philo, Pseudo-Philo, Josephus, and the Rabbis. *ZAW* 115:401–22.
———. 2004. *"Remember Amalek!": Vengeance, Zealotry, and Group Destruction in the Bible According to Philo, Pseudo-Philo, and Josephus*. Cincinnati: Hebrew Union College Press.
Feldman, Louis H., and John R. Levison, eds. 1996. *Josephus' Contra Apionem: Studies in Its Character and Context with a Latin Concordance to the Portion Missing in Greek*. Leiden: Brill.
Fink, Josef. 1955. *Noe der Gerechte in der Frühchristlichen Kunst*. Beihefte zum Archiv für Kulturgeschichte 4. Münster: Böhlen.
Finney, Paul C. 1994. *The Invisible God: The Earliest Christians on Art*. New York: Oxford University Press.
Fishbane, Michael. 1998. *The Exegetical Imagination: On Jewish Thought and Theology*. Cambridge: Harvard University Press.
Fitzmyer, Joseph A. 1965. The Aramaic "Elect of God" Text from Qumran Cave 4. *CBQ* 27:348–72.
———. 1981. *The Gospel according to Luke I–IX*. AB. Garden City, N.Y.: Doubleday.
———. 2000. Genesis Apocryphon. *EDSS* 1:302–6.
———. 2004. *The Genesis Apocryphon of Qumran Cave 1 (1Q20): A Commentary*. 3rd ed. Rome: Editrice Pontificio Istituto Biblico.
Flemming, Johann, and Ludwig Radermacher. 1901. *Das Buch Henoch*. GCS 5. Leipzig: Hinrichs.
Flesher, Paul V. M. 2005. Pentateuchal Targums as Midrash. Pages 630–46 in vol. 2 of *Encyclopaedia of Midrash: Biblical Interpretation in Formative Judaism*. Edited by Jacob Neusner and Alan J. Avery-Peck. Leiden: Brill.

Fletcher-Louis, Crispin H. T. 2002. *All The Glory of Adam: Liturgical Anthropology in the Dead Sea Scrolls*. STDJ 42. Leiden: Brill.
Fraade, Steven D. 1987. Interpreting Midrash 2: Midrash and Its Literary Contexts. *Prooftexts* 7/3:284–300.
———. 1992. Rabbinic Views on the Practice of Targum, and Multilingualism in the Jewish Galilee of the Third-Sixth Centuries. Pages 253–86 in *The Galilee in Late Antiquity*. Edited by Lee I. Levine. New York: Jewish Theological Seminary.
———. 2007. Rabbinic Polysemy and Pluralism Revisited: Between Praxis and Thematization. *AJSR* 31:1–40.
Franxman, Thomas W. 1979. *Genesis and the "Jewish Antiquities" of Flavius Josephus*. Biblica et Orientalia 35. Rome: Biblical Institute Press.
Freedman, Harry. 1939. *Genesis*. Midrash Rabbah 1. London: Soncino.
Frenkel, Yonah. 1996. *Midrash and Agadah* [Hebrew]. 3 vols. Tel Aviv: Open University.
Freudenthal, Jacob. 1874–75. *Hellenistische Studien: Alexander Polyhistor und die von ihm erhaltenen Reste jüdischer und samaritanischer Geschichtswerke*. 2 vols. Breslau: Skutsch.
Frey, Jörg. 1997. Zum Weltbild im Jubiläenbuch. Pages 261–92 in *Studies in the Book of Jubilees*. Edited by Matthias Albani, Jörg Frey, and Armin Lange. TSAJ 65. Tübingen: Mohr Siebeck.
Friedlander, Gerald, trans. and annotator. 1916. *Pirkê de Rabbi Eliezer (The Chapters of Rabbi Eliezer the Great) according to the Text of the Manuscript Belonging to Abraham Epstein of Vienna*. New York: Sepher-Hermon.
———. 1981. *Pirke de Rabbi Eliezer: The Chapters of Rabbi Eliezer the Great*. 4th ed. New York: Sepher-Hermon.
Fröhlich, Ida. 1998. "Narrative Exegesis" in the Dead Sea Scrolls. Pages 81–99 in Stone and Chazon 1998.
Gafni, Isaiah M. 1981. Nestorian Literature as a Source for the History of the Babylonian *Yeshivot* [Hebrew]. *Tarbiz* 51:567–76.
Galavaris, George. 1969. *The Illustrations of the Liturgical Homilies of Gregory Nazianzenus*. Studies in Manuscript Illumination 6. Princeton: Princeton University Press.
García Avilés, Alejandro. 1997. Alfonso X y el *Liber Razielis*: Imágenes de la magia astral judía en el *scriptorium* alfonsí. *Bullentin of Hispanic Studies* 74:21–39.
García Martínez, Florentino. 1981. 4Q Mes. Aram y el Libro de Noe. *Salamanticensis* 28:195–232.
———. 1992. *Qumran and Apocalyptic: Studies on the Aramaic Texts from Qumran*. STDJ 9. Leiden: Brill.
———. 1999. Interpretations of the Flood in the Dead Sea Scrolls. Pages 86–108 in García Martínez and Luttikhuizen 1999.
———. 2003. Eve's Children in the Targumim. Pages 27–45 in *Eve's Children: The Biblical Stories Retold and Interpreted in Jewish and Christian Traditions*. Edited by Gerard P. Luttikhuizen. Themes in Biblical Narrative 5. Leiden: Brill.
———. 2004. Samma'el in Pseudo-Jonathan and the Origin of Evil. *Journal of Northwest Semitic Languages* 30:19–41.

García Martínez, Florentino, and Gerard P. Luttikhuizen, eds. 1999. *Interpretations of the Flood.* Themes in Biblical Narrative 1. Leiden: Brill.
Gardner, Iain M. F., and Samuel N. C. Lieu, eds. 2004. *Manichaean Texts from the Roman Empire.* Cambridge: Cambridge University Press.
Garsoïan, Nina G. 1989. *The Epic Histories Attributed to P'awstos Buzand (Buzandaran Patmut'iwnk').* Harvard Armenian Texts and Studies 8. Cambridge: Harvard University Press.
Gaster, Moses. 1893. Hebrew Visions of Hell and Paradise. *Journal of the Royal Asiatic Society* 1893:571–611.
———. 1925-28. *Studies and Texts in Folklore, Magic, Mediaeval Romance, Hebrew Apocrypha.* New York: Maggs. Repr., New York: Ktav, 1971.
———. 1927. *The Asatir: The Samaritan Book of the "Secrets of Moses."* London: Royal Asiatic Society.
Gatch, Milton Mc. 1975. Noah's Raven in Genesis A and the Illustrated Old English Hexateuch. *Gesta* 14/2:3–15.
Gaylord, Harry E. 1983. The Slavonic Version of III Baruch. Ph.D. diss., Hebrew University of Jerusalem.
Gelb, Ignace J. 1962. Minni. *IDB* 3:392.
Geljon, Albert C. 2002. *Philonic Exegesis in Gregory of Nyssa's De Vita Moysis.* BJS 333. Providence, R.I.: Brown Judaic Studies.
Georgi, Dieter. 1986. *The Opponents of Paul in Second Corinthians.* Edinburgh: T&T Clark.
Gero, Stephen. 1980. The Legend of the Fourth Son of Noah. *HTR* 73:321–30.
Gilhus, Ingvild Saelid. 1985. *The Nature of the Archons: A Study in the Soteriology of a Gnostic Treatise from Nag Hammadi. CC II,4.* Studies in Oriental Religions 12. Wiesbaden: Harrassowitz.
Ginzberg, Louis. 1906a. Aaron's Rod. *JE* 1:5–6.
———. 1906b. Asaph ben Berechiah. *JE* 1:162–63.
———. 1909-38. *The Legends of the Jews.* 7 vols. Philadelphia: Jewish Publication Society.
———. 1912. Mabbul shel Esh [Flood of Fire] [Hebrew]. *Ha-Goren* 8:35–51. Repr. as pages 205–19 in *Al Halakhah ve-Aggadah: Massah u-Mehkar.* Tel Aviv: Dvir, 1960.
Goldberg, Arnold. 1977. Entwurf einer formanalytischen Methode für die Exegese der rabbinischen Traditionsliteratur. *Frankfurter Judaistische Beiträge* 5:1–41.
———. 1999. *Rabbinische Texte als Gegenstand der Auslegung: Gesammelte Schriften II.* Edited by Margarete Schlüter and Peter Schäfer. TSAJ 73. Tübingen: Mohr Siebeck.
Goldberg, Arnold, and Erwin R. Goodenough. 1953. *The Archeological Evidence from the Diaspora.* Vol. 2 of *Jewish Symbols in the Greco-Roman Period:* New York: Pantheon.
Goldin, Judah. 1955. *The Fathers according to Rabbi Nathan.* Yale Judaica Series 10. New Haven: Yale University Press.
Gould, Stephen Jay. 1985. Adam's Naval. Pages 99–103 in *The Flamingo's Smile: Reflections in Natural History.* New York: Norton.
Grabar, André. 1951. Images bibliques d'Apamée et fresques de la synagogue de Doura. *Cahiers Archeologiques* 5:9–14. Repr. as pages 114–19 in *No Graven*

Images: Studies in Art and the Hebrew Bible. Edited by Joseph Gutmann. New York: Ktav.

Grabbe, Lester L. 1988. *Etymology in Early Jewish Interpretation: The Hebrew Names in Philo.* BJS 115. Atlanta: Scholars Press.

Grant, Robert M. 1961. *Gnosticism: An Anthology.* London: Collins.

———. 2003. *Second-Century Christianity: A Collection of Fragments.* 2nd ed. Louisville: Westminster John Knox.

Greenberg, Moshe. 1983. *Ezekiel 1–20.* AB 22. Garden City, N.Y.: Doubleday.

Greenfield, Jonas C. 1973. Prolegomenon. Pages xi–xlvii in *3 Enoch or the Hebrew Book of Enoch.* Edited by Hugo Odeberg. New York: Ktav.

———. 1979. Early Aramaic Poetry. *JANESCU* 11:49–51.

———. 1988. The Words of Levi Son of Jacob in Damascus Document 4.15–19. *RevQ* 13:319–22.

Greenfield, Jonas C., and Elisha Qimron. 1992. The Genesis Apocryphon Col. XII. Pages 70–77 in *Studies in Qumran Aramaic.* Edited by Takamitsu Muraoka. AbrNahrainSup 3. Leuven: Peeters.

Greenfield, Jonas C., and Michael E. Stone. 1979. The Books of Enoch and the Traditions of Enoch. *Numen* 26:89–103.

Greenfield, Jonas C., Michael E. Stone, and Esther Eshel. 2004. *The Aramaic Levi Document: Edition, Translation, Commentary.* SVTP 19. Leiden: Brill.

Grelot, Pierre. 1975. Hénoch et ses écritures. *RB* 82:481–500.

———. 1978. Daniel 7,9–10 et le livre d'Hénoch. *Semitica* 28:59–83.

Grossfeld, Bernard. 1988. *The Targum Onqelos to Genesis.* Aramaic Bible 6. Wilmington, Del.: Glazier.

Gruenwald, Ithamar. 1970. Further Jewish Physiognomic and Chiromantic Fragments [Hebrew]. *Tarbiz* 40:301–19.

Gunkel, Hermann. 1997. *Genesis.* Translated by Mark E. Biddle. Mercer Library of Biblical Studies. Macon, Ga.: Mercer University Press.

Gutmann, Joseph. 1966. The Illustrated Jewish Manuscript in Antiquity: The Present State of the Question. *Gesta* 5:39–44. Repr. as pages 232–48 in *No Graven Images: Studies in Art and the Hebrew Bible.* Edited by Joseph Gutmann. New York: Ktav, 1971.

———. 1977. Noah's Raven in Early Christian and Byzantine Art. *Cahiers archéologiques* 26:63–71.

———. 1983. The Illustrated Midrash in the Dura Europos Synagogue Paintings: A New Dimension for the Study of Judaism. *PAAJR* 50:100–104.

Haaland, Gunnar. 2006. Beyond Philosophy. Studies in Josephus and His *Contra Apionem.* Ph.D. diss., Norwegian School of Theology, Oslo.

Hachlili, Rachel. 1996. Synagogues in the Land of Israel: The Art and Architecture of Late Antique Synagogues. Pages 96–129 in *Sacred Realm: The Emergence of the Synagogue in the Ancient World.* Edited by Steven Fine. New York: Oxford University Press and the Yeshiva University Museum, 1996.

Hahn, Scott Walker. 2005. Noah's Nakedness and the Curse on Canaan (Gen 9:20–27). *JBL* 124:25–40.

Hakobyan, T'. X., S. T. Melik'-Baxšyan, and H. X Barsełyan. 1991. *Dictionary of Topon-*

ymy of Armenian and Adjacent Territories [Armenian]. Vol. 3. Erevan: Erevan State University.
Halbertal, Moshe. 1997. *Interpretative Revolutions in the Making: Values as Interpretative Considerations in Midrashei Halakah* [Hebrew]. Jerusalem: Magnes.
Halivni, David W. 1991. *Peshat and Derash: Plain and Applied Meaning in Rabbinic Exegesis*. Oxford: Oxford University Press.
Halpern-Amaru, Betsy. 1999. *The Empowerment of Women in the Book of Jubilees*. JSJSup 60. Leiden: Brill.
Harl, Marguerite. 1987. Le nom de l'arche de Noé dans la Septante: Les choix lexicaux des traducteurs alexandrins, indices d'interprétations théologiques? Pages 15–43 in *Alexandrina: Hellénisme, judaïsme et christianisme à Alexandrie. Mélanges offerts au P. Claude Mondésert*. Edited by Jean Pouilloux. Paris: Cerf.
Harlow, Daniel C. 1996. *The Greek Apocalypse of Baruch (3 Baruch) in Hellenistic Judaism and Early Christianity*. SVTP 12. Leiden: Brill.
Hassett, Maurice M. 1911. Orans. In *The Catholic Encyclopedia*. New York: Appleton. Online: http://www.newadvent.org/cathen/11269a.htm.
Haug, Walter. 1977. *Das Mosaic von Otranto: Darstellung, Deutung und Bilddokumentation*. Wiesbaden: Reichert.
Head, Barclay V. 1906. *Catalogue of the Greek Coins of Phrygia*. London: British Museum.
Hedrick, Charles W., ed. 1990. *Nag Hammadi Codices XI, XII, XIII*. NHS 28. Leiden: Brill.
Heine, Ronald E., trans. 1982. *Origen, Homilies on Genesis and Exodus*. FC 71. Washington, D.C.: Catholic University of America.
Heinemann, Joseph. 1974. *Aggadah and Its Development* [Hebrew]. Jerusalem: Keter.
Helderman, Jan 1997. Die Bundeslade Κιβωτός: Ihre Geschichte als eine Metapher in der Umwelt der Manichäer. Pages 125–47 in *Atti del Terzo Congresso Internazionale di Studi "Manicheismo e Oriente Cristiano Antico." Arcavacata di Rende Amantea, 31 agosto–5 settembre 1993*. Edited by Luigi Cirillo and Alois van Tongerloo. Manichaean Studies 3. Leuven: Brepols.
Helm, Rudolf, and Adolf Bauer, 1955. *Hippolytus Werke: Die Chronik*. Berlin: Akademie-Verlag.
Hempel, Charlotte. ed. Forthcoming. *The Dead Sea Scrolls: Texts and Context*. STDJ. Leiden: Brill.
Hendel, Ronald S. 1995. 4Q252 and the Flood Chronology of Genesis 7–8: A Text-Critical Solution. *DSD* 2:72–79.
Hendrick, Charles W. 1980. *The Apocalypse of Adam: A Literary and Source Analysis*. SBLDS 46. Chico, Calif.: Scholars Press.
Henze, Matthias. 2005. Enoch's Dream Visions and the Visions of Daniel Reexamined. Pages 17–22 in Boccaccini 2005.
Hewsen, Robert. 2001. *Armenia: A Historical Atlas*. Chicago: University of Chicago Press.
Hidal, Sven. 1974. *Interpretatio Syriaca: Die Kommentare des heiligen Ephräm des Syrers zu Genesis und Exodus mit besonderer Berücksichtigung ihrer auslegungsgeschichtlichen Stellung*. ConBOT 6. Lund: Gleerup.

Hiebert, Robert J. V. 2007. To the Reader of Genesis. Pages 1–6 in *A New English Translation of the Septuagint and the Other Greek Translations Traditionally Included under That Title*. New York: Oxford University Press.

Higden, Ranulf. 1482. *Polycronicon*. Translated by John Trevisa. Westminster: Caxton.

Hilhorst, André. 1999. The Noah Story: Was It Known to the Greeks? Pages 56–65 in García Martínez and Luttikhuizen 1999.

Hillel, Vered. 2002. Naphtali: A "Proto-Joseph" in the Greek Testament of Naphtali. M.A. thesis. Hebrew University, Jerusalem.

———. 2007. Naphtali: A "Proto-Joseph" in the Testaments of the Twelve Patriarchs. *JSP* 16:171–201.

Himmelfarb, Martha. 1993. *Ascent to Heaven in Jewish and Christian Apocalypses*. Oxford: Oxford University Press.

———. 1994. Some Echoes of *Jubilees* in Medieval Hebrew Literature. Pages 115–41 in *Tracing the Threads: Studies in the Vitality of the Jewish Pseudepigrapha*. Edited by John C. Reeves. SBLEJL 6. Atlanta: Scholars Press.

———. 2006. *A Kingdom of Priests: Ancestry and Merit in Ancient Judaism*. Philadelphia: University of Pennsylvania Press.

Hoffmann, Georg. 1880. *Auszüge aus syrischen Akten persischer Märtyrer*. Abhandlungen für Kunde des Morgenlandes der Deutschen Morgenländischen Gesellschaft 7.3. Leipzig: Brockhaus. Repr., Nendeln: Kraus, 1966.

Holl, Karl, ed. 1915. *Ancoratus und Panarion*. GCS 25. Leipzig: Hinrich.

Holladay, William L. 1986. *Jeremiah 1: A Commentary on the Book of the Prophet Jeremiah Chapters 1–25*. Hermeneia. Minneapolis: Fortress.

Hollander, Harm W., and Marinus de Jonge. 1985. *The Testaments of the Twelve Patriarchs: A Commentary*. SVTP 8. Leiden: Brill.

Holst, Søren, and Jesper Høgenhaven. 2006. Phsyiognomy and Eschatology: Some More Fragments of 4Q561. *JJS* 57:26–43.

Hohenheim, Paracelsus von. *Hermetic and Alchemical Writings of Paracelsus*. Edited by Arthur E. Waite. Klia, Mont.: Kessinger, 2002.

Horst, Pieter Willem van der. 2002. *Japheth in the Tents of Shem: Studies on Jewish Hellenism in Antiquity*. Contributions to Biblical Exegesis and Theology 32. Leuven: Peeters.

———. 2003. A Note on the Evil Inclination and Sexual Desire in Talmudic Literature. Pages 99–106 in *Der Mensch vor Gott: Forschungen zum Menschenbild in Bibel, antikem Judentum und Koran. Festschrift für Hermann Lichtenberger zum 60. Geburtstag*. Edited by Ulrike Mittmann-Richert, Friedrich Avemarie, and Gerbern S. Oegema. Neukirchen-Vluyn: Neukirchener.

Huggins, Ronald V. 1995. Noah and the Giants: A Response to John C. Reeves. *JBL* 114:103–10.

Hughes, H. Maldwyn. 1913. The Greek Apocalypse of Baruch or III Baruch. Pages 527–41 in *The Apocrypha and the Pseudepigrapha of the Old Testament in English*. Edited by R. H. Charles. Oxford: Clarendon.

Hughes, Paul E. 1997. Moses' Birth Story: A Biblical Matrix for Prophetic Messianism. Pages 10–22 in *Eschatology, Messianism, and the Dead Sea Scrolls*. Edited by Craig A. Evans and Peter W. Flint. Grand Rapids: Eerdmans.

Isaac, E. 1983. 1 (Ethiopic Apocalypse of) Enoch. *OTP* 1:5–89.
Ibn Kathīr, Ismā'īl ibn 'Umar. 1968. Qisas Al-Anbiyā'. Al-Qāhirah: Dār al-Kutub al-Hadīthah.
James, Montague R. 1893. A Fragment of Enoch in Latin. Pages 146–50 in *Apocrypha Anecdota*. Texts and Studies 2.3. Cambridge: Cambridge University Press.
———. 1920. *The Lost Apocrypha of the Old Testament: Their Titles and Fragments*. Translations of Early Documents 1. London: SPCK.
Jastrow, Marcus. 1950. *A Dictionary of the Targumim, the Talmud Babli and Yerushalmi, and the Midrashic Literature*. New York: Pardes.
Jeffreys, Elizabeth, Michael Jeffreys, and Roger Scott. 1986. *The Chronicle of John Malalas*. Byzantina Australiensia 4. Sydney: Australian Association for Byzantine Studies.
Jellinek, Adolph. 1938. *Bet Ha-Midrasch*. 6 vols. Jerusalem: Bamberger & Wahrmann. Repr. of the 1853 edition.
Jones, F. Stanley. 1995. *An Ancient Jewish Christian Source on the History of Christianity: Pseudo-Clementine Recognitions 1.27–71*. SBLTT 37. Atlanta: Scholars Press.
Jonge, Marinus de. 1953. *The Testaments of the Twelve Patriarchs: A Study of Their Text, Composition and Origin*. Assen: Van Gorcum.
Jonge, Marinus de, et al. 1978. *The Testaments of the Twelve Patriarchs: A Critical Edition of the Greek Text*. PVTG 1.2. Leiden: Brill.
Jongeling, Bastiaan, et al. 1976. *Aramaic Texts from Qumran with Translations and Annotations*. Semitic Study Series 4. Leiden: Brill.
Kahle, Paul E., ed. 1954. *Bala'izah: Coptic Texts from Deir el-Bala'izah in Upper Egypt*. 2 vols. London: Oxford University Press.
Kalimi, Isaac. 2002. "He Was Born Circumcised": Some Midrashic Sources, Their Concept, Roots and Presumably Historical Context. *ZNW* 93:1–12.
Kalmin, Richard. 1990. Saints or Sinners, Scholars or Ignoramuses? Stories about the Rabbis as Evidence for the Composite Nature of the Babylonian Talmud. *AJSR* 15:179–205.
———. 1992. Talmudic Portrayals of Relationships between Rabbis: Amoraic or Pseudepigraphic? *AJSR* 17:165–97.
Kaplan, Chaim. 1931. The Flood in the Book of Enoch and Rabbinics. *JSOR* 15:22–24.
Karr, Don. 2001. Liber Lunae and Other Selections from British Library, MS. Sloane 3826. *Esoterica: The Journal of Esoteric Studies*. 3:295–318.
Kasher, Rimon. 2000. The Aramaic Targums of the Hebrew Bible [Hebrew]. *Pe'amim* 83:70–107.
Kaufman, J. 1932. Adambuch. Pages 788–92 in vol. 1 of *Encyclopedia Judaica*. Berlin: Eschkol.
Kensky, Alan. 1993. Moses and Jesus: The Birth of the Savior. *Judaism* 42:43–49.
Kessler, Herbert L. 1990. Program and Structure. Pages 153–64 in *The Frescoes of the Dura Synagogue and Christian Art*. Edited by Kurt Weitzmann and Herbert L. Kessler. Dumbarton Oaks Studies 28. Washington, D.C.: Dumbarton Oaks Research Library and Collection.

Kikawada, Isaac M., and Lloyd R. Bailey. 1992. Noah and the Ark. *ABD* 4:1122–31.
Kindler, Arie. 1971. A Coin-Type from Apameia in Phrygia (Asia Minor) Depicting the Narrative of Noah [Hebrew]. *Museum Haaretz Bulletin* 13: 24–32.
King, Karen L. 1988. Revisiting Norea. Pages 265–75 in *Images of the Feminine in Gnosticism*. Edited by Karen L. King. Studies in Antiquity and Christianity. Philadelphia: Fortress.
———. 1994. The Book of Norea, Daughter of Eve. Pages 66–85 in vol. 2 of *Searching the Scriptures : A Feminist Commentary*. Edited by Elisabeth Schüssler Fiorenza. London: SCM.
———. 2003. *What Is Gnosticism?* Cambridge: Harvard University Press.
Kister, Menahem. 1992. Some Aspects of Qumranic Halakha. Pages 581–86 in vol. 2 of *The Madrid Qumran, Congress*. Edited by J. Trebolle Barrera and L. Vegas Montaner. STDJ 11.2. Leiden: Brill.
———. 1998. *Studies in Avot de-Rabbi Nathan: Text, Redaction and Interpretation* [Hebrew]. Jerusalem: Hebrew University, Department of Talmud, and Yad Ben Zvi.
Klijn, A. F. J. 1981. An Analysis of the Use of the Flood in the Apocalypse of Adam. Pages 218–26 in *Studies in Gnosticism and Hellenistic Religions Presented to Gilles Quispel on the Occasion of His 65th Birthday*. Edited by Roelof van den Broek and Maarten J. Vermaseren. Études préliminaires aux religions dans l'Empire romaine 91. Leiden: Brill.
Knibb, Michael A. 1978. *The Ethiopic Book of Enoch*. 2 vols. Oxford: Clarendon.
Koch, Klaus. 2007. Der "Menschensohn" in Daniel. *ZAW* 119:369–87.
Koltun-Fromm, Naomi. 1997. Aphrahat and the Rabbis on Noah's Righteousness in Light of the Jewish-Christian Polemic. Pages 57–71 in *The Book of Genesis in Jewish and Oriental Christian Interpretation*. Edited by Judith Frishman and Lucas van Rompay. Traditio Exegetica Graeca 5. Leuven: Peeters.
Kreitzer, Larry J. 1999. On Board the Eschatological Ark of God: Noah-Deucalion and the "Phrygian Connection" in 1 Peter 3:19-22. Pages 228-72 in *Baptism, the New Testament and the Church: Historical and Contemporary Studies in Honour of R. E. O. White*. Edited by Stanley E. Porter and Anthony R. Cross. Sheffield: Sheffield Academic Press.
Kronholm, Tryggve. 1978. *Motifs from Genesis 1–11 in the Genuine Hymns of Ephrem the Syrian with Particular Reference to the Influence of the Jewish Exegetical Tradition*. ConBOT 11. Lund: Gleerup.
Kroymann, Emil. 1906. *Quinti Septini Florentis Tertullian opera Pars 3*. CSEL 47. Vienna: Tempsky; Leipzig: Freytag.
Kugel, James L. 1983. Two Introductions to Midrash. *Prooftexts* 3:131–55.
———. 1998. *Traditions of the Bible: A Guide to the Bible as It Was at the Start of the Common Era*. Cambridge: Harvard University Press.
———. 2007. How Old Is the Aramaic Levi Document? *DSD* 14:291–312.
Kugler, Robert A. 2001. *The Testaments of the Twelve Patriarchs*. Guides to Apocrypha and Pseudepigrapha. Sheffield: Sheffield Academic Press.
———. 2008. Whose Scripture? Whose Community? Reflections on the Dead Sea Scrolls Then and Now, by Way of Aramaic Levi. *DSD* 15:5–23.

Kvanvig, Helge S. 1988. *Roots of Apocalyptic: The Mesopotamian Background of the Enoch Figure and the Son of Man.* WMANT 61. Neukirchen-Vluyn: Neukirchener.
Lane, Edward W. 1863–93. *An Arabic-English Lexicon: Derived from the Best and the Most Copious Eastern Sources.* 2 vols. London: Williams & Norgate.
Lange, Armin. 1996. 1QGenAp XX10–XX32 as Paradigm of Wisdom Didactive Narrative. Pages 191–204 in *Qumranstudien.* Edited by Heinz-Josef Fabry, Armin Lange, and Hermann Lichtenberger. Göttingen: Vandenhoeck & Ruprecht.
———. 1997. The Essene Position on Magic and Divination. Pages 377–435 in *Legal Texts and Legal Issues: Proceedings of the Second Meeting of the International Organization for Qumran Studies, Cambridge, 1995.* Edited by Moshe J. Bernstein, Florentino García Martínez, and John Kampen. Leiden: Brill.
Lange, Günter. 1986. "Noach im Kasten": Zum Noach-Bild der Schulbibel. *Katechetische Blätter* 111:21–26.
Langlois, Victor. 1868. *Chronique de Michel le Grand.* Venice: Académie de Saint-Lazare.
Lawlor, Hugh J. 1897. Early Citations from the Book of Enoch. *Journal of Philology* 25:164–225.
Layton, Bentley, ed. 1974; 1976. The Hypostasis of the Archons. *HTR* 67:351–425; 69:31–101.
———. 1981. *Sethian Gnosticism.* Vol. 2 of *The Rediscovery of Gnosticism: Proceedings of the International Conference on Gnosticism at Yale New Haven, Connecticut, March 28–31, 1978.* Studies in the History of Religions 41.2. Leiden: Brill.
———. 1989. *Nag Hammadi Codex II, 2–7.* 2 vols. NHS 20–21. Leiden: Brill.
Le Fèvre de la Boderie, Guy. 1993. *La Galliade (1582).* Edited by F. Roudaut. Paris: Klincksieck.
Lehmann, Manfred R. 1958. 1QGenesis Apocryphon in the Light of the Targumim and Midrashim. *RevQ* 1:249–63.
Leicht, Reimund. 2000. Gnostic Myth in Jewish Garb: Niriyah (Norea), Noah's Bride. *JJS* 51:133–40.
———. 2006. *Astrologumena Judaica: Untersuchungen zur Geschichte der astrologischen Literatur der Juden.* Texts and Studies in Medieval and Early Modern Judaism 21. Tübingen: Mohr Siebeck.
Levinson, Joshua. 2004. Dialogical Reading in the Rabbinic Exegetical Narrative. *Poetics Today* 25:497–528.
———. 2005. *The Twice-Told Tale: A Poetics of the Exegetical Narrative in Rabbinic Midrash* [Hebrew]. Jerusalem: Magnes.
Levison, John R. 2000. *Texts in Transition: The Greek Life of Adam and Eve.* SBLEJL 16. Atlanta: Society of Biblical Literature.
Lewis, Charlton Thomas, and Charles Short. 1879. *A Latin Dictionary.* Oxford: Clarendon.
Lewis, Jack P. 1968. *A Study of the Interpretation of Noah and the Flood in Jewish and Christian Literature.* Leiden: Brill.
Licht, J. 1965. Legs as a Sign of Election [Hebrew]. *Tarbiz* 35:18–26.
Lieber, Elinor. 1984. Asaf's Book of Medicines: A Hebrew Encyclopedia of Greek and

Jewish Magic, Possibly Compiled on an Indian Model. *Dumbarton Oaks Papers.* 38:233-49.

Linder, Amnon. 1987. *The Jews in Roman Imperial Legislation.* Detroit: Wayne State University Press.

Lindt, Paul van. 1992. *The Names of Manichaean Mythological Figures: A Comparative Study on Terminology in the Coptic Sources.* Studies in Oriental Religions 26. Wiesbaden: Harrassowitz.

Lipscomb, William L. 1990. *The Armenian Apocryphal Adam Literature.* University of Pennsylvania Armenian Texts and Studies 8. Atlanta: Scholars Press.

Loewe, Raphael. 2001. Ark, Archaism and Misappropriation. Pages 113-45 in *Biblical Hebrews, Biblical Texts: Essays in Memory of Michael P. Weitzman.* Edited by Ada Rapoport-Albert and Gillian Greenberg. JSOTSup 333. Sheffield: Sheffield Academic Press.

Lolos, Anastasios. 1976. *Die Apokalypse des Ps.-Methodios.* BKP 83. Meisenheim: Hain.

Lorberbaum, Yair. 2004. *Image of God: Halakah and Haggadah* [Hebrew]. Jerusalem: Schocken.

Lupieri, Edmondo. 2002. *The Mandaeans: The Last Gnostics.* Translated by Charles Hindley. Italian Texts and Studies on Religion and Society. Grand Rapids: Eerdmans.

Luttikhuizen, Gerard P. 1997. The Thought Pattern of Gnostic Mythologizers and Their Use of Biblical Traditions. Pages 89-101 in *The Nag Hammadi Library after Fifty Years: Proceedings of the 1995 Society of Biblical Literature Commemoration.* Edited by John D. Turner and Anne Marie McGuire. NHMS 44. Leiden: Brill.

———. 1999. Biblical Narrative in Gnostic Revision: The Story of Noah and the Flood in Classic Gnostic Mythology. Pages 109-23 in García Martínez and Luttikhuizen 1999.

———. 2006. *Gnostic Revisions of Genesis Stories and Early Jesus Traditions.* NHMS 58. Leiden: Brill.

Lynche, Richard. 1601. *An Historical Treatise of the Travels of Noah into Europe.* London: Islip.

Machiela, Daniel A. 2007. The Genesis Apocryphon (1Q20): A Reevaluation of Its Text, Interpretive Character, and Relationship to the Book of Jubilees. Ph.D. diss., University of Notre Dame, Notre Dame, Indiana.

———. 2008. "Each to His Own Inheritance": Geography as an Evaluative Tool in the Genesis Apocryphon. *DSD* 15:50-66.

———. 2009. *The Dead Sea Genesis Apocryphon: A New Text and Translation with Introduction and Special Treatment of Columns 13-17.* STDJ 79. Leiden: Brill.

MacRae, George W. 1970. The Jewish Background of the Gnostic Sophia Myth. *NovT* 12:86-101.

———. 1983. The Apocalypse of Adam. *OTP* 1:713-15.

MacRae, George W., and Douglas M. Parrott. 1990. The Apocalypse of Adam (V, 5). Pages 277-86 in *The Nag Hammadi Library in English.* Rev. ed. Edited by James M. Robinson. New York: Harper San Francisco.

Maher, Michael. 1992. *Targum Pseudo-Jonathan: Genesis.* Aramaic Bible 1B. Collegeville, Minn.: Liturgical Press.

Mahfouz, Najib. 1991. *The Time and the Place and Other Short Stories.* New York: Doubleday.
Marcovich, Miroslav, ed. 1986. *Refutatio omnium haeresium.* PTS 25. Berlin: de Gruyter.
———. 1988. Justin's *Baruch*: A Showcase of Gnostic Syncretism. Pages 93–119 in *Studies in Graeco-Roman Religions and Gnosticism.* Studies in Greek and Roman Religion 4. Leiden: Brill.
Marcus, David. *From Balaam to Jonah: Anti-prophetic Satire in the Hebrew Bible.* BJS 301. Atlanta: Scholars Press, 1995.
Marcus, Ralph, trans. 1961. *Philo, Supplement 1: Questions and Answers on Genesis.* LCL. Cambridge: Harvard University Press.
Margaliot, Mordecai. 1966. *Sefer Ha-Razim.* Jerusalem: American Academy of Jewish Research.
Margoliouth, Jessie Payne Smith, ed. 1903. *A Compendious Syriac Dictionary, Founded upon the Thesaurus Syriacus of R. Payne Smith, D.D.* Oxford: Clarendon.
Martens, John W. 1994. *Nomos empsychos* in Philo and Clement of Alexandria. Pages 323–38 in *Hellenization Revisited: Shaping a Christian Response within the Greco-Roman World.* Edited by Wendy E. Helleman. Lanham, Md.: University Press of America.
Martin, François. 1906. *Le Livre d'Hénoch traduit sur le texte éthiopien.* Paris: Letouzey et Ainé.
Mason, Steve. 1996. The *Contra Apionem* in Social and Literary Context: An Invitation to Judean Philosophy. Pages 187–228 in Feldman and Levison 1996.
———. 1998. Should Any Wish to Enquire Further (*Ant.* 1.25): The Aim and Audience of Josephus's Judean *Antiquities/Life.* Pages 64–103 in *Understanding Josephus: Seven Perspectives.* Edited by Steve Mason. Sheffield: Sheffield Academic Press.
———. 2000. Introduction. Pages xii–xxxvi in Feldman 2000.
———. 2001. *Flavius Josephus, Life of Josephus: Translation and Commentary.* Leiden: Brill.
———. 2003. *Josephus and the New Testament.* 2nd ed. Peabody, Mass.: Hendrickson.
Mason, T. W. 1949. *The Dictionary of National Biography, 1931–1940.* Edited by L. G. Wickham Legg. Oxford: Oxford University Press.
Mathers, Samuel L. M. 2003. *Key of Solomon the King: Clavicula Salomonis.* Kila, Mont.: Kessinger.
Mathews, Edward G., and Joseph P. Amar, eds. and trans. 1994. *St. Ephrem the Syrian: Selected Prose Works.* FOC 91. Washington, D.C.: Catholic University of America Press.
McGuire, Anne M. 1988. Virginity and Subversion: Norea against the Powers in the *Hypostasis of the Archons.* Pages 239–58 in *Images of the Feminine in Gnosticism.* Edited by Karen L. King. Studies in Antiquity and Christianity. Philadelphia: Fortress.
McNamara, Martin. 1992. *Targum Neofiti 1: Genesis.* Aramaic Bible 1A. Collegeville, Minn.: Liturgical Press.
———. 2003. Interpretation of Scripture in the Targumim. Pages 167–97 in *The Ancient Period.* Vol. 1 of *A History of Biblical Interpretation.* Edited by Alan J. Hauser and Duane F. Watson. Grand Rapids: Eerdmans.

McVey, Kathleen E., trans. 1989. *Ephrem the Syrian: Hymns.* Mahwah, N.J.: Paulist.
Mellink, Machteld. J. 1962. Ararat. *IDB* 1:194–95.
Melzer, Aviv. 1972. Asaph the Physician—the Man and His Book: A Historical-Philological Study of the Medical Treatise, the Book of Drugs. Ph.D. diss., University of Wisconsin.
Meshorer, Yaakov. 1981. An Ancient Coin Depicts Noah's Ark. *BAR* 7.5:38–39.
Migne, Jacques-Paul. 1856. *Dictionnaire des apocryphes.* 2 vols. Paris: Migne. Repr., Turnholt, Belgium: Brepols, 1989.
Milik, J. T. 1971. Problèmes de la littérature Hénochique à la lumière des fragments araméens de Qumrân. *HTR* 64:333–78.
———. 1976. *The Books of Enoch: The Aramaic Fragments of Qumrân Cave 4.* Oxford: Clarendon.
———. 1978. Écrits prééssséniens de Qumrân: D'Hénoch à Amram. Pages 91–106 in *Qumrân: Sa piété, sa théologie et son milieu, etudes présentées par M. Delcor.* Paris: Duculot.
———. 1992. Les modèles araméens du livre d'Ester dans la grotte 4 de Qumrân. *RevQ* 15:321–99.
Milik, J. T., with Matthew Black. 1976. *The Books of Enoch: Aramaic Fragments of Qumran Cave 4.* Oxford: Clarendon.
Millar, Fergus G. B. 1993. Hagar, Ishmael, Josephus and the Origins of Islam. *JJS* 44:23–45. Repr. as pages 351–77 in *The Greek World, the Jews, and the East.* Vol. 3 of *Rome, the Greek World, and the East.* Edited by Hannah M. Cotton and Guy M. Rogers. Chapel Hill: University of North Carolina Press, 2006.
Miller, James E. 1991. The Redaction of Tobit and the Genesis Apocryphon. *JSP* 8:53–61.
Mir, Mustansir. 1999. Is the Qurʾān a Shapeless Book? *Renaissance.* Online: http://www.monthly-renaissance.com/issue/content.aspx?id=684.
———. 2000. The Qurʾān as Literature." *Renaissance.* Online: http://www.monthly-renaissance.com/issue/content.aspx?id=592.
Mitchell, Charles W., ed. 1912–21. *S. Ephraim's Prose Refutations of Mani, Marcion, and Bardaisan.* 2 vols. London: Williams & Norgate.
Moberly, R. W. L. 2000. Why Did Noah Send Out a Raven? *VT* 50:345–56.
Molenberg, Corrie. 1984. A Study of the Roles of Shemihaza and Asael in I Enoch 6–11. *JJS* 35:136–46.
Morard, Françoise. 1985. *L'Apocalypse d'Adam.* Bibliothèque Copte de Nag Hammadi; "Textes" 15. Québec: L'Université Laval.
Morgan, Michael A. 1983. *Sepher Harazim: The Book of Mysteries.* SBLTT 25, PS 11. Chico, Calif.: Scholars Press.
Morgenstern, Matthew. 1996. A New Clue to the Original Length of the Genesis Apocryphon. *JJS* 47:345–47.
Morgenstern, Matthew, Elisha Qimron, and Daniel Sivan. 1995. The Hitherto Unpublished Columns of the Genesis Apocryphon. *AbrN* 33:30–54.
Morris, Jenny. 1987. Philo the Jewish Philosopher. Pages 809–89 in vol. 3.2 of Emil Schürer, *The History of the Jewish People in the Age of Jesus Christ (175 B.C.–A.D. 135).* Revised and edited by Geza Vermes and Fergus Millar. Edinburgh: T&T Clark.

Muntner, Suessmann. 1957. *Mavo Lesefer Asaph HaRofe: Hasefer harefui haivri hajkadum beyoter.* Jerusalem: Geniza.
———. 2007. Asaph Ha-Rofe. Pages 543–44 in vol. 2 of *Encyclopedia Judaica*. Edited by Fred Skolnik. 2nd ed. 22 vols. Farmington Hills, Mich.: Thomson Gale; Detroit: Macmillan Reference.
Murphy, Roland E. 1990. *The Song of Songs*. Hermeneia. Minneapolis: Fortress.
Najman, Hindy. 1999. Interpretation as Primordial Writing: Jubilees and Its Authority Conferring Strategies. *JSJ* 30:379–410.
———. 2003. Cain and Abel as Character Traits: A Study in the Allegorical Typology of Philo of Alexandria. Pages 107–18 in *Eve's Children: The Biblical Stories Retold and Interpreted in Jewish and Christian Tradition*. Edited by Gerard P. Luttikhuizen. Leiden: Brill.
Narkiss, Bezalel. 2007. *El Pentateuco Ashburnham: La Ilustración de Códices en la Antigüedad Tardía*. Valencia: Patrimonio Ediciones.
Nau, François. 1905. Traduction des lettres XII et XIII de Jacques d'Édesse. *Revue l'orient Chrétien* 10:197–208, 258–82.
Neusner, Jacob. 1984–91. *The Talmud of Babylonia: An American Translation*. BJS. Chico, Calif.: Scholars Press.
———. 1997. *The Fathers according to Rabbi Nathan*. Vol. 6 of *The Components of the Rabbinic Documents: From the Whole to the Parts*. South Florida Academic Commentary Series 84. Atlanta: Scholars Press.
Newsom, Carol A. 1980. The Development of 1 Enoch 6–19: Cosmology and Judgment. *CBQ* 42:310–29.
Nickelsburg, George W. E. 1977. Apocalyptic and Myth in 1 Enoch 6–11. *JBL* 96:383–405.
———. 1981. *Jewish Literature between the Bible and the Mishnah: A Historical and Literary Introduction*. Philadelphia: Fortress.
———. 1992a. Enoch, First Book of. *ABD* 2:509–10.
———. 1992b. Son of Man. *ABD* 6:137–50.
———. 1998. Patriarchs Who Worry about Their Wives—A Haggadic Tendency in the Genesis Apocryphon. Pages 137–58 in Stone and Chazon 1998.
———. 1999. Seeking the Origins of the Two Ways Tradition. Pages 95–108 in *A Multiform Heritage: Studies on Early Judaism and Christianity in Honor of Robert A. Kraft*. Edited by Benjamin G. Wright III. Atlanta: Scholars Press.
———. 2000. Enoch, Books of. *EDSS* 1:249–53.
———. 2001. *1 Enoch 1: A Commentary on the Book of 1 Enoch*. Hermeneia. Minneapolis: Fortress.
Nickelsburg, George W. E., and Robert A. Kraft, eds. 1986. *Early Judaism and Its Modern Interpreters*. Atlanta: Scholars Press; Philadelphia: Fortress.
Nickelsburg, George W. E., and James C. VanderKam. 2004. *1 Enoch: A New Translation*. Minneapolis: Fortress.
Niehoff, Maren R. 2003. Circumcision as a Marker of Identity—Philo, Origen and the Rabbis on Gen 17:1–14. *JSQ* 10:89–123.
Nikiprowetzky, Valentin. 1987. La Sibylle juive et le "Troisième Livre" des "Pseudo-Oracles Sibyllins" depuis Charles Alexandre. *ANRW* 2.20.1:460–542.

Nöldeke, Theodor. 1909. *Geschichte des Qorans*. Leipzig: Weicher.
Noort, Ed. 1999. The Stories of the Great Flood: Notes on Gen 6:5–9:17 in Its Context of the Ancient near East. Pages 1–38 in García Martínez and Luttikhuizen 1999.
Noth, Martin. 1951. Noah, Daniel und Hiob in Ezechiel XIV. *VT* 1:251–60.
O'Connor, John J. 1956. The Astrological Background of the Miller's Tale. *Speculum* 31:120–25.
O'Neill, John C. 1992. History of Biblical Criticism. *ABD* 1:726–30.
Orlov, Andrei A. 2000a. Melchizedek Legend of 2 (Slavonic) Enoch. *JSJ* 31:23–38.
———. 2000b. "Noah's Younger Brother": The Anti-Noahic Polemics in *2 Enoch*. *Henoch* 22:207–21.
———. 2003. The Flooded Arboretums: The Garden Traditions in the Slavonic Version of 3 Baruch and the Book of Giants. *CBQ* 65:184–201.
———. 2005. *The Enoch-Metatron Tradition*. TSAJ 107. Tübingen: Mohr Siebeck.
———. 2007. *From Apocalypticism to Merkabah Mysticism: Studies in the Slavonic Pseudepigrapha*. JSJSup 114. Leiden: Brill.
Papoutsakis, Emmanuel. 2004. Ostriches into Sirens: Towards an Understanding of a Septuagint Crux. *JJS* 55:25–36.
Parisot, D. John, ed. 1894. *Aphraates sapientis persae, Demonstrationes*. Patralogia Syriaca: Tomus Primus. Paris: Firmin-Didot.
Parrott, Douglas M., ed. 1979, *Nag Hammadi Codices V,2–5 and VI with Papyrus Berolinensis 8502, 1 and 4*. NHS 11. Leiden: Brill.
Parry, Donald W., and Emanuel Tov, eds. *Parabiblical Texts*. Dead Sea Scrolls Reader 3. Leiden: Brill.
Pásztori-Kupán, Istvan. 2006. *Theodoret of Cyrus*. The Early Church Fathers. London: Routledge.
Pearson, Birger A. 1977. The Figure of Norea in Gnostic Literature. Pages 143–52 in *Proceedings of the International Colloquium on Gnosticism: Stockholm, August 20–25, 1973*. Edited by Geo Widengren. Filologisk-filosofiska serien 17. Stockholm: Almqvist & Wiksell; Leiden: Brill.
———. 1981. *Nag Hammadi Codices IX and X*. NHS 15. Leiden: Brill.
———. 1988a. Revisiting Norea. Pages 265–75 in *Images of the Feminine in Gnosticism*. Edited by Karen L. King. Studies in Antiquity and Christianity. Philadelphia: Fortress.
———. 1988b. Use, Authority and Exegesis of Mikra in Gnostic Literature. Pages 635–52 in *Mikra: Text, Translation, Reading and Interpretation of the Bible in Ancient Judaism and Early Christianity*. Edited by Martin J. Mulder. CRINT 2.1. Assen: Van Gorcum; Philadelphia: Fortress.
———. 1990a. Jewish Elements in Gnosticism and the Development of Gnostic Self-Definition. Pages 124–35 in idem, *Gnosticism, Judaism, and Egyptian Christianity*. Minneapolis: Fortress. Originally published as pages 151–80 in *Jewish and Christian Self-Definition*. Edited by E. P. Sanders. London: SCM, 1980.
———. 1990b. Jewish Haggadic Traditions in *The Testimony of Truth* from Nag Hammadi (CG IX 3). Pages 39–51 in idem, *Gnosticism, Judaism, and Egyptian Christianity*. Minneapolis: Fortress. Originally published in *Ex orbe religionum* 1 (1972): 457–70.

———. 1996. *Nag Hammadi Codex VII.* NHS 30. Leiden: Brill.
Philo of Alexandria. 1929–68. *Philo in Ten Volumes and Two Supplementary Volumes.* Translated by Francis H. Colson, George H. Whitaker, and Ralph Marcus. 12 vols. LCL. London: Heineman.
Pietersma, Albert. 2006. Introduction: A New Archimedean Point for Septuagint Studies? *BIOSCS* 39:1–11.
Pietersma, Albert, and Benjamin G. Wright III. 2007. To the Reader of NETS. Pages xiii–xx in *A New English Translation of the Septuagint and the Other Greek Translations Traditionally Included under That Title.* New York: Oxford University Press.
Plato. 1929. *Timaeus.* LCL. Translated by Robert G. Bury. New York, Heinemann.
Pope, Marvin H. 1977. *Song of Songs.* AB 7C. Garden City, N.Y.: Doubleday.
Popović, Mladen. 2006. Physiognomic Knowledge in Qumran and Babylonia: Form, Interdisciplinarity, and Secrecy. *DSD* 13:150–76.
———. 2007. *Reading the Human Body: Physiognomics and Astrology in the Dead Sea Scrolls and Hellenistic-Early Roman Period Judaism.* STDJ 67. Leiden: Brill.
Puech, E. 2001. *Qumran Cave 4. XXII: Textes araméens, première partie: 4Q529–549.* DJD 31. Oxford: Clarendon.
Qurṭubī, Muhammad ibn Ahmad. 1967. *Al-Jāmi' Li-Ahkām Al-Qur'ān.* 10 vols. Al-Qāhirah: Dār al-Kātib al-'Aribī.
Rajak, Teresa. 2002. *Josephus: The Historian and His Society.* 2nd ed. London: Duckworth.
Ramsay, William M. 1897. *West and West-Central Phrygia.* Part 2 of *The Cities and Bishoprics of Phrygia.* Oxford: Clarendon.
Rappaport, Salomo. 1930. *Agada und Exegese bei Flavius Josephus.* Vienna: Verlag der Alexander Kohut Mermorial Foundation.
Rasimus, Tuomas. 2005. Ophite Gnosticism, Sethianism and the Nag Hammadi Library. *VC* 59:235–63.
Reed, Annette Yoshiko. 2005. *Fallen Angels and the History of Judaism and Christianity.* Cambridge: Cambridge University Press.
Reeves, John C. 1992. *Jewish Lore in Manichaean Cosmogony: Studies in the Book of Giants Traditions.* Monographs of the Hebrew Union College 14. Cincinnati: Hebrew Union College Press.
———. 1993. Utnapishtim in the Book of Giants? *JBL* 112:110–15.
———. 1999. Exploring the Afterlife of Jewish Pseudepigrapha in Medieval Near Eastern Religious Traditions: Some Initial Soundings. *JSJ* 30:148–77.
Reicke, Bo. 1964. *The Epistles of James, Peter, and Jude: Introduction, Translation, and Notes.* AB 37. Garden City, N.Y.: Doubleday.
Reinach, Théodore. 1903. *Jewish Coins.* London: Lawrence & Bullen.
Reid, Stephen Breck. 2004. *Enoch and Daniel: A Form Critical and Sociological Study of the Historical Apocalypses.* BIBAL Monograph Series 2. 2nd ed. North Richland Hills, Tex.: BIBAL.
Reinink, Gerrit J. 1975. Das Land "Seiris" (Šir) und das Volk der Serer in jüdischen und christlichen Traditionen. *JSJ* 6:72–85.
Rendsburg, Gary A. 2007. The Biblical Flood Story in the Light of the Gilgameš Flood Account. Pages 115–27 in *Gilgameš and the World of Assyria: Proceedings of the*

Conference Held at Mandelbaum House, the University of Sydney, 21–23 July, 2004. Edited by Joseph Azize and Noel Weeks. Leuven: Peeters.

Rendtorff, Rolf. 1999. Noah, Abraham and Moses: God's Covenant Partners. Pages 127–30 in *In Search of True Wisdom: Essays in Old Testament Interpretation in Honour of Ronald E. Clements*. Edited by Edward Ball. JSOTSup 300. Sheffield: Sheffield Academic Press.

Ri, Su-Min. 1987. *La Caverne des Tresors: Les deux recensions Syriaces*. CSCO 486–487; Scriptores Syriaci 207–208. Leuven: Peeters.

Roberge, Michel, ed. 2000. *La Paraphrase de Sem (NH VII,1)*. Bibliothèque copte de Nag Hammadi, Section "Textes" 25. Québec: Les Presses de l'Université Laval; Leuven: Peeters.

Robinson, Neal. 2003. *Discovering the Qur'an: A Contemporary Approach to a Veiled Text*. Washington, D.C.: Georgetown University Press.

Rofé, Alexander. 1998. 4QMidrash Samuel? Observations concerning the Character of 4QSam[a]. *Textus* 19:63–74.

Rokeah, David, trans. 1971. *Celsi Alethes Logos*. Arranged by Otto Glöckner. Jerusalem.

Rompay, Lucas van. 1986. *Le commentaire sur Genèse–Exode 9,32 du manuscrit (Olim) Diyarbakir*. CSCO 483–484; Scriptores Syri 205–206. Leuven: Peeters.

Rösel, Martin. 1995. Die Chronologie der Flut in Gen 7–8: Keine neuen textkritischen Lösungen. *ZAW* 110:590–93.

Rousseau, Adelin, and Louis Doutreleau, eds. 1979. *Irénée de Lyon, Contre les hérésies: Livre I*. SC 263–64. 2 vols. Paris: Cerf.

Rubenstein, Jeffrey L. 1996. From Mythic Motifs to Sustained Myth: The Revision of Rabbinic Traditions in Medieval Midrashim. *HTR* 89:131–59.

———. 2001. The Bavli's Ethic of Shame. *Conservative Judaism* 53:27–39.

———, ed. 2005. *Creation and Composition: The Contribution of the Bavli Redactors (Stammaim) to the Aggada*. TSAJ 114. Tübingen: Mohr Siebeck.

Ruiten, Jacques T. A. G. M. van. 1999. The Interpretation of the Flood Story in the Book of Jubilees. Pages 66–85 in García Martínez and Luttikhuizen 1999.

———. 2000. The Division of the Earth. Pages 295–319 in idem, *Primeval History Interpreted: The Rewriting of Genesis 1–11 in the Book of Jubilees*. JSJSup 66. Boston: Brill.

Rutgers, Leonard V. 2000. *Subterranean Rome: In Search of the Roots of Christianity in the Catacombs of the Eternal City*. Leuven: Peeters.

Safrai, Zeev. 2006. The Targums as Part of Rabbinic Literature. Pages 243–78 in *The Literature of the Sages, Second Part: Midrash and Targum, Liturgy, Poetry, Mysticism, Contracts, Inscriptions, Ancient Sience and the Languages of Rabbinic Literature*. Edited by Shmuel Safrai et al. CRINT 2.1. Assen: Van Gorcum; Philadelphia: Fortress.

Salter, M., L. Salter, and Jeremy Schonfeld. 2003. *The North French Hebrew Miscellany: British Library Add. MS 11639*. 2 vols. Vol. 1 edited by M. and L. Salter; vol. 2 edited by Jeremy Schonfeld. London: Facsimile Editions.

Sanders, E. P. 1977. *Paul and Palestinian Judaism*. Philadelphia: Fortress.

Sandt, Huub van de, and David Flusser. 2002. *The Didache: Its Jewish Sources and*

Its Place in Early Judaism and Christianity. Assen: Van Gorcum; Minneapolis: Fortress.

Sarna, Nahum M. 1989. *Genesis.* JPS Torah Commentary. Philadelphia: Jewish Publication Society.

Satlow, Michael L. 2006. Rabbinic Views on Marriage, Sexuality, and the Family. Pages 612–26 in *The Late Roman-Rabbinic Period.* Vol. 4 of *The Cambridge History of Judaism.* Edited by Steven T. Katz. Cambridge: Cambridge University Press.

Schäfer, Peter. 1984. *Geniza-Fragmente zur Hekhalot-Literatur.* TSAJ 6. Tübingen: Mohr Siebeck.

———. 1988. Ein neues Fragment zur Metoposkopie und Chiromantik. Pages 84–95 in idem, *Hekhalot Studien.* TSAJ 19. Tübingen: Mohr Siebeck.

———. 2007. *Jesus in the Talmud.* Princeton: Princeton University Press.

Schäfer, Peter, and Shaul Shaked, eds. 1999. *Magische Texte aus der Kairoer Geniza.* Vol. 3. TSAJ 72. Tübingen: Mohr Siebeck.

Schalit, Abraham. 1944. *Josephus: Antiquitates Judaicae* [Hebrew]. Jerusalem: Mosad Bialik.

Schenke, Hans-Martin. 1974. Das Sethianische System nach Nag-Hammadi Handschriften. Pages 165–73 in *Studia Coptica.* Edited by Peter Nagel. Berliner byzantische Arbeiten 45. Berlin: Akademie-Verlag.

Schiffman, Lawrence H. 1987. The Conversion of the Royal House of Adiabene in Josephus and Rabbinic Sources. Pages 293–312 in *Josephus, Judaism, and Christianity.* Edited by Louis H. Feldman and Gohei Hata. Leiden: Brill.

———. 2004. Pseudepigrapha in the Pseudepigrapha: Mythical Books in Second Temple Literature. *RevQ* 21:429–38.

Schiffman, Lawrence H., and Michael D. Swartz. 1992. *Hebrew and Aramaic Incantation Texts from the Cairo Genizah: Selected Texts from Taylor-Schechter Box K1: Semitic Texts and Studies 1.* Sheffield: Sheffield Academic Press.

Schmidt, Nathaniel. 1926. The Apocalypse of Noah and the Parables of Enoch. Pages 111–23 in *Oriental Studies Published in Commemoration of the Fortieth Anniversary of Paul Haupt.* Edited by Cyrus Adler and Aaron Ember. Baltimore: Johns Hopkins University Press.

Scholem, Gershom. 1953. Physiognomy and Chiromancy [Hebrew]. Pages 459–95 in *Sefer Assaf.* Edited by Umberto Cassuto, Yehoshua Gutman, and Josef Klausner. Jerusalem: Mossad Harav Kook.

———. 1987. *Origins of the Kabbalah.* Translated by Allan Arkush. Princeton: Princeton University Press.

Schwartz, Baruch J. 2007. The Flood-Narratives in the Torah and the Question of Where History Begins [Hebrew]. Pages 139–54 in *Shai le-Sara Japhet: Studies in the Bible, Its Exegesis and Its Language.* Edited by Mosheh Bar-Asher et al. Jerusalem: Bialik.

Schwartz, Daniel R. 1990. *Agrippa I: The Last King of Judaea.* TSAJ 23. Tübingen: Mohr Siebeck.

———. 1996. Temple or City: What Did Hellenistic Jews See in Jerusalem? Pages

114–27 in *The Centrality of Jerusalem: Historical Perspectives*. Edited by Marcel Poorthuis and Ch. Safrai. Kampen, The Netherlands: Kok Pharos.

———. 2002. Wo wohnt Gott? Die Juden und ihr Gott zwischen Judenstaat, Diaspora und Himmel. Pages 58–73 in *Gottesstaat oder Staat ohne Gott*. Edited by Severin J. Lederhilger, Frankfurt am Main: Lang.

———. 2004. The Jews of Egypt between the Temple of Onias, the Temple of Jerusalem, and Heaven [Hebrew]. Pages 37–55 in *Center and Diaspora: The Land of Israel and the Diaspora in the Second Temple, Mishnah and Talmud Periods*. Edited by Isaiah M. Gafni. Jerusalem: Merkaz Zalmon Shazar. [English summary: vi–vii]

———. 2007. Josephus on the Pharisees as Diaspora Jews. Pages 137–46 in *Josephus und das Neue Testament*. Edited by Christfried Böttrich and Jens Herzer, with Torsten Reiprich. WUNT 209. Tübingen: Mohr Siebeck.

———. 2008. *Life of Josephus* [Hebrew]. Jerusalem: Yad Ben Zvi.

Schwartz, Joshua J. 1991. *Lod (Lydda), Israel: From Its Origins through the Byzantine Period, 5600 B.C.E.–640 C.E.* British Archaeological Reports, International Series 571. Oxford: Tempus Reparatum.

Schwartz, Seth. 1990. *Josephus and Judean Politics*. Columbia Studies in the Classical Tradition 18. Leiden: Brill.

Scott, James M. 1997a. The Division of the Earth in Jubilees 8:11–9:15 and Early Christian Chronography. Pages 295–323 in *Studies in the Book of Jubilees*. Edited by Matthias Albani, Jörg Frey, and Armin Lange. TSAJ 65. Tübingen: Mohr Siebeck.

———. 1997b. Geographic Aspects of Noachic Materials in the Scrolls at Qumran. Pages 368–81 in *The Scrolls and the Scriptures*. Edited by Stanley E. Porter and Craig A. Evans. Sheffield: Sheffield Academic Press.

———. 2002. *Geography in Early Judaism and Christianity: The Book of Jubilees*. SNTSMS 113. Cambridge: Cambridge University Press.

Sed-Rajna, Gabrielle. 1982. The Paintings of the London Miscellany. *Journal of Jewish Art* 9:18–30.

Segal, Michael. 2007. *The Book of Jubilees: Rewritten Bible, Redaction, Ideology and Theology*. JSJSup 117. Leiden: Brill.

Sevrin, Jean-Marie. 1975. À propos de la Paraphrase de Sem. *Le Muséon* 88:69–96.

Shapira, Amnon. 2004. Mirror Story: The Book of Esther as a Moral Correction of the Amalek Affair [Hebrew]. *Mo'ed* 14:36–48.

Shinan, Avigdor. 1992a. The Aramaic Targum as a Mirror of Galilean Jewry. Pages 242–51 in *The Galilee in Late Antiquity*. Edited by Lee I. Levine. New York: Jewish Theological Seminary.

———. 1992b. *The Embroidered Targum: The Aggadah in Targum Pseudo-Jonathan of the Pentateuch* [Hebrew]. Publication of the Perry Foundation for Biblical Research. Jerusalem: Magnes.

———. 1994. The Aggadah of the Palestinian Targums of the Pentateuch and Rabbinic Aggadah: Some Methodological Considerations. Pages 203–17 in *The Aramaic Bible: Targums in Their Historical Context*. Edited by Derek R. G. Beattie and Martin J. McNamara. JSOTSup 166. Sheffield: JSOT Press.

———. 1997. The Birth of Moshe Rabenu in Rabbinic Literature [Hebrew]. *Rimonim* 5:4–7.

Siegert, Folker, Heinz Schreckenberg, and Manuel Vogel. 2001. *Flavius Josephus: Aus meinem Leben (Vita)*. Tübingen: Mohr Siebeck.
Skinner, John. 1910. *A Critical and Exegetical Commentary on Genesis*. ICC. Edinburgh: T&T Clark.
Small, Jocelyn Penny. 2003. *The Parallel Worlds of Classical Art and Text*. Cambridge: Cambridge University Press.
Sokoloff, Michael. 1976. 'ămar něqē', "Lamb's Wool" (Dan. 7:9). *JBL* 95:277–79.
———. 1992. *A Dictionary of Jewish Palestinian Aramaic of the Byzantine Period*. Ramat-Gan: Bar Ilan University Press.
Sparks, H. F. D. 1984. *The Apocryphal Old Testament*. Oxford: Oxford University Press.
Speiser, Ephraim A. 1964. *Genesis*. AB 1. Garden City, N.Y.: Doubleday.
Sperber, Daniel. 1995. The Prayer of Moses in the *London Miscelleny* and the Uplifting of Hands in Prayer. Pages 71–75 in vol. 4 of *The Customs of Israel: Origins and History*. Jerusalem: Mosad Harav Kook.
Speyer, Wolfgang. 1970. *Bücherfunde in der Glaubenswerbung der Antike*. Hypomnemata: Untersuchungen zur Antike und zu ihrem Nachleben 24. Göttingen: Vandenhoeck & Ruprecht.
———. 1971. *Die Literarische Fälschung im heidnischen und christlichen Altertum: Ein Versuch ihrer Deutung*. Munich: Beck.
Spiegel, Shalom. 1945. Noah, Daniel and Job. Pages 305–55 in *Louis Ginzberg Jubilee Volume: On the Occasion of His Seventieth Birthday*. Edited by Saul Lieberman et al. New York: American Academy for Jewish Research.
Spilsbury, Paul. 1998. *The Image of the Jew in Flavius Josephus' Paraphrase of the Bible*. TSAJ 69. Tübingen: Mohr Siebeck.
Starcky, Jean. 1964. Un texte messianique araméen de la Grotte 4 de Qumrân. Pages 51–66 in *Mémorial du cinqantenaire de l'École des Langues Orientales de l'Institut Catholique de Paris*. Travaux de l'Institut Catholique de Paris 10. Paris: Bloud & Gay.
Steiner, Richard C. 1991. The Mountains of Ararat, Mount Lubar, and הר הקדם. *JJS* 42:247–49.
———. 1995. The Heading of the *Book of the Words of Noah* on a Fragment of the Genesis Apocryphon: New Light on a "Lost" Work. *DSD* 2:66–71.
Steinsaltz, Adin. 1989–99. *The Talmud: The Steinsaltz Edition*. New York: Random House.
Steinschneider, Moritz. 1965. *Zur pseudepigraphischen Literatur des Mittelalters*. Amsterdam: Philo.
Stephens, Walter. 2005. Livres de haulte gresse: Bibliographic Myth from Rabelais to Du Bartas. *Modern Language Notes Supplement* 120:60–83.
Sterling, Gregory E. 1992. *Historiography and Self-Definition: Josephos, Luke-Acts and Apologetic Historiography*. NovTSup 64. Leiden: Brill.
Stern, David. 1988. Midrash and Indeterminacy. *Critical Inquiry* 15:132–61.
Stern, Menahem. 1974. *Greek and Latin Authors on Jews and Judaism*. 3 vols. Jerusalem: Israel Academy of Sciences and Humanities.
Sternberg, Meir. 1985. *The Poetics of Biblical Narrative: Ideological Literature and the Drama of Reading*. Bloomington: Indiana University Press.

Stichel, Rainer. 1974. Ausserkanonische Elemente in byzantinischen Illustrationen des Alten Testaments. *Römische Quartalschrift für christliche Altertumskunde und Kirchengeschichte* 69:159–81.

———. 1979. *Die Namen Noes, seines Bruders und seiner Frau. Ein Beitrag zum Nachleben jüdischer Überlieferungen in der außerkanonischen und gnostischen Literatur und in Denkmälern der Kunst*. Abhandlungen der Akademie der Wissenschaften in Göttingen, Philologisch-Historische Klasse 3.112. Göttingen: Vandenhoeck & Ruprecht.

Stone, Michael E. 1971. Noah, Books of. Page 1189 in vol. 12 of *Encyclopedia Judaica*. Edited by Cecil Roth. 16 vols. Jerusalem: Keter.

———. 1981. *Signs of the Judgment, Onomastica Sacra and the Generations from Adam*. University of Pennsylvania Armenian Texts and Studies 3. Chico, Calif.: Scholars Press.

———. 1982a. *Armenian Apocrypha Relating to the Patriarchs and Prophets*. Jerusalem: The Israel Academy of Sciences and Humanities.

———. 1982b. The Metamorphosis of Ezra: Jewish Apocalypse and Mediaeval Vision. *JTS* 33:14–15.

———. 1984a. Apocalyptic Literature. Pages 383–441 in in Stone 1984b.

———, ed. 1984b. *Jewish Writings of the Second Temple Period: Apocrypha, Pseudepigrapha, Qumran Sectarian Writings, Philo, Josephus*. CRINT 2.2. Assen: Van Gorcum; Philadelphia: Fortress.

———. 1990. *Fourth Ezra: A Commentary on the Book of Fourth Ezra*. Hermeneia. Minneapolis: Fortress.

———. 1996a. *Armenian Apocrypha: Relating to Adam and Eve*. SVTP 14. Leiden: Brill.

———. 1996b. The Dead Sea Scrolls and the Pseudepigrapha. *DSD* 3:270–95.

———. 1999. The Axis of History at Qumran. Pages 133–49 in Chazon and Stone 1999.

———. 2000. Noah, Texts of. *EDSS* 2:613–15.

———. 2006a. The Book(s) Attributed to Noah. *DSD* 13:4–23.

———. 2006b. Pseudepigraphy Reconsidered. *Review of Rabbinic Judaism* 9:1–15.

———. 2007a. Enoch's Date in Limbo; or, Some Considerations on David Suter's Analysis of the Book of Parables. Pages 444–49 in Boccaccini 2007.

———. 2007b. The Interpretation of Song of Songs in *4 Ezra*: *JSJ* 38:226–33.

Stone, Michael E., and Esther G. Chazon, eds. 1998. *Biblical Perspectives: Early Use and Interpretation of the Bible in Light of the Dead Sea Scrolls: Proceedings of the First International Symposium of the Orion Center, 12–14 May, 1996*. STDJ 28. Leiden: Brill.

Stone, Michael E., and Jonas C. Greenfield. 1996. Aramaic Levi Document. Pages 2–72 in *Qumran Cave 4, XXI, Parabiblical Texts, Part 3*. DJD 22. Oxford: Clarendon.

Stone, Michael E., Benjamin G. Wright III, and David Satran. 2000. *The Apocryphal Ezekiel*. SBLEJL 18. Atlanta: Society of Biblical Literature.

Stone, N. 1999. Apocryphal Elements in Christian Bible Illumination. Pages 161–69 in *Apocryphes arméniens: Transmission—traduction—création—iconographie*. Edited by Valentina Calzolari Bouvier, Jean-Daniel Kaestli, and Bernard Outtier. Lausanne: Zèbre.

Stopford, J. T. Sarsfield, trans. 1983. *Gregory the Great, Ephraim Syrus, Aphrahat.* NPNF 2/13. Grand Rapids: Eerdmans.
Strack, Hermann L., and Günter Stemberger. 1992. *Introduction to the Talmud and Midrash.* Translated and edited by M. Bockmuehl. Minneapolis: Fortress.
Stroumsa, Guy G. 1984. *Another Seed: Studies in Gnostic Mythology.* NHS 24. Leiden: Brill.
Stuckenbruck, Loren. 1997. The Throne-Theophany of the Book of Giants: Some New Light on the Background of Daniel 7. Pages 211–20 in *The Scrolls and the Scriptures: Qumran Fifty Years After.* Edited by Stanley E. Porter and Craig A. Evans. JSPSup 26. Sheffield: Sheffield Academic Press.
———. 2000. The "Angels" and "Giants" of Genesis 6:1–4 in Second and Third Century BCE Jewish Interpretation: Reflections on the Posture of Early Apocalyptic Traditions. *DSD* 7:354–77.
———. 2001. Daniel and Early Enoch Traditions in the Dead Sea Scrolls. Pages 368–86 in vol. 2 of *The Book of Daniel: Composition and Reception.* Edited by John J. Collins and Peter W. Flint. VTSup 83. Leiden: Brill.
———. 2004. The Origins of Evil in Jewish Apocalyptic Tradition: The Interpretation of Genesis 6:1–4 in the Second and Third Centuries B.C.E. Pages 87–118 in *The Fall of the Angels.* Edited by Christoph Auffarth and Loren T. Stuckenbruck. Themes in Biblical Narrative 6. Leiden: Brill.
———. 2007. *1 Enoch 91–108.* Commentaries on Early Jewish Literature. Berlin: de Gruyter.
Suter, David W. 1979a. Fallen Angel, Fallen Priest: The Problem of Family Purity in *1 Enoch* 6–16. *HUCA* 50:115–35.
———. 1979b. *Tradition and Composition in the Parables of Enoch.* SBLDS 47. Missoula, Mont.: Scholars Press.
———. 2007. Enoch in Sheol: Updating the Dating of the Book of Parallels. Pages 415–43 in Boccaccini 2007.
Swartz, Michael D. 1994. Book and Tradition in Hekhalot and Magical Literatures. *Journal of Jewish Thought and Philosophy* 3:189–229.
Ṭabarī, Muhammad ibn Jarīr. 1965. *Tārīkh Al-Rusul Wa-Al-Mulūk.* Bayrut: Maktabat Khayyat.
———. 1969. *Tafsīr Al-Tabarī: Jāmi' Al-Bayān 'an Ta'wīl Al-Qur'ān.* Al-Qāhirah: Dār al Ma'ārif.
Tameanko, Marvin. 2000. Noah and the Ark on Ancient Coins. *The Shekel.* 33.4:4–9.
Taylor, Jerome. 1991. *The Didascalicon of Hugh of Saint Victor: A Guide to the Arts.* New York: Columbia University Press.
Tcherikover, Victor. 1956. Jewish Apologetic Literature Reconsidered. *Eos* 48:169–93.
Thackeray, H. St. John. 1926 *Josephus: Jewish Antiquities, Books I–IV.* London: Harvard University Press.
———. 1929. *Josephus: The Man and the Historian.* New York: Ktav. Repr., 1967.
———. 1930. *Josephus: Jewish Antiquities. Books I–III.* LCL 242. Cambridge: Harvard University Press.
Theodor, Julius, and Chanock Albeck. 1996. *Midrash Bereshit Rabbah* [Hebrew]. Jerusalem: Shalem.

Thomson, Robert W. 1978. *Moses Khorenats'i: History of the Armenians.* Cambridge: Harvard University Press.
Tisserant, Eugene. 1921. Fragments syriaques du Livre des Jubilés. *RB* 30:55–86, 206–32.
Torijano, Pablo A. 2002. *Solomon, the Esoteric King: From King to Magus, Development of a Tradition.* JSJSup 73. Leiden: Brill.
Tov, Emanuel. 2004. *Scribal Practices and Approaches Reflected in the Texts Found in the Judean Desert.* STDJ 54. Leiden: Brill.
Trebilco, Paul R. 1991. *Jewish Communities in Asia Minor.* Cambridge: Cambridge University Press.
Trever, John C. 1965. Completion of the Publication of Some Fragments from Qumran Cave 1. *RevQ* 5:323–44.
Turner, John D. 1995. Typologies of the Sethian Gnostic Treatises from Nag Hammadi. Pages 169–217 in *Les textes de Nag Hammadi et le problème de leur classification: Actes du colloque tenu à Québec du 15 au 10 Septembre 1993.* Edited by Louis Painchaud and Anne Pasquier. Bibliothèque copte de Nag Hammadi, Section "Études" 3. Quebec: Les Presses de l'Université Laval.
Turner, Martha L. 1996. *The Gospel according to Philip: The Sources and Coherence of an Early Christian Collection.* NHMS 38. Leiden: Brill.
Tuval, Michael. Forthcoming. A Jewish Priest in Rome. In *Making History: Josephus and Historical Method II.* Edited by J. Pastor et al. Leiden: Brill.
Uhlig, Siegbert. 1984. Das Äthiopische Henochbuch. Pages 471–780 in Apokalypsen. Vol. 5 of *Jüdische Schriften aus hellenistisch römischer Zeit.* Gütersloh: Mohn.
Ulrich, Eugene. 2003. The Non-attestation of a Tripartite Canon in 4QMMT. *CBQ* 65:202–14.
Unger, Dominic J., trans., 1992. *St. Irenaeus of Lyons, Against the Heresies.* Vol. 1, Book 1. Ancient Christian Writers 55. New York: Paulist.
Unger, Richard W. 1991. *The Art of Medieval Technology: Images of Noah the Shipbuilder.* New Brunswick, N.J.: Rutgers University Press.
VanderKam, James C. 1978. The Textual Affinities of the Biblical Citations in the Genesis Apocryphon. *JBL* 97:45–55.
———. 1980. The Righteousness of Noah. Pages 13–32 *Ideal Figures in Ancient Judaism.* Edited by George W. E. Nickelsburg and John J. Collins. SBLSCS 12. Chico, Calif.: Scholars Press, 1980.
———. ed. and trans. 1989. *The Book of Jubilees.* 2 vols. CSCO 510–511; Scriptores Aethiopici 87–88. Leuven: Peeters.
———. 1992a. The Birth of Noah. Pages 213–31 in *Intertestamental Essays in Honour of Józef Tadeusz Milik.* Edited by Zdzisław Jan Kapera. Krakow: Enigma. Repr. as pages 396–412 in VanderKam 2000a.
———. 1992b. Righteous One, Messiah, Chosen One, and Son of Man in 1 Enoch 37–71. Pages 169–91 in *The Messiah: Developments in Earliest Judaism and Christianity.* Edited by James H. Charlesworth. Minneapolis: Fortress.
———. 1993. Biblical Interpretation in 1 Enoch and Jubilees. Pages 96–125 in *The Pseudepigrapha and Early Biblical Interpretation.* Edited by James H. Charlesworth and Craig A. Evans. Sheffield: JSOT Press. Repr. as pages 276–304 in VanderKam 2000a.

———. 1994. Putting Them in their Place: Geography as an Evaluative Tool. Pages 46–69 in *Pursuing the Text: Studies in Honor of Ben Zion Wacholder on the Occasion of His Seventieth Birthday*. Edited by John C. Reeves and John Kampen. JSOTSup 184. Sheffield: Sheffield Academic Press. Repr. as pages 133–49 in VanderKam 2000a.
———. 1996. Jubilees' Exegetical Creation of Levi the Priest. Pages 359–73 in *Homage à Jozef T. Milik*. *RevQ* 17. Repr. as pages 545–62 in VanderKam 2000a.
———. 1999. Charles, Robert Henry (1855–1931). Page 176 in vol. 1 of *Dictionary of Biblical Interpretation*. Edited by John H. Hayes. Nashville: Abingdon.
———. 2000a. *From Revelation to Canon: Studies in the Hebrew Bible and Second Temple Literature*. JSJSup 62. Leiden: Brill.
———. 2000b. Jubilees. *EDSS* 1:434–38.
———. 2001. *The Book of Jubilees*. Guides to the Apocrypha and Pseudepigrapha. Sheffield: Sheffield Academic Press.
———. 2006. Daniel 7 in the Similitudes of Enoch (1 Enoch 37–71). Pages 291–307 in *Biblical Traditions in Transmission: Essays in Honour of Michael A. Knibb*. Edited by Charlotte Hempel and Judith M. Lieu. JSJSup 111. Leiden: Brill.
Vermes, Geza. 1973. *Scripture and Tradition in Judaism: Haggadic Studies*. 2nd ed. StPB 4. Leiden: Brill.
Vermes, Mark, trans. 2001. *Hegemonius, Acta Archelai (The Acts of Archelaus)*. Manichaean Studies 4. Turnhout: Brepols, 2001.
Vosté, Jacques-Marie, and Ceslas van den Eynde. 1950–55. Genèse. Vol. 1 of *Commentaire d'Išo'dad de Merv sur l'Ancien Testament*. 2 vols. CSCO 126, 156; Scriptores Syri 67, 75. Leuven: Durbecq.
Wacholder, Ben Zion. 1962. *Nicolaus of Damascus*. University of California Publications in History 75. Berkeley and Los Angeles: University of California Press.
———. 1968. Biblical Chronology in Hellenistic World Chronicles. *HTR* 61:451–81.
Wahl, Harald-Martin. 1992. Noah, Daniel und Hiob in Ezechiel XIV 12 20 (21–3): Anmerkungen zum traditionsgeschichtlichen Hintergrund. *VT* 42:542–53.
Waldstein, Michael, and Frederick Wisse, eds. 1995. *The Apocryphon of John: Synopsis of Nag Hammadi Codices II,1; III,1; and IV,1 with BG 8502,2*. NHMS 33. Leiden: Brill.
Wandrey, Irina. 2004. *"Das Buch des Gewandes" und "Das Buch des Aufrechten": Dokumente eines magischen spätantiken Rituals ediert, kommentiert und überstezt*. TSAJ 96. Tübingen: Mohr Siebeck.
Wansbrough, John E. 1977. *Quranic Studies: Sources and Methods of Scriptural Interpretation*. London Oriental Series 31. Oxford: Oxford University Press.
———. 1978. *The Sectarian Milieu*. London Oriental Series 34. Oxford: Oxford University Press.
Wasserstrom, Steven M. 1994. Jewish Pseudepigrapha in Muslim Literature: A Bibliographical and Methodological Sketch. Pages 87–114 in *Tracing the Threads: Studies in the Vitality of Jewish Pseudepigrapha*. Edited by John C. Reeves. SBLEJL 6. Atlanta: Scholars Press.
Watt, W. Montgomery. 1970. *Bell's Introduction to the Qur'an*. Edinburgh: Edinburgh University Press.

Weigold, Matthias. 2007. The Deluge and the Flood of Emotions: The Use of Flood Imagery in 4 Maccabees in Its Ancient Jewish Context. Pages 197–210 in *The Books of the Maccabees: History, Theology, Ideology: Papers of the Second International Conference on the Deuterocanonical Books, Pápa, Hungary, 9–11 June, 2005.* Edited by Géza G. Xeravits and József Zsengellér. JSJSup 118. Leiden: Brill.

———. 2008. Noah in the Praise of the Fathers: The Flood Story in Nuce. In *Studies in the Book of Ben Sira: Papers of the Third International Conference on the Deuterocanonical Books, Shime'on Centre, Pápa, Hungary, 18–20 May, 2006.* Edited by Géza G. Xeravits and József Zsengellér. JSJSup 127; Leiden: Brill.

Weitzmann, Kurt. 1947. *Illustrations in Roll and Codex: A Study of the Origin and Method of Text Illustration.* Princeton: Princeton University Press.

Weitzmann, Kurt, and Herbert L. Kessler. 1986. *The Cotton Genesis: British Library, Codex Cotton Otho B VI.* The Illustrations in the Manuscripts of the Septuagint 1. Princeton: Princeton University Press.

Weitzmann, Kurt, and Massimo Bernabò, with the collaboration of Rita Tarasconi. 1999. *The Byzantine Octateuchs.* The Illustrations in the Manuscripts of the Septuagint 2. 2 vols. Princeton: Princeton University Press.

Welch, Alford T. 2000. Formulaic Features of the Punishment-Stories. Pages 77–116 in *Literary Structures of Religious Meaning in the Qur'an.* Edited by Issa J. Boullata. Richmond, Surrey: Curzon.

Wellesz, Emmy. 1960 *The Vienna Genesis: With an Introduction and Notes.* New York: Yoseloff.

Weltecke, Dorothea. 1997. The World Chronicle by Patriarch Michael the Great (1126–1199): Some Reflections. *Journal of Assyrian Academic Studies* 11:6–30.

Wenham, Gordon J. 1978. The Coherence of the Flood Narrative. VT 28:336–48. Repr. as pages 436–47 in *I Studied Inscriptions from before the Flood: Ancient Near Eastern, Literary, and Linguistic Approaches to Genesis 1–11.* Edited by Richard S. Hess and David T. Tsumara. Sources for Biblical and Theological Study 4. Winona Lake, Ind.: Eisenbrauns, 1994.

Werman, Cana. 1999. Qumran and the Book of Noah. Pages 171–81 in Chazon and Stone 1999.

Westermann, Claus. 1974. *Genesis 1–11.* BKAT 1.1. Neukirchen-Vluyn: Neukirchener.

———. 1984. *Genesis 1–11: A Commentary.* Translated by John J. Scullion. Continental Commentary. Minneapolis: Augsburg.

Wevers, John W. 1993. *Notes on the Greek Text of Genesis.* SBLSCS 35. Atlanta: Scholars Press.

Wheeler, Brannon M. 2002. *Prophets in the Quran: An Introduction to the Quran and Muslim Exegesis.* New York: Continuum.

Whitney, K. William, Jr. 2006. *Two Strange Beasts: Leviathan and Behemoth in Second Temple and Early Rabbinic Judaism.* HSM 63. Winona Lake, Ind.: Eisenbrauns.

Williams, Francis E. 2001. *Mental Perception: A Commentary on NHC VI, 4, The Concept of Our Great Power.* NHMS 51. Leiden: Brill.

Williams, Frank, trans. 1994. *The Panarion of Epiphanius of Salamis, Books II and III.* NHMS 36. Leiden: Brill.

Williams, Michael Allen. 1996. *Rethinking "Gnosticism": An Argument for Dismantling a Dubious Category.* Princeton: Princeton University Press.

———. 2005. Sethianism. Pages 32–63 in *A Companion to Second-Century Christian "Heretics."* Edited by Antti Marjanen and Petri Luomanen. VCSup 76. Leiden: Brill.

Wilpert, Josef. 1891. *Ein Cyclus christologischer Gemälde aus der Katakombe der Hl. Petrus und Marcellinus.* Freiburg: Herder.

Winston, David. 1985. *Logos and Mystical Theology in Philo of Alexandria.* Cincinnati: Hebrew Union College Press.

Winston, David, and John Dillon. 1983. *Two Treatises of Philo of Alexandria: A Commentary on De Gigantibus and Quod Deus sit immutabilis.* BJS 25. Chico, Calif.: Scholars Press.

Wintermute, Orval S., trans. 1983. Jubilees. *OTP* 2:35–142.

Wise, Michael, Martin Abegg, and Edward Cook. 1996. *The Dead Sea Scrolls: A New Translation.* San Fransisco: HarperSanFrancisco.

Witakowski, Witold. 1993. The Division of the Earth between the Descendants of Noah in Syriac Tradition. *ARAM* 5:635–56.

Witherup, Ronald D. Functional Redundancy in the Acts of the Apostles: A Case Study. *JSNT* 48:67–86.

Wittig, Susan. 1973. Formulaic Style and the Problem of Redundancy. *Centrum* 1:123–36.

Wright, Benjamin G., III. 2008. The Septuagint and Its Modern Translators. Pages 103–14 in *Die Septuaginta—Texte, Kontexte, Lebenswelten.* Edited by Wolfgang Kraus and Martin Karrer. WUNT 219. Tübingen: Mohr Siebeck.

Wright, William. 1867. Two Epistles of Mar Jacob, Bishop of Edessa. *The Journal of Sacred Literature and Biblical Record* 38 [NS 10]:430–60.

Wutz, Franz X. 1915. *Onomastica Sacra: Untersuchungen zum Liber Interpretationis Nominum Hebraeorum des Hl. Hieronymous.* Texte und Untersuchungen 41.2. Leipzig: Hinrichs.

Yadin, Azzan. 2003. The Hammer on the Rock: Polysemy and the School of Rabbi Ishmael. *JSQ* 10:1–17.

Yadin, Yigael. 1962. *The Scroll of the War of the Sons of Light against the Sons of Darkness.* Oxford: Oxford University Press.

Zakovitch, Yair. 1995. *Through the Looking Glass: Reflection Stories in the Bible* [Hebrew]. Tel Aviv: ha-Kibbutz ha-Meuchad.

Zakovitch, Yair, and Avigdor Shinan. 2004. *That's Not What the Good Book Says* [Hebrew]. Tel Aviv: Yediot Ahronot.

Zellentin, Holger M. 2007. Late Antiquity Upside-Down: Rabbinic Parodies of Jewish and Christian Literature. Ph.D. diss., Princeton University.

Zimmerli, Walther. 1969. *Ezechiel.* BKAT 13.1. Neukirchen-Vluyn: Neukirchener.

———. 1979. *Ezekiel 1.* Translated by Ronald E. Clements. Hermeneia. Philadelphia: Fortress.

Zimmermann, Johannes. 1998. *Messianische Texte aus Qumran: Königliche, priesterliche und prophetische Messiasvorstellungen in den Schriftfunden von Qumran.* WUNT 2/104. Tübingen: Mohr Siebeck.

Zycha, Joseph. 1891–92. *Sancti Aureli Augustini de utilitate credendi, de duabus animabus, contra Fortunatum, contra Adimantum, contra epistolam fundamenti, contra Faustum.* CSEL 25.1–2. 2 vols. Vienna: Tempsky.

Contributors

Aryeh Amihay is a Ph.D. candidate in the Department of Religion at Princeton University. He holds a B.A. (magna cum laude) in biblical studies from the Hebrew University of Jerusalem and is a graduate fellow at the Center for Jewish Law of the Cardozo Law School (2009–2010) and the Center for Human Values at Princeton University (2010–2011).

Ruth Clements (Th.D., Harvard Divinity School, 1997) is Head of Publications for the Orion Center for the Study of the Dead Sea Scrolls, at the Hebrew University of Jerusalem. She has written on early Jewish and Christian biblical interpretation and has recently co-edited (with Daniel R. Schwartz) *Text, Thought, and Practice in Qumran and Early Christianity* (Brill, 2010).

Esther Eshel (Ph.D., Hebrew University of Jerusalem, 2000) is a Senior Lecturer in the Bible Department of Bar Ilan University. She has been a Harry Starr Fellow at Harvard University, a Visiting Scholar at University of Michigan, and a fellow at the Oxford Centre for Hebrew and Jewish Studies. Her publications include editions of some of the Cave 4 fragments and epigraphic material from Maresha and Kuntillet-'Ajrud.

Albert C. Geljon studied classics and philosophy at Vrije Universiteit Amsterdam and wrote a dissertation on Philo and Gregory of Nyssa (Leiden, 2000). He is currently a teacher of classical languages at the Christelijk Gymnasium Utrecht, The Netherlands.

Vered Hillel, Ph.D. (2009) Hebrew University of Jerusalem, is Senior Lecturer in Second Temple Period Studies at Israel College of the Bible, Netanya. She has written articles on the Testaments of the Twelve Patriarchs and related literature, as well as collaborated with Michael Stone on the publication of *The Armenian Version of the Testaments of the Twelve Patriarchs: Edition, Apparatus, Translation and Commentary*.

Daniel A. Machiela received his Ph.D. from the University of Notre Dame in 2007. He is currently Assistant Professor of Religious Studies (Early Judaism) at McMaster University in Ontario, Canada. His recent publications have focused on the Aramaic Dead Sea Scrolls and the Genesis Apocryphon (1Q20) in particular, on which he published a monograph that includes a new edition of the scroll (Brill, 2009). His broader interests lie in the many aspects of Second Temple Judaism, but especially the development of sacred traditions and scriptural interpretation during that period.

Erica L. Martin, Ph.D., teaches Hebrew Bible, New Testament, Qurʾān, and Biblical Languages in the Theology and Religious Studies department of Seattle University and the graduate School of Theology and Ministry at Seattle University, in addition to serving as Affiliate Chaplain for Jewish Life at the University of Puget Sound.

Sergey Minov, currently a Ph.D. student at the Hebrew University of Jerusalem, is writing a dissertation on the following subject: "The *Cave of Treasures* in Context: Polemical Historiography and Formation of Syriac Christian Identity in the Fifth-Sixth Centuries." Main research interests are Syriac Christianity, Jewish-Christian relations in late antiquity, apocryphal and pseudepigraphical literature, and Jewish and Christian biblical exegesis.

Jeremy Penner, M.A. (2003), is a Ph.D. candidate in the Religious Department at McMaster University, Hamilton, Ontario. His dissertation is on early Jewish prayer.

Claire Pfann (M.A., 1985, Graduate Theological Union, Berkeley) is Academic Dean and Instructor in New Testament at the University of the Holy Land in Jerusalem. She is currently working on her dissertation, "The Levites in the Late Second Temple Period: Their Presence and Social Function in Eretz Israel and the Diaspora," at the Hebrew University under the direction of Prof. Michael Stone.

Rebecca Scharbach is a doctoral student in History of Religions at the University of Chicago Divinity School. She holds a masters degree in Jewish Studies from the Hebrew University of Jerusalem and a bachelors degree in medieval history from the University of Chicago. She is currently working on the influence of popular practice and belief on rabbinic tradition formation.

Nadav Sharon, M.A. (2006), is a doctoral student of Jewish history at the Hebrew University of Jerusalem, researching the early years of Judea under Roman rule (63–37 B.C.E.).

Michael E. Stone (b. England 1938) received his B.A. (Hons.) degree in 1960 from University of Melbourne. In 1964 he was awarded a Ph.D. in Near Eastern Languages and Literatures by Harvard University and in 1985 the earned, senior doctorate, D.Litt., by the University of Melbourne. He holds honorary doctorates from Hebrew Union College and the National Academy of Sciences of Armenia. He is a Foreign Member of the Australian Humanities Academy, the Royal Netherlands Academy of Sciences, and the Academia Lombarda (Italy). He has been awarded the major Israeli National Prize, the Landau Prize for Contribution to the Humanities. He taught at the Hebrew University of Jerusalem from 1966 to 2007, where he was Gail Levin de Nur Professor of Religious Studies and Professor of Armenian Studies. He is now retired.

Moshe Tishel, Ph.D. (1967, Michigan State University), is a special student at the Hebrew University of Jerusalem.

Michael Tuval is a lecturer at the Department of Jewish History at the Hebrew University in Jerusalem. He is currently completing his Ph.D. on the religious paradigms in the writings of Flavius Josephus and Second Temple Diaspora literature.

Benjamin G. Wright III is Professor of Religion Studies at Lehigh University, Bethlehem, Pennsylvania. His research focuses mostly on Judaism in the Second Temple period. His research has concentrated on three areas: (1) Jewish wisdom literature of the period, especially the Wisdom of Jesus Ben Sira; (2) the translation of Jewish literature from Hebrew into Greek; and (3) the Dead Sea Scrolls. He most recently completed, as co-editor with Albert Pietersma of the University of Toronto and translator, *A New English Translation of the Septuagint* (Oxford University Press, 2007), the first translation into English since 1841 of the Septuagint/Old Greek translations.

Index of Ancient Sources

Hebrew Bible

Genesis

Ref	Pages
1:4	62
1:26–27	295
1:27	194, 195
1:28	141, 163
4:2	189, 191
4:12	189
4:17	315, 316
4:20–21	189
4:20–22	66
4:22	233
4:26	184
5	109, 111
5–15	77
5:1	110, 111
5:3	194
5:9	147
5:18–15:5	78
5:18	153
5:20	153
5:21	153
5:22	89, 140
5:22–23	29
5:24	89, 140, 157, 184
5:25	153
5:28	137, 153
5:28–29	53, 55
5:29	64, 152, 185, 197, 303
5:32	29, 83, 184, 201
6:1–2	241
6:1–4	54, 56, 139, 148, 208, 222, 224
6:1–5	78
6:2–4	56, 57
6:3	139, 148, 158, 224
6:4	139, 142, 295
6:5–7	149, 215
6:6–7	83, 140
6:7	224
6:8	83, 88, 89, 187, 202
6:9	83, 85, 89, 111, 140, 153, 156, 157, 184, 185, 191, 194, 196, 198, 199, 201, 202, 204, 252, 303
6:10	83
6:11	140, 148
6:11–17	83
6:14	188
6:14–16	158
6:15	226
6:16	158, 207
6:18	140, 208
7:1	153, 201, 206
7:2	188
7:4	157
7:7	206, 239
7:10	157
7:11–12	84, 158
7:12	206
7:13	206, 226
7:17–18	159
7:17–20	158
7:23	207
7:24	158
8:2–3	158
8:4	84, 198, 308, 314
8:6–12	160
8:7	225
8:16	206, 208, 209
8:18	206, 240
8:19	208
8:20	84, 161, 201, 210, 211
8:21	198
8:21–22	84

Genesis (cont.)		Exodus	
9	137, 198, 212	2:2	62, 195
9:1	141, 208	2:19	202
9:1–2	83, 163	4:1–9	205
9:1–7	84	17	297
9:4	307	24:4–9	294
9:5	137	33:17	187
9:18	84	34:29–35	61
9:20	84, 155, 161, 189, 191, 199, 202		
9:20–21	191	Leviticus	
9:20–22	189	3:1	196
9:20–23	241	3:6	196
9:21	85, 155, 190	19:23–25	161
9:22	212		
9:24	85, 190, 213	Numbers	
9:25	245, 248	13:22	139
9:27	246	13:33	139
10	16, 92, 244, 250	16:22	33
10:1–11:11	84	21:14	107
10:8–11	139	21:33	207
10:10–11	316	24:4	195
10:24	147	24:6	205
10:25	246, 249		
11:4	315	Deuteronomy	
11:12	147	1:2	220
11:12–13	148	2:1–5	220
12:1	185	3:11	207
13:17	81, 140	30:15	87
14:6	220	30:15–30	86
14:18	100, 194, 211	33:1	202
15	80	33:2	220
15:1			
81		Joshua	
17	297	10:5	228
17:1	89, 140, 196	15	93
18	209	24:4	220
24:40	140		
24:48	86	1 Samuel	
25:27	194	2:26	195
26:24	81	15	207
30:31–31:13	150	15:32–33	297
32:21	89		
34:2	212	1 Kings	
37:2	194	22	205
39:1	187		
48:15	89, 140	2 Kings	
		19:37	312

INDEX OF ANCIENT SOURCES

Isaiah		16:1	195
1:18	59	37:37	196
24:17–23	44	56:9	106
37:38	309, 312	74:14	40
42:1	98, 105	80	205
45:4	105	89:4	105
54:9	209	92:13	205
61:1	98	104:16	205
65:9	105	106:23	105
65:15	105		
65:22	105	Proverbs	
		1–8	87
Jeremiah		Job	
1:5	195	1:8	194
11:16	91	12:5	204
21:8	87		
37	205	Song of Songs	
51:27	312–314	5:10	58
51:27–28	313	5:11–12	59
Ezekiel		Lamentations	
4:4	85	4:7	59
14:12–20	65		
14:14	66, 154	Ecclesiastes	
14:20	154	10:4	206
35:2–3	220		
35:7	220	Esther	
35:15	220	2:17	89
		6:11	297
Amos		8:3	297
4:3	314		
7:10–17	205	Daniel	
		2	90
Jonah		4	90
1–4	205	7	34, 35, 72, 91
		7:1	85
Micah		7:9	34, 59
7:12	314	7:10	106
		10:5	61
Haggai			
2:23	195	Apocryphal/Deuterocanonical Books	
Zechariah			
2:1–3	41	Tobit	
		1:3	87
Psalms		4:5–6	87
1:1–3	201	4:6	89

4:10	88	PSEUDEPIGRAPHA		
4:12	97, 155			
4:19	88	Apocalypse of Abraham		
Wisdom of Solomon		23:4–9	163	
10:1–2	154	Aramaic Levi Document		
10:1–4	151	3:4–9	87	
10:4	108, 154, 159, 217	3:17	88	
14:1–7	160	4:3	85	
14:6	150, 151	4:4	85	
14:6–7	154, 160	4:13	81, 90	
		6:1–10:10	13, 17	
1 Maccabees		10:3	13	
16:24	50	10:10	7, 12, 13, 18, 27, 109	
		10:11–14	13	
2 Maccabees		11	86	
3:24	33	11:8	86	
		11:10	86	
3 Maccabees		12:4	86	
2:4	150	13	86	
		13:4	18, 247	
4 Maccabees		2 Baruch		
7:1–3	287	29:4	40, 41	
15:29–32	160	56	154	
15:31	163	56:10–16	149	
15:31–32	286			
16:20–21	286	3 Baruch		
		4	130	
Sirach		4:8–17	161–162, 212	
42:20	247	4:9–15	162	
44:16	89	4:10	150	
44:17	97, 154			
44:20	65	4 Baruch		
46:1	105	7:8	154	
4 Ezra		1 Enoch		
3:9–11	149, 154	1	19	
3:10–11	141	1–5	48, 49	
3:11	304	1–16	36	
3:14	119	1–36	47	
4:1–28	60	1:1	105, 106	
6:49–52	40	1:4	81	
6:51	41	1:8	81	
9:4–22	60	1:8–9	105, 106	
12:35–39	119	3	19	
14	119	4:12	78	

INDEX OF ANCIENT SOURCES

5:4–9	106	47:3	34, 106
6–11	27, 47, 48, 49, 51, 98, 149	48:1–2	106
6–16	88	48:2	34
6–19	24, 107	48:2–10	35
6:1	48, 107	51:3	100
6:1–4	49	52:1–2	36
6:3	32	52–54	36
6:6	79, 153	53:1–3	36
6:6–8	43	53:1–54:6	37
6:7	31	53:3	30, 31, 33
7	19	54	98
7:21–25	49	54:1	145
8–10	37	54:1–2	36
8:1–3	31, 32	54:1–55:1	9, 27, 44
8:1	32	54:3	38
8:2	31	54:5–7	145
8:3	32	54:7–55:2	27, 29, 32, 33, 34, 36, 37–38, 44
9:6	32		
9:7	32	54:5	32
10:3	163	54:6	30, 37, 38
10:4–9	32	55–62	43
12	49	55:1	34
12–16	78	55:2	37
12:1–2	48	55:3	37, 38
12:4	105	55:3–4	43
12:4–13:10	157	55:4	32
13:1–2	32	56:1	30, 31, 33
17–36	36	58–69	37
22	19	58:1–3	39
22:4	78	59	42
25:4–5	106	59:1–3	39
25:5	105	60	9, 27, 29, 30, 32, 34,35, 36, 38–42, 44
32:3–6	163	60:1–6	39
37–71	27	60:1	29, 30, 41, 109
37:1–4	37	60:2	34
38–44	36, 37	60:6	33, 40
38:2–4	106	60:7–10	39, 40
39:6–7	106	60:8	29, 30, 41
40:7	30, 31	60:9	40
41:3–8	36	60:10	34, 35
43–44	36	60:11–13	39
45–57	37	60:11–23	39, 40
46:1	34	60:11–24	36
46:2	100	60:24	39, 40
46:2–7	35	60:25	33, 39, 40
46:3	100	61	39, 42
46:3–4	105	61:1–5	39, 41

1 Enoch (cont.)

61:12–13	106	69:4–6	32
61:15	106	69:4–12	32
62–63	43	69:4–15	31
62:5–14	35	69:6	31, 32
62:11	30	69:13	32
62:12–15	106	69:22–24	36
63–70	43	69:24	34
63:1	31, 33	69:26–29	35
63:11–12	35	70	37
64	43	70–71	35, 37, 56
64:1–2	42	70:3	106
64:1–69:12	44	71:1–17	37
65–67	36, 43, 44	71:10	34
65–69	32, 44, 98, 109	71:12	34
65:1–2	42	71:13	34
65:1–3	42	71:14	35
65:1–67:3	42	72–82	24, 47
65:1–68:1	30	81:1–2	106
65:1–68:2	42	83–84	36, 42
65:1–69:25	9, 27, 29, 30, 34, 36, 42–44	83–90	60
65:2–68:1	42	86–88	88
65:6	30, 31, 33	89:1	56
65:6–12	42	89:1–9	65, 195
65:9–11	34	89:2–4	159
65:12	33	89:7–8	159
66	145	90:17	106
66:1	31, 32, 33	91:15	78
66:1–2	42	93:3	105, 106
66:3	42	94:4	105
67	36, 42	106	59, 61, 75
67:1	66	106–107	9, 10, 19, 27, 36, 48, 53, 54, 58, 67, 68, 69, 71, 72, 75, 83, 195
67:2	163	106–108	98
67:4–13	145	106:1	54
67:4–5	36	106:2	58, 61
67:4–68:1	42	106:2–3	103
67:7	33	106:2–4	104
67:8	33, 34, 43	106:3	103
68–69	43, 44	106:5	58, 61, 63
68:1	16, 18, 42, 43, 67	106:5–6	55
68:2–5	43	106:8–18	104
68:2–69:25	30, 42, 44	106:13	79, 153
69	31, 32, 43	106:13–16	149
69:1	33	106:15	146
69:2	31	106:15–18	66
69:2–3	31	106:17–18	105
69:4	31, 32	106:18	55, 64, 104, 152, 303

# INDEX OF ANCIENT SOURCES 361

106:19	66, 67	6:5–9	84
107:3	55, 64, 66, 67, 152	6:15–16	84
108:1	16, 67	7:1	15, 311
108:3–5	146	7:1–2	77, 84
		7:1–5	161
2 Enoch		7:13–17	243
22:11–23	119	7:15	15
23	57	7:16	316
23:5	101	7:17	311
23:22	63	7:20–39	27, 98
33	147	7:20	108
33:3	147	7:20–26	292
33:8–12	119	7:26–38	108
33:10	147	7:35–37	161
33:12	147	7:35	243
35:1	154	7:38	16
47–48	119	7:38–39	13, 107
67:2	158	8–9	92
69–73	99	8:10–9:15	17
70:8	159	8:11–12	17
71	10, 99	8:11–9:15	244
71:18–19	75	8:11	8, 17
73:1	158	8:12	17, 248, 249
		8:12–21	82
Jubilees		8:13	147
4:15	153	8:18	109
4:17	106	8:22–23	248
4:17–22	106	8:30	248
4:18	106, 108	9:14–15	248
4:19	107, 108	10	24, 119
4:21–22	107, 108	10:1–14	14, 15, 18, 115
4:22–23	153	10:1–15	27, 98
4:24	157	10:3	27
4:28	55, 64, 303	10:4	14
4:33	83, 155	10:10	14, 115
4:33–5:2	153	10:11–12	18
5	149	10:12–13	109
5:5	83, 88, 89	10:13	14, 18
5:19	83, 88, 89, 105, 154	10:14	15, 66, 69, 115, 121
5:24	159	10:15	15, 311
5:24–27	84	10:17	83
5:28	15, 84, 311	10:21	18
5:29	159	10:28–34	92
6:1–2	84	10:29	248
6:1–3	161	10:30–32	248
6:2–3	84	19:24	97
6:4	84	21	18

Jubilees (cont.)		Testament of Benjamin	
21:1–10	13, 98	7:3–4	2, 151
21:10	16, 18, 27, 30, 109	10:6	155
23:25	60		
23:26–28	60	Testament of Levi	
30:22	106	2:3	18
45:16	14	9:3	13
		10:5	18
Life of Adam and Eve		16:1	18
21:3	61, 63	18:2	18
49:2–3	3, 151		
50:1	3, 147	Testament of Naphtali	
		3:4–5	2, 149, 151
Pseudo-Philo, *Liber Antiquitatum Biblicarum*		Testament of Reuben	
3:2	158	5:6–7	2, 150, 151
3:4	155		
4:1–10	92	DEAD SEA SCROLLS	
49:2–50:2	144		
50:1–2	147	CD/Damascus Document	
		4:15–19	50
Sibylline Oracles		10:6	106
1:73–124	153	16:3	50
1:125–126	153		
1:125–127	154	1QpHab	
1:128–130	157	X:13	105
1:147–198	218		
1:150–170	157	1Q19	
1:171–172	157	frag. 1	71, 72, 73
1:174–198	157	frags.1–12	72, 73
1:217–224	159	frag. 2	71, 72
1:225–229	160	frag. 3	10, 19, 53, 72, 73, 103, 104
1:242–256	161	frag. 3:5	61
1:269–274	163	frag. 13	73
1:280	154	frags. 13–21	72, 73
1:321–325	282	frag. 15	73
1:340	161		
3:93–161	60	1Q20/1QapGen/Genesis Apocryphon	
3:110–114	92	0	77, 79
3:110–155	245	0:2	80
3:823–825	154, 160	0:2–3	78
3:827	163	0:8	78, 80
		0:12	80
Testament of Adam		0–I	78, 79
3	144	0–V:27	79
3:5	152	I	58
		I:2	80

INDEX OF ANCIENT SOURCES

I:3	80	VI:16	109
I:7	80	VI:19	90
I–XVII	9	VI:19–20	79
II	10, 58, 79, 83, 104	VI:23	83, 89
II:1	79	VI:24	83
II:1–3	55, 58	VII:5	81
II:4	59	VII:6	83
II:9	54	VII:7–9	83
II:13	54	VII:10–15	83
II:16	79	VII:16–IX	84
II:21	80	VII:19	90
II:24–25	55	VIII:33–34	81
II–III	10, 19	IX–X:1	84
II–V	9, 53	X–XVI	94
III:3	79	X:1–10	84
V–VI	10	X:2	10
V–XVII	8–9, 17	X:11–12	84
V:2–23	79	X:12–13	84
V:3–4	55, 79	X:13–17	84
V:5	58	X:18	84
V:7	58	XI–XII:6	84
V:10	58	XI:1–10	84
V:12	61, 103	XI:7–9	84
V:16	58	XI:11	81
V:16–19	78	XI:11–12	84
V:21	80	XI:12–14	84
V:25	81	XI:15	81, 82, 84
V:26–27	79	XII	17
V:28	79	XII–XIV	90
V:29	8, 9, 10, 11, 12–13, 27, 69, 82, 109	XII:8–9	243
V:29–36	83	XII:9–12	84
V:29–XVIII:22	79	XII:13	84, 311
VI	77	XII:13–14	84
VI:1	83, 105	XII:13–15	77
VI:1–2	154	XII:13–16	161
VI:1–5	83, 86	XII:13	15
VI:2	89	XII:14–19	84
VI:3	89	XII:16–17	161
VI:4	80, 108	XII:19–XV:21	84
VI:6–7	83	XIII–XV	242
VI:7–8	83	XIII:8–12	90
VI:8–9	83	XIII:13–17	90
VI:9–22	83	XIII:16	91
VI:11	89, 109	XIII:18–XIV:8	91
VI:11–12	89	XIV:9–19	91
VI:12	81	XIV:10	82, 91
VI:15	90	XIV:11	91

1Q20 (cont.)		1QH^a	
XIV:12	82, 91	13:38	81
XIV:13	82, 91	24:9	81
XIV:17	92		
XV–XVII:24	84	4Q186/4QHoroscope	
XV:21	85, 92	1 ii:5	110
XV:21–22	82	1 ii:7–8	110
XV:23	85	1 ii:8	110
XV:23–36	85	1 ii:9	110
XVI:12	249	1 iii:3	110
XVI:14	80	1 iii:4	110
XVI–XVII	17, 92, 244	1 iii:8–9	110
XVII	94	2 i:5	110
XVII–XVIII	82	2 i:7	110
XVII–XXII	94		
XVII:10	93	4Q196/4QpapTob^a ar	
XVII:11–15	82	2:4	309, 312
XVII:16	80		
XVIII:23	79	4Q201/4QEn^a ar	
XVIII:23–24	79	1 iii:4–5	79
XVIII:24–XX	79	iv:4–5	81, 85
XIX:14–21	82		
XIX:25	107	4Q203/4QEnGiants^a ar	
XX	19	5 ii:17–18	79
XXI:13–14	81	8	153, 157
XXI:15–16	81		
XXI:16–19		4Q206	
XXI:23	78	frags. 2–3	78
XXII	77		
		4Q212	
1Q27/1QMysteries		frag. 1	78
1 i:2	81		
		4Q228	
1QS/Community Rule		frag. 1 i:4	11
III–IV	110, 111		
III:13	110	4Q244	
III:19	110	frag. 8	243
IV:15	110	frag. 8:3	15, 311
1Q28a/1QSa		4Q252	
i:7	106	1:1–3	158
		1:10	309
1Q33/1QM/War Scroll			
2:10–14	92	4Q270/4QD^e	
10:14–15	92	frag. 6 ii:17	11

INDEX OF ANCIENT SOURCES

4Q271/4QD^f		4Q530/4QEnGiants^b ar	
frag. 4 ii:5	11	2ii 6–12	145–146
4Q384			
frag. 9:2	11	4Q561	
4QMMT		1 i 3	110
C 9–10	102	6:4	110
C 10–11	102		
4Q534		6Q8	
frags. 1–2	98	26:1	311
frag. 1, col. i:1	110		
frag. 1, col. i:1–2	61	Other Scrolls	
frag. 1, col. i:1–3	103	1QIsa^a	95
frag. 1, col. i:2	110	2Q26	148
frag. 1, col. i:3	110	4Q158, 364–367(4QRP^{a-e})	95
frag. 1, col. i:4–5	101	4Q186	98, 99, 102, 109, 111, 112
frag. 1, col. i:4–8	66	4Q246	72, 75
frag. 1, col. i:6	106, 109	4Q252–254	27
frag. 1, col. i:7–8	107	4Q415–418, 423 (4QInstruction)	72
frag. 1, col. i:8	67, 108	4Q369	109
frag. 1, col. i:9	100	4Q561	98, 99, 102, 109, 111, 112
frag. 1, col. i:10	104, 110	11Q13/11QMelch	100
frag. 1, col. i:12	109	11Q19/11QT	95
frag. 1, col. ii:1–5	103		
frag. 1, col. ii:14	100, 109	JOSEPHUS	
frag. 1, col. ii:15	100, 109		
frag. 1, col. ii:16	100	*Against Apion*	
frag. 1, col. ii:18	100	1.1	171
frag. 7:1–6	108	1.1–2.144	173
		1.47–56	169
		1.50–51	168
4Q535		1.128–131	2, 177
frag. 1, col. i:8	98	1.129–131	178
frag. 1, col. :8	98	1.130–131	170
frag. 2:1	110	2.1	171
frag. 3:1–6	103	2.45–47	172
frag. 3:2	110, 197	2.145–296	173
4Q536		*Judean Antiquities*	
frag. 1:1–2	103	1.5–6	172
frag. 2, col. 1:1	109	1.8	171, 172
frag. 2, col. 1:8	109	1.9–12	172
frag. 2, col. 1:13	109	1.14	171
frag. 2, col. 2	108	1.23–24	172, 178
frag. 2, col. 2:11	66	1.63–148	173
frag. 2, col. 2:11	108	1.69	147, 174
frags. 2+3, col. 1:8–9	67	1.70	131, 174
		1.70–71	144–45, 147

Judean Antiquities (cont.)		17–18	184
1.71	220	27	108, 152, 184, 185, 186
1.72–74	2, 153, 178–79	31	108, 156, 184, 185
1.72–108	299	31–37	156
1.74	157, 218	32	185
1.75	154	34	184
1.77	158	35–36	185
1.82	175	36	184
1.88	175	37–38	185, 187
1.90	309	42–43	158–59
1.91	160	46	163, 185
1.92	160, 161	47–48	184
1.92–95	2, 176–77, 309–10	56	163
1.96–99	174, 240		
1.96–103	179	*Agriculture*	
1.104–108	175–76	1–7	189
1.105–108	2	10–11	189
1.106	97, 174	125	189
1.110–112	2, 180	181	189
1.121	174		
1.122–138	174	*Allegorical Interpretation*	
1.122–147	92	1.96	187
1.129	174	2.60	190
1.140	161, 179	3.24	305
1.141	156	3.73	187
1. 143	93	3.77	185
1.143–147	174	3.78	184, 186
1.148	175		
3.84	180	*Cherubim*	
3.87	170, 180	27	187
3.88	180		
12.12–118	172	*Confusion*	
20.25	170, 176	2	188
20.262–267	169	23–25	189
20.263–265	172	105	184
		105–107	188
Life of Josephus			
1	169	*Creation*	
342	168	8	187
358	168	143	186
361–363	168		
430	169, 171	*Drunkenness*	
		4	190
PHILO OF ALEXANDRIA			
		Flight	
Abraham		192	189
4–5	184, 305		

INDEX OF ANCIENT SOURCES

Giants
3   184
5   184
58   188

Heir
260 184

Migration
2   185
16   298
125 184

Moses
1.25–26
1.48
1.154
2.2
2.59–60
2.59–65
2.60
2.62
2.63
2.65
2.263

Planting
185
163–164

Posterity
48
172
173
175

Preliminary Studies
24
61
90
94
103–105

Questions on Genesis
1.45
1.87
1.91

1.97
2.1   184
2.2   184
2.4   188
2.9
2.13
2.18
2.19
2.45
2.47
2.49
2.66
2.68
2.68–69
         186
         186
         186
         186
         156
         188
         158
         163
         159
         163
         145

Rewards
11–14
15–21
22
23

Sacrifices
1–4
45
59–60
102–103

Sobriety
190   190
30

Unchangeable
104–116
107
107–113
116
118
140

         184
         185
         184, 185
         184

         185
         188
         184, 185
         185
         185

Virtues
201

Worse
28
109
111
121

         152
         152
         158

184, 185
188
188
188
189
157
189
188
156, 185
163
239–40
189
190
156

184
184
185
152, 188, 283

185
185
187
184

190

186
184
186–87
187
184
184

185

184
185
305
65, 185

Worse (cont.)	
121–122	185
167–173	188
170	184, 188

New Testament

Matthew
1:18–2:12	56

Luke
1:5–78	56
2:5–20	56
23:35	98, 105

John
1:34	98, 105

Acts
2:9–11	92

2 Thessalonians
1:5–78	81

1 Peter
3:20	157, 293
3:20–21	294

2 Peter
2:5	109, 157, 218
3:5–7	146

Revelation
1:12–16	61

Greco-Roman Authors

Apollodorus, *Bibliotheca*
1.7.2	298
2.4.1	298

Appolonius of Alexandria, *Homeric Lexicon*
	298

Aristotle, *Symposium*
3	190

Ovid, *Metamorphoses*
	281

Pausanias, *Description of Greece*
3.2.4.1	298
10.14.1	298

Plato, *Laws*
677a	145

Plato, *Timaeus*
22c	145, 146
23a–b	148
29d	186

Plutarch, *Parallel Lives*
5	281

Stoics (*SVF*)
1:126	186
2:836	188
3:76	186
3:299	186
3:332	186
3:448	186
3:462	186
3:476	186
3:560	186
3:619	186
3:622	186
3:643	186
3:661	186
3:677	186
3:682	186

Early Christian Writings

Ambrose, *Paradise*
3.19	305

Aphrahat, *Demonstrations*
3	238
13:5–6	238
18	238

Apocalypse of Adam
3	146
3:8	152
5:10	146

INDEX OF ANCIENT SOURCES

69:2–71:26	218	Ephrem the Syrian, *Nisibene Hymn*	239, 304
70:4–71:26	218–219		
72:15–74:26	245	Epiphanius of Salamis, *Panarion*	
		2.26.1.3–9	229
Apocalypse of Paul		3.39.5.2–3	228
50	218	33.27.1	235
		66.83.3–85.7	245
Apocryphon of John			
BG 72:12–73:18	217	Gospel of the Egyptians	
BG 72:17–19	234	61:1–22	220
NHC 29, 1–2	234	72:10–73:6	220
Asclepius		Gospel of Philip	
73:23–34	224	84:21–85:1	226–227
Augustine, *De civitate Dei*		Hegemonius, *Acta Archelai*	
18.38	25	9.1	235
Augustine, *Against Faustus the Manichaean*		Hippolytus of Rome, *Apostolic Tradition*	
12.20	225	23	294
Cave of Treasures	239, 243, 251	Hippolytus of Rome, *Refutatio omnium haeresium*	
17	295	5.26.17–18	224
1 Clement		Hypostasis of the Archons	
7:6	218	91:34–92:3	230
9:1	218	92:3–15	219
		92:14–93:14	231
Concept of Our Great Power		96:17–28	234
37:12–23	223		
38:17–39:15	223	Irenaeus of Lyon, *Adversus haereses*	
38:25–28	218	1.18.3–4	226
40:31–41:2	223	1.30.9	228
43:17–22	223	1.30.10	216–17
Didache		Isidore of Seville, *Chronicon*	
1–6	87	1.5	131
Ephrem the Syrian, *Commentary on Genesis*		Justin Martyr, *Apology*	
6	65	2.7.2	283
6.12	239		
7.1–2	244	*Kephalaia*	
Ephrem the Syrian, *Discourses to Hypatius*		3	235
3	235	29	235
Ephrem the Syrian, *Hymn* 2	294		

Manichaean Psalms	
157:19–21	226, 235
177:1–11	226
On the Origins of the World	
102:10–11	230
Origen, *Homiliae in Genesim*	
2	65
2.1–2	284
2.2	227
Panarion	
2.26.1.3–9	229
Paraphrase of Shem	
25:7–15	220
28:5–22	220–221
Pseudo-Clementines, *Recognitiones*	
1.30.2–31.2	245
Pseudo-Tertullian, *Adversus omnes haereses*	
2.8–9	222
Right Ginza	
18	225
2.1.121	232
Septimus Severus, *Historia Augusta*	282
Severus of Antioch	
Homily 123	222
Sulpitius Severus, *Chronicle*	
1.3	225
Tertullian, *De cultu feminarum*	
3	25
Theodoret of Cyr, *Haereticarum fabularum compendium*	
1.14	221
1.26	221

Theophilus of Antioch, *Autolyctum*	
3.19	239, 304
Thought of Norea	
27:11–12	234
29:3	230
Valentinian Exposition	
38:34–39	222

Rabbinic Literature

m. Pesaḥim	
4:9	116
4:10	117
m. Nedarim	
3:11	196
m. 'Abot	
5:6	128
t. Soṭah	
10:2	65
y. Terumot	
45.4	200
y. Roš Haššanah	
2.58	210
y. Taʿanit	
1.64d	240
y. ʿAbodah Zarah	
41.2	200
b. Berakot	
10b	116
40a	130, 163
b. ʿErubin	
18b	201
b. Roš Haššanah	
20b	210

INDEX OF ANCIENT SOURCES

b. Taʿanit		31.14	120
2a	130	31.16	205
		32.6	205
b. Ketubbot		33.3	304
112a	210	34.4	206
		34.6	240
b. Nedarim		34.7	240–241
32b	100	34.9	211
		24.6	209
b. Soṭah		36.3	202, 212
12a–13a	62	36.4	155
		36.7	201
b. Giṭṭin		37.1–8	92
47a	200	46.4	196
68b	122		
		Exodus Rabbah	
b. B. Meṣiʿa		8.3	121, 129
84a	150, 200		
		Numbers Rabbah	
b. B. Batra		4.8	127
74a	40		
		Ecclesiastes Rabbah	
b. Sanhedrin		6.3	151
11a	210	9.15	218
70a	130, 212, 213		
70a–b	163	Midrash Tehillim	
108a	153, 199	9.1	121, 128
108b	207–9, 218, 240		
113b	65	Pesikta Zutra	
		Gen 7	127
Abot de-Rabbi Natan			
A 2:50–55	194–97	Pirqe de Rabbi Eliezer	
32	158	4	62
		7	126
Genesis Rabbah		8	21, 211
15.7	130	20	119
22.8	152	21	57, 62, 152, 295
23.4	144	22	292, 295
25	65	23	120, 204, 205, 207, 225, 241, 279
25.2	197, 304	24	127–28
26.1	201, 211	39	128
28.2	64	46	121
29.5	202		
30.2	202	Sekhel Tov	
30.7	120, 204, 212, 218	Exod 12	127
30.9	199		
31.11	120, 121		

Tanḥuma
  Noah 14   208
  Noah 11–12   240–241
  Vayetze 16   130
  Vaera 9   128

Aggadat Bereshit
  43   128

Tanna Debe Eliyahu
  Pirkei Hayeridot 2   128

Yalkut Shimoni
  Noah 61   163
  Esther B1   126

Targum Neofiti
  Gen 14:18   99
  Gen 6:9   203
  Gen 9:20   212

Targum Onqelos
  Gen 6:9   203
  Gen 6:16   207
  Gen 8:4   309

Targum Pseudo-Jonathan
  Gen 4:1   56
  Gen 5:29   197
  Gen 6:9   203
  Gen 6:20   205
  Gen 7:4   158
  Gen 7:10   158
  Gen 8:4   311, 312, 316
  Gen 8:20   211
  Gen 9:20   130, 163, 212
  Gen 9:22   213
  Gen 9:24   242
  Gen 14:18   99
  Josh 15:1   80
  Josh 16:1   80

Qur'ān
  Sūra 7   253–55, 261, 267, 268–69
  Sūra 10   253–55, 267–68
  Sūra 11   253–61, 266–67, 271, 272
  Sūra 23   253–55, 257–59, 260, 263, 265–66, 271
  Sūra 26   253–55, 257–58, 260, 61–263, 268
  Sūra 54   253–55, 259, 260–61, 270, 272
  Sūra 66   267, 273
  Sūra 71   253–55, 256, 260, 263–64

MEDIEVAL WRITINGS

Book of Asaṭir   24, 107, 129, 245

Key of Solomon   123

Sefer Asaf Harofe   14, 24, 113, 114–17

Sefer Habahir   236

Sefer Hamalbush   118–20, 125

Sefer Harazim   21, 22, 119, 121–22

Sefer Hayashar   124, 125, 241, 304

Sefer Raziel   21, 22–23, 113, 117–24, 125

Tashbetz Qatan   116

Zohar
  1.37b   25, 119
  1.55b   25, 118–19, 129
  1.58b   119, 129
  1.73a   130
  1.76a   119, 129

MEDIEVAL COMMENTATORS

Eliezer of Beaugency
  Ezek 14:14   65

Ibn Ezra
  Gen 7:11   127

Nachmanides
  Gen 4:3   126
  Gemul 102a   114

INDEX OF ANCIENT SOURCES

Ovadiah of Bertinoro
    m. Pesaḥim 4:10   117

Rashi (Rabbi Shlomo Yiṣḥaqi)
    Gen 9:20   212
    Ezek 14:14   65

Radak (David Kimchi)
    Ezek. 14:14   65
    Hos. 14:8   114
    Hos. 15:15   114

Yossef Kara
    Ezek 14:14   65

Index of Authors

Aaron, David H. 201
Abegg, Martin 97, 99
Adler, William 14, 15, 241, 249, 282, 295, 310, 315
Al-Gezzar, Ahmed ibn 114
Albani, Matthias 110
Albeck, Chanock 155
Alexander, Philip 58, 59, 93, 102, 110, 203, 217, 244, 282, 289
Allberry, Charles R. C. 226, 235
Allison, Dale C. 56
Alter, Robert 274
Amar, Joseph P. 239
Amihay, Aryeh 2, 11, 53, 71, 154, 193, 241, 251, 252, 304
Amit, Yairah 207
Andersen, Francis I. 158
Anderson, Gary A. 2, 61, 144, 238, 239
Aphrahat 238, 239, 241
Apollonius of Alexandria 298
Aquila 142
Attridge, Harold W. 168, 170, 171, 178
Auerbach, Erich 274
Avi-Yonah, Michael 288
Avigad, Nachman 53, 54
Baer, Richard A. 184
Baily, Loyld R. 303
Bakhos, Carol 194
Barclay, John M.G. 2, 169, 177, 178
Baron, Salo Wittmayer 126
Barselyan, H. X. 308, 310
Barthélemy, Dominique 10, 61, 68, 71
Baskin, Judith R. 214
Bauer, Adolf 249
Baumgarten, Albert I. 150, 193, 198, 199
Baxter, Wayne 68
Becker, Hans-Jürgen 195

Beeson, Charles H. 235
Bekker, Immanuel 249
Bekkum, Wout J. van 198, 199, 208
Ben-Hayyim, Zeev 24
Bergren, T. A. 315
Bergsma, John S. 213
Berman, Samuel A. 241
Bernabò, Massimo 279, 295
Bernstein, Moshe J. 50, 51, 55, 68, 77, 78, 81, 85, 193
Berossus 160, 177, 178, 310
Berthelot, Katell 102
Beyer, Klaus 53
Bezold, Carl 239
Bhayro, Siam 68, 198, 205
Bickerman, Elias J. 174
Bigg, Charles 157
Bilde, Per 168
Black, Matthew 27, 28, 31, 34, 37, 38, 40, 41, 42, 43, 53, 64, 234
Blau, Ludwig 22, 118
Bloch, Ariel A. 205
Boccaccini, Gabriele 16, 35, 36
Böhlig, Alexander 220
Boor, Carl de 249
Bousset, Wilhelm 40, 232
Boyarin, Daniel 194, 196, 200, 209, 242, 251
Brakke, David 216
Braverman, Jay 214
Brenner, Athalya 58
Brière, Maurice 222
Brock, Sebastion P. 237, 239, 244, 251
Brooke, George J. 201
Brown, Raymond 105
Brownlee, William H. 65
Bruye, Domitien de 315

Buber, Solomon 240, 241, 245
Budge, E. A. Wallis 239, 243, 244, 251
Bullard, Roger A. 219, 232, 234
Caquot, André 97, 100, 101
Carmignac, Jean 97, 106
Casey, Maurice 35
Cassuto, Umberto 53, 197
Celsus 146, 148, 152
Chabot, Jean-Baptiste 248, 249, 250
Chadwick, Henry 294
Charles, Robert H. 9, 13, 14, 17, 27, 28, 30–38, 40, 41, 43, 44, 45, 47, 48, 49, 53, 68, 108, 149
Charlesworth, James H. 27
Chilton, Bruce 172
Clarke, Ernest G. 56, 203, 212, 242
Clements, Ruth 2, 164, 277, 286
Cohen, Shaye J. D. 168, 169
Cohn, Norman 307
Collins, John J. 27, 35, 47, 48, 59, 60, 154, 161, 163, 245, 282
Colson, Francis H. 190
Conzelmann, Hans 169
Cook, Edward M. 97, 99, 146
Cotton, Hannah M. 171
Cowan, J. Milton 271
Cowley, Roger W. 17
Coxe, A. Cleveland 304
Cross, Samuel H. 245
Dalbert, Peter 169
Dan, Joseph 236
Davidson, Maxwell J. 56, 68
Davies, W. D. 56
Davila, James 97, 101, 102, 106
Dillmann, August 29, 34, 40, 41
Dillon, John 186
Dimant, Devorah 10, 18, 19, 29, 42, 44, 48, 49, 50, 51, 57, 63, 68, 97, 109, 193
DiTommaso, Lorenzo 11, 18, 27, 48,
Dix, Gregory 294
Donzel, Emeri J. van 269
Doutreleau, Louis 217
Drijvers, Hans J. W. 251
Driver, Samuel R. 199, 206
Eck, Werner 171
Edmondson, Jonathan 168
Eichrodt, Walther 65

Eid, Volker 288
Elior, Rachel 120
Elman, Yaakov 194
Ephraim the Syrian. *See* Ephrem the Syrian
Ephrem the Syrian 65, 235, 239, 240, 241, 244, 251, 294, 304
Epiphanius 229, 230–35
Eshel, Esther 12, 17, 18, 53, 56, 77, 85, 86, 87, 91, 92, 244, 247
Evans, Craig A. 97
Eynde, Ceslas van den 242
Fabricius, Johann Albert 20
Falconieri, Ottavio 284
Falk, Daniel K. 60, 68, 78, 83
Feldman, Louis H. 2, 62, 93, 145, 148, 160, 169–73, 175, 176, 177, 179, 180, 183, 188, 193
Fink, Joseph 283, 284, 285
Finney, Paul Corbey 286
Fishbane, Michael 196
Fitzmyer, Joseph A. 11, 53, 55, 56, 58, 59, 64, 68, 77, 85, 87, 90, 93, 95, 97, 98, 99, 101, 104, 105, 106, 243
Flesher, Paul V. M. 203
Fletcher-Louis, Crispin H. T. 19, 58, 68, 72, 104
Flusser, David 87
Fraade, Steven D. 194, 198, 203
Franxman, Thomas W. 170
Freedman, Harry 196, 204
Frenkel, Yonah 196
Freudenthal, Jacob 177
Frey, Jörg 60
Friedlander, Gerald 21, 204, 210
Frölich, Ida 68
Gafni, Isaiah M. 251
Galavaris, George 296
García Avilés, Alejandro 118
García Martínez, Florentino 9, 10, 17, 49, 57, 66, 68, 97, 98, 101, 104, 106
Gardner, Iain 228
Garsoïan, Nina G. 308, 309
Gaster, Moses 124, 126, 245
Gaylord, Harry E. 162
Gelb, Ignace J. 313
Geljon, Albert 2, 152, 156, 183, 186, 197

INDEX OF AUTHORS

George Cedrenus 249
George Syncellus (Synkellos) 14, 15, 178, 214, 249, 282, 310
George the Monk (Hamartolos) 249
Georgi, Dieter 169
Gero, Stephen 201, 213
Gilhus, Ingvild Saelid 219, 232, 233, 234
Ginzberg, Louis 117, 128, 130, 145, 146, 147, 163, 241
Goldberg, Arnold 164, 206
Goldin, Judah 195
Goodenough Erwin R. 163, 164
Gould, Stephen 307
Grabar, André 280, 281, 283, 284
Grabbe, Lester L. 185
Grant, Robert M. 223, 224, 227
Greenberg, Moshe 65
Greenfield, Jonas C. 11, 12, 18, 53, 85, 86, 87, 97, 99, 100, 107, 247
Grelot, Pierre 59, 97, 98, 106, 107
Gressmann, Hugo 40
Grossfeld, Bernard 207
Gruenwald, Ithamar 101
Gunkel, Hermann 56, 199, 206
Gutmann, Joseph 278, 279
Haaland, Gunnar 169, 171
Hachlili, Rachel 288
Hahn, Scott Walker 213
Hakobyan, T'. X. 308, 310
Halbertal, Moshe 194
Halivni, David 194
Halpern-Amaru, Betsy 14, 155
Harl, Marguerite 298
Harlow, Daniel C. 162
Hassett, Maurice M. 285
Haug, Walter 288, 289
Hedrick, Charles W. 222
Heine, Ronald E. 65
Heinemann, Joseph 198
Helderman, Jan 226, 227
Helm, Rudolf 249
Hendel, Ronald S. 206
Hendrick, Charles W. 245
Henze, Matthias 59
Hewsen, Robert 308, 309, 310
Hidal, Sven 237
Hiebert, Robert 137, 138

Higden, Ranulf 132
Hillel, Vered 2, 9, 13, 16, 27, 64, 143, 150, 198, 303
Himmelfarb, Martha 14, 15, 17, 57, 115, 121, 212, 245
Hippolytus of Rome 249, 294
Hoffmann, Georg 243
Høgenhaven, Jesper 102, 110
Holl, Karl 229, 235
Holladay, William L. 87
Hollander, Harm W. 2, 149, 151, 155
Holst, Søren 102, 110
Horst, Pieter Willem van der 147, 148, 209
Huggins, Ronald V. 198
Hughes, H. Maldwyn 162
Hughes, Paul 62
Ibn Ezra 127
Ibn Kathīr 269, 270, 271, 273, 275
Isaac, Ephraim 53
Jacob of Edessa 245, 248, 251, 252
Jacob of Serug 251
James, Montague R. 9, 10
Jastrow, Marcus 314
Jeffreys, Elizabeth 315
Jeffreys, Michael 315
Jellinek, Adolph 14, 15, 21, 22, 62, 63, 119
Jones, F. Stanley 245
Jonge, Marinus de 2, 11, 27, 149, 151, 155
Jongeling, Bastiaan 53
Josephus, Flavius 125, 131, 143–47, 149, 152, 160, 161, 167, 168, 169, 170, 171, 172, 174, 175, 176, 177, 178, 179, 180, 181, 299, 310
Kahle, Paule E. 216
Kalimi, Isaac 196
Kalmin, Richard 200
Kaplan, Chaim 193
Karr, Don 122
Kasher, Rimon 203
Kaufman, J. 11
Kensky, Alan 62
Kessler, Hebert L. 279, 290, 291, 295
Kikawada, Isaac M. 303
Kimchi, David 114
Kindler, Arie 279
King, Karen L. 215, 231
Kister, Menahem 77, 195

Klijn, A. F. J. 215, 216
Knibb, Michael 28, 31, 38, 39, 40, 53
Koch, Klaus 59
Koltun-Fromm, Naomi 193, 197, 199, 201, 203, 208, 209, 238
Kraft, Robert 28
Kreitzer, Larry J. 280, 283, 284
Kronholm, Tryggve 237
Kroymann, Emil 223
Kugel, James L. 7, 198, 277
Kugler, Robert A. 11, 12
Kvanvig, Helge S. 30
Lane, Edward W. 271
Lange, Armin 79, 110
Langlois, Victor 248
Lawlor, Hugh J. 11, 25
Layton, Bentley 217, 219, 228, 230, 231
Le Fèvre de la Boderie, Guy 131
Lehmann, Manfred 68
Leicht, Reimund 116, 236
Levinson, Joshua 169, 196, 198
Levison, John R. 12
Lewis, Charlton Thomas 228
Lewis, Jack P. 14, 65, 68, 139, 142, 143, 150, 162, 183, 193, 197, 294, 311
Licht, Jacob 110
Lieber, Elinor 114
Lieu, Judith 228, 251
Linder, Amnon 282
Lindt, Paul van 234, 235
Lipscomb, William L. 316
Loewe, Raphael 298
Lolos, Anastasios 243
Lorberbaum, Yair 209
Lowrie, Walter 280
Lupieri, Edmondo 225, 232
Luttikhuizen, Gerard P. 215, 216, 219
Lynche, Richard 131
Machiela, Daniel A. 53, 55, 68, 71, 77, 85, 154, 208, 237, 242, 243, 244, 251, 311
MacRae, George W. 146, 217, 245
Maher, Michael 197, 203, 211
Malalas, John 314, 315
Mahfouz, Najib 240
Marcovich, Miroslav 224
Marcus, David 205, 240
Margaliot, Mordechai 21, 22, 118, 119, 120
Margoliouth, Jessie Payne Smith 272
Martens, John W. 183
Martin, Erica 2, 253
Martin, François 38
Mason, Steve 167, 168, 169, 171, 172
Mathews, Edward G. 239
McGuire, Anne M. 231
McNamara, Martin 203, 212
McVey, Kathleen E. 239
Melikʻ-Baxšyan 308, 310
Mellink, Machteld J. 308, 313
Melzer, Avi 15, 114
Michael the Syrian 237, 248, 249, 250
Migne, Jacques-Paul 20
Milik, Józef T. 10, 11, 24, 37, 41, 47, 48, 61, 67, 68, 71, 72, 73, 78, 97, 98, 99, 106, 107
Millar, Fergus G. B. 174
Miller, James E. 68,
Minov, Sergey 215, 279
Mitchell, Charles W. 235
Moberly, R. W. L. 65
Molenberg, Corrie 48
Morard, Françoise 245
Morgan, Michael 21
Morgenstern, Mathew 9, 53, 94, 95
Morris, Jenny 183
Moses of Choren 244
Muntner, Suessmann 15, 114, 115, 117
Murphy, Roland 58
Nachmanides 114, 126
Najman, Hindy 8
Narkiss, Bezalel 291, 292, 293, 294
Nau, Françoise 245
Nazianzus, Gregory 296
Neusner, Jacob 195, 199
Newsom, Carol A. 48
Nickelsburg, George W. E. 28, 35, 39, 41, 47, 48, 53, 54, 55, 56, 59, 60, 63, 64, 65, 67, 68, 87, 103, 104
Niehoff, Maren 196
Nikiprowetzky, Valentin 60
Noort, Ed 193, 198
Noth, Martin 65
O'Connor, John J. 130
O'Neil, John C. 28
Origen 65, 130, 227, 284, 305

INDEX OF AUTHORS

Orlov, Andrei A. 10, 11, 13, 20, 27, 30, 57, 100, 163, 193, 211
Papoutsakis, Emmanuel 233
Paracelsus 131, 132
Parisot, D. John 238
Parrott, Douglas M. 218, 219, 224, 245
Parry, Donald W. 122, 146
Pásztori-Kupán, Istvan 221
Pearson, Birger A. 215, 217, 220, 221, 230, 232, 233, 234
Penner, Jeremy 11, 61, 62, 97, 129, 197
Peters, Dorothy M. 1
Pfann, Claire 71
Pfann, Stephen J. 72, 73
Philo of Alexandria 2, 65, 108, 145, 146, 148, 152, 155–59, 183–91, 197, 239, 240, 241 298, 303, 309
Pietersma, Albert 137, 138
Plato 145, 146, 148
Polyhistor 177
Pope, Marvin H. 58
Puech, E. 68, 97, 99, 101, 105, 106, 109
Qimron, Elisha 9, 53
Qurṭubī, Muhammad ibn Ahmad 269, 270, 271, 272, 273, 275
Rajak, Teresa 168
Ramsay, William M. 281, 283
Rappaport, Salomo 170
Rasimus, Tuomas 221
Reed, Annette Yoshiko 139
Reeves, John C. 119, 198, 222
Reicke, Bo 157
Reid, Stephen Breck 59
Reinach, Théodore 283
Reinink, Gerrit J. 220
Rendsburg, Gary A. 198
Rendtorff, Rolf 63
Ri, Su-Min 239, 243
Rives, James 168
Roberge, Michael 221
Rofé, Alexander 200
Rompay, Lucas van 242
Rösel, Martin 206
Rousseau, Adelin 217
Rubenstein, Jeffrey L. 194, 204, 210
Ruiten, Jacques T. A. G. M. van 60, 93
Rutgers, Leonard 283

Safrai, Zeev 203
Salter, M. 297
Salter, L. 297
Sanders, Ed Parish 28
Sandt, Huub van de 87
Sarna, Nahum M. 53
Satlow, Michael L. 209
Schäfer, Peter 101, 214, 236
Schalit, Abraham 170
Scharbach, Rebecca 63, 113
Schenke, Hans-Martin 217
Schiffman, Lawrence H. 18, 118, 170
Schmidt, Nathaniel 16, 20, 68
Scholem, Gershom 101, 110, 111, 236
Schonfeld, Jeremy 297
Schreckenberg, Heinz 169
Schwartz, Baruch J. 206
Schwartz, Daniel R. 50, 167, 169, 179
Schwartz, Joshua J. 246
Schwartz, Seth 168
Scott, James M. 9, 16, 17, 68, 244, 245, 315
Scott, Reginald 123
Sed-Rajna, Gabrielle 297
Segal, Michael 60, 68, 193
Septimius Severus 279, 280, 282
Sevrin, Jean-Marie 221
Sextus Julius Africanus 282, 314
Shaked, Shaul 236
Shapira, Amnon 207
Sharon, Nadav 9, 141, 143, 179, 193, 204, 212
Sherbowitz-Wetzor, Olgerd 245
Shinan, Avigdor 56, 62, 203, 209
Short, Charles 228
Siegert, Folker 169
Sivan, Daniel 9, 53
Skinner, John 53, 148, 206
Small, Jocelyn P. 277, 278
Sokoloff, Michael 60, 233
Solomon of Basrah 243
Sparks, H. F. D. 13, 14
Speiser, Ephraim A. 199, 201
Sperber, Daniel 297
Speyer, Wolfgang 50
Spiegel, Shalom 65
Spilsbury, Paul 173
Starcky, Jean 97, 98, 99

Steiner, Richard	8, 9, 15, 68, 69, 83	Turner, Martha I.	227
Steinsaltz, Adin	199	Tuval, Michael	47, 143, 167, 172
Steinschneider, Moritz	114	Uhlig, Siegbert	48
Stemberger, Günter	241	Ulrich, Eugene	102
Stephanus of Byzantium	281	Unger, Richard W.	217
Stephens, Walter	132	VanderKam, James C.	14, 28, 35, 53, 54, 59, 60, 64, 65, 68, 80, 89, 121, 154, 194, 197, 242, 243, 244, 247, 248,
Sterling, Gregory E.	170		
Stern, David	194		
Stern, Menahem	309, 310	Vermes, Mark	234, 235
Stevens, Lauren	2	Vermes, Geza	194
Stichel, Rainer	228, 232	Vidas, Moulie	193
Stone, Michael E.	1, 2, 8, 9, 12, 13, 16, 17, 18, 20, 27, 30, 37, 50, 51, 53, 58, 60, 61, 63, 64, 68, 71, 72, 79, 83, 85, 86, 87, 93, 105, 107, 111, 115, 118, 119, 121, 129, 143, 144, 149, 154, 162, 193, 198, 210, 214, 244, 247, 252, 303, 306, 307, 310	Vogel, Manuel	169
		Vosté, Jacques-Marie	242
		Wacholder, Ben Zion	175, 310
		Wahl, Harald-Martin	65
		Waldstein, Michael	217, 234,
		Wandrey, Irina	124, 125
Stone, Nira	279	Wansbrough, John E.	274
Stopford, J. T.	304	Wasserstrom, Steven M.	236
Strack, Hermann, L.	241	Weitzmann, Kurt	278, 290, 291, 295
Stroumsa, Guy G.	232, 233	Welch, Alford	253, 261, 264, 266
Strugnell, John	7	Wellesz, Emmy	295
Stuckenbruck, Loren	53, 54, 56, 58, 59, 60, 61, 63, 64, 65, 68, 69, 139	Wenham, Gordon J.	206
		Werman, Cana	9, 10, 14, 18, 49, 50, 51, 68
Suidas	281	Westermann, Claus	56, 206
Suter, David W.	29, 31, 32, 44, 48, 56, 105	Wevers, John W.	138, 139, 140, 141, 142
Swartz, Michael D.	15, 22, 118	Weyer, Johann	123, 124
Syncellus, George	14, 15, 178, 249	Wheeler, Brannon M.	270
Ṭabarī, Muhammad ibn Jarīr	269, 270, 271, 272, 273, 274, 275	Whitney, K. William Jr.	39, 40, 41, 42
		Williams, Francis E.	223, 224, 229, 245
Tameanko, Marvin	279	Williams, Michael Allen	215, 217
Tcherikover, Victor	169	Wilpert, Josef	2, 285
Theordor, Julius	155	Winston, David	186, 187
Theodore Bar Koni	251	Wintermute, Orval S.	107
Theodoret of Cyr	221	Wise, Michael	97, 99
Thackeray, H. St. John	152, 168, 174, 220	Wisse, Frederik W.	217, 220, 234
Theophilus of Antioch	239, 283, 304	Witakowski, Witold	249, 250
Thomson, Robert W.	244	Wright, William	137, 245
Tishel, Moshe	9, 141, 143, 179, 204, 212	Wright, Benjamin G. III	1, 2, 137, 138
Tisserant, Eugene	247, 248	Wutz, Franz X.	303, 304, 305
Torijano, Pablo A.	121, 122	Yadin, Azzan	194
Tov, Emanuel	95, 146	Yadin, Yigal	53, 54, 92, 194
Trebilco, Paul	279, 280, 281, 282, 283, 298	Zakovitch, Yair	209
Trever, John C.	71	Zellentin, Holger M.	213
Trevisa, John	132	Zenobius	282
Tuffin, Paul	14, 15, 249, 282, 310, 315	Zimmerli, Walther	65
Turner, John D.	217	Zimmermann, Johannes	97, 99, 100

www.ingramcontent.com/pod-product-compliance
Lightning Source LLC
Chambersburg PA
CBHW021114300426
44113CB00006B/149